The Law of ESG Derivatives

This book weaves together a comprehensive legal analysis of sustainable finance regimes governing Environment, Social and Governance (ESG) derivatives, with insightful sociological perspectives on risks and uncertainties.

Sustainable finance offers a unique chance to channel capital towards sustainability goals, with ESG derivatives emerging as potent catalysts for a transition to a more sustainable economy. Beyond amplifying capital flow, they strategically align with effective ESG risk and uncertainty management. The book explores how integrating ESG derivatives can strategically serve sustainable investment, offering insights into optimal risk management. The work not only outlines challenges but presents potential solutions, highlighting ESG derivatives' role in addressing market failures affecting sustainable finance, which is an aspect often overlooked by regulators in the EU, the UK, and the US. Serving as a strategy guide for countries adopting a diverse sustainable finance portfolio, the book targets policy practitioners and advocacy specialists, catering to a broad multidisciplinary audience amid the increasing interest in ESG-related products.

The book's dual emphasis on financial derivatives for ESG risk management and sociological perspectives positions it as an ideal resource for scholars, experts, practitioners, researchers, and curious minds across law, business, management, and sociological studies.

Ligia Catherine Arias Barrera holds a Ph.D. in law from the University of Warwick, and an LL.M in commercial and corporate law from Queen Mary University of London. She is Associate Professor at the School of Law of the Externado de Colombia University, Private Consultant in Financial Law Services in Colombia, the UK and the EU, and Member of the Group of Experts in Capital Markets and Financial Regulation at the Ibero-American Institute for Law and Finance.

Routledge Research in Finance and Banking Law

Global Finance in the 21st Century
Stability and Sustainability in a Fragmenting World
Steve Kourabas

Banking Regulation in Africa
The Case of Nigeria and Other Emerging Economies
Folashade Adeyemo

Crypto-Finance, Law and Regulation
Governing an Emerging Ecosystem
Joseph Lee

Regulation and Governance of Mutual Funds
United Kingdom and United States of America Perspectives on Investor Protection
Mohammed Khair Alshaleel

Regulation of Debt Collection in Europe
Understanding Informal Debt Collection Practices
Cătălin-Gabriel Stănescu

The Regulation of Megabanks
Global Systemically Important Banks and their Legal Frameworks
Katarzyna M. Parchimowicz

Regulating Open Banking
Comparative Analysis of the EU, the UK and Taiwan
Chang-Hsien Tsai and Kuan-Jung Peng

The Law of ESG Derivatives
Risk, Uncertainty and Sustainable Finance
Ligia Catherine Arias-Barrera

For more information about this series, please visit: www.routledge.com/Routledge-Research-in-Finance-and-Banking-Law/book-series/FINANCIALLAW

The Law of ESG Derivatives

Risk, Uncertainty and Sustainable Finance

Ligia Catherine Arias-Barrera

Routledge
Taylor & Francis Group
LONDON AND NEW YORK

First published 2025
by Routledge
4 Park Square, Milton Park, Abingdon, Oxon OX14 4RN

and by Routledge
605 Third Avenue, New York, NY 10158

Routledge is an imprint of the Taylor & Francis Group, an informa business

British Library Cataloguing-in-Publication Data
A catalogue record for this book is available from the British Library

ISBN: 978-1-032-42995-3 (hbk)
ISBN: 978-1-032-42996-0 (pbk)
ISBN: 978-1-003-36524-2 (ebk)

DOI: 10.4324/9781003365242

Typeset in Times New Roman
by Apex CoVantage, LLC

This work is dedicated to my family.

Contents

Figures

Cases

Advertising Standards Authority (ASA) v HSBC [2022]. ASA Ruling on HSBC UK Bank plc.

Amber Corp. and Olga Kiiker [2023] Case No. 230422073P1 Alberta Court of Justice.

American Petroleum Institute v. EPA [2015] Case No. 15–1020. District of Columbia Circuit.

ASA Ruling on Ryanair Ltd t/a Ryanair Ltd. [2019] Complaint No. G19–1035778.

Australian Centre for Corporate Responsibility v. Santos [2021]. NSD858/2021.

Commonwealth v. Exxon Mobil Corp [2019] Case No. SJC-13211. Massachusetts High Court.

Earth Island Institute v The Coca-Cola Company. [2021] Case N. 2021 CA 001846 B. Superior Court of the District of Columbia. Civil Division.

Future Generations v Ministry of Environment and Others [2018] Colombian Supreme Court. Case No. 11001-22-03-000-2018-00319-01.

Greenpeace France and Others v. Total Energies Electricité Gaz France [2022].

Hoosier Energy Rural Elec. Coop. v. John Hancock Life Ins. Co. No. 1:08-cv-1560-DFH-DML, 2008 U.S. Dist. LEXIS 10.

In re Tesla Motors, Inc. Stockholder Litigation [2023] Case No. 181, 2022 Delaware Supreme Court.

Maria Guadalupe Ellis v Nike USA, Inc and Nike Retail Services, Inc [2023] Case N. 4:2023cv00632. District Court Eastern District of Missouri Division.

Public Defender's Office of the State of Pará v. Associacao dos Ribeirinhos e Moradores and Others [2022] (Project 2620 carbon credits and "forest carbon grabbing).

Mario Atencio and others v *The State of New Mexico and others* [2023] State of New Mexico, County of Santa Fe, First Judicial District Court.

Texas v. Securities & Exchange Commission [2023] Case No. 23–60079.5th Cir.

Verbraucherzentrale Banden- Württemberg e.V. v. Commerz Real Fund Management S.à.r.l. [2022]. Regional Court of Stuttgart.

Acknowledgements

Above all, I want to express my gratitude to God and my family.

I extend heartfelt gratitude to my friends and colleagues at Externado de Colombia University and the University of Warwick for their support in shaping both my professional and personal trajectory. I feel truly blessed to be surrounded by such a supportive network.

Abbreviations

AAUs	Assigned Amount Units
AIFs	Alternative Investment Funds
CAs	Corresponding Adjustments
CAT Swaps	Catastrophe Swaps
CCA 2008	Climate Change Act 2008
CCPs	Core Carbon Principles
CDM	Clean Development Mechanism
CDR	Carbon Dioxide Removal
CRD IV	Capital Requirements Directive IV
CRR II	Capital Requirements Regulation
CRU	Climate Risk Unit
CSDDD	Corporate Sustainability Due Diligence Directive
CSDR	Corporate Sustainability Reporting Directive
DACS	Direct Air Capture and Storage
DTRs	Disclosure Guidance and Transparency Rules
ELS	Event Loss Swaps
EMIR	Regulation on OTC Derivatives, Central Counterparties and Trade Repositories
ERA	Environmental Risk Assessment
ESG	Environmental, Social, and Governance
ESRS	European Sustainability Reporting Standards
FM	Frontier Markets
FSMA 2000	Financial Services and Markets Act
GCF	Green Climate Fund
GFS	UK Government's Green Finance Strategy
GGR	Greenhouse Gas Removal
GHG	Greenhouse Gases
GRI	Global Reporting Initiative
GTAG	Green Technical Advisory Group
GWP	Global Warming Potential
IET	International Emissions Trading
ILS	Insurance-linked Securities
IOSCO	International Organization of Securities Commission
IPCC	Intergovernmental Panel for Climate Change
ISDA	International Swaps and Derivatives Association

ISSB	International Sustainability Standards Board
ITMOs	Internationally Transferred Mitigation Outcomes
JI	Joint Implementation
KPIs	Key Performance Indicators
LDCs	Least Developed Countries
MiFID I & II	Market and Financial Instruments Directive I & II
MiFIR	Market and Financial Instruments Regulation
Nbs	Nature-based solutions
NDCs	Nationally Determined Contributions
NFRD	European Nonfinancial Reporting Directive
NGFS	Network for Greening Financial Services
OTF	Organised Trading Facility
PCAF	Partnership for Carbon Accounting Financials
PPAs	Power Purchase Agreements Futures
PRI	Principles for Responsible Investment
RECs	Renewable Energy Certificates
RINs	Renewable Identification Numbers
SASB	Sustainability Accounting Standards Board
SBS	Security-based Swap
SDGs	Sustainable Development Goals
SECR	Streamlined Energy and Carbon Reporting
SFDR	Sustainable Finance Disclosure Regulation
SIDS	Small Island Developing States
SLDs	Sustainability-linked derivatives
TCFD	Task Force on Climate-related Financial Disclosures
TNFD	Task Force on Nature-related Financial Disclosures
TPT	UK Transition Planning Taskforce
TSC	Technical Screening Criteria
UCITS	Undertakings for Collective Investment in Transferable Securities
UKCGC	UK Corporate Governance Code 2018
UKSC	UK Stewardship Code 2020
UNFCCC	United Nations Framework Convention on Climate Change
VCM	Voluntary Carbon Markets
VCMD	Voluntary Carbon Market Derivatives
VPPA	Virtual PPA

1 Introduction

The Chapters in Outline

Sustainable finance emerges as an opportunity to channel capital towards the achievement of sustainability goals. Within this landscape, environmental, social, and governance ESG derivatives stand out as catalysts, with the potential to strengthen the transition to a more sustainable economy, amplifying the flow of capital and aligning it strategically with the effective management of ESG risks and uncertainties. Financial markets are focused on promoting the issuance of loans, debt instruments, and equity aligned with the UN sustainable development goals (SDGs). The core argument of the research and discussion of this book is to explore the critical role that ESG derivatives perform in any economic activity considering meeting sustainability objectives. Our primary focus is to analyse how the reasoning behind risks and uncertainties linked to ESG factors forms the bedrock for ESG derivative design. This foundational discussion unveils a critical perspective, revealing the current inadequacies of the EU, UK, and US regimes governing ESG derivatives in fostering market growth. Significantly, our work highlights, for the first time, the intricate relationship between ESG *risks* and the role of ESG *derivatives*. Our central hypothesis embraces a risk-based approach as a tool to comprehend how ESG derivatives can significantly contribute to achieving the objectives of sustainable finance. To foster the widespread use of ESG derivatives embedded with clear sustainability-aligned key performance indicators (KPIs), the risk-based approach must carefully consider the nuances of both risks and uncertainties, including how they are best managed and controlled.

We adopt the risk-based approach as our methodological compass, pioneering the first comprehensive study into the primary risks and uncertainties linked with each of the ESG factors. Our inquiry extends to discerning how the integration of ESG derivatives can serve as a strategic tool in sustainable investment strategies, offering insights into the optimal management of these risks and uncertainties. This pioneering study highlights not only the challenges, but also the potential solutions that ESG derivatives bring to the forefront in enhancing the management of risks associated with ESG factors.

This book stands as a distinctive contribution to the field, weaving together a legal analysis of pertinent sustainable finance regimes, governing ESG derivatives

DOI: 10.4324/9781003365242-1

and sociological perspectives on risks and uncertainties. Additionally, we examine regulatory frameworks and explore comprehensive sustainability-related policy considerations. Our focus is on understanding the dynamics among state regulation, self-regulatory instruments, and contractual mechanisms as essential tools for promoting behavioural change in accordance with the urgent imperatives embedded in sustainability goals. In this context, we advocate for the significant role that ESG derivatives should play in the establishment of a social licence for finance and the creation of value for all stakeholders. The primary contribution of this study lies in its theoretical exploration, shedding light on the risks and uncertainties that ESG derivatives have the potential to address. This includes tackling market failures affecting sustainable finance, a dimension that has been largely overlooked by regulators in the EU, the UK, and the US.

In Chapter 2, we define the scope of sustainability within the confines of ESG factors. This enables us to delve into the characteristics that currently shape sustainable finance. Our examination of the interplay between sustainability and ESG factors propels the discourse investigating priorities established by international organisations concerning pressing environmental concerns – particularly the commitments aimed at addressing climate change and net-zero targets. This introduction serves as a gateway for identifying common ground within the existing regulatory landscape, while also offering a lens to envision areas ripe for enhancement. Our exploration delineates the manifestation of sustainability within the spectrum of ESG factors, emphasising the significance of distinguishing between green and dirty finance, and establishing measures to avert the risk of greenwashing. Within this context, our objective is to precisely define the boundaries and functions of financial derivatives, elucidating how they can seamlessly align with sustainability objectives.

Chapter 3 outlines the concepts of financial derivatives as hedging instruments, and the functioning of the market. The exposition underscores the adaptability of this type of contract to serve diverse objectives – in this context, the SDGs. At the core of our argument are two pillars: an analysis of the regulatory regimes governing traditional and ESG derivatives in the EU, UK, and US markets, and an exploration of the role of the contract, as a legal institution facilitating behaviour modification. In our legal analysis of the existing regulations applicable to ESG derivatives, we highlight the prevailing uncertainty regarding their acknowledgment as instruments of sustainable finance in the EU and the UK. Conversely, the US approach appears more open to endorsing the use of diverse financial contracts geared towards ESG objectives. We contend that the adaptability of financial derivatives presents a significant opportunity for sustainable finance. Their substantial flexibility, intertwined with the diverse variables influencing sustainability goals, aligns effectively with a market fundamentally rooted in contractual freedom. However, to mitigate the risk of greenwashing, we emphasise the critical need to draft ESG derivatives with explicit and quantifiable ESG targets, articulated through measurable KPIs. Ensuring transparency regarding the underlying purpose of each derivative transaction is crucial to facilitate their seamless integration into sustainable investment portfolios, and broader corporate sustainability strategies.

Seeking to articulate the current types of ESG derivatives with sustainable finance objectives, Chapter 4 explores the capacity of current derivatives to effectively hedge ESG risks. Here, we conduct a comprehensive examination of the pivotal role played by sustainability-linked derivatives in steering the transition toward a more sustainable economy. We also analyse the importance of voluntary carbon credits derivatives markets, emphasising the imperative to strengthen the foundational primary market, optimising its efficacy in advancing sustainability. In essence, the chapter endeavours to throw some light onto the untapped potential within ESG derivatives to propel sustainability goals. We see how ESG derivatives can play a pivotal role in addressing the deficiencies of lack of standardisation and inconsistent disclosure levels within sustainable finance, and explore how their distinctive attributes position them as instruments capable of both enhancing transparency in underlying markets, and establishing more robust risk-management methodologies.

Following this ESG factor analysis, Chapter 5 focuses attention on the convergence between environmental issues and the sociological categories of risks and uncertainties. The selection of environmental impacts for risk assessment typically encompasses factors such as energy efficiency, emissions, waste, climate change, and various environmental programmes. Consequently, the formulation of a risk-management strategy involves a comprehensive examination of past liabilities, current challenges, and future risk scenarios. However, the adequate identification of material environment risks and uncertainties is often guided by the information collected according to diverse ESG reporting standards. This could lead to errors in judgement – where certain issues are considered extremely risky when they are not, and vice versa. To overcome such difficulties in building an environmental risk corporate strategy, thereby promoting the adoption of relevant financial instruments, we argue in favour of the implementation of regulatory impact analysis from a risk-based approach perspective.

Chapter 6 presents a thought-provoking double-edged hypothesis, in which we explore the relevance of social factors in the rationale of sustainable finance. We argue that sustainability is instrumental in actualising a *social licence* for finance – and financial derivatives could play a pivotal role in making this a reality. While the derivatives market currently functions as a platform for assigning value to capital exposed to risk, there is potential for it to transform into a catalyst for amplifying social wealth. The reconfiguration of financial derivatives to pursue positive social impact requires transforming them from activities centred on value extraction to instruments focused on value creation. This transformation hinges on establishing clear regulatory expectations related to social issues, and recognising the role of ESG derivatives as contracts that both complement and reinforce the development and implementation of a social licence.

There is nascent attention arising in the interaction between governance and financial derivatives, and Chapter 7 explores this discourse, particularly in the correlation between the use of derivatives contracts and firm value. We examine how the interaction between derivatives and governance serves as a benchmark for various sustainable investment strategies. Recognising the significance of ESG reporting, we investigate how certain corporations and investors derive advantages from self-regulatory instruments crafted within capital markets. Given the intimate connection between the evolution of governance and investors' fiduciary duties, the concluding section contemplates whether these duties need to be reconfigured to align with broader ESG objectives.

Scope and Preliminary Considerations

Financial derivatives constitute a market that allows and incentivises creativity and financial innovation[1] *– but could it become a credible path towards reliable sustainable finance?*

To understand the potential of ESG derivatives for strengthening sustainable finance goals, it is helpful to explain the features of sustainability within the context of ESG. This allows us to identify the opportunities for this type of contract to effectively manage ESG risks and uncertainties.

Sustainable Finance

Sustainable finance is the driving force behind achieving sustainability goals within the framework of ESG factors. In recent years, market development has primarily centred around environmental objectives, particularly in climate finance. Notably, commitments in this domain have led to a significant increase, reaching an annual average of USD 1.3 trillion in 2021/2022, compared to USD 653 billion in 2019/2020.[2] At COP28, Germany and Canada declared that global climate finance targets for 2022 and 2023 had been achieved. Such progress, while noteworthy, remains insufficient, and unevenly distributed across sectors and regions. Developed economies continue to mobilise most climate finance, leaving developing and least developed countries (LDCs) with inadequate funding. According to the Climate Policy Initiative, less than 3% of the global total (USD 30 billion) was allocated to LDCs.[3] The imperative to improve access to both public and private sources of finance is driven by the need to address challenges related to obtaining verifiable data across sectors and regions; enhance local ecosystems for climate investment; and integrate climate adaptation and resilience into financial systems.

In the area of nature and biodiversity, the stark reality of a world experiencing one of the most profound extinction crises in history[4] has propelled international

1 Alastair Hudson, *The Law on Financial Derivatives* (2nd edn, Sweet & Maxwell, 1998) 7.

2 Climate Policy Initiative, 'Global Landscape of Climate Finance 2023', November 2023. www.climatepolicyinitiative.org/publication/global-landscape-of-climate-finance-2023/ accessed 30th November 2023.

3 ibid.

4 A. Deutz, G. M. Heal, R. Niu, E. Swanson, T. Townshend, L. Zhu, A. Delmar, A. Meghji, S. A. Sethi and J. Tobin-de la Puente, *Financing Nature: Closing the Global Biodiversity Financing Gap* (The Paulson Institute, The Nature Conservancy, and the Cornell Atkinson Center for Sustainability, 2020).

endeavours to establish a collective agreement on necessary actions. This culminated in the 15th Conference of the Parties to the UN Convention on Biological Diversity in 2022 and 2023. What emerged was an imperative to enhance financial flows towards investments capable of producing tangible and verifiable advancements in the global status of biodiversity. The overarching goal is to completely bridge the biodiversity financing gap by 2030, estimated to be in the range of USD 598–824 billion annually.[5]

The inadequacy in accurately assessing biodiversity within our financial markets and economic frameworks arises from multiple market failures.[6] A significant portion of biodiversity benefits qualify as public goods, making them undervalued in markets due to their non-excludable and non-rivalrous nature.[7] Additionally, the impacts of biodiversity conservation and loss extend to third parties, resulting in external benefits and costs. This classic market failure leads to insufficient financial rewards for biodiversity conservation efforts, and inadequate financial penalties for those causing harm.[8] Furthermore, the absence of well-defined property rights exacerbates biodiversity market failures, as no entity possesses a direct financial interest or incentive to conserve these resources, or allocate them to their most valuable use.[9]

In addition to the funding required for mitigation and adaptation efforts,[10] the significance of sustainable finance is intertwined with the broader global economic ramifications stemming from both persistent and severe physical climate risks, as well as biodiversity loss. Projections from the International Monetary Fund (IMF) indicate that sectoral productivity shifts resulting from chronic climate risks (such as alterations in temperature and precipitation, along with extreme climate conditions like heat waves, floods, and droughts) could incur an average annual cost of 1.2% and 3.2% of global GDP, respectively, over the period from 2021–2100.[11] Moreover, economic value generation amounting to USD 44 trillion – representing

5 ibid.

6 C. Herweijer et al., 'Nature Risk Rising: Why the Crisis Engulfing Nature Matters for Business and the Economy', World Economic Forum, 2020. www.weforum.org/publications/nature-risk-rising-why-the-crisis-engulfing-nature-matters-for-business-and-the-economy/#:~:text=Nature%20Risk%20Rising%2C%20produced%20in,and%20services%20within%20the%20broader accessed 30th November 2023.

7 Charles Perrings and others, 'The Economics of Biodiversity and Ecosystem Services', in Shahid Naeem and others (eds), *Biodiversity, Ecosystem Functioning, and Human Wellbeing: An Ecological and Economic Perspective* (Oxford University Press, 2009; online edn, Oxford Academic, 1 September 2009).

8 Lucy Emerton, 'Using Economic Incentives for Biodiversity Conservation', IUCN, The World Conservation Union, 2000. https://portals.iucn.org/library/sites/library/files/documents/PDF-2000-002.pdf accessed 30th November 2023.

9 A. Deutz et al., *Financing Nature: Closing the Global Biodiversity Financing Gap* (n 4).

10 University of Cambridge Institute for Sustainability Leadership (CISL), *Risk Sharing for Loss and Damage: Scaling Up Protection for the Global South* (University of Cambridge Institute for Sustainability Leadership, 2023).

11 Caterina Lepore and Roshen Fernando, 'Global Economic Impacts of Physical Climate Risks', WP/23/183, September 2023.

over half of the world's total GDP – is moderately or highly dependent on nature and its services.[12] Consequently, this substantial portion of the global economy is susceptible to risks arising from the loss of biodiversity.

Notwithstanding the urgency of attending to such environmental risks, there are other concerns surrounding ESG factors. In this sense, sustainable finance is still in its infancy, creating financial products that address the social phase that ESG derivatives may potentially promote, as well as their role in encouraging the improvement of corporate governance structures considerate of stakeholders' interests.

Why ESG Derivatives?

We ask whether and how we might repurpose the use of financial derivatives to satisfy sustainability needs in three key areas – Environment, Social, and Governance

Derivative contracts are the result of combining certain features to raise capital and manage credit risk. Most characteristics of these transactions respond to specific client or investor interests, and in the derivatives market, any transaction can be perfectly reshaped to satisfy the client's needs. Achieving the UN SDGs will support global progress towards more sustainable growth. In this context, the role of finance can contribute by serving as a more effective allocator of capital, to supporting transition to a greener and low-carbon economy.

Over the past few years, some international regulators have attempted to promote sustainable finance, particularly focusing on bonds, equities, and loan markets – but this progress should be strengthened by a *complete financial product catalogue*. Aiming at being environmentally responsible is both a virtue and a necessity. However, there are multiple difficulties faced by the ESG movement in finance – starting with the absence of awareness of environmental risk; limited understanding of the transmission mechanism between ESG-related risk and financial risks; the ability to quantify those risks, gaps in methodologies and data quality; and a lack of regulatory expectations and incentives. This book is focused on how to set out a route–map for those expectations, as they concern the role of ESG derivatives. The proposal is to borrow the sociological concepts of risk and uncertainty, to understand how they fit into the ESG finance narrative. This argument provides the basis to discuss how financial derivatives are useful tools to manage, control, and mitigate ESG-related risks and uncertainties. As investor demand increases, regulation is expected to be the moderating voice, establishing a clear and common framework to support the rising appetite for ESG products.

The current interest in bonds, equities, and loans as primary instruments to develop sustainability in finance falls short. This environment seems to leave us with an incomplete picture of the necessary tools to 'solve the future', and to better manage the ever more prominent risks. If a concept common to climate

12 WEF, 'Nature Risk Rising: Why the Crisis Engulfing Nature Matters for Business and the Economy', June 2020.

change, environmental crisis, social distress, unemployment, corporate disorder, unsustainable growth, health crisis is *risk*, and the 'unknowns' brought by future events, it seems only rational to consider that, along with finance and credit products, capital markets support the development of financial products that help to *manage and mitigate* those risks and uncertainties. The best fit-for-purpose instruments are financial derivatives. Therefore, the addition of ESG derivatives is another tool, to grant access to the market and solve the deficiencies of sustainable finance.

The demand for ESG products comes from portfolio managers, ETF market makers, and the structured products sector.[13] Clients on the buy-side tend to favour ESG investment, because they perceive such factors will lead to long-term investment returns, as well as having a positive impact on their reputation, and contribute to mitigate investment risk.[14] Part of the EU and UK regulatory response is focused on securities that can invest directly on the activities – either green or dirty – leaving derivatives inappropriately excluded from the disclosure regime. This book acknowledges the need for a coherent regulatory approach, to open up the debate on how derivatives serve the orderly growth of ESG finance.

There are several ways to use financial derivatives, and perhaps the growing interest in ESG investing is an opportunity for a primer on them?[15] Derivatives contribute to improve price discovery and transparency, strengthen risk management, facilitate more efficient asset allocation, help participants hedge ESG-related risks, and promote longtermism.[16]

Primarily, derivatives are used to control and reallocate risks.[17] They are also instruments to obtain funding at a preferential rate,[18] or to take speculative advantage of a movement in a financial market for the investing.[19] However, the most important function of derivatives is to hedge the risk generated in any other type of contract. Indeed, most companies and shareholders[20] use derivatives to control

13 Eurex, 'The Changing Shape of Derivatives Markets: A Deep Dive into ESG Investing', 2020. www.eurexchange.com/resource/blob/1680460/2aa48304dc6662065a81e880e720bd9d/data/A_Deep_dive_into_ESG.pdf accessed 29th November 2023.

14 ibid.

15 Fisher Black, 'Foreword: The Many Faces of Derivatives', in Jack Clark Francis, William W. Toy and J. Gregg Whittaker (eds), *Handbook of Equity Derivatives* (Wiley Series on Financial Engineering, 2000) ix.

16 ISDA, 'Overview of ESG-Related Derivatives Products and Transactions', January 2021. www.isda.org/a/qRpTE/Overview-of-ESG-related-Derivatives-Products-and-Transactions.pdf accessed 29th November 2023.

17 Henry T. C. Hu, 'Misunderstood Derivatives: The Causes of Informational Failure and the Promise of Regulatory Incrementalism', *The Yale Law Journal* 102 (1993): 1457, 1464–1465.

18 Peter A. Abken, 'Over-the-Counter Financial Derivatives: Risky Business?', *Federal Reserve Bank of Atlanta Economic Review* (March–April 1994): 5.

19 Alastair Hudson, *The Law of Financial Derivatives* (n 1) 9.

20 Kimberly D. Krawiec, 'Derivatives, Corporate Hedging, and Shareholder Wealth: Modigliani-Miller Forty Years Later', *University of Illinois Law Review* (1998): 1039.

business risks by 'hedging'.[21] Meaning 'protecting',[22] hedging is the process by which 'an exposed entity enters into a transaction that will generate profit in the exact circumstances that would generate a loss under the exposure'.[23] Therefore, the nature of hedging is to reduce rather than to create risk[24] – it reallocates (though it does not eliminate) risk from one party to another. Nevertheless, this benign tool might not always operate in the way anticipated at the time of its creation, transforming it in to a 'risk-bearing' instrument.[25]

An important concept in derivatives transactions is *risk*. Risk refers to randomness that is quantifiable in terms of probability distributions[26] – it suggests volatility. Risk acts as a 'driver' of market transactions, and in every transaction, there is a continuous exchange of risks between counterparties. Derivatives have proved to be among the most effective tools for isolating and transferring those financial risks. In ESG finance, derivatives are the perfect tool to manage project risk, interest risk, and currency risk.[27]

A parallel concept in derivatives transactions that must not be overlooked is *uncertainty*. We here draw a famous distinction between (unknowable) uncertainty and (measurable) risk. This difference is not a bright line, but a sliding scale of confidence as to the reliability of models to predict the future.

Financial derivatives assume a vital role in capital markets, exerting a substantial impact on the broader economy. When employed prudently,[28] they offer substantial advantages. Companies strategically use derivatives as a safeguard against a diverse array of risks inherent to their business operations;[29] their allure primarily stems from their flexibility, serving as a versatile tool for institutional and corporate investors to hedge a wide spectrum of risks.[30] Our inquiry is focused on examining how financial derivatives can be reimagined and repurposed to effectively address sustainability risks.

21 Lee Berton, 'Experts Shed Light on the Murky and Complex World of Derivatives', *Wall Street Journal*, 16 June 1994.

22 Carolyn H. Jackson, 'Have You Hedged Today? The Inevitable Advent of Consumer Derivatives', *Fordham Law Review* 67 (1999): 3206.

23 Norman Menachem Feder, 'Deconstructing Over-the-Counter Derivatives', *Columbia Business Law Review* (2002): 677, 717.

24 ibid.

25 Richard Dale, *Risk and Regulation in Global Securities Market* (John Wiley & Sons Ltd, 1996) 153.

26 William F. Sharpe, 'Nuclear Financial Economics', in William H. Beaver and George Parker (eds), *Risk Management: Problems and Solutions*, vol. 17 (McGraw-Hill, 1995) 34 and Peter H. Huang, 'A Normative Analysis of New Financially Engineered Derivatives', *Southern California Law Review* 73 (March 2000): 471, 477.

27 ISDA, 'Overview of ESG-related Derivatives Products and Transactions' (n 16).

28 Christian A. Johnson, 'At the Intersection of the Bank Finance and Derivatives: Who Has the Right Way?', *Tennessee Law Review* 66 (Fall 1998): 23.

29 Anatoli Kuprianov, 'The Role of Interest Rate Swaps in Corporate Finance', *Federal Reserve Bank of Richmond Economic Quarterly* (Summer 1994): 53–58.

30 Christopher Culp, 'The Social Functions of Financial Derivatives', in Robert Kolb and James Overdahl (eds), *Financial Derivatives Pricing and Risk Management* (Kolb Series in Finance, 2011) 59. www.semanticscholar.org/paper/The-Social-Functions-of-Financial-Derivatives-Culp-Kolb/180efffbdfbfb699080f5f80823c034a6f7a1f1b accessed 30th November 2023.

Indeed, derivatives improve economic efficiency by breaking risk apart, and parcelling it out to those parties that are the cheapest and most willing risk bearers.[31] However, promoting the use and expansion of ESG derivatives requires us to recognise the most prominent challenges. There is a need to improve disclosure and transparency, and to enhance standardisation – whilst bearing in mind that tailored solutions tend to be regarded as better able to meet clients' interests. Moreover, the industry calls for increased accessibility to market for investors, by increasing liquidity compared to non-ESG well-established derivatives. Similarly, granting broader access is linked to ensuring global exposure, as well as country-level exposure to both new green investment and transition products.

The development of novel ESG-related derivatives is an ongoing and dynamic process. Thus far, the International Swaps and Derivatives Association (ISDA) has underscored advancements such as negotiations involving a range of instruments (such as sustainability-linked derivatives, ESG-related credit default swap indices, exchange-traded derivatives based on listed ESG-related equity indices, emissions trading derivatives, renewable energy, and renewable fuels derivatives, as well as catastrophe and weather derivatives).[32] A common thread among these products is the adoption of an incentive system, aimed at fostering the attainment of sustainability goals. The objective is to tailor transactions and incorporate KPIs that gauge client capacity and dedication to achieving sustainability outcomes.[33] Performance evaluation directly influences the conditions of the derivatives contracts. In recognising the pivotal role of the contract as a legal institution in behaviour modification, it becomes essential to grasp the transformative potential that ESG derivatives offer to sustainability objectives.[34]

Having clear guidance on the regulatory treatment of ESG derivatives is crucial for fostering market growth. The regulatory framework inherited from derivatives markets, particularly in over-the-counter transactions, appears to be applicable to these transactions. Consequently, regulations such as MiFID I and II, as well as EMIR and the revised CRR II and CRD V packages, are extended to encompass ESG derivatives.[35]

Furthermore, market participants engaging in ESG derivatives will need to adhere to ESG frameworks that encompass reporting obligations. However, there is notable uncertainty regarding widespread acknowledgment of ESG derivatives as sustainable investment instruments. Presently, the EU and UK regimes, unlike

31 David Mullins, 'Remarks on the Global Derivatives Study Sponsored by the Group of Thirty', ISDA Summer Conference, 1993. https://fraser.stlouisfed.org/title/statements-speeches-david-w-mullins-912/remarks-global-derivatives-study-sponsored-group-thirty-international-swaps-derivatives-association-summer-conference-new-york-ny-35397#scribd-open accessed 29th November 2023.

32 ISDA, 'Overview of ESG-Related Derivatives Products and Transactions' (n 16).

33 European Commission, 'Guidelines on Non-Financial Reporting (Methodology for Reporting Non-Financial Information)', 26 June 2017. C (2017) 4234 final. P. 21.

34 ISDA, 'Overview of ESG-related Derivatives Products and Transactions' (n 16).

35 Markets in Financial Instruments Directive 2014 (2014/65/EU), Regulation on OTC Derivatives, Central Counterparties and Trade Repositories known as EMIR Regulation (EU) No 648/2012, last reviewed in August 2022, and CRR II Regulation ((EU) 2019/876) and the CRD V Directive ((EU) 2019/878). The Regulation and the Directive amended the Capital Requirements Regulation (575/2013) (CRR) and the CRD IV Directive (2013/36/EU) respectively.

the US, categorically exclude ESG derivatives from such recognition. This initial standpoint poses a dual challenge, limiting not only the expansion of sustainable finance, but also impeding the optimisation of ESG risk-management strategies.

Remarks and Considerations

Considering the failures affecting the rapid growth and expansion of sustainable finance, along with the urgent risks involved in the term 'ESG', the promotion of more financial products aligned with sustainability seems adequate. In this context, ESG derivatives emerge as a distinctive trend, envisioning the need to manage the myriad of risks and uncertainty encompassed by sustainability issues.

The argument in favour of accepting the potential of ESG derivatives to strengthen sustainable finance is based on the most prominent features of these transactions. Derivatives provide counterparties with avenues for both capital raising and risk management. Moreover, their ample flexibility allows them to be meticulously tailored to align with the specific interests of clients and investors. Our inquiry delves into the fundamental exploration of the feasibility and methodology of redirecting the use of financial derivatives, to effectively address sustainability imperatives across three pivotal areas of ESG factors. This reorientation is propelled by the overarching goal of advancing a more sustainable trajectory. Within this overarching framework, the financial sector assumes a pivotal role in augmenting its contribution, by serving as a more adept allocator of capital, thereby catalysing the transition toward a greener and more circular economy.

To attain this objective, regulators should explore the potential of ESG derivatives in addressing inefficiencies within sustainable finance. These inefficiencies often stem from information asymmetries, occasionally exacerbated by inconsistent disclosure requirements; inadequate and inaccurate analysis of nonfinancial data hindering clear assessments of materiality, insufficient standardisation; and a lack of transparency mechanisms for pricing underlying assets and markets. However, positioning ESG derivatives as a distinct category of contracts not only hinges on regulatory reforms, but also necessitates a reimagining of the use of derivatives contracts, as instruments to yield clear and substantial behaviour modification.

The central argument advanced in this work elucidates the methodology of drafting these contracts to effectively produce consistent and measurable KPIs. The critical analysis of this argument leads us to unravel a cohesive progression across six chapters, intricately intertwining the concepts of risks, uncertainties, ESG criteria, and the potential of financial derivatives in fulfilling sustainability goals.

Bibliography

Books

Black, F., 'Foreword: The Many Faces of Derivatives' in Francis, J.C., Toy, William W., & Whittaker, J.G. (eds.), *Handbook of Equity Derivatives* (Wiley Series on Financial Engineering 2000).

Culp, C., 'The Social Functions of Financial Derivatives' in Robert Kolb, R., and Overdahl, J. (eds.), *Financial Derivatives Pricing and Risk Management* (Kolb Series in Finance 2011).

Dale, R., *Risk and Regulation in Global Securities Market* (John Wiley & Sons Ltd 1996).

Hudson, A., *The Law on Financial Derivatives* (2nd edn, Sweet &Maxwell 1998).

Perrings, C. *et al.*, 'The Economics of Biodiversity and Ecosystem Services' in Naeem, S. *et al.* (eds.), *Biodiversity, Ecosystem Functioning, and Human Wellbeing: An Ecological and Economic Perspective* (Oxford University Press 2009).

Articles

Deutz, A., Heal, G.M., Niu, R., Swanson, E., Townshend, T., Zhu, L., Delmar, A., Meghji, A., Sethi, S.A., and Tobin-de la Puente, J., 'Financing Nature: Closing the Global Biodiversity Financing Gap' *The Paulson Institute, The Nature Conservancy, and the Cornell Atkinson Center for Sustainability* (2020) 5.

Feder, N.M., 'Deconstructing Over-the-Counter Derivatives' *Columbia Business Law Review* (2002) 677.

Gardiner, S.M., and Hartzell-Nichols, L., 'Ethics and Global Climate Change' 3(10) *Nature Education Knowledge* (2012) 5.

Henry, T.C.Hu, 'Misunderstood Derivatives: The Causes of Informational Failure and the Promise of Regulatory Incrementalism' 102 *The Yale Law Journal* (1993) 1457.

Huang, P., 'A Normative Analysis of New Financially Engineered Derivatives' 73 *Southern California Law Review* (2000) 477.

Jackson, CH., 'Have You Hedged Today? The Inevitable Advent of Consumer Derivatives' 67 *Fordham Law Review* (1999) 3206.

Krawiec, K.D., 'Derivatives, Corporate Hedging, and Shareholder Wealth: Modigliani-Miller Forty Years Later?' *University of Illinois Law Review* (1998) 1039.

Kuprianov, A., 'The Role of Interest Rate Swaps in Corporate Finance' *Federal Reserve Bank of Richmond Economic Quarterly* (1994) 53.

Lee, MT., and Suh, I., 'Understanding the Effects of Environment, Social, and Governance Conduct on Financial Performance: Arguments for a Process and Integrated Modelling Approach' 1(1) *Sustainable Technology and Entrepreneurship* (2022) 100004.

Working Papers

Eurex, 'The Changing Shape of Derivatives Markets: A Deep Dive into ESG Investing' (2020) <www.eurexchange.com/resource/blob/1680460/2aa48304dc6662065a81e880e720bd9d/data/A_Deep_dive_into_ESG.pdf> accessed 29th November 2023.

Lepore, C., and Roshen, F., 'Global Economic Impacts of Physical Climate Risks', WP/23/183 (September 2023).

University of Cambridge Institute for Sustainability Leadership (CISL), 'Risk Sharing for Loss and Damage: Scaling Up Protection for the Global South', November 2023.

International Organizations Policy Documents and Reports

Climate Policy Initiative, Global Landscape of Climate Finance 2023 (November 2023) <www.climatepolicyinitiative.org/publication/global-landscape-of-climate-finance-2023/> accessed 30th November 2023.

Emerton, L., 'Using Economic Incentives For Biodiversity Conservation', IUCN, The World Conservation Union (2000) <https://portals.iucn.org/library/sites/library/files/documents/PDF-2000-002.pdf> accessed 30th November 2023.

WEF, 'Nature Risk Rising: Why the Crisis Engulfing Nature Matters for Business and the Economy, World Economic Forum' (2020) <www.weforum.org/publications/nature-risk-rising-why-the-crisis-engulfing-nature-matters-for-business-and-the-economy/#:~:text=Nature%20Risk%20Rising%2C%20produced%20in,and%20services%20within%20the%20broader> accessed 30th November 2023.

Conference Papers

Mullins, D., 'Remarks on the Global Derivatives Study Sponsored by the Group of Thirty' (1993) ISDA Summer Conference.

EU Legislation

Directive 2014/65/EU of the European Parliament and of the Council of 15 May 2014 on Markets in Financial Instruments and Amending Directive 2002/92/EC and Directive 2011/61/EU.

European Commission, 'Guidelines on Non-Financial Reporting (Methodology For Reporting Non-Financial Information)'26 June 2017. C (2017) 4234.

Regulation on OTC Derivatives, Central Counterparties and Trade Repositories known as EMIR Regulation (EU) No 648/2012.

2 The Rationale of Sustainable Finance

Introduction

This introductory chapter seeks to offer a concise and critical overview of ongoing developments in sustainable finance, focusing on the perspective of a risk-based approach to regulation. It sheds light on the potential of sustainable finance as an opportunity to redirect capital flows towards sustainable investments; to address financial risks arising from climate change, resource depletion, social issues, and more; and to support the long-term transition to a sustainable society.

We begin by examining how sustainability is reflected in environmental, social, and governance (ESG) factors, and explore the importance of distinguishing between dirty (or nongreen) and green finance. In addition, we examine the defining characteristics of both physical and transition risks, address the complexities of net-zero targets, and assess the challenges related to avoiding 'greenwashing'. In light of the global commitment to achieving net-zero emissions, we explore the essential aspects of both scientific and regulatory definitions. Furthermore, we thoroughly analyse the implications of greenwashing on the pursuit of sustainability goals. The main objective here is to establish a comprehensive foundation for understanding the principles of sustainable finance, and to underscore critical elements that will be further explored in the subsequent chapters. Specifically, our goal is to delineate the framework in which ESG financial derivatives can function and collaborate with other financial instruments, to advance the objectives of sustainable finance.

This introductory chapter sets the stage for our exploration of areas of alignment within the existing regulatory landscape and offers insights into potential enhancements concerning ESG derivatives contracts in the subsequent chapters. The methodological lens of our study is the risk-based approach to regulation.

Sustainability and ESG Factors

The notion of sustainability is set to be delimited from the outset, as it is a contention point among regulators, academics, and practitioners dealing with ESG factors. A common understanding of the term leads us to assert that 'sustainability is a measure of whether or to what extent a particular process or practice can

DOI: 10.4324/9781003365242-2

continue'.[1] Certainly, sustainability is not a new concept, as the answer to questions about whether any process can continue is at the core of any business strategy.[2] In that sense, the recent adoption of the term 'sustainability' in relation to environmental, social, and governance factors responds to the fact that ESG issues are drawn upon several kinds of interconnected processes that are urgent in the current state of the planet.[3]

The query for sustainability disrupts longstanding ideas about the opposite relationship between profitability and stakeholders' interests. From climate-related problems to social instability,[4] progress in the economy, society, and the environment can no longer be regarded as in conflict with sustainable growth.[5] This discussion will be covered in the following chapters, but let us begin by considering the reason behind the common trend on sustainable finance, closely related to the priorities set out in Article 2.1 (c) of the Paris Agreement.[6] The commitment for financial institutions to develop capacity and capabilities that enable them to identify, disclose, assess, and manage climate, environmental, and sustainability risks[7] is central to every decision in financial services.[8] However, the unsolved query regarding sustainable finance is how to ensure its goals are achieved with integrity and coherence, avoiding the risk of greenwashing. Certainly, until now, sustainable finance regulation has largely focused on providing an extensive and comprehensive framework. It covers a considerable range of benchmarks that provide the minimum standards for market participants to design and implement their own sustainability strategies.

Understanding that '*global problems require global solutions*', current international commitments towards the achievement of SDGs involve an ever-growing range of regulatory tools. One of the initiatives focused on capital markets are

1 Paul Thomson and Patricia E. Norris, *Sustainability: What Everyone Needs to Know* (Oxford University Press, 2021) 2.

2 Maha Faisal Alsayegh, Rashidah Abdul Rahman and Saeid Homayoun, 'Corporate Economic, Environmental, and Social Sustainability Performance Transformation Through ESG disclosure', *Sustainability* 12.9 (2020): 3910.

3 H. Ahmad, M. Yaqub and S. H. Lee, 'Environmental-, Social-, and Governance-Related Factors for Business Investment and Sustainability: A Scientometric Review of Global Trends', *Environment, Development and Sustainability* 26 (2023): 2965–2987.

4 Muhammad Ikram et al., 'The Social Dimensions of Corporate Sustainability: An Integrative Framework Including COVID-19 Insights', *Sustainability* 12.20 (2020): 8747.

5 Michael T. Lee and Suh Ikseon, 'Understanding the Effects of Environment, Social, and Governance Conduct on Financial Performance: Arguments for a Process and Integrated Modelling Approach', *Sustainable Technology and Entrepreneurship* 1.1 (2022): 100004.

6 Paris Agreement to the United Nations Framework Convention on Climate Change, 12 December 2015, T.I.A.S. No. 16-1104.

7 Simon Thompson, 'Green and Sustainable Finance: Principles and Practice in Banking, Investment and Insurance', *Chartered Banker* (2nd edn, Kogan Page, 2023) 1.

8 Speech Marck Carney, 'Speaking at the Re-Launch of the All-Party Parliamentary Group (APPG) for the Environment on Tuesday', 15 September 2020. www.edie.net/mark-carney-climate-considerations-must-be-embedded-in-every-financial-decision-for-a-truly-green-recovery/ accessed 13th June 2023.

the IOSCO's unification efforts to address issues around sustainability and climate change.[9] The Financial Stability Board (FSB) and the Network for Greening Financial Services (NGFS) have taken the lead in coordinating and harmonising responses to climate and other environmental and sustainability risks. The narrative in this scenario highlights the multiple regulatory instruments issued in the European Union market, amongst them the EU Taxonomy,[10] the European Non-Financial Reporting Directive (NFRD),[11] EU climate benchmarks,[12] the European Green Bond standard, science-based targets, and transition plans. Instruments also include the European Green Deal, the EU Sustainable Finance Action Plan, the Climate Delegated Act, and the Environmental Delegated Act, as well as the amendments to the Disclosures Delegated Act. Likewise, there is a range of proposed regulation on ESG ratings.[13] We will analyse some of these instruments when exploring the regime for ESG derivatives, as they represent the growing interest in delimiting and supporting the expansion of sustainable finance. It might be anticipated that the rationale of these regulatory efforts in the EU go beyond its borders, as they are meant to increase the transparency of the social and environmental impacts of firms' activities worldwide.[14]

Furthermore, UK regulatory initiatives should also be considered, starting with the intertwined relationships among the UK Government's Green Finance Strategy (GFS),[15] the joint work of the Financial Conduct Authority (FCA),[16] and the Prudential Regulation Authority (PRA), developing an approach that enhances the UK financial system's resilience to climate change. Also, let us consider the Bank of England's[17] objective to play a leading role in this movement. The Bank

9 IOSCO, 'Sustainable Finance and the Role of Securities Regulators and IOSCO: Final Report', FR04/2020, April 2020. www.iosco.org/library/pubdocs/pdf/IOSCOPD652.pdf accessed 1st July 2023.

10 European Commission, Joint Research Centre, S. Battiston et al., 'The EU Sustainability Taxonomy: A Financial Impact Assessment', Publications Office, 2020. https://data.europa.eu/doi/10.2760/347810 accessed 2nd November 2023.

11 Directive 2014/95/EU of October 22, 2014.

12 EU Climate Transition Benchmark (EU CTB) and the EU Paris-Aligned Benchmark (EU PAB). EU Technical Expert Group on Sustainable Finance, 'Report on Benchmarks: On Climate Benchmarks and Benchmarks', ESG Disclosures, September 2019. https://finance.ec.europa.eu/system/files/2019-09/190930-sustainable-finance-teg-final-report-climate-benchmarks-and-disclosures_en.pdf; www.unepfi.org/wordpress/wp-content/uploads/2022/02/Climate-Benchmarks_all-members-presentation.pdf.

13 European Commission, 'Sustainable Finance: Investing in a Sustainable Future', June 2023.

14 A. F. Cicchiello, F. Marrazza and S. Perdichizzi, 'Non-Financial Disclosure Regulation and Environmental, Social, and Governance (ESG) Performance: The Case of EU and US Firms', *Corporate Social Responsibility and Environmental Management* 30.3 (2023): 1121–1128. https://doi.org/10.1002/csr.2408.

15 HM Government, 'Mobilising 2023 Green Finance Strategy', March 2023. www.gov.uk/government/publications/green-finance-strategy accessed 1st July 2023.

16 FCA, 'Climate Change and Green Finance', Discussion Paper DP18/8, October 2018. www.fca.org.uk/publication/discussion/dp18-08.pdf accessed 1st July 2023.

17 Bank of England, 'Our Response to Climate Change'. www.bankofengland.co.uk/climate-change accessed 1st July 2023.

aims – through the Climate Financial Risk Forum,[18] its policies, and operations – to ensure the macroeconomy, the financial system, and the Bank itself are resilient to the risks from climate change, and to support the transition to a net-zero economy.

US regulators have also promoted several proposals and regulatory instruments regarding ESG regulation, such as the CFTC report on 'Managing Climate Risk in the US Financial System'[19], and the SEC 2021 announcement of their intention to develop a comprehensive ESG disclosure framework. This proposal would amend rules and forms under both the Investment Advisers Act of 1940 ('Advisers Act') and the Investment Company Act of 1940 ('Investment Company Act') to require registered investment advisers, certain advisers that are exempt from registration, registered investment companies, and business development companies all to provide additional information regarding their ESG investment practices.[20] Furthermore, recognising the leading role of the private sector regarding the advancement of the ESG agenda, we will analyse private sector commitments on designing ESG measuring and disclosure methodologies, such as the Principles for Responsible Investment (PRI), the Task Force on Climate-related Financial Disclosures (TCFD), and the Task Force on Nature-related Financial Disclosures (TNFD).

As may be anticipated, sustainable finance regulation – at least in the three jurisdictions studied in this book (i.e., the EU, UK, and US) – aims at improving disclosure of nonfinancial information, strengthening strategies of returns on ESG investments, and reframing ESG factors. However, in doing so, sustainable finance regulation has overlooked alternatives to equities, bonds, and credit markets, and particularly hedge products, given the greater complexity of strategies and asset classes.[21] Lately, a nascent interest has arisen in exploring the role of short selling in sustainable finance. In the third chapter, in which the role of derivatives in ESG is explained, we will expand on the opportunities hedging products bring to sustainable investment strategies. In particular, we will study how old and new derivatives products serve a wide range of purposes,[22] and delve into 'the channels

18 Climate Financial Risk Forum Guide 2020, June 2020. www.fca.org.uk/publication/corporate/climate-financial-risk-forum-guide-2020-summary.pdf.

19 CFTC, 'Managing Climate Risk in the U.S. Financial System', 2020. www.cftc.gov/sites/default/files/2020-09/9-9-20%20Report%20of%20the%20Subcommittee%20on%20Climate-Related%20Market%20Risk%20-%20Managing%20Climate%20Risk%20in%20the%20U.S.%20Financial%20System%20for%20posting.pdf accessed 17th December 2023.

20 SEC, '17 CFR Part 200, 230, 232, 239, 249, 274, and 279 [Release No. IA-6034; IC-34594; File No. S7-17-22] RIN: 3235-AM96, Enhanced Disclosures by Certain Investment Advisers and Investment Companies about Environmental, Social, and Governance Investment Practices', 25 May 2022. www.sec.gov/rules/proposed/2022/ia-6034.pdf.

21 Jason Mitchell, 'To Net or Not to Net, that is the Question: A Regulatory Review for Calculating the ESG Impact of Hedge Fund Portfolios', *The Journal of Impact & ESG Investing* 3.4. Special Issue in Greenwashing. www.pm-research.com/content/pmrjesg/3/4 accessed 13th June 2023.

22 Dean Naumowicz and Delyth Hughes, 'The Role of Sustainability-Linked Derivatives in Meeting Global ESG Goals', *Butterworths Journal of International Banking and Financial Law* (October 2021): 628.

of influence, the efficacy of short selling to affect the cost of capital, the time-varying feature of short selling, and the limitations of short sellers when engaging corporates'.[23]

The clarity regarding mainstream definitions is the first step towards building the discourse around risk and uncertainties as the methodological lens of this study. To understand how the theory of risk[24] can provide the grounds for a more fruitful discussion, let us first throw some light onto the intertwined notions of sustainable, green, and dirty (or nongreen) finance.

Sustainable Finance

The notion of sustainable finance is an ever-growing concept that has its most accepted roots in the 1987 UN Report on the Environment and Development,[25] which stated

> *Sustainable finance is finance that meets the social, environmental, and livelihood needs of the present generation without compromising the ability of future generations to meet their own needs, and that creates a fair balance between societies in the north and the south.*

Hence, sustainable finance encompasses two pillars.[26] On the one hand, making the activities and operations of financial institutions more sustainable, as they consider broader economic, environmental, and social factors as a part of the institution's strategy and management. On the other hand, financing sustainable economic, environmental, and social objectives delimited in the UN Sustainable Development Goals (SDGs).[27] Hence, the successful combination of management and financing following the SDGs might help us to delineate the boundaries of sustainable finance. In this scenario, the label 'ESG' has gained some traction,[28] in considering how organisations manage *environmental*, *social*, and *governance* factors in their activities.[29] The origin of the ESG concept comes from the field of socially

23 Jason Mitchell, 'To Net or Not to Net, that is the Question: A Regulatory Review for Calculating the ESG Impact of Hedge Fund Portfolios' (n 21).

24 See Ulrich Beck and Mark Ritter, *Risk Society: Towards a New Modernity* (Sage Publications, 1992–2009).

25 United Nations, 'Report of the World Commission on Environment and Development: Our Common Future', 1987. https://sustainabledevelopment.un.org/content/documents/5987our-common-future.pdf accessed 14th June 2023.

26 A. Fatemi and I. J. Fooladi, 'Sustainable Finance: A New Paradigm', *Global Finance Journal* 24.2 (2013): 101–113.

27 United Nations, 'The 2030 Agenda and the Sustainable Development Goals: An Opportunity for Latin America and the Caribbean', LC/G. 2681-P/Rev.

28 European Social Investment Forum (EUROSIF), 'European SRI Study', 2014. www.eurosif.org/wp-content/uploads/2022/03/Eurosif-SRI-Study-2014.pdf accessed 12th May 2023.

29 There is also a trend to use sustainable and ESG interchangeably.

responsible investments (SRI),[30] and thus some authors[31] judge it to be an evolution of socially responsible conduct in business, as it was originally conceived in the early 1980s. However, the current ESG trend covers a much broader programme.[32] It now includes good principles of sustainable development based on strategies to generate long-term competitive financial returns and positive social effects.[33] Our purpose in using the term 'ESG' is to include both factors[34] that influence activities and corporate decision-making[35], as well as the risks[36] that illustrate the way finance supports the achievement of sustainable goals. We also accept the assertion of academics like Edmans,[37] who argue that ESG is both 'extremely important and nothing special' – economically, at least. This means accepting that ESG is no different to other intangible assets and investments that create long-term financial and social value.[38]

The quest for ESG consolidation, aggravated due to recent comments from industry leaders,[39] indicating that the term ESG is losing momentum as it has been strongly politicised, strives for a balance between corporate traditional priorities and meeting expectations of long-term impact and returns from sustainable corporate strategies and investment. The significant impact that ESG factors can have on the value of companies and securities requires higher levels of transparency and strict reporting methodologies for comparable ESG data. Therefore, sustainable finance regulation is expected to channel its efforts towards providing greater

30 Iwona Bak and Katarzyna Cheba, 'ESG Risk as a New Challenge for Financial Markets', in Magdalena Ziolo (ed), *Finance and Sustainable Development: Designing Sustainable Financial Systems* (Routledge International Studies in Money and Banking, 2021) 22.

31 Jason M. Ribando and George Bonne, 'A New Quality Factor: Finding Alpha with Asset4 ESG Data', Thomson Reuter, Startmine Research Note. www.thomsonreuters.com/content/dam/openweb/documents/pdf/tr-com-financial/report/starmine-quant-research-note-on-asset4-data.pdf accessed 13th May 2023.

32 Martina K. Linnenluecke, Tom Smith and Brent McKnight, 'Environmental Finance: A Research Agenda for Interdisciplinary Finance Research', *Economic Modelling* 59 (2016): 124–130.

33 Iwona Bak and Katarzyna Cheba, 'ESG Risk as a New Challenge for Financial Markets' (n 30) 22.

34 Zhao Changhong, Yu Guo, Jiahai Yuan, Mengya Wu, Daiyu Li, Yiou Zhou and Jiangang Kang, 'ESG and Corporate Financial Performance: Empirical Evidence from China's Listed Power Generation Companies', *Sustainability* 10.8 (2018): 1–18.

35 Since 1992, the UNEP FI has been advocating for financial institutions to integrate ESG factors into the decision-making process.

36 Magdalena Ziolo, Iwona Bak, Ria Sinha and Manipadma Datta, 'ESG Risk Perception in Sustainable Financial Decisions. Quantitative Methods Perspective', in Kesra Nermed and Malgorzata Latuszynska (eds), *Experimental and Quantitative Methods in Contemporary Economics: Computational Methods in Experimental Economics (CMEE) 2018 Conference* (Springer, 2020) 157.

37 Alex Edmans, 'The End of ESG', *Financial Management* 52 (2023): 3– 17. https://doi.org/10.1111/fima.12413.

38 Alex Edmans, 'Applying Economics – Not Gut Feel – To ESG', SSRN, March 16, 2023. https://ssrn.com/abstract=4346646.

39 Ananya Bhattacharya, 'BlackRock CEO Larry Fink is Focusing on Goals Other than "ESG": Fink Said the ESG Debate Has been "misused" by Both Conservatives and Liberals', 27 June 2023. https://qz.com/blackrock-ceo-larry-fink-is-focusing-on-goals-other-tha-1850580124 accessed 3rd June 2023.

clarity around reporting, assessment, comparability, and ESG data relevance. The problem, however, is that – despite the broad range of sustainable finance regulatory instruments – ESG data methodologies have been developed by market participants before regulatory instruments were in place. Hence, there is an overproduction of assessment methodologies of ESG data that renders complex material information for reporting, analysis, and understanding by the market, investors, and corporates. As a result, some market actors[40] deemed the inclusion of credit rating agencies as positive and necessary,[41] because of the centrality of ratings to the investment process.[42] However, there is a downside: an overreliance on the role of credit ratings, as regulators have a tendency to incorporate credit ratings to a point whereby they end up outsourcing their responsibilities to private market actors.[43]

Building a sustainable financial system involves a group of diverse actors. These include intergovernmental organisations, national governments, central banks and financial regulators, international financial institutions and multilateral development banks, scientific organisations, financial services firms, and nongovernmental organisations. Among them, intergovernmental bodies, national governments, and regulatory authorities have a particularly important role in leading the speed of progress. The driving force of change is to consolidate financial systems that are designed for sustainability, and not just stability. Indeed, the 2007 Global Financial Crisis was the turning point that forced financial markets, regulators, and companies to rethink not only systemic risk, but how the creation of value to society must involve the stakeholder triple line of people, planet, and profit.[44] Therefore, a financial system is regarded as sustainable only when it actively 'contributes to the needs of the society by supporting sustainable and equitable economies, while protecting the natural environment'.[45] In this context, ESG factors emerge as key parameters to assess how companies manage their contribution to sustainable development, and how financial institutions are important catalysts for supporting it.[46] The assessment of a company's purpose, following a value-based-management approach,[47] drives the push towards a more sustainable economy.

40 The Principles for Responsible Investment.

41 Hanna Silvola and Tiina Landau, *Sustainable Investing: Beating the Market with ESG* (Palgrave McMillan, 2021) 71.

42 Daniel Cash, 'Sustainable Finance Ratings as the Latest Symptom of "Rating Addiction" ', *Journal of Sustainable Finance & Investment* 8.3 (2018): 242–258.

43 ibid., 244.

44 Peter Fisk, *People Planet Profit: How to Embrace Sustainability for Innovation and Business Growth* (Kogan Page Publishers, 2010) 5.

45 UN PRI Initiative, 'Blueprint for Responsible Investment'. www.unpri.org/about-us/a-blueprint-for-responsible-investment accessed 13th June 2023.

46 Nihat Aktas, Eric De Bodt and Jean Gabriel Cousin, 'Do Financial Markets Care About SRI? Evidence from Mergers and Acquisitions', *Journal of Banking and Finance* 35 (2011): 1753–1761. www.sciencedirect.com/science/article/abs/pii/S037842661000453X accessed 13th June 2023.

47 Michael Burkert and Rainer Lueg, 'Differences in the Sophistication of Value-based Management – The Role of Top Executives', *Management Accounting Research* 24.1 (2013): 3–22. https://doi.org/10.1016/j.mar.2012.10.001 accessed 12th May 2023.

In this context, green finance has taken the lead. The three major international agreements[48] supporting sustainability objectives are focused on environmental issues, especially those related to combating climate change. This might be a reason to equate sustainable finance to green finance. However, conceptual clarity regarding the issues embedded in ESG factors is key to understanding how a risk-based approach helps to unfold the purpose of finance in terms of promoting sustainability.

This book will also define how sustainability is reflected in ESG factors, why it is important to differentiate the dirty (or nongreen) and green finance, and how to prevent the risk of 'greenwashing'. The concepts of green and dirty finance represent contrasting approaches to financial investments and their environmental impact. *Green finance* aims to channel capital towards environmentally friendly and sustainable projects, while *dirty finance* refers to investments that are associated with high carbon emissions and environmental degradation.

Green Finance

Green finance is a financial framework that prioritises investments in projects and activities that have positive environmental benefits. It seeks to support the transition to a low-carbon and sustainable economy, by directing capital towards renewable energy, energy efficiency, sustainable infrastructure, and other environmentally friendly sectors.

Green finance integrates environmental considerations into investment decision-making, assessing projects based on their environmental impact, carbon footprint, and sustainability credentials before allocating funds. It underscores the importance of measuring and disclosing environmental impact, advocating the use of indicators and reporting frameworks to monitor and evaluate the environmental performance of investments. Various financial instruments, such as green bonds, green loans, sustainability-linked loans, and innovative financing mechanisms, support sustainable investments aligned with environmental goals. Governments and regulatory bodies play a crucial role by implementing supportive policies and regulations. These measures may include tax incentives, subsidies, and mandatory reporting requirements, aiming to encourage the widespread adoption of sustainable practices within the context of green finance.

Probably the most comprehensive definition of green finance[49] encompasses various aspects related to the financing of environmentally sustainable investments and initiatives. This includes financing green investments, financing public policies, and the creation of financial instruments for green investments. Green

48 United Nations Climate Convention on Climate Change (UNFCCC) 1992; Kyoto Protocol 1997, Paris Agreement 2015.

49 Nannette Lindenberg, 'Definition of Green Finance', April 2014. https://web.archive.org/web/20180721183829id_/www.die-gdi.de/uploads/media/Lindenberg_Definition_green_finance.pdf accessed 4th July 2023.

finance also involves providing financial resources for both public and private sector investments that have positive environmental impacts. These investments can include funding projects related to the management of water resources, the protection of biodiversity and landscapes, and other activities aimed at preserving and improving the environment. Moreover, it covers financing initiatives focused on minimising and compensating for environmental and climate-related damage.

Green finance also extends to the financing of public policies that encourage the implementation of environmental projects and initiatives. Examples of such policies can include feed-in tariffs that promote the use of renewable energies and other measures to mitigate environmental damage. Additionally, green finance involves specific components within the financial system that are dedicated to supporting and facilitating green investments, such as the Green Climate Fund (GCF), a financial institution established to provide financial resources to developing countries for projects that address climate change mitigation and adaptation.

The creation of financial instruments for green investments encompasses various financial products and mechanisms designed to fund green projects. Examples include green bonds, and structured green funds that pool investments specifically for green initiatives. Later in the book, we will argue the benefits of designing financial derivatives as a hedging tool for the myriad ESG risks.

The landscape of debt-finance instruments used to raise private funds for sustainable development has evolved significantly.[50] While green bonds were once the primary choice, the sustainable-debt market has expanded rapidly, witnessing a remarkable 26% growth between 2017 and 2018, with a total issuance of sustainable debt products amounting to USD 247 billion.[51] Moreover, this market has experienced diversification over the past four years,[52] introducing four additional instruments: sustainability bonds, social bonds, green loans, and sustainability-linked loans (also known as sustainability-improvement loans or ESG-linked loans).

Within the context of green finance, there are other subcategories proposed, to categorise the type of risks they aim to manage. Nature-based and biodiversity-based finance have entered the regulatory dialogue. When discussing finance for nature, we are addressing both public and private funding directed towards nature-based solutions (NbS) that are aimed at addressing pressing global issues such as biodiversity loss, land degradation, and climate change.[53] As defined by the UN Environment Assembly, NbS encompasses all efforts to safeguard,

50 Mathias Lund Larsen, 'A Growing Toolbox of Sustainable Finance Instruments', 22 November 2019. https://greenfdc.org/a-growing-toolbox-of-sustainable-finance-instruments/?cookie-state-change=1688514773379#_ftn8 accessed 4th July 2023.

51 Bloomberg, 'Sustainable Debt Market Sees Record Activity in 2018', 2019. https://about.bnef.com/blog/sustainable-debt-market-Sees-record-activity-2018/ accessed 4th July 2023.

52 Mathias Lund Larsen, 'A Growing Toolbox of Sustainable Finance Instruments' (n 50).

53 UNEP, ELD, 'State of Finance for Nature 2022', 1 December 2022. https://wedocs.unep.org/bitstream/handle/20.500.11822/41333/state_finance_nature.pdf?sequence=3 accessed 2nd November 2023.

preserve, rehabilitate, and responsibly exploit natural or altered land, water, coastal, and marine environments. These actions aim to tackle social, economic, and environmental issues adeptly and efficiently, while concurrently enhancing human welfare, ecosystem services, and bolstering resilience and biodiversity.[54] Despite the broad and daily attention to climate-related risk policies and mitigation strategies, the UNEP reports that we are far behind in terms of NbS financing. For 2022, NbS financial support amounted to USD 154 billion annually, falling short of the required investment by some way – estimated at USD 384 billion per year by 2025, and USD 484 billion per year by 2030.[55] This financing disparity is disproportionate to the substantial potential in addressing climate change from NbSs, which (according to the World Bank) have the capacity to contribute up to 37% of the necessary mitigation efforts by 2030, to meet the objectives outlined in the Paris Agreement.[56] This gap illustrates that, while there is a widespread acknowledgment of climate-related risks and the role of NbS in mitigating them, the implementation of requisite actions is hindered by considerable uncertainty for corporations, organisations, and markets in taking concrete and quantifiable steps. In the context of a risk society,[57] it appears that there is a disconnect between the awareness of these risks and the measures put in place to effectively manage them.

Along with the NbS, solutions based on the use of technology are also being considered in the fight against climate change. The United Nations Framework Convention on Climate Change (UNFCCC) refers to these as *climate technologies*. Climate technologies aimed at reducing greenhouse gas (GHG) emissions involve renewable energy sources like wind, solar, and hydropower. Additionally, climate technologies focused on adapting to the impacts of climate change include resilient crops, early warning systems, and infrastructure such as sea walls. Moreover, 'soft' climate technologies involve practices promoting energy efficiency and training for efficient equipment tilization.[58] The UN has developed a series of frameworks to facilitate the identification of the opportunities that technology can bring to tackling climate change. In 2010, the Conference of the Parties (COP) established the Technology Mechanism™, designed with the primary aim of expediting and improving the development and transfer of climate-related tech.[59] Then, in 2023, as part of the Joint Work

54 UNEP, 'Fifth Session of the United Nations Environment Assembly (UNEA-5)', February 2021. www.unep.org/environmentassembly/unea5 accessed 2nd November 2023.

55 UNEP, ELD, 'State of Finance for Nature 2022' (n 53).

56 WB, 'What You Need to Know About Nature-Based Solutions to Climate Change', 19 May 2022. www.worldbank.org/en/news/feature/2022/05/19/what-you-need-to-know-about-nature-based-solutions-to-climate-change accessed 2nd November 2023.

57 See Ulrich Beck, *Risk Society: Towards a New Modernity* (Sage, 1992).

58 UNFCCC, 'Technology and the UNFCCC: Building the Foundation for Sustainable Development', 2016. https://unfccc.int/ttclear/misc_/StaticFiles/gnwoerk_static/NAD_EBG/54b3b39e25b84f96aeada52180215ade/b8ce50e79b574690886602169f4f479b.pdf accessed 2nd November 2023.

59 UNFCCC, 'Support for Implementing Climate Technology Activities', 2010. https://unfccc.int/ttclear/support/technology-mechanism.html accessed 2nd November 2023.

Programme for the Technology Mechanism (2023–2027),[60] the TM initiated the 'Artificial Intelligence for Climate Action' project. This project is exploring the potential of AI as a potent tool for advancing and amplifying transformative climate solutions, with a specific emphasis on mitigating and adapting to climate change in developing countries, particularly Least Developed Countries (LDCs) and Small Island Developing States (SIDS).[61]

Closely related to nature finance is the category of biodiversity finance. It encompasses the use of capital to finance biodiversity conservation and restoration.[62] According to the World Wildlife Fund (WWF), there has been a 69% average decline in global populations of mammals, fish, birds, reptiles, and amphibians since 1970.[63] The report characterises the present situation as a 'code red' warning for humanity, and alerts us that, while conservation efforts are helping, urgent action is required if we are to reverse nature loss.[64] Along with the tragic consequences for human life and planetary boundaries, the diminishing of biodiversity poses an existential peril to the worldwide economy, given that over half of the world's GDP relies on nature and the invaluable services it offers.[65] Despite the undeniable need to focus attention on developing instruments and markets to finance biodiversity, there is not enough research in finance[66] explaining how to articulate the flow of private capital towards biodiversity conservation and restoration.

Biodiversity credits have emerged as a globally embraced financial instrument. These credits serve as an asset originating from investments dedicated to the enhancement, preservation, and advancement of biodiversity within a defined geographical area.[67] It is subsequently traded on local and global platforms, catering to businesses seeking to acquire assets that align with their corporate ESG commitments. Essentially, the asset's value is contingent on the documented and verified advancements in enhancing the ecological health of a specific ecosystem and/or the abundance of designated species in the predetermined region.[68]

60 UNFCC, 'Programme of Work 2023–2027', 2023. https://pow.ctc-n.org/programme.html accessed 2nd November 2023.

61 UNFCCC, 'Technology Mechanism Initiative on Artificial Intelligence for Climate Action', 2023. https://unfccc.int/ttclear/artificial_intelligence accessed 2nd November 2023.

62 Caroline Flammer, Thomas Giroux and Geoffrey Heal, 'Biodiversity Finance', NBER Working Paper No. 31022, March 2023. www.nber.org/system/files/working_papers/w31022/w31022.pdf accessed 3rd November 2023.

63 WWF, 'Living Planet Report 2022'. https://livingplanet.panda.org accessed 3rd November 2023.

64 ibid.

65 ibid.

66 Laura Starks, 'Sustainable Finance and E, S, & G Issues: Values Versus Value (Presidential Address at the 2023 American Finance Association Meetings)', *Journal of Finance* (forthcoming, 2023).

67 Tulkin Radjabov, 'Biodiversity Credit – An Effective Trade-Off Mechanism', 13 July 2023. www.undp.org/uzbekistan/blog/biodiversity-credit-effective-trade-mechanism accessed 5th December 2023.

68 ibid.

In this context, Flamer, Giroux, and Heal[69] introduce a pioneering approach for structuring biodiversity finance, based on two fundamental pillars: blended finance and pure private capital. Blended finance leverages funds from public and philanthropic sectors to enhance private sector investments in sustainable development. The Convention on Biological Diversity Global Biodiversity Framework[70] has endorsed blended finance as an effective means to augment the capital pool aimed at implementing nature-positive solutions through multi-sectoral collaborations. From a risk perspective, it is essential to identify how biodiversity finance can deliver financial benefits to investors. Like other aspects of market development, the focus is not solely on satisfying greater humanity concerns, but also revolves around materialising financial returns. This leads us to examine the potential monetisation of biodiversity.

While attributing an instrumental value to biodiversity may appear presumptuous, considering nature's intrinsic or ethical value,[71] the necessity to attract investment in biodiversity validates such a notion. Linking the value of biodiversity to financial outcomes can be seen in multiple ways – it might be considered, for instance, that protecting bees can significantly enhance agricultural productivity.[72] Preserving coastal ecosystems can effectively reduce the risks of flooding; conserving forest ecosystems can generate valuable carbon credits.[73] This broad spectrum of opportunities offers a direct avenue for biodiversity conservation projects to attract private capital.

There remains a significant opportunity for further advancements in the field of blended finance concerning biodiversity. Nonetheless, there are challenges that must be addressed to fully realise this potential. The most relevant difficulty is how to enhance risk management in this type of investment. Empirical evidence suggests that blending is typically used when the expected biodiversity impact is high, but the financial return is too low to be financed by pure private capital.[74] Some participants in the blended finance ecosystem argue that enhancing market practices is essential to mitigate both perceived and actual risks, while also improving expected investment returns.[75]

A risk-based approach to addressing the limitations of blended finance can be effectively adopted through a four-stage strategy. First, *concessional capital*[76]

69 Caroline Flammer, Thomas Giroux and Geoffrey Heal, 'Biodiversity Finance' (n 62) 4.

70 Convention of Biological Diversity, 'COP15: Nations Adopt Four Goals, 23 Targets for 2023 in Landmark Biodiversity Agreement', 19 December 2022. www.cbd.int/article/cop15-cbd-press-release-final-19dec2022 accessed 3rd November 2023.

71 P. A. L. D. Nunes and J. C. J. M. van den Bergh, 'Economic Valuation of Biodiversity: Sense or Nonsense?', *Ecological Economics* 39 (2001): 205. Elsevier.

72 Caroline Flammer, Thomas Giroux and Geoffrey Heal, 'Biodiversity Finance' (n 62) 6.

73 ibid.

74 R. Gibson-Brandon, S. Glossner, P. Matos and T. Steffen, 'Do Responsible Investors Invest Responsibly?', *Review of Finance* 26.6 (2022): 1389–1432.

75 Convergence Blending Global Finance, 'State of Blended Finance 2023', 25 October 2023. www.convergence.finance accessed 3rd November 2023.

76 ibid.

is provided by public or philanthropic entities, offering loans with interest rates below the market average. This structure reduces the overall cost of capital, mitigates the risk of default, and enables private investors to earn a return similar to market rates on their loans. Second, *guarantee protection* comes into play, with public or philanthropic entities committing to cover private debt obligations, in the case of nonpayment or reimbursing private equity funders for any asset value loss. This provides private investors extending debt or equity finance with a safety net if issues arise during the project; furthermore, development finance institutions, such as MIGA, USAID, and SIDA may offer financial guarantees to compensate private investors if the expected rate of return is not met.[77] Third, *incorporating provisions for technical assistance funds* in various project phases is advisable. These funds enhance technical expertise for project implementation, and the skills development and capacity-building supported by grants have a lasting impact.[78] Finally, to ensure the success and sustainability of development projects, it's crucial to consider *design-stage funding*. This approach, proposed by the global network for blended finance, Convergence, aims to enhance the overall sustainability, and safeguard the returns for investors at every stage of a biodiversity-related project.[79]

Dirty Finance

In contrast to green finance and its related categories of nature and biodiversity finance, 'dirty finance' refers to investments that are associated with high carbon emissions and environmental degradation. Dirty finance[80] supports industries and activities that contribute to pollution, deforestation, fossil fuel extraction, and other environmentally harmful practices. This type of finance perpetuates carbon-intensive activities and exacerbates climate change. Investments in coal-fired power plants, oil and gas exploration, and other carbon-intensive industries contribute to GHG emissions, leading to global warming and its associated impacts. Moreover, dirty or 'non-sustainable' finance often supports activities that result in deforestation, habitat destruction, and biodiversity loss. Industries such as mining, logging, and intensive agriculture can have severe ecological consequences, leading to irreversible damage to ecosystems. Furthermore, as we will explain later, the transition to a low-carbon economy poses risks to dirty finance. As the world moves towards cleaner energy sources and sustainable practices, investments in

77 Caroline Flammer, Thomas Giroux, and Geoffrey Heal, 'Biodiversity Finance' (n 62) 12.

78 Convergence Blending Global Finance, 'State of Blended Finance 2023' (n 75).

79 ibid.

80 See Elysha Davila and Caroline Dreyer, 'Why We No Longer Use the Phrase "Brown Finance" ', 14 September 2020. www.climatechangenews.com/2020/09/14/no-longer-use-phrase-brown-finance/ accessed 3rd November 2023. See also, Laura Cerami and Domenico Fanizza, 'A Market for Brown Assets to Make Finance Green', WP/23/11, January 2023. www.imf.org/en/Publications/WP/Issues/2023/01/20/A-Market-for-Brown-Assets-To-Make-Finance-Green-528413 accessed 3rd November 2023.

carbon-intensive assets may become stranded, losing their economic value and becoming financially unsustainable.

Recognising the risks associated to focusing finance strategy solely on green financial instruments and markets, there are proposals for the construction of a secondary market for nongreen assets.[81] The rationale behind the proposal is that of the *green paradox*[82] – to understand that climate and sustainability-guided policies that overly concentrate on bolstering the green economy (while deliberately neglecting carbon-intensive infrastructure and activities) could hasten the devaluation of dirty assets within significantly shorter timeframes than necessary to ensure a seamless and effective transition.[83] Researchers at the IMF propose that a promising strategy for mobilising private capital and supporting the transition to a carbon-neutral economy would be to transfer carbon-intensive assets from banks' balance sheets to portfolios managed by dedicated green investors.[84] They contend that the establishment of a secondary market for these assets allows banks to offload a portion of their carbon-intensive exposures, thereby freeing up risk-based capital that can be redirected towards funding new green initiatives. Furthermore, this emerging market expands the range of investment opportunities accessible to green asset managers, going beyond the limitations imposed by environmentally conscious investors. In essence, this approach aims to enhance the efficiency and effectiveness of capital allocation in the context of sustainable finance.[85]

As may be anticipated, the establishment of financial markets designed to facilitate a well-organised transition is eminently suitable, and contributes to a consistent and secure realisation of sustainable finance objectives. In a risk-based framework, this approach involves the identification and management of one of the most significant transition risks.

The Problems of Sustainable Finance

The rationale of ESG, responsible investment, and sustainable finance encompasses the incorporation of ESG considerations into investment decision-making and their inclusion in investment portfolios. The aim is to make financers and investors adopt one of two positions (either *avoiding* or *reducing* exposure to investments that pose higher ESG risks), while influencing the recipient companies and projects of the investment to take action to reduce ESG risks and create a positive social impact. In the broader context, sustainable finance is meant to enhance the funding of genuine transition initiatives, improving accessibility for individuals, small and medium-sized enterprises (SMEs), and public entities, to harness available opportunities in

81 ibid.

82 Svenn Jensen, Kristina Mohlin, Karen Pittel and Thomas Sterner, 'An Introduction to the Green Paradox: The Unintended Consequences of Climate Policies', *Review of Environmental Economics and Policy* 9.2 (Summer 2015).

83 ibid.

84 Laura Cerami and Domenico Fanizza, 'A Market for Brown Assets to Make Finance Green' (n 80).

85 ibid.

sustainability. This will bolster the financial sector's ability to withstand climate and environmental risks and enhance its sustainability impact, and ultimately, establish ambitious and cohesive standards across all global forums to achieve ESG targets. Unfortunately, progress has been slow and there are serious difficulties.

The worldwide scope of sustainability challenges underscores the importance of assessing the most effective allocation of available capital. Navid Hanif, Director of Financing for the Sustainable Development Office at the UN, advocates for a shift in perspective among capital-exporting countries. While these nations typically refer to 'emerging markets' (EMs), this designation encompasses only around 20 countries. However, there are still 91 nations that remain underserved in terms of capital inflows. There is a clear imbalance between the shared purpose of sustainable finance and the way capital is being directed.[86] In this scenario, the call is to consider the difficulties faced by frontier markets and EM economies[87] in accessing capital for sustainability purposes. It is the frontier markets (FMs) that require investment most urgently.[88] A frontier market is characterised as a low-income, high-growth economy that falls below the classification of an EM due to its relatively small size, perceived risk, or limited liquidity.[89] FM funding has notably decreased after the COVID-19 pandemic.[90] A significant portion of the capital raised for the 2030 Agenda falls short in its efforts to achieve high-impact outcomes related to the SDGs.[91]

The constrained access to capital in FMs is particularly concerning, because they encompass a substantial share of the global population, accounting for one-third of the world's inhabitants.[92] However, according to the UBS Frontier Market report of 2020, their contribution to the global economy is relatively small, accounting for only 3.5% of the total global GDP, and possessing an equity market

86 UN, 'Opening Statement by Mr. Navid Hanif Assistant Secretary-General for Economic and Social Development', 2 August 2023. https://financing.desa.un.org/document/opening-statement-mr-navid-hanif-assistant-secretary-general-economic-and-social accessed 3rd November 2023.

87 Deepali Gautam, Rohit Goel, Fabio Natalucci, 'Sustainable Finance in Emerging Markets is Enjoying Rapid Growth, But May Bring Risks', 1 March 2022. www.imf.org/en/Blogs/Articles/2022/03/01/sustainable-finance-in-emerging-markets-is-enjoying-rapid-growth but may bring-risks accessed 3rd November 2023.

88 UN, 'Opening Statement by Mr. Navid Hanif Assistant Secretary – General for Economic and Social Development' (n 86).

89 Lalith P. Samarakoon, 'Stock Market Interdependence, Contagion, and the U.S. Financial Crisis: The Case of Emerging and Frontier Markets', *Journal of International Financial Markets, Institutions and Money* 21.5 (2011): 724–742.

90 Jay Collins, 'Unlocking Private Climate Finance for Emerging Markets', Panel Discussion Vice Chairman, Banking, Capital Markets and Advisory, Citi, Online, 2 October 2023. www.iif.com/events/2023IMF/meetingid/a8ea5909-e557-ee11-be6f-000d3a99aa70 accessed 3rd November 2023.

91 Natasha White, 'Citi Executive Backs Pause Clauses for Emerging-Market Debt', 23 June 2023. www.bloomberg.com/news/articles/2023-06-23/citi-executive-backs-pause-clauses-for-some-emerging-market-debt?embedded-checkout=trueaccessed 3rd November 2023.

92 IMF, 'World Economic Outlook', Population Metrics, October 2023. www.imf.org/external/datamapper/LP@WEO/OEMDC/ADVEC/WEOWORLD accessed 3rd November 2023.

capitalisation that makes up just 0.6% of the worldwide total.[93] The UN projects that the proportion of the working-age population in FMs will remain stable at 67% in 2030, mirroring the current level.[94] This highlights that a significant segment of the global population is not experiencing the positive effects that sustainable finance aims to deliver. This issue doesn't stem from longstanding global capital inequality, but rather from the failure to address global challenges with a comprehensive and inclusive approach.

The counterargument might rationalise that the unequal distribution of capital for sustainability projects and initiatives revolves around the issue of trust. Insufficient access to sustainability-related data hinders the fair allocation of financing. While most sustainable regulations are primarily focused on developed economies, EMs and FMs have been slower in adopting relevant reporting requirements. Consequently, there is an undeniable information asymmetry that steers financiers and investors towards markets with higher levels of transparency – or at least, those with more structured disclosure mechanisms. In addition to the data disparity and the challenges of comparing markets, the problem is exacerbated by legal uncertainty. A crucial aspect of this issue is the need for certainty regarding regulatory and policy frameworks, an environment that governments must urgently foster. While the common ground for sustainability-related projects is the guideline of the SDGs, building trust through robust regulatory and self-regulatory instruments is essential to attract financiers.[95]

As the significance of sustainability grows, there is an increasing demand from various stakeholders, including investors, consumers, and society at large, for companies and projects to openly demonstrate and disclose their sustainability impact.[96] In response, companies are actively heeding this demand and swiftly taking measures to communicate their positive contributions. To assist in this endeavour, international standards organisations (such as the TCFD, PRI, Sustainability Accounting Standards Board (SASB), the International Sustainability Standards Board (ISSB) with the IFRS S1 General Requirements for Disclosure of Sustainability-related Financial Information and IFRS S2 Climate-related Disclosures, and the UN SDGs) have put forth frameworks that companies and financial institutions

93 UBS, '2020 Strategic Asset Allocation and Capital Market Assumptions Update', 16 April 2020. www.ubs.com/content/dam/WealthManagementAmericas/documents/2020-cma-whitepaper.pdf accessed 3rd November 2023.

94 UN, 'Frontier Technology Issues: Harnessing the Economic Dividends from Demographic Change', 6 July 2023. www.un.org/development/desa/dpad/publication/frontier-technology-issues-harnessing-the-economic-dividends-from-demographic-change/ accessed 3rd November 2023.

95 Rohit Goel, Deepali Gautam and Fabio M. Natalucci, 'Sustainable Finance in Emerging Markets: Evolution, Challenges, and Policy Priorities', IMF Working Papers, 9 September 2022. www.imf.org/en/Publications/WP/Issues/2022/09/09/Sustainable-Finance-in-Emerging-Markets-Evolution-Challenges-and-Policy-Priorities-521689 accessed 3rd November 2023.

96 Jay Gelb, Rob McCarthy, Werner Rehm and Andrey Voronin, 'Investors Want to Hear from Companies About the Value of Sustainability', 15 September 2023. www.mckinsey.com/capabilities/strategy-and-corporate-finance/our-insights/investors-want-to-hear-from-companies-about-the-value-of-sustainability accessed 3rd November 2023.

can utilise to assess, manage, and report their progress.[97] Governments are intensifying their efforts to establish taxonomies[98] that will standardise the specifics of what sustainability entails, and how it can be uniformly measured. However, corporate strategies, regulations, and the expectations of stakeholders are all advancing more rapidly than the data needed to support these initiatives.[99]

Multiple challenges exist in the context of sustainability data. Firstly, ESG data often lacks the necessary level of detail at the company level. The concept of measuring sustainability is relatively new, and has not been comprehensively measured in terms of both depth and breadth.[100] Even when ESG data is available,[101] significant inconsistencies frequently emerge.[102] Companies within the same sector may employ varying methods to measure and collect data, or they may prioritise different sustainability factors based on their perceived relevance. This is because the narrative of sustainability responds to different perceptions of risks – while SDGs and the Paris Agreement seem to provide a benchmark for sustainable strategies, the interpretation of these instruments, as well as the selection of the most prominent risk, is not uniform. Data providers and rating agencies also employ different methodologies for generating ESG data through modelling and estimation. Consequently, each data provider can calculate significantly different data and 'scores' for the same company.

Moreover, there are misalignments in how companies aggregate data for different reporting purposes. This leads to internal discrepancies, as the ESG reporting framework may substantially differ from the financial reporting framework. These misalignments are further compounded by seemingly minor but quantifiably significant variations between multiple 'generally accepted' ESG frameworks (such as TCFD, PRI, SASB, ISSB, the SDGs, and the EU Taxonomy). Additionally, current ESG data management processes tend to be highly manual, susceptible to human error, and infrequently verified by third-party assessments, raising concerns about data quality. Regrettably, there are no straightforward solutions to address these challenges, and they are already requiring substantial investments of

97 Cristina Alexandrina Stefanescu, 'Linking Sustainability Reporting Frameworks and Sustainable Development Goals', *Accounting Research Journal* 35.4 (2022): 508–525.

98 See World Bank, 'Colombia: Leading the Path to Sustainability in Latin America', 7. September 2022. www.worldbank.org/en/news/feature/2022/08/31/colombia-leading-the-path-to-sustainability-in-latin-america accessed 3rd November 2023.

99 William Easterly, 'How the Millennium Development Goals are Unfair to Africa', *World Development* 37.1 (2009): 26–35.

100 William Easterly, 'The Trouble with the Sustainable Development Goals', *Current History* 114.775 (2015): 322.

101 Nadia Albu, Nicolae Catalin, Madalina Dumitru and Valentin Dumitru, 'Plurality or Convergence in Sustainability Reporting Standards?', *Amfiteatru Economic Journal* 15.7 (2013): 729–742. The Bucharest University of Economic Studies.

102 Hai-Anh Dang, Haishan Fu and Umar Serajuddin, 'Tracking the Sustainable Development Goals: Emerging Measurement Challenges and Further Reflections', GLO Discussion Paper No. 327, 2019. Global Labor Organization (GLO).

capital and resources to implement systems that can automate and oversee ESG data management.

The predominant challenge lies in the expenses incurred by individual companies and projects when acquiring data. However, this goes beyond the basic costs of accessing, managing, and disclosing ESG data. The true expense arises from the effort needed to integrate ESG factors into a company's existing business model and infrastructure, which is essential for generating the required data.[103] Effective integration must commence at the strategic and policy levels, and permeate throughout management activities, process restructuring, and system modifications.[104] Only through this comprehensive approach can the relevant ESG data be generated and disclosed, meeting the expectations of stakeholders and regulators concerning a company's sustainability performance. This burden is particularly onerous for SMEs, as the cost of integration often exceeds their scale.[105] Private companies not subject to nonfinancial data disclosure regulations, like the NFRD,[106] also bear a significant weight in this regard.

Additionally, strengthening the scalability of sustainability-related projects is important to enhance risk management.[107] To reshape the risk-return profile of projects that might be deemed unsuitable for investment, it is vital to efficiently merge both public and private capital. This is why blended finance is seen as a promising avenue for sustainable financing. Nevertheless, even with a substantial pool of funds, deploying this capital can be a formidable task without a consistent stream of feasible investment prospects. Therefore, partnering with local and development banks possessing a profound grasp of the SDGs is pivotal to establish a pipeline of projects that meet the criteria for investment.[108] Likewise, governments have a significant role to play in reducing the risks associated with these opportunities.

103 Sara Bernow, Jonathan Godsall, Bryce Klempner and Charlotte Merten, 'More Than Values: The Value-Based Sustainability Reporting That Investors Want', in *Sustainability and Private Equity & Principal Investors Practices* (McKinsey & Company, July 2019). www.mckinsey.de/~/media/McKinsey/Business%20Functions/Sustainability/Our%20Insights/More%20than%20values%20The%20value%20based%20sustainability%20reporting%20that%20investors%20want/More%20than%20values-VF.pdf accessed 3rd November 2023.

104 Carol Adams and Patty McNicholas, 'Making a Difference: Sustainability Reporting, Accountability and Organisational Change', *Accounting, Auditing & Accountability Journal* 20.3 (2007): 382–402.

105 Marika Arena and Giovanni Azzone, 'A Process-Based Operational Framework for Sustainability Reporting in SMEs', *Journal of Small Business and Enterprise Development* 19.4 (2012): 669–686.

106 Ries Breijer and René P. Orij, 'The Comparability of Non-Financial Information: An Exploration of the Impact of the Non-Financial Reporting Directive (NFRD, 2014/95/EU)', *Accounting in Europe* 19.2 (2022): 332–361.

107 Aurélien Acquier, Valentina Carbone and David Massé, 'How to Create Value (s) in the Sharing Economy: Business Models, Scalability, and Sustainability', *Technology Innovation Management Review* 9.2 (2019).

108 IDB, 'IDB Calls for Greater Collaboration with Public Development Banks to Mobilize Resources for SDGs, Climate Change', 4 September 2023. www.iadb.org/en/news/idb-calls-greater-collaboration-public-development-banks-mobilize-resources-sdgs-climate accessed 3rd November 2023.

They can address issues, such as currency convertibility, and provide guarantees. Additionally, it is essential to ensure that investors can clearly perceive a direct connection between the projects and their contributions to the SDGs.

Considering this context, the concepts and topics introduced in this section serve to frame the discussion about how financial instruments – particularly financial derivatives – can enhance the effectiveness of sustainable finance. As our argument unfolds, the concepts, attributes, and challenges described here offer additional insights into how certain issues have been addressed through regulations, or the advancement of sustainability-linked financial transactions.

Furthermore, sustainability, within the realm of ESG, should not solely revolve around environmental factors. It must also include social and governance, as we will discuss in Chapters 6 and 7. However, in 2015, the Paris Agreement established a framework that outlined a set of priorities for regulators, industries, markets, and society to address the most pressing climate risk, which is climate change. Therefore, the following section examines various categories of climate risks.

Climate Risks

Physical Climate Risks

Within the context of environmental risks, climate-related risks are a priority, as these are imperative to understanding and addressing the impacts of changing climate. Physical climate risks have become a pressing global concern as the planet experiences the effects of climate change. These risks encompass a range of adverse impacts, including extreme weather events, sea level rise, heat waves, droughts, and flooding, which have far-reaching implications for human societies, ecosystems, and economies. Understanding physical climate risks means to explore the nature of physical climate risks, their implications, and the strategies needed to respond to these challenges with mitigation, adaptation, or both.

In 1979, the Intergovernmental Panel for Climate Change (IPCC)[109] defined climate change broadly as 'any change in climate over time whether due to natural variability or as a result of human activity'. The term refers to long-term shifts in weather patterns and average temperatures that can be triggered by human activities and/or natural changes.[110] Then, in 1992, the UNFCCC[111] made industrial country signatories commit themselves to 'the aim of returning individually or jointly to their 1990 levels these anthropogenic emissions of carbon dioxide and other greenhouse gases'. Climate change is not just an environmental issue for scientists to discuss, thereby creating certainties or uncertainties (the heavily contested climate change discourse can create certainty about what to do in some areas, yet simultaneously, alert us to the uncertainties of planetary changes not yet possible

109 Intergovernmental Panel on Climate Change (IPCC).

110 Roger A. Pielke, Jr., 'What is Climate Change?', *Energy & Environment* 15.3 (2004): 518.

111 UNFCCC, Article 4, Paragraph 2b.

to fully anticipate or manage). Thus, climate change requires a transversal dialogue on risks to highlight the role that business, society, and individuals play in creating and solving the problem.

In its submission to the Earth Summit, in Rio de Janeiro in 1992, the World Business Council for Sustainable Development (WBCSD) brought attention to the complex and seemingly contradictory relationship between business and climate change. Acknowledging that industrial activity, predominantly driven by business, is the primary contributor to anthropogenic CO_2 emissions – and that consequently, addressing climate change requires a profound transformation in industrial structure and operations – the WBCSD also recognised the importance of economic development in fostering innovation, clean technology, green investment, adaptation, and ultimately achieving climate protection. To accomplish these objectives, the WBCSD proposed a paradigm shift for businesses, emphasising a departure from the often adversarial relationship between business and government on environmental matters, and advocating for a more collaborative approach.[112] The multidimensional character of climate change is reflected in various approaches, being regarded as an environmental threat, an ethical dilemma,[113] a sociological problem,[114] and – due to its economic implications – also a market failure.[115] Regardless of the dimension adopted, policymakers and scientific communities accept that the main reason for the current state of climate change is human activity, primarily GHG emissions. Rising atmospheric concentrations of carbon dioxide and other GHGs lead to global warming and alter the Earth's climate system, triggering various physical climate risks.

Physical climate risks manifest in diverse forms. The first and most notorious of these are extreme weather events. Climate change intensifies the frequency and intensity of extreme weather events such as hurricanes, cyclones, wildfires, and heavy rainfall. These events can result in extensive property damage, loss of life, and disruption to critical infrastructure, affecting communities and economies. Following this, sea level rise is the next most significant risk. As global temperatures rise, glaciers and polar ice caps melt, leading to a rise in sea level. Higher sea levels increase the risk of coastal flooding and erosion, submerging low-lying areas, threatening coastal communities, and impacting coastal ecosystems and economies. Another significant physical climate risk is heat wave/drought. The increasing frequency and severity of these events in the last 40 years is alarming. Such extreme weather is reported to have been responsible for half a trillion euros in

112 C. Okereke, B. Wittneben and F. Bowen, 'Climate Change: Challenging Business, Transforming Politics', *Business & Society* 51.1 (2012): 7–30.

113 S. M. Gardiner and L. Hartzell-Nichols, 'Ethics and Global Climate Change', *Nature Education Knowledge* 3.10 (2012): 5.

114 A. Giddens, *The Politics of Climate Change* (Polity, 2009).

115 John Chung-En Liu, Yoram Bauman and Yating Chuang, 'Climate Change and Economics 101: Teaching the Greatest Market Failure', *Sustainability* 11.5 (2019): 1340. https://doi.org/10.3390/su11051340 accessed 1st July 2023.

economic losses, and between 85,000–145,000 human fatalities, whilst heat waves alone have caused tens of thousands of premature deaths just in Europe since 2000.[116] Heat waves pose risks to human health, exacerbate water scarcity, and strain agricultural systems. Droughts can result in crop failures,[117] reduced water availability, and food security challenges.[118]

Flooding and heavy precipitation is another physical climate risk. Warmer temperatures enhance evaporation, increasing the capacity of the atmosphere to hold moisture. This leads to more intense rainfall events and the potential for widespread flooding, putting communities at risk, damaging infrastructure, and disrupting economic activities.[119]

Implications of physical climate risks are severe for human societies and natural ecosystems. The frequency and intensity of extreme weather events can result in the loss of lives, displacement of populations, and destruction of infrastructure. Ecosystems face disruption and degradation, leading to the loss of biodiversity, altered habitats, and ecological imbalances. Moreover, physical climate risks have profound economic ramifications. The destruction of infrastructure, disruptions to supply chains, and reduced agricultural productivity can result in significant financial losses. Industries such as tourism, agriculture, and insurance face increased volatility, while vulnerable communities may struggle to recover from the socioeconomic impacts. Although the extent of impact is severe across the entire planet, physical climate risks exacerbate existing inequalities and vulnerabilities. They disproportionately affect marginalised communities, low-income populations, and developing countries. Limited access to resources, inadequate infrastructure, and socioeconomic disparities make these communities more susceptible to the adverse impacts of climate change.

The identification and assessment of physical climate risks prompts the design of mitigation and adaptation strategies, many of them guided by regulatory instruments such as green taxonomies. Whilst *mitigation* strategies aim to reduce GHG emissions and limit further climate change, *adaptation* refers to adjustments in ecological, social, or economic systems, in response to actual or expected climatic stimuli and their impact.[120] In the Glasgow – Sharm el-Sheikh work programme on

116 European Environment Agency, 'Extreme Weather: Floods, Droughts and Heatwaves', 14 June 2023. www.eea.europa.eu/en/topics/in-depth/extreme-weather-floods-droughts-and-heat waves accessed 1st July 2023.

117 Teresa Armada Brás et al., 'Severity of Drought and Heatwave Crop Losses Tripled Over the Last Five Decades in Europe', *Environmental Research Letters* 16 (2021): 065012. https://doi.org/10.1088/1748-9326/abf004.

118 World Bank, 'Food Security Update | World Bank Response to Rising Food Insecurity', 9 November 2023. https://thedocs.worldbank.org/en/doc/40ebbf38f5a6b68bfc11e5273e1405d4-0090012022/related/Food-Security-Update-XCV-11-9-23.pdf accessed 29th November 2023.

119 T. Bauer, V. Ingram, W. De Jong and B. Art, 'The Socio-Economic Impact of Extreme Precipitation and Flooding on Forest Livelihoods: Evidence from the Bolivian Amazon', *International Forestry Review* 20.3 (September 2018): 314–331.

120 United Nations Climate Change, 'Adaptation and Resilience'. <>https://unfccc.int/topics/adaptation-and-resilience/the-big-picture/introduction#:~:text=Adaptation%20refers%20to%20

the global goal on adaptation,[121] the aim regarding adaptation is to enhance adaptative capacity, strengthen resilience and reduce vulnerability to climate change. The adaptation strategy is planned with a view to contribute to sustainable development, and framed within the context of the mitigation goal of keeping temperature rise to a maximum of 1.5°C or 2°C. Therefore, adaptation implies *changes in processes, practices, and structures* to moderate potential damages or to benefit from opportunities associated with climate change.

Key mitigation actions include transitioning to renewable energy.[122] Shifting from fossil fuels to renewable energy sources, such as solar and wind power, reduces carbon emissions and promotes a low-carbon energy system. Moreover, energy efficiency and conservation[123] requires improving energy efficiency in buildings, transportation, and industries to reduce energy consumption and associated GHG emissions. Policies around reforestation and afforestation[124] are also central to mitigate climate change. Expanding forests through such efforts helps sequester carbon dioxide from the atmosphere, mitigating climate change. Promoting sustainable agricultural practices[125] such as precision farming and agroforestry reduces emissions from agricultural activities and enhances carbon sequestration in soils.

Adaptation strategies are focused on enhancing adaptive capacity, strengthening resilience, and reducing vulnerability to climate change. Thus, designing and retrofitting infrastructure to withstand climate-related hazards (such as increased precipitation, storm surges, and heat waves) helps build resilience and minimise damage. Likewise, developing and strengthening early warning systems allows for timely response to extreme weather events, providing communities with crucial information, and reducing the loss of lives and assets. In this scenario, implementing sustainable water management practices is also key. This includes water conservation, watershed management, and investment in water infrastructure, as these help mitigate the impacts of droughts and floods. Finally, conserving and restoring ecosystems (such as wetlands and mangroves) can enhance natural resilience,

---

adjustments%20in,opportunities%20associated%20with%20climate%20change> accessed 1st July 2023.

121 UNFCC, 'Glasgow – Sharm el-Sheikh Work Programme on the Global Goal on Adaptation Referred to in Decision 7/CMA.3. Draft Conclusions Proposed by the Chairs', 15 June 2023. https://unfccc.int/documents/629445 accessed 1st July 2023.

122 Richard York, Shannon Elizabeth Bell, 'Energy Transitions or Additions? Why a Transition from Fossil Fuels Requires More Than the Growth of Renewable Energy', *Energy Research & Social Science* 51 (2019): 40–43.

123 Patrick Moriarty and Damon Honnery, 'Energy Efficiency or Conservation for Mitigating Climate Change?', *Energies* 12.18 (2019): 3543.

124 Antonio Trabucco, Robert J. Zomer, Deborah A. Bossio, Oliver van Straaten and Louis V. Verchot, 'Climate Change Mitigation Through Afforestation/Reforestation: A Global Analysis of Hydrologic Impacts with Four Case Studies', *Agriculture, Ecosystems & Environment* 126.1–2 (2008): 81–97.

125 V. Piñeiro et al., 'A Scoping Review on Incentives for Adoption of Sustainable Agricultural Practices and Their Outcomes', *Nature Sustainability* 3.809–820 (2020).

provide coastal protection, and support biodiversity, benefiting both human communities and the environment.

To promote a risk-based approach to effectively manage these physical climate risks, we need the cohesive lead of international cooperation and policy frameworks. The first one of the regulatory instruments that contributes to that process is the Paris Agreement, a global climate accord that aims to limit global temperature rise to well below 2°C and pursue efforts to limit it to 1.5°C. The Agreement emphasises the need for adaptation measures and sets the stage for international collaboration in addressing physical climate risks. The relevance of the Paris Agreement is that it helps us to understand *how to agree on common principles to intervene and act*. We argue that the occurrences of the risks described previously, and other newfound risks, are closely related to the process of building regulation as an intervention tool. As Archer[126] argues, in her work on the development of morphogenesis in the face of the crisis of normativity, a situation of social conflict or an encounter of multiple diverse interests – e.g., agreeing on physical risk and how to adopt mitigation and adaptation measures – must be solved based on the *binding nature of normativity*. In all cases, we must avoid this becoming a predatory regime.[127] To successfully create a new binding norm implies reaching a high level of legitimacy in regulatory decisions. It requires recognising the interests of all the regulatees, including the 'conventional morality'[128] created in specific cultural systems. Seeking agreement between normativity and legal order requires considering that initially there was a unitary and unifying normative source to which legal validity was subscribed and, therefore, certain obligations were binding to all in society. Then, we evolved towards the concept of a legal order that revolves around a minimum acceptance by regulated individuals – a view supported by Ross,[129] Hart, Dworkin, and Habermas.[130] Consequently, we accepted that, in the regulatory decision-making process, it is necessary to find foundations of compatible ideals[131] and thus achieve normative validity and social effectiveness.

Alongside this framework, international collaborations such as the UNFCCC facilitate information sharing, financial support, and capacity-building initiatives to assist developing countries in adapting to physical climate risks. Also, national and local governments play a crucial role in implementing policies and regulations that incentivise climate resilience, promote sustainable practices, and provide support to vulnerable communities. As we will explore further on, the role of regulation is to set clear expectations about how risks and uncertainties should be identified, assessed, and managed. The adoption of the risk-based approach to regulation is meant to facilitate the treatment of physical climate

126 Margaret Archer, *Morphogenesis and the Crisis of Normativity* (Springer Nature, 2016).

127 ibid.

128 ibid.

129 A. Ross, *Directives and Norms* (Routledge and Kegan Paul, 1968).

130 David Ingram, 'Dworkin, Habermas, and the CLS Movement on Moral Criticism in Law', *Philosophy & Social Criticism* 16.4 (1990): 237–268.

131 P. Koller, 'On the Nature of Norms', *Ratio Juris* (2014): 155–175.

risks and the significant challenges they pose to human societies, ecosystems, and economies. Understanding these risks from different perspectives – their implications and the strategies for their mitigation and adaptation – is crucial for building resilience and fostering sustainable development. The integration of diverse perceptions of risks is a duty not only of the public sector but society as a whole.[132] By taking comprehensive actions at local, national, and international levels, we can navigate the challenges posed by physical climate risks, safeguard vulnerable communities, and ensure a sustainable future for generations to come. Those changes that primarily appear as exclusively focused on climate risks will progressively become impacts of sustainability trends.[133] Such trends may materialise as either long-term drivers of change, or possibly (also) as sudden shocks and shifts, when complex developments occur. That's why, along with physical risks, the progress towards a more sustainable society requires us to tackle transition risks.

Transition Climate Risks

Talking about transition risks means navigating challenges in the shift to a low-carbon economy. Such a transition is essential for mitigating the impacts of climate change and achieving global sustainability goals; however, this transition poses its own set of risks, known as transition climate risks. These encompass the economic, financial, social, and political challenges associated with active intervention to mitigate and adapt current practices to move towards a low-carbon economy. Transition risks arise from the necessary changes in policies, regulation, technologies, and business conduct aimed at reducing GHG emissions and promoting sustainable practices.

The advancement towards a low-carbon economy is a dynamic process. Hence, the identification of transition climate risks is a continuous task. We could argue that the most recognised transition risks include stranded assets,[134] disruptions to industries and employment,[135] market and financial volatility,[136] and social and political changes.[137]

132 Tarja Halonen, President of Finland 2000–2012.

133 Hanna Silvola and Tiina Landau, *Sustainable Investing: Beating the Market with ESG* (Palgrave MacMillan, 2021) 205.

134 Ben Caldecott, Elizabeth Harnett, Theodor Cojoianu, Irem Kok and Alexander Pfeiffer, 'Stranded Assets: A Climate Risk Challenge', in Ana Rios (ed), *IDB Monograph* (Inter-American Development Bank, 2016) 481. https://publications.iadb.org/en/publications/english/viewer/Stranded-Assets-A-Climate-Risk-Challenge.pdf accessed 1st July 2023.

135 Martina K. Linnenluecke, Alexander Stathakis and Andrew Griffiths, 'Firm Relocation as Adaptive Response to Climate Change and Weather Extremes', *Global Environmental Change* 21.1 (2011): 123–133.

136 Irene Monasterolo, 'Climate Change and the Financial System', *Annual Review of Resource Economics* 12.299–320 (October 2020).

137 Thomas Dietz, Rachael L. Shwom and Cameron T. Whitley, 'Climate Change and Society', *Annual Review of Sociology* 46.135–158 (July 2020).

As the transition progresses, certain high-carbon assets (like fossil fuel reserves or infrastructure) may become economically unviable due to increased regulation,[138] changing market dynamics, or shifting investor preferences. In this context, a broad definition of *stranded assets* identifies them as 'assets that have suffered from unanticipated or premature write-downs, devaluations, or conversion to liabilities'.[139] A significant portion of the literature is centred around two interrelated concepts: unburnable carbon and the carbon bubble. Unburnable carbon refers to the situation where global fossil fuel assets currently hold a higher value than their actual commercial viability, under stringent carbon budget constraints.[140] This notion highlights the risk of stranded assets and the potential disconnect between the current value of fossil fuel reserves and their future feasibility.[141] The discussion surrounding unburnable carbon has stimulated considerable debate on the perils associated with fossil fuel investments, and has catalysed the emergence of the fossil fuel divestment campaign. The carbon bubble proposes the hypothesis that the overvaluation of fossil fuel assets,[142] stemming from the notion of unburnable carbon, had led to the formation of a financial bubble[143] that could potentially have systemic implications for the global financial system. In broader terms, however, transition risks may also represent increased costs to fund the transition to new, more sustainable business models not related to fossil fuels, such as the risks related to physical climate change, biodiversity loss, and litigation related to environmental factors.[144] In all those cases the common denominator is that for some sectors and firms, the transition to net zero and the commitment to environmental sustainability may lead to significant losses in economic value.[145]

Disruptions to industries and employment poses another major risk. Transitioning away from carbon-intensive industries, such as coal mining or fossil fuel extraction, can result in job losses and economic upheaval in affected regions. Retraining

138 Ben Caldecott, Alex Clark, Krister Koskelo, Ellie Mulholland and Conor Hickey, 'Stranded Assets: Environmental Drivers, Societal Challenges, and Supervisory Responses', *Annual Review of Environment and Resources* 46.417–447 (October 2021).

139 Ben Caldecott, *Stranded Assets and the Environment: Risk, Resilience and Opportunity* (Routledge, 2018).

140 Atif Ansar, Ben Caldecott and James Tilbury, *Stranded Assets and the Fossil Fuel Divestment Campaign: What Does Divestment Mean for the Valuation of Fossil Fuel Assets?* (Representative Smith School of Enterprise and the Environment, University of Oxford, 2013). https://www.smithschool.ox.ac.uk/sites/default/files/2022-03/SAP-divestment-report-final.pdf.

141 Carbon Tracker Initiative, 'Unburnable Carbon 2013: Wasted Capital and Stranded Assets'. https://www.lse.ac.uk/GranthamInstitute/wp-content/uploads/2014/02/PB-unburnable-carbon-2013-wasted-capital-stranded-assets.pdf.

142 Frederick van der Ploeg and Armon Rezai, 'Stranded Assets in the Transition to a Carbon-Free Economy', *Annual Review of Resource Economics* 12 (October 2020): 281–298.

143 Ben Caldecott, 'Why High-Carbon Investment Could Be the Next Sub-Prime Crisis', *The Guardian*, 12 July 2011.

144 Ben Caldecott, Alex Clark, Krister Koskelo, Ellie Mulholland and Conor Hickey, 'Stranded Assets: Environmental Drivers, Societal Challenges, and Supervisory Responses' (n 138) 7.

145 Simon Thompson, 'Green and Sustainable Finance: Principles and Practice in Banking, Investment and Insurance' (n 7) 217.

and supporting workers in transitioning to new industries is crucial to minimise social and economic impacts. In addition to the risk of job losses, there is a potential for energy price increases that could disproportionately impact lower-income households. Furthermore, the rapid expansion of renewables and other low-carbon energy sources, if not carefully managed, may compromise land rights and livelihoods without adequate consideration for the rights of those affected.[146] It is in this scenario where we argue that the adoption of a risk-based approach to regulation would help to rebalance the conflicting interests of several stakeholders, as well as the trade-offs between environmental and social factors. Hence, it is crucial for governments to collaborate closely with businesses, local communities, and labour representatives to develop long-term visions for successful and just transitions.[147] In doing so, it is essential to ensure that the voices of all stakeholders are considered, fostering a just and inclusive process.

Regarding *market and financial volatility*, the transition adds to the debate the dichotomy of risk and uncertainty. From sociological studies, Giddens[148] offers insights into the distinction between these two categories. On the one hand, *risk* refers to situations where the potential outcomes and their probabilities are known, allowing for the calculation and management of risks based on available data and expertise. In other words, risks are events or situations that can be assessed and measured, and their consequences can be predicted with a certain level of confidence. On the other hand, *uncertainty*, as defined by Giddens,[149] refers to situations where the potential outcomes and their probabilities are unknown or difficult to determine. Unlike risks, uncertainties are characterised by a lack of sufficient information or established patterns to make reliable predictions. Uncertainties often emerge in complex, rapidly changing, or ambiguous situations where multiple factors interact and the future is inherently unpredictable. Giddens' distinction between risk and uncertainty provides a framework for this study to analyse and understand how individuals, groups, regulators, and societies navigate and respond to different types of transition risk challenges.[150] It underscores the need for reflexivity and adaptive strategies in the face of uncertainties, recognising that social interactions, collective actions, regulatory decisions, and the construction of shared meanings play a crucial role in addressing the complexities of an uncertain future. The juxtaposition of these concepts allows us to argue that transition climate risks

146 Gambhira Ajay, Green Fergus and Peter J. G. Pearson, 'Towards a Just and Equitable Low-Carbon Energy Transition', Imperial College London, Grantham Institute Briefing Paper No. 26, August 2018. www.imperial.ac.uk/media/imperial-college/grantham-institute/public/publications/briefing-papers/26.-Towards-a-just-and-equitable-low-carbon-energy-transition.pdf accessed 1st July 2023.

147 Anabella Rosemberg, 'Building a Just Transition: The Linkages Between Climate Change and Employment', *International Journal of Labour Research* 2.2 (2010): 125–161. www.proquest.com/openview/8c63a878479bc23b643b71ebcdc2a2e9/1?pq-origsite=gscholar&cbl=226543 accessed 18th August 2023.

148 A. Giddens, 'Risk and Responsibility', *The Modern Law Review* 62.1 (1999): 1–10.

149 ibid.

150 A. Giddens, *The Politics of Climate Change* (Polity Press, 2013).

can introduce uncertainties into financial markets. These risks could trigger fluctuations in the value of carbon-intensive assets, the emergence of new investment opportunities, and the need for increased transparency in reporting climate-related risks.

The last type of transition risks that we consider in this book is that associated with *social and political challenges*. Transition may encounter social and political resistance. It cannot be denied that, in terms of sustainability, all of humanity is acting outside safe planetary boundaries.[151] Notwithstanding this truth, the most notorious contradictors of economic transition to sustainable practices might be those in regions and activities heavily reliant on carbon-intensive industries. Hence, balancing the interests of various stakeholders, ensuring a just transition, and garnering public support are essential for a smooth and inclusive shift. Abson et al. propose to focus research – and, we would add, the regulatory effort – on transformational 'sustainability interventions' which reconnect people to nature, restructure institutions, and rethink how knowledge is created and used in pursuit of sustainability.[152] We borrow these concepts to explain that a risk-based approach to regulation is flexible enough to promote the adoption and implementation of regimes that blend the politics of risk and uncertainty[153] as the building blocks of sustainable finance. The building up of a regime that seeks transformational actions relies on the best alignment possible of incentives towards a common end.

The risk-based approach to regulation is the regulatory strategy and the route–map to navigate not only transition climate risks, but the entire sustainable finance path. It encompasses policy and regulatory frameworks, innovation and technology, stakeholder engagement and collaboration, and financial sector alignment.

As will be discussed later, clear and consistent policy signals, along with supportive regulatory frameworks, are crucial for managing transition climate risks. Long-term emission reduction targets, carbon-pricing mechanisms, and regulations promoting sustainable practices provide stability and guide investment decisions. Also, investing in research and development of low-carbon technologies and innovative solutions is essential for a successful transition.[154] Encouraging technological advancements in renewable energy, energy efficiency, and sustainable agriculture[155] can facilitate the adoption of cleaner practices and drive economic growth.

151 W. K. Steffen et al., 'Planetary Boundaries: Guiding Human Development on a Changing Planet', *Science* 347 (2015): 1259855.

152 D. J. Abson et al., 'Leverage Points for Sustainability Transformation', *AMBIO* 46.30–39 (2017). https://doi.org/10.1007/s13280-016-0800-y.

153 Julia Black, 'The Emergence of Risk-Based Regulation and the New Public Risk Management in the United Kingdom', *Public Law* 512 (2005): 535.

154 Robyn Owen, Geraldine Brennan and Fergus Lyon, 'Enabling Investment for the Transition to a Low Carbon Economy: Government Policy to Finance Early-Stage Green Innovation', *Current Opinion in Environmental Sustainability* 31 (2018): 137–145. https://doi.org/10.1016/j.cosust.2018.03.004.

155 Shiva Gorjian, Hossein Ebadi, Laxmikant D. Jathar and Laura Savoldi, 'Solar Energy for Sustainable Food and Agriculture: Developments, Barriers, and Policies', in Shiva Gorjian and Pietro Elia

Another area of special attention for designing an effective risk-based approach to sustainable finance and the management of transition climate risk is *stakeholder engagement and collaboration.*[156] This requires identifying convergent and diverse groups of interests,[157] including businesses, communities, and civil society organisations. Collaboration fosters trust, enables knowledge sharing, and ensures that the transition is inclusive and equitable.[158]

The contribution of a risk-based approach to regulation in terms of stakeholder engagement is pivotal to the line of thought defended in this book. A risk-based approach to regulation is a framework that focuses on identifying, assessing, and managing risks associated with various activities, industries, or sectors. Rather than applying a uniform set of rules and regulations to all entities, a risk-based approach allows regulators to allocate resources and prioritise their efforts based on the level of risk posed by different factors.[159] The identification of those different levels of risks requires cooperation and dialogue. It aims at engaging with relevant stakeholders, including industry representatives, experts, and the public. This helps in gathering valuable insights, expertise, and diverse perspectives to inform risk assessments,[160] regulatory decisions, and the development of effective risk-management strategies. High levels of cooperation allow regulators to tailor regulations and compliance requirements according to the level of risk identified.[161] Furthermore, by focusing the intervention on several levels of risks and uncertainties, regulators can prioritise their enforcement efforts and allocate resources more effectively. This ensures that regulatory interventions are directed where they are most needed, to mitigate potential harm or adverse consequences.[162]

The appeal of a risk-based approach to regulation stems from its emphasis on striking a balance between crucial aspects – such as public safety, environmental protection, and fostering innovation and economic growth. By prioritising the most

---

Campana (eds), *Solar Energy Advancements in Agriculture and Food Production Systems* (Academic Press, 2022) 1–28. https://doi.org/10.1016/B978-0-323-89866-9.00004-3.

156 Henry Rothstein, Phil Irving, Terry Walden and Roger Yearsley, 'The Risks of Risk-Based Regulation: Insights from the Environmental Policy Domain', *Environment International* 32.8 (2006): 1056–1065. https://doi.org/10.1016/j.envint.2006.06.008.

157 Christopher M. Taylor et al., 'Environmental Regulation in Transition: Policy Officials' Views of Regulatory Instruments and Their Mapping to Environmental Risks', *Science of the Total Environment* 646 (2019): 811–820. https://doi.org/10.1016/j.scitotenv.2018.07.217.

158 A. Gouldson, A. Morton and S. J. T. Pollard, 'Better Environmental Regulation – Contributions from Risk-Based Decision-Making', *Science of the Total Environment* 407.19 (2009): 5283–5288. https://doi.org/10.1016/j.scitotenv.2009.06.013.

159 H. Rothstein, O. Borraz and M. Huber, 'Risk and the Limits of Governance', *Regulation & Governance* 7 (2013): 215–235. https://doi.org/10.1111/j.1748-5991.2012.01153.x.

160 D. Iverson, 'Governance Risk', in D. Iverson (ed), *Strategic Risk Management* (2013). https://doi.org/10.1002/9781118638828.ch2.

161 J. Black and R. Baldwin, 'When Risk-Based Regulation Aims Low: Approaches and Challenges', *Regulation & Governance* 6 (2012): 2–22. https://doi.org/10.1111/j.1748-5991.2011.01124.x.

162 ibid.

significant risks,[163] this approach fosters effective risk management, strengthens compliance, and contributes to the establishment of a more efficient and adaptable regulatory framework. These elements are pivotal for cultivating an efficient and sustainable finance regime, ensuring the alignment of financial activities with long-term sustainability objectives.

Finally, alignment of the financial sector is of paramount importance in effectively managing transition climate risks and successfully fulfilling the aim of sustainable finance.[164] As the world strives to transition to a low-carbon and sustainable economy, the financial sector plays a critical role in allocating capital, assessing risks, and supporting the necessary investments and innovations.[165]

Capital allocation[166] is the first of many reasons why financial sector alignment is crucial in managing transition climate risks. The financial sector has a significant role in directing capital towards sustainable and climate-friendly projects and businesses. By aligning financial flows with climate objectives, such as supporting renewable energy projects or energy-efficient infrastructure, the sector can facilitate the transition to a low-carbon economy.[167] Likewise, financial institutions need to assess and manage climate-related risks to protect their investments and ensure long-term sustainability.[168] This includes evaluating the potential impacts of climate change on asset valuations, credit risks, and operational risks.[169] Through robust risk assessment frameworks, the financial sector can make informed decisions, adjust investment strategies, and contribute to the mitigation of transition climate risks.

163 J. Black and R. Baldwin, 'Really Responsive Risk-Based Regulation', *Law & Policy* 32 (2010): 181–213. https://doi.org/10.1111/j.1467-9930.2010.00318.x.

164 H. Ahlström and D. Monciardini, 'The Regulatory Dynamics of Sustainable Finance: Paradoxical Success and Limitations of EU Reforms', *Journal of Business Ethics* 177.193–212 (2022). https://doi.org/10.1007/s10551-021-04763-x.

165 Umberto Pisano, André Martinuzzi and Bernulf Bruckner, 'The Financial Sector and Sustainable Development: Logics, Principles and Actors', ESDN Quarterly Report No. 27, December 2012, 4. www.researchgate.net/profile/Umberto-Pisano/project/European-Sustainable-Development-Network-ESDN/attachment/587f307108aefb94deda9f2b/AS:451806535917568@1484730480978/download/2012-December-The_Financial_Sector_and_Sustainable_Development.pdf accessed 1st July 2023.

166 Yue Zhu, Juntao Zhang and Caiquan Duan, 'How Does Green Finance Affect the Low-Carbon Economy? Capital Allocation, Green Technology Innovation and Industry Structure Perspectives', *Economic Research-Ekonomska Istraživanja* 36 (2023): 2. https://doi.org/10.1080/1331677X.2022.2110138.

167 Y. Bian, K. Song and J. Bai, 'Market Segmentation, Resource Misallocation and Environmental Pollution', *Journal of Cleaner Production* 228 (2019): 376–387. https://doi.org/10.1016/j.jclepro.2019.04.286.

168 Isaac Akomea-Frimpong, David Adeabah, Deborah Ofosu and Emmanuel Junior Tenakwah, 'A Review of Studies on Green Finance of Banks, Research Gaps and Future Directions', *Journal of Sustainable Finance & Investment* 12.4 (2022): 1241–1264. https://doi.org/10.1080/20430795.2020.1870202.

169 Gunnar Friede, Timo Busch and Alexander Bassen, 'ESG and financial Performance: Aggregated Evidence from More Than 2000 Empirical Studies', *Journal of Sustainable Finance & Investment* 5.4 (2015): 210–233. https://doi.org/10.1080/20430795.2015.1118917.

Disclosing and reporting material data play a crucial role in enabling sustainable finance to fulfil its catalyst function.[170] Transparent and standardised climate-related disclosures are indispensable for investors, regulators, and other stakeholders to comprehend the climate risks and opportunities associated with financial institutions and their portfolios.[171] Embracing enhanced reporting requirements, such as those articulated by frameworks like the TCFD (among other regulatory instruments to be explored later), fosters a deeper understanding of transition climate risks and encourages responsible investment practices. However, there are considerable concerns[172] regarding the extent to which ESG reporting guidelines enhance information disclosure from businesses.

In essence, by directing capital, conducting risk assessments, promoting transparency, and engaging with stakeholders, the financial sector can make a significant contribution to the transition toward a low-carbon and resilient economy, all while safeguarding financial stability and long-term sustainability. Implications of transition climate risks and the potential for losses do not only affect asset owners. It is estimated that financial institutions worldwide have lending and investment portfolios currently aligned with a global warming trajectory of more than 3°C to 3.75°C.[173] This substantial misalignment far exceeds the objectives set by the Paris Agreement, indicating that most institutions are currently exposed to significant levels of transition risk.

Economic and social negative impact are additional implications of transition risks. Such negative consequences particularly affect those communities dependent on carbon-intensive industries. Job losses and economic dislocation can lead to aggravated social inequalities and challenges in ensuring a just transition. Addressing these challenges requires robust social policies, retraining programmes, and support for affected communities.

Finally, ensuring the stability of the financial system becomes a paramount concern when addressing transition risks. These risks have the potential to generate systemic implications for the financial system, as the revaluation of carbon-intensive assets and exposure to climate-related liabilities can impact financial institutions. Therefore, the implementation of robust risk assessment frameworks and stress-testing measures becomes crucial in enhancing the resilience of the financial sector to climate-related shocks. Empirical evidence[174] suggests that at an individual

170 Michael D. Kimbrough, Xu (Frank) Wang, Sijing Wei and Jiarui (Iris) Zhang, 'Does Voluntary ESG Reporting Resolve Disagreement Among ESG Rating Agencies?', *European Accounting Review* (2022). https://doi.org/10.1080/09638180.2022.2088588.

171 ibid.

172 N. Darnall, H. Ji, K. Iwata and T. H. Arimura, 'Do ESG Reporting Guidelines and Verifications Enhance Firms' Information Disclosure?', *Corporate Social Responsibility and Environmental Management* 29.5 (2022): 1214–1230. https://doi.org/10.1002/csr.2265.

173 Simon Thompson, 'Green and Sustainable Finance: Principles and Practice in Banking, Investment and Insurance' (n 7) 221.

174 Laura Chiaramonte, Alberto Dreassi, Claudia Girardone and Stefano Piserà, 'Do ESG Strategies Enhance Bank Stability During Financial Turmoil? Evidence from Europe', *The European Journal of Finance* 28.12 (2022): 1173–1211. https://doi.org/10.1080/1351847X.2021.1964556.

level, ESG strategies can serve as a risk mitigation tool for banks during periods of financial distress, acting akin to insurance. This can be attributed to the notion that engaging in environmental, social, and corporate governance practices fosters more prudent banking activities, cultivating stable relationships with relevant communities, and bolstering a bank's reputation.[175] Thus, enhancing ESG engagement in the banking sector not only yields benefits in terms of environmental and societal impact, but also fortifies the sector's resilience in times of financial crisis.[176]

Litigation or Liability Risks

Communities and individuals are increasingly resorting to legal action to hold governments and high-emitting corporations responsible for the negative impacts of climate change, and they are beginning to achieve some notable successes. As a result, corporations now face a growing risk of climate litigation, which can further amplify the well-documented physical and transition risks associated with climate change. However, there is still limited understanding of the specific effects and costs of climate litigation on corporations.[177]

In many jurisdictions, financial regulators acknowledge the potential financial risks associated with climate change litigation. One notable example is the Network for Greening the Financial System (NGFS), which recognises the emergence of legal cases related to climate change as a specific type of risk called 'liability risk'. This risk is identified as a subset of the broader categories of physical and transition risks, which are the primary drivers of financial impacts resulting from climate change.[178] The NGFS merely identifies liability risk as a potential form of 'operational risk' without further exploration. As a result, financial regulators that rely on the NGFS framework to develop their own approaches to climate-related financial risks often do not go beyond this level of understanding.

It is crucial for financial regulators and policymakers to delve deeper into the nature of liability risk stemming from climate change litigation.[179] By examining the specific legal and financial implications of such cases, regulators can gain a more nuanced understanding of the potential financial risks faced by governments, firms, and investors. This deeper understanding can facilitate the development of more robust frameworks for assessing and addressing climate-related financial risks. The analysis of the effects on how climate litigation risks materialise can be assisted by the adoption of a risk-based approach.

175 ibid.

176 ibid.

177 Javier Solana, 'Research Article: Climate Change Litigation as Financial Risk', *Green Finance* 2.4: 344–372. https://eprints.gla.ac.uk/225765/1/225765.pdf accessed 3rd July 2023.

178 Network for Greening the Financial System, 2019.

179 Misato Sato, Glen Gostlow, Catherine Higham, Joana Setzer and Frank Venmans, 'Impacts of Climate Litigation on Firm Value', Centre for Climate Change Economics and Policy Working Paper No. 421, Grantham Research Institute on Climate Change, and the Environment Working Paper No. 397, May 2023.

In the context of financial institutions, the specific challenges associated with climate-related risks often extend beyond their planning horizons. The PRA in the UK, for instance, has assessed that the planning horizons for the banking sector typically span around four years. This implies that risks may not be fully realised and stringent climate policies may not yet have taken effect within this timeframe. As a result, financial institutions face the complex task of managing climate-related risks that may materialise over longer-term periods, necessitating forward-looking strategies to address these challenges effectively. Therefore, the adoption of a risk-based approach to give dynamism and continue to review risks, the probability of their occurrence, and tools for risk management is central to achieving the best possible results.

Until now, the most comprehensive effort to articulate the potential financial impact of climate change litigation is the TCFD, an initiative of the FSB.[180] The TCFD aims to establish consistent disclosures of climate-related financial risks for companies, banks, and investors. In its final recommendations, the TCFD provides insight into the financial implications of climate change litigation by highlighting three potential costs. These include regulatory fines or court-ordered payments, increased insurance premiums, and reduced demand for products and services (which can indicate reputational costs). However, the TCFD's articulation of these costs remains limited, as they are merely listed in a table without further elaboration on how they may unfold. Although the TCFD's scope of analysis is helpful, it is important to recognise that climate change litigation is a complex and multifaceted phenomenon, likely to give rise to various types of costs beyond those so far identified by the TCFD. The financial impact of litigation can extend beyond the immediate costs mentioned, and may encompass factors such as legal fees, damages awarded, resource allocation for legal defence, potential loss of investor confidence, and the overall impact on a company's financial stability and long-term viability.[181]

To fully understand and address the financial implications of climate change litigation, it is crucial to consider a broader range of potential costs and their interconnections. This entails exploring the indirect consequences, systemic risks,[182] and cascading effects that may result from legal actions related to climate change. Financial institutions, companies, and investors can better assess and manage the financial risks associated with climate change litigation by taking a more comprehensive and integrated approach based on risk.

Financial regulators acknowledge the liability risk linked to climate change litigation,[183] but there is a necessity for additional in-depth exploration and analysis

180 Task Force on Climate-related Financial Disclosures, 'Final Report: Recommendations of the Task Force on Climate-Related Financial Disclosures', June 2017. www.fsb-tcfd.org/publications/final-recommendations-report/ accessed 3rd July 2023.

181 Javier Solana, 'Research Article: Climate Change Litigation as Financial Risk' (n 177) 345.

182 Francesco Lampertia, Valentina Bosettib, Andrea Roventinia, Massimo Tavonibe and Tania Treibicha, 'Three Green Financial Policies To Address Climate Risks', *Journal of Financial Stability* 54 (2021): 100875.

183 Prudential Regulatory Authority, 'Transition in Thinking: The Impact of Climate Change on the UK Banking Sector', 2018. www.bankofengland.co.uk/prudential-regulation/publication/

of this specific risk category. Conducting more comprehensive studies is crucial to formulate more effective strategies for managing these risks. Seeking to contribute to the ongoing debate on climate liability risks, Sato et al.[184] conducted a study to measure the financial market's reaction to climate litigation, by constructing a comprehensive dataset encompassing a wide range of corporate litigation cases against major publicly listed corporations on US and European stock exchanges. The dataset covers the period 2005–2021, providing a near-universe representation of climate litigation within the specified timeframe. By including a diverse range of cases, we can estimate the aggregate market-wide effect, which offers valuable insights into the overall impact of climate litigation on firm value. Despite the heterogeneity of climate lawsuits, an important finding of this study highlights the growing significance of climate litigation as a tool to influence climate governance, reshape company behaviour, and transform business models.[185] While the earliest recorded corporate climate litigation case dates back to 1995,[186] it is in more recent years that climate litigation has gained recognition for its potential to impact the trajectory and effectiveness of climate governance. The purpose of these lawsuits is to drive changes in companies' behaviour, and encourage the adoption of sustainable business models, marking a significant shift in the role and impact of climate litigation.

The Net-Zero Target: A Pathway to a Sustainable Future

The concept of achieving net-zero carbon emissions has its roots in the realm of physical climate science. However, its practical implementation is intricately intertwined with social, political, and economic systems, and more concretely, with the ESG factors.

As a fundamentally scientific concept, 'net zero' stems from the understanding that, to limit the increase in global average temperatures to specific thresholds, there exists a finite budget for carbon dioxide and other GHGs that can be emitted into the atmosphere.[187] Once this budget is depleted, any additional emissions must be offset by removing an equivalent amount from the atmosphere, through various sinks.

Net-zero emissions will be attained when the total emissions generated by human activities are offset by removing carbon from the atmosphere through a process called *carbon removal*. To achieve net zero, a two-part approach is necessary.[188]

2018/transition-in-thinking-the-impact-of-climate-change-on-the-uk-banking-sector accessed 3rd July 2023.

184 Misato Sato, Glen Gostlow, Catherine Higham, Joana Setzer and Frank Venmans, 'Impacts of Climate Litigation on Firm Value' (n 179).

185 ibid., (n 179) 5.

186 Sabin Center for Climate Change Law, *About, Climate Litigation Databases* (Sabin Center for Climate Change Law, 2022). http://climatecasechart.com/about/ accessed 3rd July 2023.

187 R. Black et al., *Taking Stock: A Global Assessment of Net Zero Targets* (ECIU and Oxford Net Zero, 2021).

188 Kelly Levin, Taryn Fransen, Clea Schumer, Chantal Davis and Sophie Boehm, 'What Does "Net-Zero Emissions" Mean? 8 Common Questions, Answered', World Resources Institute,

Firstly, emissions originating from human activities (such as those produced by vehicles powered by fossil fuels and industrial facilities) must be significantly reduced, ideally approaching zero. Secondly, any remaining emissions should be counterbalanced by an equal amount of carbon removal. This can be accomplished through natural methods like reforestation and ecosystem restoration, as well as through technological solutions like direct air capture and storage (DACS)[189] – directly extracting carbon from the atmosphere and securely storing it.

Determining the acceptable level of temperature rise is a decision shaped by society, albeit one that is informed by climate science. The Paris Agreement, which has been ratified by 197 countries, aims to constrain global warming to well below 2°C, and strives for efforts to limit it to 1.5°C.[190] Adhering to this budget necessitates peaking CO_2 emissions before 2030 and reaching net-zero emissions around 2050.

While the term 'net zero' is not explicitly mentioned in the 2015 Paris Agreement, a careful reading of Articles 2 and 4, in consideration of the best available scientific knowledge, provides an interpretative context for understanding the concept and significance of net zero within the agreement. The 2021 Glasgow Climate Pact (a nonbinding decision by the Parties to the Paris Agreement) makes reference to net zero in the context of implementing the agreement, and contributes to defining the practical implications of the concept within the UN climate framework.

Article 2 of the Paris Agreement establishes the global temperature objective, aiming to limit the increase in global average temperature to 'well below 2°C above preindustrial levels' and pursue efforts to achieve a temperature limit of 1.5°C. This temperature goal builds upon the 1992 UNFCCC's objective of preventing dangerous human interference with the climate system, by quantifying the limits of what can be considered dangerous in terms of temperature rise. By defining the temperature goal, scientists are able to estimate, with some uncertainties, a global carbon budget and the necessary pathways for global emissions reductions to stay within that budget.

It is important to interpret the temperature goal of the Paris Agreement as a single goal, encompassing both the aspirational 1.5°C goal *and* the 'well below 2°C' goal, which are inseparable in the agreement's text.[191] The language and order of prominence given to the 'well below 2°C' goal indicate its significance. While

---

20 March 2023. www.wri.org/insights/net-zero-ghg-emissions-questions-answered accessed 2nd July 2023.

189 Christian Breyer, Mahdi Fasihi, Cyril Bajamundi and Felix Creutzig, 'Commentary: Direct Air Capture of CO: A Key Technology for Ambitious Climate Change Mitigation', *Joule* 3 (18 September 2019): 2053–2065. www.cell.com/joule/pdf/S2542-4351(19)30413-1.pdf accessed 2nd July 2023.

190 IPCC, *Special Report on Global Warming of 1.5°C*. V. Masson-Delmotte et al. (eds) (WMO, 2018).

191 Myles R. Allen, Pierre Friedlingstein, Cécile A. J. Girardin, Stuart Jenkins, Yadvinder Malhi, Eli Mitchell-Larson, Glen P. Peters and Lavanya Rajamani, 'Net Zero: Science, Origins, and Implications', *Annual Review of Environment and Resources* 47 (2022): 872.

Article 2.1(a) aims to *hold the temperature increase* to well below 2°C, it only aims to pursue efforts to *limit the increase* to 1.5°C. It is worth noting that at the time of negotiating the Paris Agreement, countries were not on track to achieve either goal, and this provision sets a global direction for future actions. The implications are best understood as NASA explains them. With a warming of 1.5°C, approximately 14 percent of the global population will face severe heat waves at least once every five years. This figure increases significantly to 37 percent at a warming of 2°C, signifying a widespread occurrence of extreme heat waves.[192]

Allen et al.[193] argue that interpreting the temperature goal of the Paris Agreement as a single goal (spanning from 1.5°C to 'well below' 2°C) allows for scientific advancements to influence the specific target within that range over time. As scientific understanding evolves, it can inform and shape the trajectory that countries should strive for within this temperature range.

These scientific and societal considerations underscore the importance of embracing the attributes of net zero as a framework for effective climate action.[194] Indeed, in the aftermath of the Paris Agreement, the pursuit of achieving net-zero emissions has emerged as a defining framework for climate action. In an exhaustive analysis, Hale et al.[195] conducted a study encompassing more than 4,000 countries, companies, and subnational governments (which collectively account for a significant share of global emissions). The study observed that 769 of these entities have set net-zero targets. However, upon closer examination, they discovered that only 152 of them meet the minimum criteria for robustness.[196] These criteria encompass factors such as the clarity of timing, current status, breadth of coverage, utilisation of offsets, and effectiveness of governance structures.[197] The statistics reveal that, while the concept of net zero has gained widespread recognition, its practical implementation is still in its nascent stages.

The level of compliance to net-zero policies and commitments varies across different countries. Despite the ongoing increase in global GHG emissions, several countries have demonstrated a sustained commitment to reducing their emissions.[198] Furthermore, the annual reductions in emissions achieved by certain countries fall within the range required to limit global warming to 2°C. However, this progress is

192 Alan Buis, 'A Degree of Concern: Why Global Temperatures Matter'. https://climate.nasa.gov/news/2865/a-degree-of-concern-why-global-temperatures-matter/.

193 ibid.

194 S. Fankhauser et al., 'The Meaning of Net Zero and How to Get It Right', *Nature Climate Change* 12 (2022): 15–21. https://doi.org/10.1038/s41558-021-01245-w.

195 Thomas Hale, Stephen M. Smith, Richard Black, Kate Cullen, Byron Fay, John Lang and Saba Mahmood, 'Assessing the Rapidly-Emerging Landscape of Net Zero Targets', *Climate Policy* 22.1 (2022): 18–29. https://doi.org/10.1080/14693062.2021.2013155.

196 ibid.

197 ibid.

198 See William F. Lamb, Michael Grubb, Francesca Diluiso and Jan C. Minx, 'Countries with Sustained Greenhouse Gas Emissions Reductions: An Analysis of Trends and Progress by Sector', *Climate Policy* 22.1 (2022): 1–17. https://doi.org/10.1080/14693062.2021.1990831.

not uniform across all countries or sectors, and more consistent and comprehensive efforts are needed to address the full spectrum of emissions sources.

The net-zero target is vital for mitigating climate change impacts by balancing carbon emissions and removals. It helps limit global temperature rise, decrease extreme weather events, and protect ecosystems and communities. Despite its importance, the Paris Agreement delegates the responsibility to signatory countries to set emissions pathways and the nationally determined contributions (NDCs) toward global net zero. There is no standardised benchmark for assessing sufficiency, ambition, or equity, relying instead on an ongoing review process for evaluation.

Regular stocktakes are designed to stimulate ambitious action, and facilitate the convergence of national emissions pathways towards a global state of net zero that aligns with the long-term temperature objectives.[199] Through these stocktakes, countries can assess their progress, share best practices, and enhance their climate commitments over time. This iterative process fosters a collective effort to continuously raise the level of ambition and ensure a coordinated global response to climate change.[200] The flexible approach championed by the Paris Agreement recognises the diverse circumstances and capabilities of different countries, while striving for a collective trajectory that is consistent with long-term climate goals.

Implementing the Net-zero Target

The adoption to net zero is largely left to individual emitters and self-regulated voluntary codes.[201] There are, however, key contested areas to consider in a net-zero strategy.[202] A fundamental aspect of achieving the net-zero target is transitioning from fossil fuel-based energy systems to renewable and clean energy sources. This entails scaling up investments in renewable energy technologies, promoting energy efficiency measures, and phasing out the use of coal and other high-emission fuels. Moreover, decarbonising transportation requires the widespread adoption of more sustainable forms of transportation, investment in sustainable public transportation, and the development of infrastructure to support zero-emission transportation systems. Similarly, addressing emissions from land use and agriculture is essential in achieving the net-zero target. This involves adopting sustainable farming practices, reducing deforestation, promoting reforestation and afforestation efforts, and enhancing carbon sequestration in soils through regenerative agricultural practices. Furthermore, carbon capture and storage (CCS) technologies play a crucial role in

199 See United Nations, 'Race to Zero Campaign'. https://racetozero.unfccc.int/system/race-to-zero/?_gl=1*d0655d*_ga*MTUwMjMyNzYwNy4xNjg4MjI2ODIx*_ga_7ZZWT14N79*MTY4ODI1NTYxNC4zLjAuMTY4ODI1NTYxNC4wLjAuMA accessed 1st July 2023.

200 S. Fankhauser et al., 'The Meaning of Net Zero and How to Get It Right' (n 194) 9.

201 J. Rogelj, O. Geden, A. Cowie and A. Reisinger, 'Three Ways to Improve Net-Zero Emissions Targets', *Nature* 591 (2021): 365–368.

202 Dr. James Hansen's Testimony before the US Senate Committee on Energy and Natural Resources, 23 June 1988. www.sealevel.info/1988_Hansen_Senate_Testimony.html accessed 1st July 2023.

achieving the net-zero target. As will be analysed later in the study of the carbon credits market, CCS involves capturing carbon dioxide emissions from industrial processes or power generation, and storing them underground. This technology can help offset emissions from sectors where complete decarbonisation is challenging.

As may be anticipated, the transition to a net-zero economy poses both challenges and opportunities. It requires technological advancements and significant investment. Developing and scaling up clean energy technologies, carbon capture and storage systems, and sustainable infrastructure poses challenges in terms of cost, technical feasibility, and the need for supportive policies and incentives. However, the 'net zero' target as a transformative strategy in addressing the urgent challenges of climate change brings along opportunities. By balancing emissions and removals, it offers a pathway to a sustainable future, reducing the risks posed by global warming and fostering resilience. While implementation presents challenges, the net-zero target presents significant opportunities for technological advancements, social equity, and international cooperation. By collectively embracing this target, we contribute to build the road towards a more sustainable, low-carbon, and prosperous world for future generations.

To overcome some of the uncertainties regarding net-zero policies, Fankhauser et al.[203] propose seven reliable attributes for a successful net-zero framework. The proposal includes three segments: the urgency of zero, the integrity of 'net', and the consistency with sustainable development objectives. For our analysis, we adopt four of the seven attributes. The *urgency of zero* starts with the attribute of front-loaded emission reductions. Implementing early and significant emission reductions serves to preserve flexibility and optionality in climate action. By front-loading these reductions, we retain the ability to potentially revise and tighten future carbon budgets based on emerging scientific insights.[204] For instance, if new findings reveal the occurrence of carbon cycle feedbacks, such as accelerated thawing of permafrost, leading to additional emissions, we can adapt our strategies accordingly. This notion is consistent with one of the features of the risk-based approach to regulation. The continuous review and assessment of initial parameters of intervention ought to be updated, according to newfound or newly discovered risk.

Front-loading emission reductions allows us to proactively address the evolving understanding of climate dynamics and potential feedback loops. This concept aligns with Ulrich Beck's theory of *risk society*[205] and the notion of latency within the reflexivity of modernisation. According to Beck, as society undergoes reflexive modernisation, its structural social conditions are significantly transformed.[206] As risks associated with modernisation become more scientifically recognised,

203 S. Fankhauser et al., 'The Meaning of Net Zero and How to Get It Right' (n 194) 13.

204 T. Gasser et al., 'Path-Dependent Reductions in CO_2 Emission Budgets Caused by Permafrost Carbon Release', *Nature Geoscience* 11 (2018): 830–835.

205 Ulrich Beck, *Risk Society: Towards a New Modernity* (n 57) 154.

206 ibid.

adopting front-loaded emissions reduction strategies reduces the latency period – the time between a stimulus and its result.

By taking ambitious action early on, we acknowledge that the relationship between early emission reductions and their outcomes can help mitigate risks associated with unforeseen amplifications of GHG emissions. This proactive approach allows us to adapt to emerging knowledge and scientific insights, ensuring that our strategies and policies remain aligned with the goals of climate stability and sustainability. By reducing latency, we enhance our ability to address the complex and interconnected challenges posed by climate change, fostering a more resilient and adaptable society.

Incorporating the concept of latency within the framework of front-loading emission reductions underscores the importance of timely action in risk-based regimes. By embracing the reflexive nature of modernisation and integrating scientific understanding, we can navigate the uncertainties and complexities of climate change more effectively. This approach not only safeguards against potential future risks, but also enables us to foster a sustainable and thriving society for generations to come.[207]

The second attribute of the 'urgency of zero' segment is that of *a comprehensive approach to emission reductions*.[208] A fundamental aspect of net zero is its comprehensive approach to emissions abatement. Unlike partial emissions targets (which allowed challenging emission sources to be offset by residual emissions) net zero requires addressing all emissions sources. This eliminates the option of leaving certain sources unaddressed, except for the potential utilisation of carbon removal techniques.

The comprehensive nature of net zero necessitates addressing emissions from all sectors, extending beyond the traditional focus on energy-related emissions. The advancements in renewable energy and the impending transformation of the automotive industry demonstrate positive momentum towards achieving net zero. By adopting a holistic approach that targets all emissions sources, we can effectively mitigate climate change and pave the way towards a sustainable and carbon-neutral future.

In designing such a holistic approach, we can benefit from the features of a risk-based regime, which strengthens the scientific and social understanding of net-zero-related risks. The rationale behind promoting a target-all-emissions approach stems from recognising that science plays a crucial role – as a cause, as a means of defining the problem, and as a source of solutions to risks.[209] Consequently, society and the market undergo a process of 'scientisation', where scientific knowledge shapes decision-making processes. However, there is a potential danger associated with

207 A. Averchenkova, S. Fankhauser and J. J. Finnegan, 'The Impact of Strategic Climate Legislation: Evidence from Expert Interviews on the UK Climate Change Act', *Climate Policy* 21 (2021): 251–263.

208 S. Fankhauser et al., 'The Meaning of Net Zero and How to Get It Right' (n 194) 16.

209 Ulrich Beck, *Risk Society: Towards a New Modernity* (n 57) 156.

this approach. The construction of a target-all-emissions policy may inadvertently become entangled in the contradictory cycle of science that in turn will inform policy[210] and investment.[211] In this cycle, science presupposes and conducts a critique of itself and the existing practices of experts, leading to a period of introspection within the scientific community.[212] This self-reflection may introduce additional uncertainty and risks, potentially undermining the stability and effectiveness of the target-all-emissions policy. Therefore, it is essential to navigate this complex landscape carefully, acknowledging the potential challenges and uncertainties that may arise from the scientific and societal processes. By doing so, we can foster a more resilient and adaptive approach to addressing net-zero-related risks, ensuring that the path towards a sustainable future is robust and well informed.

The second segment of the solution proposed by Fankhauser et al.[213] is the integrity of 'net'. According to this segment, the cautious use of carbon dioxide removal is the third attribute of an effective net-zero strategy. Carbon dioxide removal (CDR) has garnered significant attention and is often seen as a component of greenhouse gas removal (GGR).[214] GGR encompasses not only carbon dioxide, but also other GHGs like methane (CH_4). In the Kyoto Agreement, the concept of Assigned Amount Units (AAUs) was introduced.[215] These units do not pertain exclusively to carbon dioxide, but encompass various GHGs, with their quantities made equivalent based on their Global Warming Potential (GWP).[216]

CDR techniques generate valuable climate outcomes, by physically extracting carbon dioxide from the atmosphere and relocating it elsewhere for storage. By reducing the concentration of atmospheric carbon dioxide, the rate of global warming can be slowed down, provided that the carbon dioxide remains removed from the atmosphere. Ensuring the appropriate duration of carbon storage is a crucial concern, because temporary removals yield only temporary advantages. However, numerous cost-effective CDR options available today predominantly offer only temporary carbon removal. Assessing the cost of various CDR strategies becomes challenging, due to variations in the permanence or duration of carbon removal.

210 Geoffroy Dolphin, Michael Pahle, Dallas Burtraw and Mirjam Kosch, 'A Net-Zero Target Compels a Backwards Induction Approach to Climate Policy', Resources for the Future, WP 22, 18 October 2022. https://media.rff.org/documents/WP_22-18.pdf accessed 2nd July 2023.

211 IEA, *World Energy Outlook 2021* (IEA, 2021). www.iea.org/reports/world-energy-outlook-2021 accessed 2nd July 2023.

212 Ulrich Beck, *Risk Society: Towards a New Modernity* (n 57) 150.

213 S. Fankhauser et al., 'The Meaning of Net Zero and How to Get It Right' (n 194) 25.

214 Guy Lomax, Mark Workman, Timothy Lenton, Nilay Shah, 'Reframing the Policy Approach to Greenhouse Gas Removal Technologies', *Energy Policy* 78 (2015): 125–136. https://doi.org/10.1016/j.enpol.2014.10.002.

215 IPCC, *Appendix II Glossary. IPCC Third Assessment Report – Climate Change 2001 Working Group III: Mitigation* (Cambridge University Press, 2001).

216 United States Environmental Protection Agency, 'Understanding Global Warming Potentials'. www.epa.gov/ghgemissions/understanding-global-warming-potentials#:~:text=The%20Global%20Warming%20Potential%20(GWP,carbon%20dioxide%20(CO_2) accessed 2nd July 2023.

The differing timeframes over which carbon is effectively removed make it difficult to make direct cost comparisons among different CDR approaches.

Additionally, accurately quantifying carbon dioxide removal presents another significant challenge that is often overlooked. Certain approaches, especially those related to biological systems, require advanced scientific knowledge and innovative technologies to effectively understand and assess the carbon cycle impacts resulting from changes in land management. This process is crucial for obtaining reliable and cost-effective measurements of carbon dioxide removal.

Distinguishing carbon dioxide removal from traditional carbon offsets is essential. The carbon offset concept emerged to reduce the costs of compulsory carbon-pricing schemes. Back then,[217] global taxation or carbon-trading systems were considered the most viable strategies to combat GHG emissions. Offsets played a role in keeping mitigation costs manageable, by permitting cost-effective emission reductions from external sources to offset the expense of domestic reductions.

Carbon removal stands at a crucial crossroads. Various promising approaches are currently being field-tested, while both public and private stakeholders recognise the necessity of scaling removal to tackle unavoidable emissions in the coming decades. However, there is a significant concern regarding the risk of equating carbon removal with traditional offsets.[218] The private market for carbon-removal credits is largely intertwined with the existing carbon-offsetting industry. This poses a challenge, because traditional offsets give credit to activities that avoid or reduce CO_2 emissions, potentially conflicting with climate mitigation efforts, whereas carbon removal addresses a distinct issue – cleaning up pollution from sources that persist or cannot be sufficiently reduced, even after substantial mitigation has been achieved.[219]

The conflicting and unsolved issues of carbon removal justify the need for a complete risk-based regime. Risk-based regulation allows a scaling prioritisation of risks, in line with regulatory objectives. As CDR is gaining prominence alongside mitigation and adaptation as a vital component of the climate response portfolio, the risk-based approach would broaden the debate to understand that CDR should be studied from both sides. With the growing importance of CDR, and the emergence of mature approaches in early-stage deployment, researchers and analysts are now investigating the interactions between carbon removal and mitigation.[220] These explorations include questions about whether CDR might

217 Sofia Pyrgioti, 'There and Back Again: The History of Offsets by Mark Trexler, the Ph.D. of the First Offset Project', 10 February 2023. https://carboncloud.com/2023/02/10/offset-history-trexler/ accessed 2nd July 2023.

218 Frances Wang, Danny Cullenward, Jeremy Freeman and Jan Mazurek, 'Addressing Critical Challenges in Carbon Dioxide Removal', Climate Works Foundation, 10 December 2020. www.climateworks.org/blog/addressing-critical-challenges-in-carbon-dioxide-removal/ accessed 2nd July 2023.

219 ibid.

220 D. P. McLaren, D. P. Tyfield, R. Willis, B. Szerszynski and N. O. Markusson, 'Beyond "Net-Zero": A Case for Separate Targets for Emissions Reduction and Negative Emissions', *Frontiers in Climate* 1 (2019): 4.

discourage mitigation efforts,[221] the role of carbon capture and use in decarbonisation, and how carbon removal can synergise with mitigation in the context of energy systems.[222] At this juncture, however, Buck et al.[223] argue that there are compelling reasons for both scientific research and policymaking to closely examine carbon *removal* and *adaptation*[224] in tandem. One of the most significant advantages of conducting joint analyses is that adaptation literature sheds light on the social dimensions of climate response, which are sometimes overlooked in technical assessments of carbon removal potentials. By integrating vulnerability analysis,[225] we gain insights into why certain communities are at risk, directing our attention to social conditions that would both shape and be influenced by the deployment of CDR technologies. This integrated approach enables us to recognise the interplay between social and environmental factors, fostering more impactful and fair climate solutions. By incorporating various risk perspectives, including the *environmental* and *social* aspects of ESG, we can develop CDR policies that not only address existing and emerging social vulnerabilities, but also align with its technical potential. In a risk-based approach, the objectives would aim to identify opportunities for adaptive CDR in planning, and assess the adaptive value of projects, while also providing recognition for the carbon that has been effectively removed.[226]

As we will develop in depth, in our analysis of voluntary carbon markets (VCMs), effective regulation of carbon offsets is the fourth attribute of an effective net-zero strategy.[227] Ensuring the social and environmental integrity of CDR is closely tied to the integrity and appropriate regulation of carbon offsets. Past experiences with carbon offset markets (such as the Clean Development Mechanism[228] or the current voluntary carbon market)[229] have highlighted the need for upgraded and strictly enforced

221 N. Markusson, D. McLaren and D. Tyfield, 'Towards a Cultural Political Economy of Mitigation Deterrence by Negative Emissions Technologies' (NETs)', *Global Sustainability* 1 (2018): e10.

222 ibid.

223 Holly J. Buck, Jay Furhman, David R. Morrow, Daniel L. Sanchez and Frances M. Wang, 'Perspective: Adaptation and Carbon Removal', One Earth 3, 23 October 2020. www.cell.com/one-earth/pdf/S2590-3322(20)30477-2.pdf accessed 2nd July 2023.

224 R. N. Cooper, J. T. Houghton, J. J. McCarthy and B. Metz, 'Climate Change 2001: The Scientific Basis', *Foreign Affairs* 81 (2002): 208.

225 Holly J. Buck, Jay Furhman, David R. Morrow, Daniel L. Sanchez and Frances M. Wang, 'Perspective: Adaptation and Carbon Removal' (n 223).

226 ibid.

227 S. Fankhauser et al., 'The Meaning of Net Zero and How to Get It Right' (n 194) 25.

228 Nathan E. Hultman, 'How Can the Clean Development Mechanism Better Contribute to Sustainable Development', *AMBIO: A Journal of the Human Environment* 38.2 (1 March 2009): 120–122. https://doi.org/10.1579/0044-7447-38.2.120.

229 Anja Kollmuss (SEI-US), Helge Zink (Tricorona), Clifford Polycarp (SEI-US), 'Making Sense of the Voluntary Carbon Market: A Comparison of Carbon Offset Standards', Stockholm Environment Institute and Tricorona, WWF Germany, March 2008. www.globalcarbonproject.org/global/pdf/WWF_2008_A%20comparison%20of%20C%20offset%20Standards.pdf accessed 2nd July 2023.

quality standards to address environmental integrity concerns.[230] Given that only a few organisations and countries will be able to achieve the balance between residual emissions and removal into sinks on their own, there is a requirement for systems that can facilitate a global balance between emission sources and carbon sinks. Risk-based regimes recognise that policy systems are most adaptable to change when risk decisions are made incrementally, considering the conflicting dynamics of a specific context.[231] This principle holds true in the context of carbon reductions, where the process of achieving carbon reduction goals involves navigating both successes and setbacks along the way. By adopting a risk-based approach, policymakers can better manage and mitigate the uncertainties and risks associated with carbon reduction efforts.

Various arrangements can be considered for this purpose. Some governments may choose to centrally procure carbon offsets through regular purchases to balance their national carbon accounts. Another option is the existence of a private market for carbon offsets. The growing ambition reflected in net-zero commitments has already generated increased demand for offsets, which has rekindled concerns regarding their effectiveness.[232] Further explanation on carbon offsets and carbon markets will be presented in the following chapters.

Greenwashing Risks

No discourse around sustainable finance is complete unless it considers the risk of greenwashing – in an era of increasing environmental awareness and consumer demand for sustainability, greenwashing has emerged as a significant risk in the business landscape. The term 'greenwashing' was coined by New York environmentalist Jay Westervelt in 1986.[233] Delmas and Cuerel[234] define it as 'the intersection of two firm behaviours: poor environmental performance and positive communication about environmental performance'. Greenwashing refers to the deceptive practice of portraying a company, product, or service as environmentally friendly or sustainable, while the reality may not align with the claims.

Although the judgement of a greenwashing practice is meant to be studied case by case, it is possible to identify the drivers behind such practices. We could delve into the infamous and now historic 2007 Shell case, to illustrate the concept of

230 Benjamin K. Sovacool, 'Four Problems with Global Carbon Markets: A Critical Review', *JSTOR: Energy & Environment* 22.6 (2011): 681–94. www.jstor.org/stable/43735038 accessed 2nd July 2023.

231 Sheila Jasanoff, 'Risk Management and Political Culture', in *Social Research Perspectives* (Occasional Reports on Current Topics, Russell Sage Foundation, 1986) 33.

232 S. Fankhauser et al., 'The Meaning of Net Zero and How to Get It Right' (n 194) 15.

233 P. Romero, 'Beware of Green Marketing, Warns Greenpeace Exec', *ABS-CBN*, 2008. www.abs-cbnnews.com/special-report/09/16/08/beware-green-marketing-warns-greenpeace-exec accessed 2nd July 2023.

234 Magali A. Delmas and Vanessa Cuerel Burbano, 'The Drivers of Greenwashing', *California Management Review* 54.1 (October 2011): 64–87. Special Issue: Environmental Management and Regulatory Uncertainty.

greenwashing and identify the actors involved. Shell's slogan, '*Don't throw anything away. There is no away.*' was displayed above a vibrant image of an industrial landscape, featuring refineries and four chimneys emitting colourful flowers into a clear blue sky. This iconic advertisement serves as a poignant example of greenwashing practices. Then, *The Guardian* published an article titled 'No bouquets for Shell press ad',[235] which strongly criticised the company for their misleading advertisement. Following its publication in the UK, environmental lobby group Friends of the Earth raised concerns about the inconsistency between Shell's communication and its actual environmental performance.[236] They lodged a complaint with the Advertising Standards Authority (ASA), the UK's self-regulatory organisation for the advertising industry. Subsequently, the advertisement was banned, and Shell publicly stated that they had no plans to reuse the advertising campaign in the future.[237]

Greenwashing encompasses various forms of misleading marketing or communication that create a false perception of environmental responsibility; it can involve exaggerated claims, ambiguous language, selective disclosure, or the omission of relevant information. As may be anticipated, the core of greenwashing is closely linked to information and how it is communicated. In essence, it could be allocated as a manifestation of information asymmetry, triggered by a misleading interest in creating 'false value'. Hence, greenwashing involves a deliberate strategy employed by companies to deceive investors and consumers into believing that the firm is committed to environmental, social, and/or governance policies that enhance the value of the company and its products or services. Maintaining the illusion involves significant costs for the firm, but these costs may seem, at least initially, outweighed by the benefits of an improved reputation in the market.[238] In essence, greenwashing involves the use of false corporate social responsibility activities to create an undeserved reputation that boosts the company's value.[239] Besides information asymmetry, greenwashing also incorporates stakeholder theory, as management must deceive not only customers, but other stakeholders, such as shareholders and debtholders, who have a direct impact on the company's value.

Delmas and Burbano[240] adopt institutional theory to identify various factors that drive greenwashing. They categorise these drivers into four main areas. The first area is *non-market external drivers*, which encompass a lenient and uncertain regulatory environment, activist groups, NGOs, and the media. These actors serve as informal

235 Chris Tryhorn, 'No Bouquets for Shell Press Ad', Wednesday 7 November 2007 10.30 GMT. www.theguardian.com/media/2007/nov/07/asa.advertising accessed 2nd July 2023.

236 P. Seele and L. Gatti, 'Greenwashing Revisited: In Search of a Typology and Accusation-Based Definition Incorporating Legitimacy Strategies', *Business Strategy and the Environment* 26 (2017): 239–252. https://doi.org/10.1002/bse.1912.

237 ibid.

238 S. V. de Freitas Netto, M. F. F. Sobral, A. R. B. Ribeiro and G. R. da Luz Soares, 'Concepts and Forms of Greenwashing: A Systematic Review', *Environmental Sciences Europe* 32 (2020): 19. https://doi.org/10.1186/s12302-020-0300-3.

239 Richard Paul Gregory, 'When is Greenwashing an Easy Fix?', *Journal of Sustainable Finance & Investment* 13:2 (2023): 919–942. https://doi.org/10.1080/20430795.2021.1907091.

240 Magali A. Delmas and Vanessa Cuerel Burbano, 'The Drivers of Greenwashing' (n 234).

monitors, scrutinising and exposing instances of firm greenwashing. The second area is *market external drivers*, which include consumer demand, investor demand, and incentives driven by competition. Firms often emulate their competitors to avoid falling behind in the market. The third area is *organisational-level drivers*, which involve firm characteristics such as size, profitability, and industry. Additionally, factors such as incentive structures, ethical climate, organisational inertia, resistance to change, and the effectiveness of internal communication play a role in driving or discouraging greenwashing practices within organisations. The fourth area is *individual-level psychological drivers*, which encompass cognitive biases such as optimistic bias, narrow decision framing, and hyperbolic intertemporal discounting. These psychological factors can influence decision-making and contribute to greenwashing behaviour at the individual level. Overall, these drivers provide insights into the multifaceted factors that contribute to the prevalence of greenwashing in various contexts.

The extensive literature[241] on greenwashing identifies several manifestations of this practice. Firstly, there is 'selective disclosure', where a firm emphasises certain information while downplaying other information.[242] Some authors[243] suggest that companies with poor environmental performance tend to engage in higher levels of selective disclosure. This is especially evident when companies adopt eco-labels from dishonest manufacturers.

Another form of greenwashing is 'decoupling', wherein companies claim to meet shareholders' expectations without genuinely altering their practices.[244] This often occurs when organisations pursue ambitious projects without adequate support from sustainable practices or sufficient funds to achieve their stated environmental goals. Similarly, 'attention deflection'[245] is a recognised form of greenwashing involving symbolic activities aimed at diverting stakeholders' attention from corrupt business actions. Likewise, 'deceptive manipulation' involves misleading communications that create a false impression that a firm's products, objectives, or policies are environmentally friendly.[246]

241 Zhi Yang, Thi Thu Huong Nguyen, Hoang Nam Nguyen, Thi Thuy Nga Nguyen and Thi Thanh Cao, 'Greenwashing Behaviours: Causes, Taxonomy and Consequences Based on a Systematic Literature Review', *Journal of Business Economics and Management* 21.5 (2020): 1486–1507. https://doi.org/10.3846/jbem.2020.13225.

242 X. Font, A. Walmsley, S. Cogotti, L. McCombes and N. Häusler, 'Corporate Social Responsibility: The Disclosure-Performance Gap', *Tourism Management* 33.6 (2012): 1544–1553. https://doi.org/10.1016/j.tourman.2012.02.012.

243 D. M. Patten, 'The Relation Between Environmental Performance and Environmental Disclosure: A Research Note', *Accounting Organizations & Society* 27 (2002): 763–773. https://doi.org/10.1016/S0361-3682(02)00028-4.

244 J. W. Meyer and B. Rowan, 'Institutionalized Organizations: Formal Structure as Myth and Ceremony', *American Journal of Sociology* 83 (1977): 340–363. https://doi.org/10.1086/226550.

245 S. Lightfoot and J. Burchell, 'Green Hope or Greenwash? The Actions of the European Union at the World Summit on Sustainable Development', *Global Environmental Change* 14 (2004): 337–344. https://doi.org/10.1016/j.gloenvcha.2004.07.002.

246 A. Siano, A. Vollero, F. Conte and S. Amabile, 'More Than Words: Expanding the Taxonomy of Greenwashing after the Volkswagen Scandal', *Journal of Business Research* 71 (2017): 27–37. https://doi.org/10.1016/j.jbusres.2016.11.002.

Finally, another avenue for greenwashing is 'authorisation to external parties', where companies replace the credibility of third-party authorisers with their own self-issued endorsements. While product- and company-level authorisations are meant to control greenwashing, alone, they cannot prevent the phenomenon effectively – they require external back-up.[247] Some companies may lobby for the establishment of third-party eco-labelling systems or stricter labelling rules to address greenwashing concerns.

Assessing the impact of greenwashing is crucial for the development of effective regulatory frameworks in sustainable finance. We argue that a risk-based approach to regulation – which fosters ongoing dialogue between regulators and stakeholders, is instrumental in tackling the challenges posed by greenwashing. Such an approach enables the identification and mitigation of adverse effects, such as misleading consumers, undermining market dynamics, and diluting the effectiveness of regulatory measures.

A risk-based regime provides a framework to address the difficulties associated with detecting and combating greenwashing. These challenges include the absence of standardised definitions, limited transparency, and verification mechanisms, as well as the complexity and scope of the issue. By adopting a risk-based perspective, regulators can proactively manage these challenges, and work towards enhancing the integrity and credibility of sustainability claims in financial markets.

Greenwashing deceives environmentally conscious consumers who strive to make sustainable choices, by concealing the true ecological consequences of products or services. When consumers fall prey to greenwashing, they unwittingly support companies that contribute to environmental degradation rather than embrace sustainable practices.[248] This erodes trust and undermines progress towards a more sustainable future. Furthermore, greenwashing can distort market forces, by creating an unfair playing field for genuinely sustainable businesses. Because being green carries potential benefits for companies, greenwashing has emerged as CSR's evil twin.[249] Companies that engage in greenwashing may momentarily gain[250] an unjust advantage over competitors who invest substantial resources into authentic sustainability practices. This hinders the growth of truly sustainable businesses and impedes the overall transition to a green economy. Moreover, greenwashing poses challenges for regulators in their efforts to enforce environmental regulations and standards. For instance, the

247 Bruce Smart. *Beyond Compliance: A New Industry View of the Environment* (World Resources Institute, 1992) 285. ISBN: 0-915825-73-2. $19.95. Bruce Smart, 'Beyond Compliance: A New Industry View of the Environment', *Bulletin of Science, Technology & Society* 13.4 (1993): 239–239. https://doi.org/10.1177/027046769301300465.

248 M. D. T. De Jong, K. M. Harkink and S. Barth, 'Making Green Stuff? Effects of Corporate Greenwashing on Consumers', *Journal of Business and Technical Communication* 32.1 (2018): 77–112. https://doi.org/10.1177/1050651917729863.

249 ibid.

250 Gergely Nyilasy, Harsha Gangadharbatla and Angela Paladino, 'Greenwashing: A Consumer Perspective', *Economics & Sociology* 5.2 (2012): 116–123. www.proquest.com/openview/ae91eb4f4c1fc46e970d3d20cbd0fbfa/1?pq-origsite=gscholar&cbl=1416337 accessed 3rd July 2023.

UK's FCA recently raised some integrity-related concerns in the sustainability-linked loan market.[251] The regulator identified weak incentives in the sustainability-related terms of the loans, and low-ambition sustainability targets and indicators chosen for the loans. Misleading claims make it arduous for regulators to differentiate between genuinely sustainable practices and superficial marketing ploys. This dilution of regulatory impact hampers endeavours to hold companies accountable for their environmental impact, and inhibits the effective implementation of policies.

The fight to eliminate greenwashing does not involve only regulatory agencies, it must also include market actors. Unfortunately, research reveals that a significant number of hedge funds that publicly endorse the United Nations Principles for Responsible Investment actually engage in greenwashing practices. These hedge funds – which present themselves as environmentally conscious – underperform both genuinely green funds and nongreen funds when adjusting for risk.[252] This underperformance is particularly pronounced in cases where there is poor alignment between fund managers' incentives and investors' interests.

As a practice where financial intermediaries fail to fulfil their commitment to responsible investing, greenwashing has the potential to hinder the envisioned process described in theoretical models[253] that propose that asset prices reflect the preferences of investors towards green and nongreen assets. By engaging in greenwashing, financial intermediaries create a disconnection between their stated commitment to responsible investment and their actual actions. This can undermine the accurate pricing of assets based on investors' genuine preferences for environmentally sustainable investments. In turn, it may impede the efficient allocation of capital to green assets, and the incorporation of investors' preferences into asset prices.[254] Therefore, it is of the utmost importance to address greenwashing, and ensure that financial intermediaries adhere to their responsible investment commitments to facilitate the integration of investors' environmental preferences into asset-pricing mechanisms.

The hedge fund industry serves as a significant segment of the market for studying greenwashing. Firstly, hedge funds are renowned for being among the world's most sophisticated investors; they collectively manage a substantial amount of assets[255] totalling approximately USD 3.6 trillion.[256] They play a crucial role in

251 FCA, 'FCA Outlines Concerns About Sustainability-Linked Loans Market', 29 June 2023. www.fca.org.uk/news/news-stories/fca-outlines-concerns-about-sustainability-linked-loans-market accessed 3rd July 2023.

252 Hao Lliang, Lin Sun and Melvyn Teo, 'Greenwashing: Evidence from Hedge Funds', *Research Collection Lee Kong Chian School of Business* (2021): 1–68. https://ink.library.smu.edu.sg/lkcsb_research/6737 accessed 3rd July 2023.

253 Lubos Pastor, Robert F. Stambaugh and Lucian A. Taylor, 'Dissecting Green Returns', University of Chicago, Becker Friedman Institute for Economics Working Paper No. 2021-70, 10 June 2022.

254 Hao Lliang, Lin Sun and Melvyn Teo, 'Greenwashing: Evidence from Hedge Funds' (n 252) 2.

255 Carl Ackermann et al., 'The Performance of Hedge Funds: Risk, Return, and Incentives', *JSTOR: The Journal of Finance* 54.3 (1999): 833–874. www.jstor.org/stable/222427 accessed 3rd July 2023.

256 K. Brunnermeier and S. Nagel, 'Hedge Funds and the Technology Bubble', *The Journal of Finance* 59 (2004): 2013–2040. https://doi.org/10.1111/j.1540-6261.2004.00690.x.

the portfolios of various institutional investors (including pension funds and sovereign wealth funds), many of whom have embraced responsible investing. This underscores the significance of hedge funds for responsible institutional investors, as evident from the PRI's provision of tools to aid in incorporating ESG factors into hedge fund selection, whereas similar tools are not available for mutual funds. Secondly, relative to mutual funds, hedge funds employ complex strategies and operate with lower levels of transparency, disclosure, and regulatory oversight.[257] These characteristics amplify the potential for agency problems and opportunistic behaviour within the industry, thereby increasing the likelihood of greenwashing practices. The intricate nature of hedge fund strategies, and the limited regulatory scrutiny create an environment where misaligned incentives and deceptive practices can more readily occur. Considering these factors, the hedge fund industry offers a unique setting to study greenwashing – due to its prominence, complex strategies, lower transparency, and the divergence of perspectives between managers and investors on the significance of ESG factors. Analysing greenwashing within hedge funds can provide valuable insights into the challenges and dynamics surrounding responsible investing, agency problems, and the potential impact on investor outcomes.

Despite the challenges in detecting and combating greenwashing, and the multiple actors involved in the process, sustainable finance – in particular green finance – may contribute to better manage this risk, if properly designed and implemented. It is in this scenario that our proposal of a risk-based approach finds place. Empirical research findings[258] demonstrate that the advancement of green finance can serve as an effective mechanism to incentivise and promote ESG performance within firms. By mitigating the potential for greenwashing, green finance initiatives contribute to more genuine and impactful actions taken by companies to address sustainability concerns. Regulation of green finance has a moderating influence on various aspects of firm behaviour.[259]

As we will explain later on in the book, innovation is one of the risks to consider when assessing the effectiveness of sustainable finance regulatory instruments. It is argued that green finance initiatives have a positive impact on fostering firms' green innovation activities. By guiding and promoting the provision of financial support and incentives specifically tailored to environmentally friendly projects and initiatives – by means of the creation of regulatory incentives – firms are encouraged to invest in the research, development, and implementation of sustainable practices. This promotes a culture of innovation, and propels firms towards the adoption of greener technologies and practices. Likewise, the presence of regulated

257 Hao Lliang, Lin Sun and Melvyn Teo, 'Greenwashing: Evidence from Hedge Funds' (n 252) 2.

258 Dongyang Zhang, 'Does Green Finance Really Inhibit Extreme Hypocritical ESG Risk? A Greenwashing Perspective Exploration', *Energy Economics* 121 (2023): 106688. https://doi.org/10.1016/j.eneco.2023.106688.

259 Simon Dikau and Ulrich Volz, 'Central Bank Mandates, Sustainability Objectives and the Promotion of Green Finance', *Ecological Economics* 184 (2021): 107022. https://doi.org/10.1016/j.ecolecon.2021.107022.

green finance is associated with improved profitability for firms.[260] Investments in sustainable and environmentally responsible activities often lead to cost savings, enhanced operational efficiency, and improved risk management.[261] As a result, firms that actively engage with green finance initiatives tend to achieve greater financial success, aligning economic prosperity with sustainable practices.[262]

Therefore, regulation acts as a promotor of green finance benefits. Green finance contributes to reducing the financial constraints faced by firms. Access to dedicated funding sources and capital specifically designated for sustainable projects helps to alleviate financial barriers that could hinder firms' ability to pursue ESG objectives. By facilitating financial resources and mechanisms tailored to sustainability, green finance empowers firms to overcome financial limitations and implement impactful ESG initiatives.[263]

As perhaps may be anticipated, we defend the important role of regulation of green finance in promoting ESG performance and mitigating greenwashing risks. The availability of green finance initiatives provides a supportive framework for firms to embrace sustainability, leading to increased green innovation, enhanced profitability, and reduced financial constraints. By encouraging genuine and impactful actions, green finance drives positive change, and contributes to the broader transition towards a more sustainable and resilient economy.

The magnitude of the greenwashing problem is revealed by the rising level of lawsuits being filed by consumer and activist groups. In 2021, a group of environmental organisations filed a lawsuit against The Coca-Cola Company, alleging that the company had engaged in false and misleading marketing practices regarding the environmental benefits of its products. The lawsuit claimed that Coca-Cola used labels such as 'ocean-bound', 'environmentally friendly', and 'recyclable', to attract consumers seeking more sustainable options, despite these claims being inaccurate. Coca-Cola also faced criticism for promoting single-use plastic bottles as an environmentally responsible choice, despite the significant contribution of these bottles to plastic waste and pollution in oceans and rivers.[264] Although Coca-

260 Chien-Chiang Lee, Chih-Wei Wang and Bui Tien Thinh, 'Green Development, Climate Risks, and Cash Flow: International Evidence', *Pacific-Basin Finance Journal* 79 (2023): 102021. https://doi.org/10.1016/j.pacfin.2023.102021.

261 U. Atz, T. Van Holt, E. Douglas and T. Whelan, 'The Return on Sustainability Investment (ROSI): Monetizing Financial Benefits of Sustainability Actions in Companies', in R. Bali Swain and S. Sweet (eds), *Sustainable Consumption and Production*, vol. II (Palgrave Macmillan, 2021). https://doi.org/10.1007/978-3-030-55285-5_14.

262 E. Albertini, 'Does Environmental Management Improve Financial Performance? A Meta-Analytical Review', *Organization & Environment* 26.4 (2013): 431–457. https://doi.org/10.1177/1086026613510301.

263 M. L. Barnett and R. M. Salomon, 'Does It Pay to Be Really Good? Addressing the Shape of the Relationship Between Social and Financial Performance', *Strategic Management Journal* 33.11 (2012): 1304–1320. https://doi.org/10.1002/smj.1980.

264 Changing Markets Foundation, 'Ground-breaking Report Reveals Hypocrisy of World's Biggest Plastic Polluters'. http://changingmarkets.org/wp-content/uploads/2020/09/Talking-Trash-FINAL.pdf.

Cola stated its commitment to reducing single-plastic use, research revealed a substantial increase in the company's virgin plastic usage between 2019 and 2021. It is worth mentioning that Coca-Cola won the lawsuits[265] – one in California, and another in the District of Columbia, DC. The court dismissed claims that Coca-Cola's sustainability statements violated DC's Consumer Protection Law. The Court held that The Coca-Cola Company's statements about its sustainability initiatives (on various platforms, such as its website and Twitter) constituted false and deceptive marketing, in violation of the District of Columbia Consumer Protection Procedures Act (CPPA).[266]

In 2023, a consumer who bought Nike's 'Sustainability Collection' products took legal action, by filing a class action complaint in the federal district court for the Eastern District of Missouri.[267] The complaint alleged that Nike made false and misleading claims about the sustainability, use of sustainable materials, and environmental friendliness of these products. The plaintiff argued that Nike labelled the products as supporting a 'Move to Zero', which represents Nike's commitment to achieving zero carbon emissions and zero waste, in order to safeguard the future of sports. The complaint accused Nike of violating Missouri's Merchandising Practices Act, and raised claims of unjust enrichment, negligent misrepresentation, and fraud.

On 10 May 2023, a lawsuit was filed in New Mexico District Court, claiming that the State of New Mexico and other defendants were in violation of the State Constitution by neglecting their constitutional responsibilities to safeguard the environment from the adverse effects of oil and gas pollution.[268] The plaintiffs consisted of 'frontline' community members residing near oil and gas production sites, Indigenous peoples, youth, and environmental organisations. The complaint argued that – despite the state's constitutional obligation to protect New Mexico's air, water, environment, and natural resources – it continued to authorise

265 *Earth Island Institute vs the Coca-Cola Company*. Case No. 2021CA001846 B. Superior Court of the District of Columbia. Civil Division. www.earthisland.org/images/uploads/suits/Earth.Island_.v_._Coca-Cola_.Complaint_.(stamped)_.pdf.

266 See Sabin Center for Climate Change Law U.S. Litigation Chart. http://climatecasechart.com/case/earth-island-institute-v-coca-cola-co/ accessed 3rd July 2023.

267 *Maria Guadalupe Ellis, on behalf of herself and all others similarly situated, vs. Nike USA, Inc, Nike Retail Services, Inc, US District Court Eastern District of Missouri Division*, 10 May 2023. http://climatecasechart.com/wp-content/uploads/sites/16/case-documents/2023/20230510_docket-423-cv-00632_complaint.pdf.

268 *State of New Mexico County of Santa Fe. First Judicial District Court, Mario Atencio; Paul and Mary Ann Atencio; Daniel Tso; Samuel Sage; Cheyenne Antonio; Kendra Pinto; Julia Bernal; Jonathan Alonzo; Pastor David Rogers; Youth United for Climate Crisis Action (yucca); Pueblo Action Alliance; Indigenous Lifeways; the Center for Biological Diversity; and Wildearth Guardians. vs. the State of New Mexico; The New Mexico Legislature; Governor Michelle Lujan Grisham; New Mexico Environment Department; Secretary James Kenney in His Official Capacity; Energy Minerals Natural Resources Department; Secretary Sarah Cottrell Propst, in Her Official Capacity; Environmental Improvement Board; and the Oil Conservation Commission.* http://climatecasechart.com/wp-content/uploads/sites/16/case-documents/2023/20230510_docket-D-101-CV-202301038_complaint.pdf accessed 2nd November 2023.

and promote oil and gas extraction, without establishing and implementing a comprehensive statutory, regulatory, and enforcement framework that ensures the preservation of New Mexico's pristine and healthful environment. The complaint alleged a breach of the Constitution's 'Pollution Control Clause' and raised concerns regarding substantive due process and equal protection violations under the New Mexico Constitution.

The increasing number of greenwashing lawsuits highlights the urgency of adopting effective strategies to address this risk. One crucial strategy is to prioritise enhanced transparency and disclosure, holding companies accountable for providing accurate and comprehensive information about their sustainability practices. This entails disclosing relevant metrics, methodologies, and certifications to substantiate their claims. Independent verification and certification by reputable standards bodies can greatly enhance credibility and build trust.

Furthermore, establishing standardised definitions, criteria, and certifications for sustainability is vital in the fight against greenwashing. Collaborative efforts among industry associations, NGOs, and regulatory bodies can develop frameworks that guide companies in adopting genuine sustainable practices, while offering consumers reliable benchmarks for evaluation.

Regulatory oversight also plays a critical role in addressing greenwashing. Regulators must enforce existing regulations and develop new ones that specifically target deceptive practices. Strengthening regulatory oversight, increasing penalties for greenwashing, and fostering collaboration between regulatory agencies can all serve as deterrents against false claims and ensure compliance.

Equally important is the work of consumer education and awareness. Empowering individuals to make informed choices and identify greenwashing is crucial. Educating consumers about sustainable practices, emphasising the importance of independent verification, and promoting critical thinking can cultivate a more discerning and knowledgeable consumer base.

Greenwashing poses significant risks to stakeholders and the environment, undermining genuine sustainability efforts. The complexity of the issue, the lack of standardised definitions, and limited transparency all contribute to the persistence of greenwashing practices. By enhancing transparency, implementing standardised criteria, strengthening regulatory oversight, and promoting consumer education, we can mitigate the risk of greenwashing. Combating greenwashing is essential to ensure the credibility of sustainability claims, foster trust, and drive meaningful change towards a more sustainable future. In later chapters we delve into several sustainable finance regulatory instruments, to understand their role in identifying and managing the risk of greenwashing.

Concluding Remarks

Sustainability, as encapsulated by the ESG framework, constitutes the core of sustainable finance. Its purpose is to navigate the multifaceted and sometimes conflicting risks and uncertainties inherent in ESG factors. Present regulatory and self-regulatory structures in the area of sustainable finance predominantly emphasise environmental considerations, with a specific focus on policies addressing climate change. Notably, climate change stands out due to its distinctive nature, as it is a structural and long-term crisis, different from any other crisis ever faced in history. The challenges brought by the climate change crisis require the action of companies, investors, and governments. All market actors must be prepared for an era of significant capital redistribution, where ouression of capital must be mostly channelled towards sustainability activities. This means that in order to attend the financing and hedging needs inherent to ESG risks, their identification, analysis, and management must be done with the same rigor as the traditional financial risks (i.e., credit, liquidity, operational risks).

In line with this reasoning, sustainable finance reflects a sincere dedication from the financial services sector to actively support clearly defined sustainability goals. Within this framework, green finance stands out as a financial model that prioritises investments in projects and activities contributing positively to the environment. Two specific subcategories gaining prominence within green finance are nature-based finance (NbF) and biodiversity finance. Both public and private financial investments in Nature-based Solutions (NbS), and their adherence to global targets, play a pivotal role in meeting the essential investment needs for reducing global warming to below 1.5°C, addressing biodiversity loss, and achieving land-degradation neutrality.

Biodiversity finance plays a crucial role in facilitating the transformative changes essential to halt and reverse the decline in biodiversity and ecosystem services. Addressing the challenges arising from the current limitations of green finance necessitates an expansion of the scope of financing strategies, specifically through the coherent integration of public and private investments. In this context, blended finance emerges as a suitable approach, leveraging funds from the public and philanthropic sectors to enhance private sector investments in sustainable development.

Theouresss of green finance faces various challenges. Sustainable finance Is not merely a process in which investors push companies to confront ESG risks. Companies have also started altering their economic practices. This encompasses the publication of annual sustainability reports, and a growing emphasis on the concerns and worth of stakeholders, while safeguarding shareholders' interests. Nevertheless, the journey to fortify reporting standards that yield comprehensive, transparent, precise, and comparable data is still under intense scrutiny.

It is crucial to recognise that beyond the anticipated role of finance in advancing sustainability objectives, enhancing the volume and accuracy of sustainability-related information can yield advantages for both companies and financial markets. It has the potential to boost liquidity for green and transition initiatives, reduce capital expenses, and enhance the efficient allocation of available capital. Nonetheless, disclosing information comes at a cost, and mandatory reporting would pose considerable implementation challenges.

The current focus on climate-related risks highlights the significance of hedging instruments like financial derivatives in advancing sustainable finance objectives. In this context, a comprehensive grasp of the concepts of physical, transition, and liability risks contributes to the formulation of the risk-based strategy advocated in this book. Physical risks involve the consequences and potential impact on the value of specific financial assets resulting from climate-related events. Transition risks encompass financial risks that emerge during the process of shifting and transforming towards a low-carbon economy. The category of liability or litigation risks pertains to the risks associated with actions that may be pursued by direct victims of climate change in seeking compensation.

The net-zero target is a vital component in mitigating the impacts of climate change. It works by achieving a balance between emissions and removals, effectively curbing the global temperature rise, reducing the frequency and intensity of extreme weather events, and protecting vulnerable ecosystems and communities from the adverse consequences of climate change. The scientific and regulatory aspects explored in this chapter serve as the foundation for comprehending the significant role that carbon credit derivatives play in enhancing net-zero strategies.

Finally, given the persistent occurrence of greenwashing in sustainable finance, assessing the repercussions of greenwashing becomes a vital element in shaping effective regulatory frameworks. We argue that a risk-based regulatory approach, promoting ongoing dialogue between regulators and stakeholders, plays a crucial role in addressing the challenges presented by greenwashing. Furthermore, the establishment of mechanisms to mitigate these risks can also be embedded in the structure of financial transactions. Consequently, the fundamental characteristics of greenwashing elucidated in this chapter serve as the foundation for comprehending how ESG derivatives contracts can function as instruments for encouraging positive corporate behaviour, in alignment with sustainability objectives.

Bibliography

Books

Archer, M., *Morphogenesis and the Crisis of Normativity* (Springer Nature 2016).

Bak, I., and Cheba, K., 'ESG Risk as a New Challenge for Financial Markets' in Ziolo, M. (ed.), *Finance and Sustainable Development: Designing Sustainable Financial Systems* (Routledge International Studies in Money and Banking 2021).

Caldecott, B., *Stranded Assets and the Environment: Risk, Resilience and Opportunity* (Routledge 2018).

Fisk, P., *People Planet Profit: How to Embrace Sustainability for Innovation and Business Growth* (Kogan Page Publishers 2010).

Giddens, A., *The Politics of Climate Change* (Polity 2009).

Silvola, H., and Landau, T., *Sustainable Investing: Beating the Market with ESG* (Palgrave Macmillan 2021).

Thompson, S., *Green and Sustainable Finance: Principles and Practice in Banking, Investment and Insurance, Chartered Banker* (2nd edn, Kogan Page 2023).

Ziolo, M., Bak, I., Sinha, R., and Datta, M., 'ESG Risk Perception in Sustainable Financial Decisions. Quantitative Methods Perspective' in Nermed, K., and Latuszynska, M. (eds.), *Experimental and Quantitative Methods in Contemporary Economics: Computational Methods in Experimental Economics* (Springer 2020).

Articles

Adams, C., and McNicholas, P., 'Making A Difference: Sustainability Reporting, Accountability and Organisational Change' 20(3) *Accounting, Auditing & Accountability Journal* (2007) 382.

Ahlström, H., and Monciardini, D., 'The Regulatory Dynamics of Sustainable Finance: Paradoxical Success and Limitations of EU Reforms' 177 *Journal of Business Ethics* (2022) 193.

Ahmad, H., Yaqub, M., and Lee, S.H., 'Environmental-, Social-, and Governance-Related Factors for Business Investment and Sustainability: A Scientometric Review of Global Trends' *Environment, Development and Sustainability* (2023) 3.

Albertini, E., 'Does Environmental Management Improve Financial Performance? A Meta-Analytical Review' 26(4) *Organization & Environment* (2013) 431.

Albu, N., Catalin, N., Dumitru, M., and Dumitru, V., 'Plurality or Convergence In Sustainability Reporting Standards?' 15(7) *Amfiteatru Economic Journal* (2013) 729.

Alsayegh, M., Faisal, R., Rahman, A., and Homayoun, S., 'Corporate Economic, Environmental, and Social Sustainability Performance Transformation Through ESG Disclosure' 12(9) *Sustainability* (2020) 3910.

Ansar, A., Caldecott, B., and Tilbury J., 'Stranded Assets and the Fossil Fuel Divestment Campaign: What Does Divestment Mean for the Valuation of Fossil Fuel Assets?' *Smith School of Enterprise and the Environment* (2023) 1.

Arena, M., and Azzone, G., 'A Process-Based Operational Framework For Sustainability Reporting in SMEs' 19(4) *Journal of Small Business and Enterprise Development* (2012) 669.

Armada Brás, T. *et al.*, 'Severity of Drought and Heatwave Crop Losses Tripled over the Last Five Decades in Europe' 16 *Environmental Research Letters* (2021) 12.

Aurélien, A., Carbone, V., and Massé, D., 'How to Create Value (S) in the Sharing Economy: Business Models, Scalability, and Sustainability' 9(2) *Technology Innovation Management Review* (2019) 1.

Burkert, M., and Lueg, R., 'Differences in the Sophistication of Value-based Management – The Role of Top Executives' 24(1) *Management Accounting Research* (2013) 3.

Caldecott, B., Clark, A., Koskelo, K., Mulholland, E., and Hickey, C., 'Stranded Assets: Environmental Drivers, Societal Challenges, and Supervisory Responses' 46 *Annual Review of Environment and Resources* (2021) 417.

Cash, D., 'Sustainable Finance Ratings as the Latest Symptom of 'Rating Addiction' 8(3) *Journal of Sustainable Finance & Investment* (2018) 242.

Changhong, Z., Yu, G, Y., Mengya, W., Daiyu, L.,ouu, Z., and Jiangang, K, 'ESG and Corporate Financial Performance: Empirical Evidence From China's Listed Power Generation Companies' 10(8) *Sustainability* (2018) 1.

Cicchiello, A.F., Marrazza, F., and Perdichizzi, S., 'Non-financial Disclosure Regulation and Environmental, Social, and Governance (ESG) Performance: The Case of EU and US Firms' 30(3) *Corporate Social Responsibility and Environmental Management* (2023) 1121.

Darnall, N., Ji, H., Iwata, K., and Arimura, T.H., 'Do ESG Reporting Guidelines and Verifications Enhance Firms' Information Disclosure?' 29(5) *Corporate Social Responsibility and Environmental Management* (2022) 1214.

Delmas, M.A., and Cuerel-Burbano, V., 'The Drivers of Greenwashing' 54(1) *California Management Review*. Special Issue: Environmental Management and Regulatory Uncertainty (2011) 64.

Easterly, W., 'The Trouble With the Sustainable Development Goals' 114(775) *Current History* (2015) 322.

Edmans, A., 'The End of ESG' 52 *Financial Management* (2023) 3.

Fankhauser, S., Smith, S.M., Allen, M. *et al*., 'The Meaning of Net Zero and How to Get It Right' 12 *Nature Climate Change* (2022) 15.

Gibson-Brandon, R., Glossner, S., Matos, P., and Steffen, T., 'Do Responsible Investors Invest Responsibly?' 26(6) *Review of Finance* (2022) 1389.

Ikram, M. *et al*., 'The Social Dimensions of Corporate Sustainability: An Integrative Framework Including COVID-19 Insights' 12(2) *Sustainability* (2020) 8747.

Linnenluecke, M.K., Smith, T., and McKnight, B., 'Environmental Finance: A Research Agenda For Interdisciplinary Finance Research' 59 *Economic Modelling* (2016) 124.

Liu, J.C.E., Bauman, Y., and Chuang, Y.T., 'Climate Change and Economics 101: Teaching the Greatest Market Failure' 11(5) *Sustainability* (2019) 1340.

Monasterolo, I., 'Climate Change and the Financial System' 12 *Annual Review of Resource Economics* (2020) 299.

Moriarty, P., and Honnery, D., 'Energy Efficiency or Conservation for Mitigating Climate Change?' 12(18) *Energies* (2019) 3543.

Nunes, P., and van den Bergh, J., 'Economic Valuation of Biodiversity: Sense Or Nonsense?' 29 *Ecological Economics* (2001) 205.

Okereke, C., Wittneben, B., and Bowen, F., 'Climate Change: Challenging Business, Transforming Politics' 51(1) *Business & Society* (2012) 7.

Piñeiro, V., Arias, J., Dürr, J. *et al*., 'A Scoping Review on Incentives for Adoption of Sustainable Agricultural Practices and Their Outcomes' 3 *Nature Sustainability* (2020) 809.

Rothstein, H., Irving, P., Walden, T., and Yearsley, R., 'The Risks of Risk-Based Regulation: Insights from the Environmental Policy Domain' 32(8) *Environment International* (2006) 1056.

York, R., and Bell, S.E., 'Energy Transitions or Additions? Why a Transition from Fossil Fuels Requires More Than the Growth of Renewable Energy' 51 *Energy Research & Social Science* (2019) 40.

Working Papers

Breyer, C., Fasihi, M., Bajamundi, C., and Creutzig, F., 'Commentary: Direct Air Capture of CO: A Key Technology for Ambitious Climate Change Mitigation' Joule 3, 2053–2065 (18 September 2019) <www.cell.com/joule/pdf/S2542-4351(19)30413-1.pdf> accessed 2nd July 2023.

Cerami, L., and Fanizza, D., 'A Market for Brown Assets To Make Finance Green' WP/23/11 (January 2023) <www.imf.org/en/Publications/WP/Issues/2023/01/20/A-Market-for-Brown-Assets-To-Make-Finance-Green-528413> accessed 3rd November 2023.

Convergence Blending Global Finance, 'State of Blended Finance 2023' (25 October 2023) <www.convergence.finance> accessed 3rd November 2023.

European Commission, Joint Research Centre, Battiston, S., Alessi, L., Roncoroni, A. *et al*., 'The EU Sustainability Taxonomy: A Financial Impact Assessment', Publications Office (2020) <https://data.europa.eu/doi/10.2760/347810> accessed 2nd November 2023.

European Social Investment Forum (EUROSIF), 'European SRI Study' (2014) <www.eurosif.org/wp-content/uploads/2022/03/Eurosif-SRI-Study-2014.pdf> accessed 12th May 2023.

Flammer, C., Giroux, T., and Heal, G., 'Biodiversity Finance', NBER Working Paper No. 31022 (March 2023) <www.nber.org/system/files/working_papers/w31022/w31022.pdf> accessed 3rd November 2023.

Goel, R., Gautam, D., and Natalucci, F., 'Sustainable Finance in Emerging Markets: Evolution, Challenges, and Policy Priorities', IMF Working Papers (9 September 2022) <www.imf.org/en/Publications/WP/Issues/2022/09/09/Sustainable-Finance-in-Emerging-Markets-Evolution-Challenges-and-Policy-Priorities-521689> accessed 3rd November 2023.

Hao, L., Lin, S., and Melvyn, T., 'Greenwashing: Evidence from Hedge Funds', 1–68. Research Collection Lee Kong Chian School of Business, 2021 <https://ink.library.smu.edu.sg/lkcsb_research/6737> accessed 3rd July 2023.

International Organizations Policy Documents and Reports

Convention of Biological Diversity, 'COP15: Nations Adopt Four Goals, 23 Targets for 2023 in Landmark Biodiversity Agreement' (19 December 2022) <www.cbd.int/article/cop15-cbd-press-release-final-19dec2022> accessed 3rd November 2023.

IDB, 'IDB Calls for Greater Collaboration with Public Development Banks to Mobilize Resources for SDGs, Climate Change' (4 September 2023) <www.iadb.org/en/news/idb-calls-greater-collaboration-public-development-banks-mobilize-resources-sdgs-climate> accessed 3rd November 2023.

IOSCO, 'Sustainable Finance and the Role of Securities Regulators and IOSCO: Final Report', FR04/2020 (April 2020) <www.iosco.org/library/pubdocs/pdf/IOSCOPD652.pdf> accessed 1st July 2023.

IPCC, 'Special Report on Global Warming of 1.5 °C (eds Masson-Delmotte, V. *et al.*)' (WMO 2018) <www.ipcc.ch/site/assets/uploads/sites/2/2019/06/SR15_Full_Report_Low_Res.pdf> accessed 1st July 2023.

Kyoto Protocol to the United Nations Framework Convention on Climate Change, 10 December 1997, 2303 U.N.T.S. 162.

Paris Agreement to the United Nations Framework Convention on Climate Change, 12 December 2015, T.I.A.S. No. 16–1104.

UN PRI Initiative, 'Blueprint for Responsible Investment' <www.unpri.org/about-us/a-blueprint-for-responsible-investment> accessed 13th June 2023.

UNEP, ELD, 'State of Finance for Nature 2022' (1 December 2022) <https://wedocs.unep.org/bitstream/handle/20.500.11822/41333/state_finance_nature.pdf?sequence=3> accessed 2nd November 2023.

UNEP, 'Fifth Session of the United Nations Environment Assembly (UNEA-5)' (February 2021) <www.unep.org/environmentassembly/unea5> accessed 2nd November 2023.

UNFCC, 'Glasgow – Sharm el-Sheikh Work Programme on the Global Goal on Adaptation Referred to in Decision 7/CMA.3. Draft Conclusions Proposed by the Chairs' (15 June 2023) <https://unfccc.int/documents/629445> accessed 1st July 2023.

UNFCCC, 'Innovative Approaches for Strengthening Coastal and Ocean Adaptation – Integrating Technology and Nature-based Solutions' (13 June 2022) <https://unfccc.int/documents/510426> accessed 23rd October 2023.

UNFCCC, 'Technology and the UNFCCC: Building the Foundation for Sustainable Development' (2016) <https://unfccc.int/ttclear/misc_/StaticFiles/gnwoerk_static/NAD_EBG/54b3b39e25b84f96aeada52180215ade/b8ce50e79b57469088660216 9f4f479b.pdf> accessed 2nd November 2023.

UNFCCC, 'Technology Mechanism Initiative on Artificial Intelligence for Climate Action' (2023) <https://unfccc.int/ttclear/artificial_intelligence> accessed 2nd November 2023.

Conference Papers

Carney, M., Speaking at the re-launch of the All-Party Parliamentary Group (APPG) for the Environment on Tuesday (15 September 2020).

Collins, J., 'Unlocking Private Climate Finance for Emerging Markets', Panel Discussion Vice Chairman, Banking, Capital Markets and Advisory, Citi, Online (2 October 2023).

UK Legislation and Policy Documents

Bank of England, *Our Response to Climate Change* (London 2023).

FCA, *Climate Change and Green Finance*, Discussion Paper DP18/8 (October 2018).

HM Government, *Mobilising 2023 Green Finance Strategy* (March 2023).

EU Legislation

Directive 2014/95/EU of 22 October 2014 as regards disclosure of non-financial and diversity information by certain large undertakings and groups.

EU Climate Transition Benchmark (EU CTB) and the EU Paris-Aligned Benchmark (EU PAB), *EU Technical Expert Group on Sustainable Finance, Report on Benchmarks: On Climate Benchmarks and Benchmarks: ESG Disclosures* (September 2019) <https://finance.ec.europa.eu/system/files/2019-09/190930-sustainable-finance-teg-final-report-climate-benchmarks-and-disclosures_en.pdf> accessed 17th October 2023.

European Commission, *Sustainable Finance: Investing in a Sustainable Future* (June 2023).

3 Contextualising Financial Derivatives and Regulation

Introduction

To understand how financial derivatives can contribute to the achievement of sustainable finance objectives, it is first important to explore the functioning of the market, to revisit the concepts of plain vanilla derivatives as hedging instruments, and to analyse the regulatory regimes applicable to traditional and ESG derivatives in the EU, UK, and US market. To that end, this chapter delves into the concept of contracts as powerful tools for behaviour change, and as complementary instruments for regulation. The goal is to establish a shared understanding of how financial derivatives contracts can be repurposed to support sustainability objectives effectively. To achieve this, ESG derivatives must be carefully designed, integrating regulatory expectations and contract terms that incentivise a shift towards sustainability. We explore the relationship between regulation and contracts as an instrument of economic and sustainable growth. One of the overarching aspects concerning the role of regulation as a means for economic progress pertains to the concept of contracts, and their function as instruments for governing private interests. In this context, our objective is to outline an approach that enables financial contracts to not only address the individual concerns of counterparties, but also to integrate sustainable development interests.

Additionally, we examine the regulatory framework for financial derivatives, commencing with a brief overview of the post-GFC regulatory changes in the over-the-counter (OTC) derivatives market. This is followed by a comprehensive examination of the existing regulations governing ESG derivatives. We apply the risk-based approach to evaluating the key characteristics of EU, UK, and US regulations.

Regulation Teleology and Its Relationship With the Contract

One of the most outstanding aspects of the regulation is the effect it seeks to have on its addressees: the change or modification of conduct. This is the point of contact between state regulation and all sources of private regulation, including the contract. The regulation seeks that 'the industry, organisations and individuals modify their conduct in favour of complying with the law, and ultimately obtaining

DOI: 10.4324/9781003365242-3

the proposed objectives'.[1] However, the regulatory environment prevents its operation from being so simple. Regulation is created, designed, and implemented in an environment where the law is imperfect, enforcement systems are limited, compliance schemes must be continually evaluated and adjusted, regulators' resources are limited, and a significant degree of discretion is conferred to the regulated entities. The dynamics of change, and the balance of the interests involved in the regulatory environment make the fundamental purpose of behaviour change an ongoing challenge. The setting of the 'rules of the game' is not exclusively in the hands of the regulatory authority – this is why the contract becomes a concurrent instrument to modify behaviour and balance the interests of those involved.[2] Later in our study, we will explore the constantly evolving regulatory landscape, where state regulatory authorities propose rules, and industry stakeholders are actively involved in shaping their own instruments, leveraging standards of conduct and contractual negotiations. We contend that both sources play a vital role in defining the actual impact of finance in promoting sustainability throughout the market. This results in the financial system fulfilling its function of driving positive social and environmental outcomes, creating a general and widespread impact for the better.

In this context, it is crucial for the regulator to acknowledge the inherent limitations and challenges of its role from the very beginning. Recognising that regulation is a dynamic process involving negotiation and strategic decision-making allows us to better understand regulators' responsibilities.[3] Successful negotiation requires considering the diverse interests of various stakeholders who will be impacted by the regulatory framework. These stakeholders include institutions, consumers of goods and services, and interest groups. Their interests often diverge, leading to conflicting collective and individual benefits, which can sometimes give rise to opportunistic behaviours.[4]

In the task of identifying these numerous and varied interests, the regulator must strive to avoid favouring a select few. Certain actors in the regulatory landscape may strategically position themselves to exert greater influence over the regulatory content. In this regard, it becomes crucial for the regulator to remain vigilant and prevent any undue influence or capture.[5] It is within this context that financial contracts can play a pivotal role as catalysts for behaviour modification, and offer an opportunity to foster stronger commitments towards ESG-related objectives.

Understanding that the regulation is aimed at *modifying the behaviour of its recipients* has allowed the construction of theories about how the regulated relate

1 Cento Veljanovski, 'Strategic Use of Regulation', in R. Baldwin, M. Cave and M. Lodge (eds), *The Oxford Handbook of Regulation* (Oxford University Press, 2010) 87.

2 Colin Scott, 'Analysing Regulatory Space: Fragmented Resources and Institutional Design', in *Public Law* (Sweet and Maxwell, 2001) 283–305.

3 Joseph William Singer, *No Freedom Without Regulation: The Hidden Lesson of the Subprime Crisis* (Yale University Press, 2015) 58.

4 O. E. Williamson, *The Economic Institutions of Capitalism* (Free Press, 1985).

5 IMF, 'Regulatory Capture in Banking', vol. 2006, issue 34. www.elibrary.imf.org/view/journals/001/2006/034/article-A001-en.xml?ArticleTabs=fulltext accessed 20th July 2023.

to the regulation. Thus, for example, within the economic theory of regulation, it is argued that regulated firms and individuals have self-interests they seek to protect through legal and economic institutions. Achieving this protection reduces – from the regulated party's perspective – the difficulties faced when executing the activities subject to regulation. These interests – of the regulated and their greater adaptability to regulatory parameters – become framed within the major justifications for intervention, such as the correction of market failures,[6] the adoption of risk-based regimes, or the redistribution of available resources under the notion of distributive justice. The juxtaposition of the interests of the regulated and the justifications for regulation sheds light on the importance stressed by Owen and Brauetigan,[7] regarding the seriousness with which the regulated should approach regulation. Their argument centres around three key aspects. Firstly, those who adhere to and comply with the regulation stand to benefit by aligning their behaviour with the established standards, rules, and principles. Secondly, the participation and lobbying efforts of the regulated during the regulatory processes, although costly, can still yield meaningful results. And thirdly, regulation is a dynamic process wherein both the industry and the regulator can influence each other. The regulator can strategically leverage its tools to effect behavioural changes and achieve its objectives, while the industry seeks to shape the regulatory landscape in its favour. The integration of diverse regulatory and self-regulatory instruments has significantly contributed to shaping the current regulatory landscape concerning ESG-related standards. This convergence of multiple regulatory approaches in the ESG domain is particularly intriguing, and underscores the complexity and importance of the regulatory framework.

Alternatively, the concept of regulation viewed through the lens of negotiation has also been likened to the rationale of a contract.[8] This perspective emphasises the idea that, like commercial contracts, regulation involves a limited number of parties with significant interests at stake. As a result, these parties must be willing to adapt to the contractual conditions and, consequently, their behaviour in response to the evolving circumstances that arise during the implementation of the regulation. This approach highlights the dynamic and iterative nature of the regulatory process, where the involved parties continuously engage and adjust their actions to meet the changing needs and challenges that emerge over time. Under this assumption, we could consider that, just as there are collaboration contracts where the parties share a common interest and tasks are distributed to better obtain the common good, in the ideal scenario of regulation, there is also cooperation in favour of the regulatory objectives. Here, both the regulator and the regulated are aligned to obtain the same benefit or objective. There are also signed bilateral contracts, where each of the parties involved is focused on obtaining an individual

6 George Stigler, *Chicago Studies in Political Economy* (University of Chicago Press, 1988).

7 B. M. Owen and R. Braeutigam, *The Regulation Game: Strategic Use of the Administrative Process* (Ballinger, 1974).

8 V. P. Goldberg, 'Regulation and Administered Contracts', *Bell Journal of Economics* 7 (1976): 426.

result. Even though the successful execution of contractual obligations will benefit both parties, there is no solidarity here. On the contrary, each one fulfils his obligations while waiting for individual compensation or benefit.

If we transfer this rationality to the field of regulation, each one of the participants in the regulated environment fulfils their role, but interests may be diametrically opposed. This way of understanding regulation will be reflected in the greater or lesser willingness of the regulated to comply with the regulation and adapt their conduct. Thus, there can be a range of responses: total adherence to the purposes of the regulation, disinterest, creative compliance where compliance is only formally met, or even resistance to what is prescribed by the regulator. Recognising these dynamics within the context of ESG regimes is crucial to anticipate that adopting a risk-based approach serves as the most effective strategy to enhance regulatory compliance. By acknowledging the diverse and evolving interests of stakeholders, regulators can prioritise and tailor their efforts to address the most significant risks and potential challenges in promoting sustainable practices. This risk-based approach allows for a more targeted and efficient allocation of regulatory resources, fostering better compliance and alignment with ESG objectives.

The interplay between regulation and behaviour has spurred studies across various disciplines. One such area is the integration of public policy design with behavioural sciences, known as 'behavioural insights' (BIs). These insights stem from lessons drawn from social and behavioural sciences, encompassing decision-making, psychology, cognitive sciences, neurosciences, and group and organisational behaviour.[9,10] The inductive methodology is employed to enlighten regulators about the actual behaviours influencing specific social and economic outcomes. Armed with this knowledge, regulators can experiment with different regulatory responses, assess their impacts, and ultimately adopt the most suitable tools or strategies for effective governance.

The use of BIs means that regulators not only have the standard of conduct of the rational individual as a point of reference, but can also consider the effects of perception errors, behaviour errors, and other variables that determine how the regulation is received, as well as the probabilities of compliance depending on the type regulated. The OECD identifies that the four forms of BI implementation are focused on simplifying information; identifying errors and promoting the most convenient solutions; increasing the visibility of public policies; and eliminating or reducing errors in decision-making.[11] In the realm of ESG regulation, the integration of BIs facilitates the examination of regulatory compliance and

9 OECD, 'Regulatory Policy Outlook 2018, Chapter: Improving Regulation and Outcomes through Behavioural Insights'. www.oecd-ilibrary.org/sites/9789264303072-10-en/index.html?itemId=/content/component/9789264303072-10-en&mimeType=text/html accessed 2nd November 2023.

10 OECD, *Behavioural Insights and Public Policy: Lessons from Around the World* (OECD Publishing, 2017). http://dx.doi.org/10.1787/9789264270480-en.

11 P. Lunn, *Regulatory Policy and Behavioural Economics* (OECD Publishing, 2014). https://doi.org/10.1787/9789264207851-en.

companies' approach to regulation. Empirical studies[12] indicate that, for instance, European reporting companies exhibit a mature, strategic, and long-term-oriented ESG approach.[13] Notably, they tend to prioritise environmental and social concerns over corporate governance targets. These companies also embrace a customised ESG strategy tailored to their specific business needs, aiming to boost organisational efficiency and competitive edge. Additionally, there seems to be a pronounced emphasis on employees, external-oriented measures, operational aspects, and process-driven enhancements in corporate ESG performance and development. However, when dealing with investors as promotors of change in corporate actions, their actual investment behaviors seem to remain inconsistent with responsible ownership.[14] As asset managers exhibit greater compliance with ESG regulation, especially reporting rules, their motivation to integrate sustainability and long-term, return-making considerations in their investment practices diminishes. This decoupling strategy within the organisation leads to a scenario where asset managers, compelled to justify responsible behaviour, may have a limited sense of responsibility for promoting long-term changes in corporate behaviour. Overall, the perception of ESG regulation among corporates, investors, and regulated actors is multifaceted, making it challenging to pinpoint a single measure or provide a simple response. Moreover, progress on ESG issues varies significantly depending on the geographical location, reflecting the diverse approaches and priorities across different regions worldwide.[15]

As we warned before, the regulation process is a two-way system. In this sense, behaviour modification is not only aimed at the regulated, but also involves the regulators. The concept of regulator responsibility – for which the term 'accountability'[16] has been coined – illustrates the way in which regulation shapes regulator behaviour. The definition of accountability is usually present when evaluating the efficiency of a regulatory and supervisory authority. Measuring their work focuses regulators on designing and continuously evaluating their policies and intervention mechanisms. However, we must note that the parameters to judge the performance of the regulator exist from the beginning. That is, when the regulator chooses a strategy and some tools, that regulator is defining a starting point of knowing exactly what it is going to do, how it is going to execute it, and what commitments

12 Irina-Eugenia Iamandi, Laura-Gabriela Constantin, Sebastian Madalin Munteanu and Bogdan Cernat-Gruici, 'Mapping the ESG Behavior of European Companies. A Holistic Kohonen Approach', *Sustainability* 11 (2019): 3276.

13 ibid.

14 K. Sakuma-Keck and M. Hensmans, 'A Motivation Puzzle: Can Investors Change Corporate Behavior By Conforming To ESG Pressures?', in *Institutional Investors' Power to Change Corporate Behavior: International Perspectives: Critical Studies on Corporate Responsibility, Governance and Sustainability*, vol. 5 (Emerald Group Publishing Limited, 2013) 367–393.

15 Dan Daugaard and Ashley Ding, 'Global Drivers for ESG Performance: The Body of Knowledge', *Sustainability* 14 (2022): 2322.

16 M. Bovens, R. E. Goodin and T. Schillemans, *The Oxford Handbook of Public Accountability* (Oxford University Press, 2014).

it is assuming towards those regulated. Such a choice not only gives content to the regulation, but also sets the conditions by which the regulator will fulfil its duties.[17]

The evaluation of regulatory strategies against behaviour modification of those regulated depends largely on their design and implementation. For example, in the case of risk-based regulation, which is mostly adopted in the financial system, it is debatable how effective such a strategy is in terms of behaviour modification.[18] This is an interesting discussion. On the one hand, the defenders of risk-based systems say that the strategy has the potential to shape the relations between regulators and those regulated, and to integrate norms of behaviour, to define and delimit the parameters of responsibility and accountability.[19] On the other hand, opponents argue that risk-based regulation is limited to part of the task, because there is a gap between the risk assessment and the implementation or enforcement system. They argue that the gaps exist precisely because intervention in these regimes is guided by risk, while enforcement seeks a regulatory response in the attitude of those regulated and their ability to comply.[20]

The connection between ESG regulatory compliance and regulatory strategies is intricately tied to ESG performance. To comprehend this landscape, scholars have identified at least four categories in the existing literature.[21] The first category delves into the fundamental discussion of laissez-faire business practices versus ESG responsibilities,[22] presenting an archetype model to comprehend the underlying issues. The second trend explores the diverse perspectives of various actors relevant to this field, such as employees, customers, and institutional investors, showcasing their heterogeneous nature. The third category centres on stakeholder theory, grappling with the delineation between stakeholders and the broader community. Lastly, the fourth trend provides an overview of innovative theories and frameworks developed to analyse, monitor, and manage businesses' social responsibilities.[23]

Despite the prevailing context, there has been limited exploration in the literature concerning the impact of regulation as a catalyst for ESG focus.[24] Given these

17 Dalvinder Singh, 'Legal Accountability of Financial Regulators', in Dalvinder Singh (ed), *Banking Regulation of UK and US Financial Markets* (Routledge, 2007) ch. 6.

18 Cento Veljanovski, 'Strategic Use of Regulation', in R. Baldwin, M. Cave and M. Lodge (eds), *The Oxford Handbook of Regulation* (Oxford University Press, 2010) 87.

19 Joanna Gray and Jenny Hamilton, *Implementing Financial Regulation: Theory and Practice* (John Wiley & Sons, Ltd, 2006) 1.

20 Julia Black and Robert Baldwin, 'When Risk-Based Regulation Aims Low: A Strategic Framework', *Regulation and Governance* 6 (2012): 132.

21 Dan Daugaard and Ashley Ding, 'Global Drivers for ESG Performance: The Body of Knowledge' (n 15) 17.

22 ibid., 18.

23 ibid.

24 *See* J. W. Meyer, 'The Effects of Education as an Institution', *American Journal of Sociology* 83 (1977): 55–77; Douglass North, *Institutions, Institutional Change and Economic Performance* (Cambridge University Press, 1990); R. La Porta, F. Lopez-de-Silanes, A. Shleifer, R. W. Vishny, 'Law and Finance', *Journal of Political Economy* 106 (1998): 1113–1155; D. Matten and J. Moon,

broader insights, it becomes crucial to delve deeper into the connection between state regulation, contracts, and the overarching goal of fostering sustainable economic development. By doing so, we can better understand the intended role of financial derivatives in accelerating ESG finance.

Regulation and Contracts as an Instrument of Economic and Sustainable Growth

We begin this discussion with one of the fundamental arguments of Thomas Piketty's work, in his recent book *Capital and Ideology*:

> An inegalitarian regime . . . is characterised by a set of discourses and institutional mechanisms that seek to justify and structure economic, social and policies of the company in question. Every regime has its weaknesses and can only survive if it is willing to continually transform itself, often in conflictual and violent ways, drawing on past experiences and acquired knowledge.[25]

In this context, the following points outline the fundamental elements of studying regulation as the foundation for economic and sustainable development. It is important to note that some of these elements have faced criticism for not presenting a balanced discourse, and thus, they should be understood within the historical context that shaped their development. Our objective is to present the backdrop in which diverse discourses on economic and sustainable development have emerged, considering regulation as a key intervention mechanism.

In general terms, it could be affirmed that the importance of regulation in economic development was ignored in economic studies prior to the 1990s. Thus, the supervening theories on economic development have focused on the role of geography, public policies, and institutions. Those theories that grounded economic development in public policy were predominant from World War II to the Washington Consensus, including the period of the Asian financial crises of the mid-1990s. Subsequently, there was a shift towards institutions as the fundamental basis for promoting economic development.

Theories rooted in geography propose that economic development is influenced by the physical advantages conferred by a location, tying it to the region's flora, fauna, climate, and geography. Jared Diamond,[26] a prominent figure in this theory, integrates biological, anthropological, and archaeological concepts to argue that specific locations can create favourable conditions for economic development.

'"Implicit" and "Explicit" CSR: A Conceptual Framework for a Comparative Understanding of Corporate Social Responsibility', *Academy of Management Review* 33 (2008): 404–424. As cited in Dan Daugaard and Ashley Ding, 'Global Drivers for ESG Performance: The Body of Knowledge' (n 15) 15.

25 Thomas Piketty, *Capital e Ideología, De la Traducción Daniel Fuentes Castro* (Editorial Planeta, 2019) 13.

26 Jared Diamond, *Guns, Germs, and Steel: The Fates of Human Societies* (W.W. Norton, 1997).

These ideas[27] were influential before the 20th century and, given the current threat of climate change, may regain significance. However, Diamond contends that the differences between economically developed, and less developed countries cannot be solely attributed to natural resources and human proactivity. Some economists emphasise human institutions, encompassing law, codes of conduct, governance, and economic structures, as pivotal to economic development. While efficient institutions motivate productivity and foster development, others contribute to poverty.[28] This recognition underscores the importance of distinguishing between institutions that promote growth and those that hinder it. Nevertheless, this explanation is deemed incomplete, prompting consideration of additional factors when discussing development.

On the one hand, there are geographical factors that determine the probability of higher or lower growth. According to Diamond's theory, it is considered that people in tropical countries spend more time sick and therefore unable to be productive, as compared to inhabitants of nontropical countries. Likewise, in tropical countries there is lower productivity in agriculture, due to lack of fertile soils and higher incidence of diseases in plants and animals. On the other hand, his theory ignores the origin of good institutions. Diamond is accused of confusing the dependent variables or proximate causes with the independent variables or ultimate causes. To explain and understand the origin of good institutions, we must explore the context and historical evolution in each society. For example, if the history of agriculture is taken as a starting point, it is possible to determine how each region and society has had different experiences with institutions, based on the distribution and uses of those resources during approximately 4,000 years in Greece and China, or in less than 30 years, in regions like New Guinea. To the extent that each experience is different, and therefore deserves numerous debates for each specific case, Diamond concludes that the main determining factors in the study of the economic development of countries are *both* institutions *and* geographical factors.

Diamond's proposals, despite receiving widespread praise from some, face significant scrutiny when evaluated as the foundation of environmental determinism.[29] Environmental determinism itself includes a range of discourses, ideas that could now be labelled as racism, imperialism, and ill-intended geopolitics. All of them were incorporated within its theoretical framework.[30] We argue here that Diamond's central ideas, such as the ones that suggest focusing on physical geography and on climate, to understand why the world is divided into rich and poor, should be re-examined in times of sustainability urgencies.

27 Thomas Piketty, *Capital e Ideología, De la Traducción Daniel Fuentes Castro* (n 25) 14.

28 Jared Diamond, *Guns, Germs, and Steel: The Fates of Human Societies* (W.W. Norton, 1997) 2017. Afterword, Rich and Poor Countries in the Light of Guns, Germs, and Steel. 7437.

29 David Correia, 'F**k Jared Diamond', *Capitalism Nature Socialism* 24.4 (2013): 1–6.

30 Stephen Frenkel, 'Geography, Empire, and Environmental Determinism', *Geographical Review* 82.2 (April 1992): 143–153.

We initiated this book by emphasising that global problems demand global solutions. This means that deterministic theories like Diamond's contradict the rationale of ESG commitments and policies. Unfortunately, environmental determinism is far from dead, and appears to be resurfacing through some recent climate-related studies. Correia[31] points out that we should acknowledge the correlation between the increasing research on historical climate collapse, and the widespread acceptance of contemporary anthropogenic climate change research.[32] However, it is essential to subject the latter to critical review and scrutiny.[33] While researchers may not explicitly state it,[34] the motivation behind historical studies linking climate and collapse – particularly among funding agencies and the public – is closely linked to the current climate crisis. However, the crucial question is whether the apocalyptic message of the climate crisis can justify 'ignoring the suffering of the marginalized and the disenfranchised'.[35] We argue that the real quest lies in pursuing radical transformation that encompasses not only addressing climate and environmental risks, but also integrating considerations of social justice. This viewpoint is one of the core reasons why this book extends beyond the study of financial instruments, to address environmental factors. Instead, it advocates for elevating the risks of social and governance aspects, included in the broader ESG phenomenon, at the forefront of sustainable finance.

We are not alone in this discourse to integrate environmental and social factors of the planetary crisis. It is worth noting the growing argument considering how anthropogenic climate change violates human rights. According to this approach, anthropogenic climate change violates – or for some, increases the risk of violating[36] – basic human rights to life, physical security, subsistence, and health.[37] Following a similar approach, the concept of climate justice has become pervasive in discussions about the current climate emergency faced by society. Although often viewed as a recent phenomenon, its roots can be traced back to environmental justice scholarship and activism in the US, where it addressed issues of environmental racism, racialised pollution, and unequal protection for communities of colour.[38] Over time, climate justice has evolved into a global area of study and a platform

31 David Correia, 'F**k Jared Diamond' (n 29) 5.

32 N. Oreskes, 'The Scientific Consensus on Climate Change: How Do We Know We're Not Wrong?', in A. Lloyd and E. Winsberg (eds), *Climate Modelling* (Palgrave Macmillan, 2018).

33 John Green, *The Anthropocene Reviewed* (Dutton Penguin Random House LLC, 2021) 17.

34 Naomi Oreskes, 'The Scientific Consensus on Climate Change', *Science* 306 (2004): 1686–1686.

35 David Correia, 'F**k Jared Diamond' (n 29) 5.

36 The IPCC reports that there is 'high confidence', which it defines as '= 8 out of 10 chance' (IPCC, 2007a, 27), that: 'The health status of millions of people is projected to be affected through, for example, increases in malnutrition; increased deaths, diseases and injury due to extreme weather events; increased burden of diarrhoeal diseases; [. . .] and the altered spatial distribution of some infectious diseases'.

37 Derek Bell, 'Does Anthropogenic Climate Change Violate Human Rights?', *Critical Review of International Social and Political Philosophy* 14.2 (2011): 99–124.

38 B. Bullard, *Unequal Protection: Environmental Justice and Communities of Color* (Random House, 1994).

for advocacy.[39] Starting from the early 2000s,[40] it also became a rallying point for environmental and climate organisations, using climate justice as a framework to highlight climate debt and historical responsibility, and advocating for justice for communities disproportionately affected by the climate crisis despite contributing the least to it.[41]

Theories that base economic development on the construction of public policies take their starting point from the end of World War II and the creation of the International Monetary Fund and the World Bank in the Bretton Woods Treaty,[42] New Hampshire in 1944. The focus of development theory, at that time, was the design and implementation of adequate intervention and aid policies, which were the foundation of the Washington Consensus,[43] expressed in stabilisation, liberalisation, and privatisation.[44] William Easterly[45] clearly identifies post-World War II public policy trends related to economic development and poverty reduction. These are foreign aid policies to balance investment and savings; investment in technology; investment in education; population control; opening of official credit lines to induce reforms in public policies; and credit amnesties to facilitate the processes of regulatory reforms. Much of the failure to achieve the expected results of these policies is related to the lack of connection between incentive systems and economic development, which, in turn, reduces poverty. In Easterly's opinion, to guarantee the success of public policies as an element of promoting economic development, it is necessary to strengthen incentive systems through their institutionalisation. The process requires working on four pillars: government actions to eliminate poverty; development and implementation of macroeconomic policies; the creation and maintenance of an adequate fiscal framework; and the defence of a political system based on public interest, aimed at reducing polarisation and inequality.

The rise of institutions as the basis of economic development occurs with the transition from state economies to market economies at the beginning of the 1990s. The question that has been discussed since the end of the '80s was: how to attend to this transition? In this context, the followers of Friedrich Hayek, Milton Friedman, and the Chicago school focused on the idea that if everything in such economies was rapidly liberalised and privatised, the market economy would develop naturally.

39 T. Sikor and P. Newell, 'Globalizing Environmental Justice?', *Geoforum; Journal of Physical, Human, and Regional Geosciences* 54 (2014): 151–157.

40 Peter Newell, 'Climate Justice', *The Journal of Peasant Studies* 49.5 (2022): 915–923.

41 P. Bond, *Politics of Climate Justice: Paralysis Above, Movement Below* (Scottsville: University of KwaZulu-Natal Press, 2012).

42 Michael D. Bordo, 'The Bretton Woods International Monetary System: A Historical Overview', in Michael D. Bordo and Barry Eichengreen (eds), *A Retrospective on the Bretton Woods System* (University of Chicago Press, 2007) 3–108.

43 John Williamson, 'A Short History of the Washington Consensus', *Law and Business Review of the Americas* 15.7 (2009): 9.

44 *See* Paul Krugman, 'Dutch Tulips and Emerging Markets', *Foreign Affairs* 32 (July–August 1995): 6.

45 William Easterly, *The Elusive Quest for Growth: Economist's Adventures and Misadventures in the Tropics* (MIT Press, 2001) 286.

However, reality proved to be more complex, and for this reason, the reformers noted the need to strengthen institutions, mainly the role of law and the protection of property, to facilitate the transition to the market economy. Thus arises the movement of 'New Institutional Economics'. For Douglass North,[46] institutions are essential for economic development, as they are the rules of the game in society,[47] and give structure to all daily activities. Private property is embedded in institutions, and institutions are the necessary structure for economic growth. Thus, under weak institutions, the invisible hand of the market acts and – as Katharina Pistor brilliantly explains in her book, *The Code of Capital* – law becomes a tool that codifies the dynamics of economic concepts and realities. These realities include capital, as well as the distribution and protection of some of its holders[48] – even the holder of the capital may end up being codified as capital themselves. North's fundamental quest is how to find the best combination of institutions to capture the gains of the free market, in the context of using incentives to make institutions increasingly efficient.[49] His study focuses on solving the problem of human cooperation, especially that which allows economies to obtain market benefits, in the sense of Adam Smith's *Wealth of Nations*.[50]

Naturally, the theories of institutions, public policies, and geography as the basis of economic development have been discussed in studies such as those by Esterly and Levine,[51] or Rodrik, Subramanian, and Trebbi.[52] However, although significant, the results are not conclusive regarding the way in which public policies and institutions should be designed; their success continues to depend on the circumstances of each economy.

As we can see, the relationship between economic development and regulation is a broad and debated area. Part of a normative approach (*what should be*) and a positive one (*what is*),[53] this relationship includes analysis of prices, access, quality, market entry and structure, empirical cost-benefit studies, as well as the development of standards, rules, and compliance mechanisms. It has been developed mainly in four areas: economic regulation, social regulation, competition law, and

46 Douglass North, *Institutions, Institutional Change and Economic Performance* (n 24) 3.

47 ibid.

48 Katharina Pistor, *The Code of Capital: How the Law Creates Wealth and Inequality* (Princeton University Press, 2019) 204.

49 Douglass North, *Institutions, Institutional Change and Economic Performance* (n 24) 1.

50 'The real wealth of a nation consists of its productive output, and the system of money which is needed as a means of easy exchange and a symbol of value'. Adam Smith, *The Wealth of Nations with an Introduction by Tom Buttler-Bowdon* (Capstone, 2010) xxvi.

51 William Easterly and Ross Levine, 'Tropics, Germs, and Crops: How Endowments Influence Economic Development', NBER Working Paper No. 9106 de 2002.

52 Dani Rodrik, Arvind Subramanian and Francesco Trebbi, 'Institutions Rule: The Primacy of Institutions over Integration and Geography in Economic Development', IMF Working Paper WP/02/189, November 2002.

53 Cento Veljanovski, 'Economic Approaches to Regulation in Robert Baldwin', in Martin Cave and Martin Lodge (eds), *The Oxford Handbook of Regulation*, (Oxford University Press, 2010) 18.

legal systems.[54] Fundamentally, the economic approach to law can be defined as the application of economic theories to examine the formation, structure, processes, and impact of law and regulatory institutions[55] – among them, the contract. Thus, concepts from price theory, such as scarcity and choice, are applied to the law-making process – and, in the context of our discourse, to the regulatory process. The scarcity of resources involves the need to make decisions, rationalising the use of regulation and assigning available resources to meet the most pressing needs. Economists mostly – although not exclusively[56] – assume that these decisions are made rationally, under the premise of incurring the lowest possible costs and maximising benefits.

One of the transversal elements to the use of regulation as a tool for economic development relates to the notion of *contract*, and its role as an instrument for regulating private interests. However, our purpose is to formulate a path that allows the function of financial contracts, not only to attend to the individual interests of the parties, but also to integrate and at the same time become a tool for reconfiguring the larger interests involved in the provision of financial services. In the context of sustainable finance, this means meeting the social, environmental, and livelihood needs of the present generation – without compromising the ability of future generations to meet their own needs.

It is in this context where the reconceptualisation of sustainable development[57] ought to be the starting point of any debate. Modern environmentalism has arisen as a critical response to the prevailing Western-centric development paradigm. However, it manifests in various forms and expressions.[58] Environmentalism highlights the shortcomings of a development model that leads to ecological devastation on a global scale. Alongside this, the model of traditional economic development also fosters social exclusion and economic alienation. Environmentalism challenges numerous fundamental assumptions made by the Western development model. These include the notions about the utilisation of nature and natural resources, the definition of progress, and the governance of society.[59] This challenge encompasses both the traditional patterns of authority within society, and the formulation and execution of public policies. Therefore, numerous environmental development models have emerged as alternatives to the traditional development paradigm. These models advocate for transformative social changes that prioritise the

54 ibid.

55 Cento Veljanovski, *Economic Principles of Law* (Cambridge University Press, 2007) ch. 2. Ver Cento Veljanovski, *The New Law and Economics – A Research Review* (Oxford Centre for Socio-Legal Studies, 1982).

56 Michel Zouboulakis, *The Varieties of Economic Rationality: From Adam Smith to Contemporary Behavioural and Evolutionary Economics* (Routledge, 2014) 2.

57 International Union for the Conservation of Nature and Natural Resources (IUCN), *World Conservation Strategy: Living Resources Conservation for Sustainable Development* (IUCN in Collaboration with UNEP and WWF, 1980).

58 J. Barry, *Environment and Social Theory* (2nd edn, Routledge, 2006).

59 Susan Baker, *Sustainable Development* (2nd edn, Routledge, 2016) 2.

fulfilment of both material and nonmaterial human needs, foster social equity, enhance organisational effectiveness, and build the necessary human and technical capacity to achieve sustainability.[60] Naturally, as a belief in the common heritage of humankind, the role of sustainable development should illustrate not only the normative dimensions of public policy, but also the design of contracts to promote long-term transformation of basic aspects of the traditional industrial economic system.

The implementation of sustainable development is often viewed as a political concept intertwined with governance considerations.[61] However, translating the commitment to sustainable development into actionable measures necessitates the involvement of various societal actors and institutions.[62] Among these, a crucial institution that plays a significant role is the *contract*. It is generally accepted that contracts are governance mechanisms in contemporary economic and social relations.[63] Nevertheless, it is essential to perceive this function of the contract as dynamic, since contractual relationships must be contextualised within an ever-changing economic and market environment.[64] Likewise, the role of contract is strengthened when viewed from the notion of freedom. This is to understand the freedom of contract as an immunity from legal reprisal for making or receiving promises, and the power of contract as a power to secure legal sanctions when another breaks his promise. Hence, the power of a contract lies in providing the promisee with legal remedies sufficient to safeguard their trust in the promise, deter gains through default, and enforce expectations, especially in cases of concealed or unverifiable reliance.[65] In this context, the use of financial derivatives as instruments to promote the achievement of sustainability goals is key.

We want to emphasise that our stance is not simply advocating for the insertion of sustainability clauses in any financial or commercial contract. Rather, our argument supports the idea that *the core focus of the contract should align with specific and measurable sustainability indicators* – the KPIs. While sustainability clauses have become prevalent,[66] their effectiveness in terms of enforcement is often lacking. Indeed, sustainability contractual clauses (SCCs) are frequently detached from the primary subject matter of the contract, and primarily serve the interests of third

60 M. Roseland, 'Sustainable Community Development: Integrating Environmental, Economic, and Social Objectives', *Progress in Planning* 54 (2000): 73–132.

61 K. N. Farrell, R. Kemp, F. Hinterberg, C. Rammel and R. Ziegler, 'From "for" to Governance for Sustainable Development in Europe: What is at Stake for Future Research?', *International Journal of Sustainable Development* 8.1–2 (2005): 127–151.

62 Susan Baker, *Sustainable Development* (n 59) 67.

63 Peter Vincent-Jones, 'Contractual Governance: Institutional and Organizational Analysis', *Oxford Journal of Legal Studies* 20.3 (Autumn 2000): 317–351.

64 ibid., 319.

65 Ian R. MacNeil, 'Power of Contract and Agreed Remedies', *The Cornell Law Quarterly* 47.495 (1961–1962).

66 V. Ulfbeck, O. Hansen and A. Andhov, 'Contractual Enforcement of CSR Clauses and the Protection of Weak Parties in the Chain', in V. Ulfbeck, A. Andhov and K. Mitkidis (eds), *Law and Responsible Supply Chain Management* (Routledge, 2019) 46–52.

parties, such as employees of suppliers, local communities affected by the contract's performance, other businesses, or the public at large.[67] While contracts have been associated with certain advancements in the sustainability performance of global supply chains, enforcement continues to be a significant challenge.[68] These type of clauses require the contractual partner to comply with specific sustainability production requirements. The requirements tend to include environmental practices, human rights protection, employees' well-being, and anti-bribery measures.[69] The issue that cuts across these clauses is *enforcement*, which has been highlighted as a major challenge. For instance, enforcement may face obstacles due to vague language used in the formulations of sustainability requirements. Additionally, enforcement by third parties may be rejected, on the grounds that the contract cannot be classified as a third-party beneficiary contract. As a result, it is argued that traditional contract law principles, as well as those of transnational instruments, might be useful but inadequate when dealing with sustainability clauses.[70]

In this context, it is important to clarify that the role of contracts in promoting compliance with sustainability goals is complementary to state and international regulation. We see no contradiction in the interaction between public policy and contracts aligned with greater sustainability objectives. Contract law is intended to facilitate and streamline the enforcement of sustainability requirements within the contract.[71] This goes beyond protecting individual interests of the parties, as it also aims to safeguard societal interests. The discourse is no longer solely focused on the quality of a product meeting a counterparty's expectations, but on ensuring that the production of such a product is done in a sustainable manner.[72]

However, the reality of making the sustainability clauses enforceable has some challenges. As Ulfbeck and Hansen posed, the first issue to overcome is the one that qualifies sustainability obligations as ethical rather than legal obligations. If we accept that sustainability obligations are legal, they will be enforceable by principle. Then, there's the challenge regarding the level of importance afforded to the sustainability clause – a real, material commitment to sustainability goals would lead us to conclude that these clauses are as important and central to the contract as commercial clauses. Finally, there is the issue of whether sustainability clauses must be expressly included in the contract, or whether implied terms are the preferable method of incorporation.

67 K. Mitkidis, 'Enforcement of Sustainability Contractual Clauses in Supply Chains by Third Parties', in V. Ulfbeck, A. Andhov and K. Mitkidis (eds), *Law and Responsible Supply Chain Management* (Routledge, 2019).

68 ibid.

69 Vibe Ulfbeck and Ole Hansen, 'Sustainability Clauses in an Unsustainable Contract Law?', *European Review of Contract Law* 16.1 (2020): 186–205.

70 F. Cafaggi, 'New Foundations of Transnational Private Regulation', in C. Scott et al. (eds), *The Challenge of Transnational Private Regulation* (Blackwell Publishers, 2011) 22.

71 A. Beckers, 'Towards a Regulatory Private Law Approach for CSR Self-Regulation? The Effect of Private Law on Corporate CSR Strategies', *European Review of Private Law* (2019): 239.

72 Vibe Ulfbeck and Ole Hansen, 'Sustainability Clauses in an Unsustainable Contract Law?' (n 69) 190.

In English law, there is a distinction between implied terms in fact, and implied terms in law. Despite this common confusion, implied terms allow for judicial intervention while maintaining the appearance of respecting the parties' self-determination.[73] This feature of implied terms becomes particularly relevant when including sustainability-related tasks in a contract. Given the evolving nature of sustainability goals, it is advantageous to adopt contractual clauses that are flexible and adaptable.

Following the European adoption of the implied terms trend, our argument gains strength. The Principles of European Contract Law[74] recognise that a contract may contain implied terms derived from the parties' intention, the nature and purpose of the contract, and principles of good faith and fair dealing. These three criteria support the adoption of sustainability clauses, as they can become a means to establish a coherent sustainability performance. In certain cases, the parties' intention, although not explicitly stated, might be inferred through the implicit adoption of trade usages in specific sectors.[75] This is the main feature of sustainability clauses; they become tools to promote greater commitment towards sustainability goals. However, they are not the only contractual instrument to achieve such a goal, which is why we argue for the adoption of *contracts* – not just clauses – as instruments for behaviour adjustment in line with greater sustainability goals.

In light of these considerations, the main focus of this work is to explore how financial derivatives contracts can contribute to achieving sustainable finance objectives. Our aim is to analyse the role of these contracts as a central instrument in the rationale of sustainable finance, using the concepts of risk and uncertainty. In the first chapter of this book, we established that the successful integration of management and financing aligned with the SDGs helps us define the scope of sustainable finance. This entails recognising the inherent interplay between risk and uncertainty, which are characteristic of the sustainability journey, and, we argue, also a feature of the use of financial contracts to hedge ESG risks. We acknowledge that despite setting common ESG targets, certain damaging events may still occur and not be preventable or efficiently managed. This is a reality that will be reflected in the use of financial derivatives for sustainability. In the context of a contract, risk calculation becomes pivotal in making decisions about entering into a contractual agreement, and doing so with the purpose of hedging. Collins[76] elucidates that the calculation of risks involves both sides of the equation. On one side, there is an

73 Hugh Collins, 'Implied Terms: The Foundation in Good Faith and Fair Dealing', *Current Legal Problems* 67.1 (2014): 297–331.

74 O. Lando and H. Beale (eds), *Principles of European Contract Law Part I and II* (Kluwer Law International, 2000) 302–305, art 6:102 Implied Terms.

75 See C. R. Drahozal, 'Usages and Implied Terms in the United States', in F. Gelinas (ed), *Usages and Implied Terms in the Age of Arbitration* (Oxford University Press, 2016) 103–124. As cited in Vibe Ulfbeck, and Ole Hansen, 'Sustainability Clauses in an Unsustainable Contract Law?' (n 69) 195.

76 Hugh Collins, *Regulating Contracts* (Oxford University Press, 2002; online edn, Oxford Academic, 1 January 2010). https://doi.org/10.1093/acprof:oso/9780199258017.001.0001 accessed 21st July 2023.

estimation of the expected benefits derived from the transaction. On the other side, there is a fear of potential betrayal or disappointment. In conducting this calculation, one crucial variable will always be the value attached to the expected benefits. In this context, the benefits derived from the contracts are not solely focused on profits, but instead serve a broader sustainability strategy. In the next chapter, we will delve into how the three forms of ESG derivatives – namely, traditional derivatives, sustainability-linked derivatives, and Carbon Credit Derivatives – function as tools for more effectively managing ESG risks.

The structure of the next section allows the reader to remember the structure and functioning of the derivatives market. This provides the basis to better understand how the ESG derivatives, analysed in Chapter 4, are integrated into the traditional market.

Physiology of the Derivatives Market

Defining Financial Derivatives

Although financial derivatives have been part of commercial life for millennia – at least since Ancient China and Mesopotamia[77] – their academic conceptualisation is more recent. The first attempts to define derivatives were comprehensive[78] of all types of transactions that serve debt financing and raising capital.[79] The mainstream definitions of financial derivatives include some common features and uses of these instruments. Hence, it has been generally accepted that derivatives might be used to serve two alternative functions: to obtain funding at a preferential rate, or to take speculative[80] advantage of a movement in a financial market for the investing institution.[81] However, this is a very restrictive approach, neglecting the role of financial derivatives as tools of efficient risk management.

One attempt to clarify the term is to define financial derivatives as 'a financial instrument whose value is derived from the performance of a secondary source such as an underlying bond, commodity or index'.[82] This definition, however, prompts more questions to be answered, if we were to reach a complete understanding of the instrument; details about the occurrence of the event, pricing and risk-hedging,

77 Satyajit Das, *Traders, Guns, and Money: Known and Unknowns in the Dazzling World of Derivatives* (Prentice Hall Financial Times, 2006) 23.

78 Timothy E. Lynch, 'Derivatives: A Twenty-First Century Understanding', Indiana Legal Studies Research Paper No. 187, 2011, 14. http://ssrn.com/abstract=1785634 accessed 23rd October 2022.

79 Schuyler Henderson, *Henderson on Derivatives* (Lexis Nexis Butterworths, 2003) 1.

80 See Lynn A. Stout, 'Why the Law Hates Speculators: Regulation and Private Ordering in the Market for OTC Derivatives', *Duke Law Journal* 48.701 (1999): 741.

81 See S. Henderson speaking on December 8, 1997, at *Legal Accounting and Control Challenges of Credit Derivatives,* IBC in Alastair Hudson, *The Law on Financial Derivatives* (2nd edn, Sweet & Maxwell, 1998) 9.

82 Bryan A. Garner and Henry Campbell Black, *Black's Law Dictionary* (9th edn, West Publishing Company, 2009), available at Westlaw Blacks.

are not included in these 'under-inclusive definitions'.[83] Alternatively, Scout defines derivatives as 'probabilistic bets on future events',[84] which potentially broadens the scheme to include as many transactions as possible[85] – this is an overinclusive definition.[86]

Authors such as Hudson offer some broader definitions. For instance,

> (A) derivative is simply a financial arrangement, the value of which is 'derived' from another financial instrument, index or measure of economic value. . . . Financial arrangement involving mutuality and valued by reference to current market rates, prices or levels . . . is a contract in which the parties only pretend to do something and allocate the risks and benefits between themselves as if they had done that something.[87]

The extent of this conceptualisation allows market actors to create any type of transaction that falls within the derivatives area. Therefore, it could be predicted that those market actors are the 'holders of knowledge' of such types of transactions, and that specialised knowledge escapes from the control of third parties, including nonspecialised market participants – and more importantly, for the purpose of this book, regulators and supervisors.

Such an assertive statement anticipates one of the lines of thought formulated within this work. Even within a sustainable finance landscape seemingly influenced by heightened state intervention through regulation, collaboration between regulators and market participants remains imperative. The use of ESG derivatives contracts serves as a complementary force to regulatory initiatives, fostering a tangible shift in the behaviour of market participants. This transformation aligns their individual interests with the broader objectives of sustainable finance. Recognising the advantages and constraints arising from the interaction between actors in the derivatives market and regulatory authorities is crucial. This acknowledgment underscores that the design, implementation, and enforcement of effective derivatives market regulations necessitate an understanding of how market participants acquire, incorporate, and navigate information in their contracts. These considerations become especially pertinent when determining the optimal approach for regulating the emerging category of ESG derivatives.

83 Timothy Lynch, 'Derivatives: A Twenty-First Century Understanding' (n 78) 14.

84 Lynn A. Stout, 'Derivatives and the Legal Origin of the 2008 Credit Crisis', *Harvard Business Law Review* 1 (2011): 1. http://ssrn.com/abstract=1874806 accessed 23rd October 2022.

85 See Randy Myers, *What Every CEO Needs to Know about Weather Risk Management* (CME Group, 2008). www.cmegroup.com/trading/weather/files/WeatherRisk_CEO.pdf accessed 23rd October 2022.

86 ibid., 18.

87 Alastair Hudson, *Credit Derivatives: Law, Regulation and Accounting Issues* (Sweet and Maxwell, 1999) 63.

The lack of certainty regarding the concept of financial derivatives has deprecated the clear notion of both regulators[88] and market actors. Indeed, the first approach adopted in the US to define financial derivatives is an illustrative case of how the absence of a comprehensive definition of these transactions adversely affects regulation. The initial legislative proceeding financial derivatives regulation started at the Senate Committee on Agriculture, Nutrition and Forestry and the House of Agricultural Committee. Those first regulations, as Lynch explains, were conceived for noncomplex transactions, mainly futures and options on agricultural commodities. Therefore, when derivatives evolved into exotic forms, like synthetic collateral debt obligations or credit default swaps,[89] that regulation proved insufficient. Obviously, further changes have been introduced to US regulation since its creation; however, not all the issues of the current complex structures have been properly addressed.[90]

Leaving aside this theoretical discussion, this work takes the mainstream definition of financial derivatives *as securities*[91] *and financial contracts*[92] *whose value is based on the level of some agreed-upon benchmark*[93] *and, in their most complex versions, are forms of 'financial engineering'*.[94] The term 'derivative transaction' includes a wide variety[95] of financial transactions.[96] Derivatives are usually defined as 'contracts whose value is derived from the value of another underlying asset';[97] these underlying assets can be bonds, shares, commodities, indexes[98] or any other financial asset, or any combination of these. Although this definition is generally true, it does not cover some OTC derivatives – for example, weather derivatives.[99]

88 Federal Reserve Bank of New York, 'Policy Perspectives on OTC Derivatives Markets', Staff Report N° 424, March 2010.

89 Timothy Lynch, 'Derivatives: A Twenty-First Century Understanding' (n 78) 9.

90 ISDA, 'Analysis After Five Years of Implementation', ISDA, 25 July 2015. http://www2.isda.org/news/dodd-frank-five-years-on-significant-progress-and-outstanding-challenges accessed 13th June 2023.

91 Robert L. Gottsfield, Michael R. Lopez and William A. Hicks, III., 'Derivatives: What They Are, What They Cause, What's The Law', *UTBJ* 15 (1 November 1996).

92 Bryan H. Booth, 'Prudence or Paranoia: Considering Stricter Regulation of the International Over-The-Counter Derivatives Market', *Duke Journal of Comparative & International Law* 499 (Spring 1995).

93 Mark A. Guinn and William L. Harvey, 'Taking OTC Derivative Contracts as Collateral', *Business Law* 57 (2002): 1127, 1129.

94 Satoshi Hosokawa and Koichi Matsumoto, 'Pricing Interest Rate Derivatives with Model Risk', *Journal of Financial Engineering* 2.1 (2015): 1–18.

95 Saul S. Cohen, 'The Challenge of Derivatives', *Fordham Law Review* (1993/1995): 63. He argues that the term 'derivatives' operates without definitional borders.

96 Board of Governors of the Federal Reserve System, Federal Deposit Insurance Corporation, and Office of the Comptroller of the Currency, 'Derivative Product Activities of Commercial Banks: Joint Study Conducted in Response to Questions Posed by Senator Riegle on Derivatives Products 2 (27 January 1993).

97 Schuyler Henderson, *Henderson on Derivatives* (n 79) 1.

98 Alastair Hudson, *Credit Derivatives: Law, Regulation and Accounting Issues* (n 87) 60.

99 Melanie Cao and Jason Wei, 'Weather Derivatives Valuation and Market Price of Weather Risk', *The Journal of Future Markets* 4.11 (2004): 1068.

In such transactions, the market itself establishes the value of the index. However, it can be generally accepted that there is a relationship between the value of the underlying asset and the value of the derivative.[100] That's why any change in the value of the underlying asset affects the value of the derivatives.

As a derivatives transaction is a contract, its settlement can be either physical or in cash.[101] When the contract calls for one of the parties to buy or sell the underlying asset, this would be a physical-settlement arrangement. Alternatively, the derivatives contract can call for one of the parties to buy or sell only the economic equivalent of ownership of the underlying; this would be a cash-settlement arrangement.

An Overview of the Use of Financial Derivatives

Derivatives perform several functions.[102] Primarily, these instruments are used to control and reallocate risks.[103] Also, they are instruments to 'obtain funding at a preferential rate',[104] or to 'take speculative advantage of a movement in a financial market for the investing'.[105] However, the most important function of derivatives is to hedge the risk generated in any other type of contract. Indeed, most companies and shareholders[106] use derivatives to control business risks by 'hedging'. Hedging means protecting;[107] it is the process by which 'an exposed entity enters into a transaction that will generate profit in the exact circumstances that would generate a loss under the exposure'.[108] For instance, where a party has an exposure to UK interest rates, a derivative can be used to generate an income which will offset any loss suffered from the movements in the interest rate.[109] Therefore, the nature of hedging, as derivatives' function of risk management, is to reduce rather than to create risk; they

100 Global Derivatives Study Group, G-30, 'Derivatives: Practices and Principles', vol. 28, 1993. http://group30.org/images/uploads/publications/G30_Derivatives-PracticesandPrinciples.pdf accessed 28th August 2022 (DSG G30).

101 Simon James, *The Law of Derivatives* (Informa Law, Routledge, 2013) 126.

102 Fisher Black, 'Foreword: The Many Faces of Derivatives in Jack Clark Francis', in William W. Toy and J. Gregg Whittaker (eds), *Handbook of Equity Derivatives* (Wiley Series on Financial Engineering, 2000) ix.

103 Henry T. C. Hu, 'Misunderstood Derivatives: The Causes of Informational Failure and the Promise of Regulatory Incrementalism', *The Yale Law Journal* 102.1457 (1993): 1464–1465.

104 Peter A. Abken, 'Over-the-Counter Financial Derivatives: Risky Business?', *Federal Reserve Bank of Atlanta Economic Review* (March–April 1994): 5.

105 Alastair Hudson, *The Law on Financial Derivatives* (n 81) 9.

106 Kimberly D. Krawiec, 'Derivatives, Corporate Hedging, and Shareholder Wealth: Modigliani-Miller Forty Years Later', *University of Illinois Law Review* (1998): 1039.

107 Carolyn H. Jackson, 'Have You Hedged Today? The Inevitable Advent of Consumer Derivatives', *Fordham Law Review* 67 (1999): 3206.

108 Norman Menachem Feder, 'Deconstructing Over-the-Counter Derivatives', *Columbia Business Law Review* (2002): 677, 717.

109 Alastair Hudson, *Credit Derivatives: Law, Regulation and Accounting Issues* (n 87) 11.

reallocate (though they do not eliminate)[110] risk from one party to another.[111] Nevertheless, this benign tool might not always operate in the way anticipated at the time of its creation,[112] transforming it in to a 'risk-bearing' instrument.[113]

Additionally, derivatives serve as instruments for speculation; they allow end users to speculate on the movements of the market.[114] This is the case when the use of a derivative contract 'enables the investor to mimic the result of trading on an underlying financial market by entering into an off-market transaction with a financial institution'.[115] In purely speculative transactions the buyer or seller of the derivative has no interest in the underlying risk or has no true exposure. Rather, his interest is on the future movements of prices and the resulting profit they can obtain.[116] In this regard, opponents argue that derivatives speculation poses significant problems for the larger economy, and they should be treated as 'unenforceable wagers'.[117] While the use of derivatives for speculation is expected from sophisticated traders, the experience shows that this is a common activity to all market participants. Amongst the most known cases in the 1990s are Orange Country, Barings Bank, and Proctor & Gamble,[118] all of them victims of the excessive seeking of high returns.

Arbitrage is another disseminated practice within derivatives traders. It consists of using the mismatches in market movements to generate profits. Arbitrageurs take advantage of either price mismatches or artificially restricted opportunities; they also stake positions before markets react to certain events.[119] Hence, it is possible for market users to take advantage of mismatches in prices or market conditions by speculating on the underlying financial products without the need to undergo the formalities of conventional market-trading.[120] Thus, arbitrage can take place in different situations according to parties' interests, but also depends on market imperfections, the speed, and opacity of the trading.[121]

To illustrate the use of derivatives for hedging risks, the most common examples can be found in commodity derivatives. For instance, *A* is an importer, refiner,

110 Norman Menachem Feder, 'Deconstructing Over-the-Counter Derivatives' (n 108).

111 ibid., 682.

112 Peter H. Huang, 'A Normative Analysis of New Financially Engineered Derivatives', *South California Law Review* 73 (2000): 471.

113 Richard Dale, *Risk and Regulation in Global Securities Market* (John Wiley & Sons Ltd, 1996) 153.

114 United States General Accounting Office (GAO), 'Financial Derivatives: Actions Needed to Protect the Financial System', 34–35 (1994) [GAO Report] 25.

115 Alastair Hudson, *Credit Derivatives: Law, Regulation and Accounting Issues* (n 87) 11.

116 Norman Menachem Feder, 'Deconstructing Over-the-Counter Derivatives' (n 108) 719; Don M. Chance, 'Losing Money with Derivatives', *Essays in Derivatives* (1998): 289, 300.

117 Lynn A. Stout, 'Derivatives and the Legal Origin of the 2008 Credit Crisis' (n 84) 11.

118 Desmond Eppel, 'Risky Business: Responding to OTC Derivatives Crises', *Columbia Journal of Transnational Law* 40 (2002): 677, 687.

119 Norman Menachem Feder, 'Deconstructing Over-the-Counter Derivatives' (n 108) 720.

120 Alastair Hudson, *Credit Derivatives: Law, Regulation and Accounting Issues.* (n 87) 12.

121 Norman Menachem Feder, 'Deconstructing Over-the-Counter Derivatives' (n 108) 720.

and retailer of petroleum products. *A* enters a bulk of derivative transactions with banks in an attempt to protect itself from the rising price of oil. These derivatives contracts require the banks to make payments to *A* when oil prices are high. Conversely, *A* is required to make payments to the banks if the price of oil falls below an agreed floor.[122]

It is also possible to structure a derivative contract to serve 'unusual' client's interests. For instance, to avoid tax laws.[123] In *Explainaway Ltd v HMRC*,[124] Explainaway and its parent company (Paul Rackham Ltd) entered two derivatives, FTSE 100 LIFFE futures contracts (one long and one short), which were in turn traded with two acquired subsidiaries, with the sole purpose of eliminating tax on the gain on its short contract.

One important concept in derivatives transactions is *risk*. Risk refers to the randomness that is quantifiable in terms of probability distributions[125] – it suggests volatility. Risk is usually understood as an element with potentially negative outcomes. However, risk is also a promise of the possibility of profits, not just losses;[126] also, it is correlated with a rate of return, so if the investment risk increases, so does its profitability. Hence, risk acts as a 'driver' of market transactions, and in every transaction, there is a continuous exchange of risks between counterparties. Derivatives have proved to be among the most effective tools for isolating and transferring those financial risks.

However, derivatives themselves can represent various types of risks,[127] including credit risk, market risk, liquidity risk, legal risk, and operational risk. Credit risk is the risk that a derivatives transaction counterparty might default.[128] Under the traditional transaction structure, before the GFC, one entity was exposed to credit risk by its counterparty. After the introduction of central counterparties (CCPs) to the OTC derivatives market, such a bilateral structure changed. Thus, as the CCP poses itself in the middle of the transaction and becomes the counterparty of the two initial counterparties, there is a change in the allocation of credit risk that is now transferred to the CCP. Then, the risk of each individual transaction is mutualised across all CCP's members.

122 Example based on *Standard Chartered Bank v Ceylon Petroleum Corp* [2011] Queen's Bench Division 11 July 2011 EWHC 1785 (Comm).

123 *Hoosier Energy Rural Electricity Cooperative v. John Hancock Life Insurance Company* is a complex dispute involving CDS contract, in which the transaction was designed to allow John Hancock to claim to be the 'owner' of the plant for tax purposes. *Hoosier Energy Rural Elec. Coop. v. John Hancock Life Ins. Co. No. 1:08-cv-1560-DFH-DML*, 2008 U.S. Dist. LEXIS 10.

124 *Explainaway Ltd v HMRC* [2012] UKUT 362.

125 Peter H. Huang, 'A Normative Analysis of New Financially Engineered Derivatives' (n 112).

126 Desmond Eppel, 'Risky Business: Responding to OTC Derivatives Crises' (n 118).

127 Brandor Becker and Francois-Ihor Mazur, 'Risk Management of Financial Derivatives Products: Who's Responsible for What?', *Journal of Corporation Law* 21.177 (Fall 1995): 183.

128 Gregory R. Duffee, 'On Measuring Credit Risks of Derivative Instruments', *Journal of Banking and Finance* 20 (1996): 805. www.econ2.jhu.edu/People/Duffee/jbf_1996.pdf accessed 16th September 2015.

Market risk reflects the risk of adverse prices, interest rates, index levels, volatility, and fluctuations in the underlying asset.[129] The common methods[130] to manage market risk include marking to market, using a portfolio approach to manage market risk, and hedging.[131]

Liquidity risk appears in two forms – market liquidity risk and funding liquidity risk.[132] Market liquidity risk refers to the risk that an entity may be unable to offset a derivatives transaction in a timely manner or at the market price.[133] Funding liquidity risk is the risk that a party cannot meet its payment obligations on the settlement date.[134] A loss of liquidity arises when the creditworthiness of any of the counterparties declines or is in a period of market distress. One example of liquidity market risk crystallising was the 1987 market crash,[135] where there was an overreliance on the insurance market, and its ability to absorb the losses of the futures and bond markets.

Legal risk emerges when there are issues affecting or impeding the enforcement of the contract[136] and, as a result, a counterparty being unable to collect on a winning position. The source of such impediments might be inadequate documentation, the uncertain legality[137] of the contract itself,[138] or the effect of insolvency laws on netting provisions.[139] To avoid the crystallisation of this risk, counterparties should develop policies and procedures to adequately determine the legality of the contract's content from the outset.

Finally, operational risk is the risk of loss resulting from inadequate or failed internal processes, people, and systems or from external events.[140] The operational management should include three elements: 'the people involved in the derivatives

129 Derivatives Policy Group, 'A Framework for Voluntary Oversight of the OTC Derivatives Activities of Securities Firm Affiliates to Promote Confidence and Stability in Financial Markets', 1995. http://ifci.ch/137790.htm accessed 16th September 2015.

130 DSG G30, 'Derivatives: Practices and Principles' (n 100).

131 Brandor Becker and Francois-Ihor Mazur, 'Risk Management of Financial Derivatives Products: Who's Responsible for What? (n 127) 190.

132 Federal Reserve System, 'Liquidity Risk, in Trading and Capital-Markets Activities Manual', September 2002. www.federalreserve.gov/boarddocs/supmanual/trading/trad_p2.pdf accessed 16th September 2015.

133 Basel Committee on Banking Supervision, 'Risk Management Guidelines for Derivatives', 1994. www.bis.org/publ/bcbsc211.pdf accessed 16th September 2015.

134 BIS, 'Central Bank Survey of Derivatives Market Activity', 1995. www.bis.org/publ/r_fx96.htm accessed 16th September 2015.

135 Gerard Gennotte and Hayne Leland, 'Market Liquidity, Hedging, and Crashes', *The American Economic Review* 80 (1990): 999.

136 Norman Menachem Feder, 'Deconstructing Over-the-Counter Derivatives' (n 108).

137 *Hazell v. Hammersmith and Fullham Borough Council*, 2 W.L.R. 372; 1 All E.R. 545 (H.L. 1991).

138 Anne Beroza and Robert M. McLaughlin, 'What General Counsels Need to Know About Derivatives: Understanding Risks Can Protect Your Company', *Corporate Legal Times*, 14 October 1994.

139 IOSCO, 'Operational and Financial Risk Management Control Mechanism for Over-the-Counter Derivatives Activities of Regulated Securities Firms', Technical Committee of International Organisation of Securities Commission Working Paper No. 3, 1994.

140 BIS, 'Principles for the Sound Management of Operational Risk', Basel Committee on Banking Supervision, 2011, 3.

transactions, the framework within which the activities are undertaken, and the systems that are used'.[141] Thus, the types of risk that can be characterised as operational are broad;[142] basically, any risk that does not fit into any of the other categories could be classified as operational.

Financial derivatives play an important role in capital markets, and in general in the broader economy. Derivatives transactions are an important component of financial markets, providing significant benefits when used prudently.[143] Companies use derivatives for protection against a myriad of risks that are inherent to their business.[144] The attractiveness of derivatives, especially the OTC derivatives market, lies principally in being a flexible tool for institutional and corporate investors to hedge a large range of risks.[145] Derivatives can also achieve legitimate business objectives,[146] often at a much lower cost than traditional investments.[147]

Indeed, derivatives improve economic efficiency, by breaking apart risk and parcelling it out to the parties who are the cheapest and most willing risk bearers.[148] Awrey argues that these benefits are identifiable in the role that OTC derivatives play in completing asset markets,[149] enhancing price discovery,[150] and absorbing systemic risk.[151] However, the role of OTC derivatives as mechanisms that help to absorb systemic risk is debatable,[152] especially after the GFC. The high level of interconnectedness and the excessive concentration of risk amongst derivatives

141 Derivatives Policy Group, 'A Framework for Voluntary Oversight of the OTC Derivatives Activities of Securities Firm Affiliates to Promote Confidence and Stability in Financial Markets' (n 129) 50.

142 Codelco Head Claims, 'Systematic Deception', *Metals Week*, 15 September 1994, 1; John McManus, 'Derivatives Dealing a Risky Business: Barings is Not the First Major Company to be Brought to Its Knees by Trading in Such Futures', *Irish Times*, 27 February 1995, 14.

143 Christian A. Johnson, 'At the Intersection of the Bank Finance and Derivatives: Who has the right way?', *Tennessee Law Review* 66 (Fall 1998): 23.

144 Anatoli Kuprianov, 'The Role of Interest Rate Swaps in Corporate Finance', *Federal Reserve Bank of Richmond Economic Quarterly* (Summer 1994): 53–58.

145 Christopher Culp, 'The Social Functions of Financial Derivatives', in Robert Kolb and James Overdahl (eds), *Financial Derivatives Pricing and Risk Management* (Kolb Series in Finance, 2011) 59. www.rmcsinc.com/articles/Soc_Fctns.pdf accessed 18th September 2015.

146 Balvinder Sangha, 'Financial Derivatives: Applications and Policy Issues', *Business Economics* 30.1 (January 1995): 46.

147 Robert L. Gottsfield, Michael R. Lopez and William A. Hicks, III., 'Derivatives: What They Are, What They Cause, What's The Law' (n 91).

148 David Mullins, 'Remarks on the Global Derivatives Study Sponsored by the Group of Thirty', ISDA Summer Conference, 1993, 1. https://fraser.stlouisfed.org/scribd/?item_id=35397&filepath=/docs/historical/federal%20reserve%20history/bog_members_statements/mullins_19930728.pdf#scribd-open accessed 18th September 2015.

149 Dan Awrey, 'The Dynamics of OTC Derivatives Regulation: Bridging the Public-Private Divide', *European Business Organization Law Review* 11 (2010).

150 ibid.

151 ibid.

152 *See* Roger Lowenstein, *When Genius Failed: The Rise and Fall of Long-Term Capital Management* (Random House Trade Paperbacks, 2000); Thomas F. Siems, '10 Myths About Financial Derivatives', *Cato Institute, Cato Policy Analysis* 283 (1997): 8–9.

dealers, even under the post-GFC regulatory framework, is the key source of potential systemic risk.

Nonetheless, derivative transactions create substantial risks[153] – among them, as explained earlier, there are market,[154] credit,[155] operational,[156] liquidity,[157] and legal[158] risks. These are like the risks banks and securities firms face in their traditional business;[159] however, OTC derivatives are differentiated from these traditional risks by virtue of their complexity, and rapid risk transformation associated with them.[160] Their complexity is in the structuring and pricing of OTC derivatives transactions; the peculiarity of tailored transactions may not be fully understood by end users and regulators. Similarly, the pricing of derivatives that is supposed to be dependent on the value of the underlying asset is not as easy to comprehend. The speed of derivatives trading[161] is reflected in the rapid risk transformation.[162] Most derivatives are traded through a standard contract, which allows counterparties to enter as many transactions as they need. These transactions are negotiated through calls, emails, and electronic platforms, and counterparties rapidly change. Therefore, the risk of every transaction in every stage of trade for OTC derivatives is neither easily identifiable nor traceable, and sometimes a trader's decision to sell or to buy derivatives takes a fraction of a second to take advantage of assets' price variations identified by computers.[163] However, this situation, regardless of its challenge, should not prevent regulators from establishing and enforcing the rules of the market.[164]

Additionally, the riskiness of the derivatives market is manifested by the high concentration of business among a few major players. Part of the explanation for

153 Saul S. Cohen, 'The Challenge of Derivatives' (n 95).

154 Adam R. Waldman, 'Comment OTC Derivatives & Systemic Risk: Innovative Finance or the Dance into the Abyss', *American University Law Review* 43 (1994): 1023, 1047. www.wcl.american.edu/journal/lawrev/43/waldman.pdf accessed 31st May 2023.

155 Jeremy A. Gluck, 'Measuring and Controlling the Credit Risk of Derivatives', in Robert A. Klein and Jess Lederman (eds), *Derivative Risk and Responsibility* (The University of Chicago Press, 1996) 121, 156–157; See Adam R. Waldman, 'Comment OTC Derivatives & Systemic Risk: Innovative Finance or the Dance into the Abyss' (n 154).

156 John C. Dugan, 'Derivatives: Netting, Insolvency, and End Users', *Banking Law Journal* 112 (1995): 638, 644–646.

157 Adam R. Waldman, 'Comment OTC Derivatives & Systemic Risk: Innovative Finance or the Dance into the Abyss' (n 154).

158 2 W.L.R. 372; 1 All E.R. 545 (H.L. 1991) (n 137).

159 Richard Dale, *Risk and Regulation in Global Securities Market* (n 113) 156.

160 ibid.

161 ibid., 157.

162 Desmond Eppel, 'Risky Business: Responding to OTC Derivatives Crises' (n 118).

163 Sara Lynch, 'CME Group Sparked Shutdown of CFTC's Academic Research Program', 2013. www.reuters.com/article/2013/04/24/us-cftc-cme-research-idUSBRE93N0YN20130424 accessed 31st May 2023.

164 Stewart Macbeth, 'Lighting the Lamp, or How Regulators Can Help Themselves Monitor global OTC Derivatives Markets', 2010. http://archive-org.com/page/2944645/2013-10-01/www.world-exchanges.org/insight/views/lighting-lamp-or-how-regulators-can-help-themselves-monitor-global-otc-derivatives accessed 21st June 2023.

this may lie in the complex information and risk-management systems that underpin the market. The failure of a large derivatives dealer may not only affect its counterparties, but the liquidity of the whole market. Furthermore, the concentration of the risk is magnified by the interconnectedness of derivatives traders[165] with the rest of the financial system, facilitating cross-market contagion of systemic defaults. Hence, attending to the repercussions of failure, large derivatives dealers have been characterised as 'too-big to fail'[166] institutions. Under the postcrisis regulatory reform, the concentration of business and risks among a few major players is changed by the concentration of a large portion of transactions in the new intermediaries of the market, the CCPs.

Finally, the importance of the OTC derivatives market is not only verified by the size of the market, but also the relevance of those who participate within it. The OTC derivatives market gathers financial and nonfinancial counterparties; they are classified as two types of participants: end users and broker–dealers. End users may be banks, securities firms, insurance companies, governments, investment funds, or commercial firms. There are dealers who develop customised derivative products for their customers and have different levels of involvement in the derivatives market.[167] Some financial institutions act as dealers by quoting prices to, buying derivatives from, and selling to end users.

Morphology of Financial Derivatives Transactions

Financial derivatives constitute a market that allows and incentivises creativity[168] and financial innovation.[169] Derivatives contracts are the result of combining certain features that allow the counterparties to look for capital raising and credit risk management. Therefore, most of the characteristics of these transactions will respond to the specific interests of the clients and investors. This explains the fact that, in the derivatives market, any transaction can be perfectly reshaped to satisfy the client's needs.[170]

Despite the differences among the different types of derivatives, there are some commonly recognised features shared by most financial derivatives contracts. Henderson,[171] one of the leading authors in the derivatives market, has set out some of the attributes of financial derivatives, warning that 'not all derivatives share all

165 Frederick Dolmer, 'A Critical Evaluation of the European Credit Default Swap Reform: Its Challenges and Adverse Effects as a Result of Insufficient Assumptions', *Journal of Banking Regulation* 14.1 (2013): 33–60.

166 Sara Lynch, 'CME Group Sparked Shutdown of CFTC's Academic Research Program' (n 163) 161.

167 Richard Dale, *Risk and Regulation in Global Securities Market* (n 113) 155.

168 M. Scholes, 'Derivatives and Financial Innovation: The Past, Present and the Future', *Tijdschrift voor Economie in Management* XLIII.4 (1998): 555. www.econ.kuleuven.be/rebel//jaargangen/1991-2000/1998/TEM1998-4/TEM1998-4_553-562p.pdf accessed 25th October 2022.

169 Alastair Hudson, *The Law on Financial Derivatives* (n 81) 7.

170 ibid., 9.

171 Schuyler Henderson, *Henderson on Derivatives* (n 79) 60.

characteristics, and the characteristics of certain types of derivatives sometimes require a little analytical thinking to spot'.[172] Therefore, the first step is to identify the form of the transaction; usually these are swaps, options, futures, or forwards.

The second stage is to identify that every derivative exists because of an underlying asset. However, this must not be confused with terms of the autonomy[173] of the derivative and the underlying asset *per se*. The underlying asset (rate, price, currency, index, security, commodity, or other economic metric) is the base of the financial derivative; although closely related, they are independent. An exception to this rule is found in the illustrative case of credit default swaps (CDS): defined as contracts where the rights and obligations of the parties derive from the credit risk of a reference entity or asset. Under a CDS, a 'protection buyer contracts with a counterparty and in return for a premium, buys protection against particular credit events which should be carefully defined in the contract'.[174] Here, the credit risk is derived from any other contract or legal agreement between counterparties that would potentially breach their commitments. Seeking to cover themselves from the consequences of the breach, they decide to enter a CDS to 'buy' protection, similar but not equal to the one provided by insurance.[175]

Derivatives take shape in different types of transactions. Within the most common types of derivatives are options, futures, swaps, and credit derivatives.

Options

Options – to sell or to buy – are transactions according to which one person buys the right to sell or to buy a specific asset, establishing a future date *(strike date)* to deliver it, but fixing the price (*strike price*) at the moment of the agreement.[176],[177] Such an agreement also includes a premium, the fee paid to the option seller. If the option is to buy, it is a call option; if the option is to sell, it is a put option.[178] The seller is the option writer or option seller, and the buyer is called the option holder or option buyer.[179] In this type of transaction, what is traded is the *right* to buy or sell[180] the specific asset, not the asset itself. The variation of the assets' real price is inherent in options, and justifies the reason they are called *contracts for differences*. The rationale is that sellers or buyers are taking the risk of price fluctuation. Hence, if the price of the asset is higher by the strike date, the seller is losing the

172 Timothy Lynch, 'Derivatives: A Twenty-First Century Understanding' (n 78).

173 See *S.C.F. Finance Co Ltd. V. Marsi* [1986] 2 Lloyd's Rep. 366.

174 David Rule, *The Credit Derivatives Market: Its Development and Possible Implications for Financial Stability* (Financial Stability Review, Bank of England, June 2001) 118.

175 IMF, *Financial Derivatives* (Eleventh Meeting of the IMF Committee on Balance of Payments Statistics, 21–23 October 1998) 3.

176 Roberta Romano, 'A Thumbnail Sketch of Derivative Securities and Their Regulation', *Maryland Law Review* 55 (1996): 1, 49.

177 John Hull, *Options, Futures & Other Derivatives* (Prentice Hall International, 2003) 194.

178 Norman Menachem Feder, 'Deconstructing Over-the-Counter Derivatives' (n 108) 692.

179 ibid.

180 Joana Benjamin, *Financial Law* (OUP, 2007) 66.

difference, while the buyer is gaining it. Contrariwise, if by the strike date, the price of the asset is lower than the strike price, the seller is profiting from the transaction while the buyer is losing the difference. Additionally, the right to sell or buy can be withdrawn without affecting the underlying asset's transaction.

Futures or Forwards

According to this type of transaction, one party agrees with another to sell specific assets at a future date at a fixed price.[181] Here, one party is assuming the *obligation* – as opposed to just the right – to exchange the asset on the future date.[182] Notwithstanding the real price that the assets might have by the fixed date, the payable price is the one agreed to at the time both parties entered the transaction.[183] This is an alternative way of financing production and industrial activities. For instance, it may be used by a farmer in funding next season's production, receiving financing, and guaranteeing the sale by the end of the specified period. The foreseeable risk is the potential default in the underlying transaction.

Swaps

Swaps are agreements between two parties to pay each other a series of cash flows, based on fixed or floating interest rates in the same or different currencies.[184] The most common swaps include interest rates, currencies, market risks, and credit risks.[185] Swaps have been used in managing financial crises.[186] An interest rate swap

> is an agreement between two parties by which each one agrees to pay the other on a specified date or dates with an amount calculated by reference to the interest which would have accrued over a given period on a notional principal sum. The rate of interest payable by each party (on the same notional sum) is different.[187]

One of these is a fixed interest rate, the other a floating interest rate. Swaps are made upon the basis to set off the object of the transaction. This is better understood with an example:

Company *A* and Company *B* have borrowed £100 from third parties. The credit taken by Company *A* was agreed with a variable interest rate (e.g., LIBOR) plus 1%. The credit of Company *B*, in the form of a bond, has a fixed rate of 10%.

181 John Hull, *Options, Futures & Other Derivatives* (n 177) 104.
182 ibid.
183 ibid.
184 Schuyler Henderson, *Henderson on Derivatives* (n 79) 33.
185 Joana Benjamin, *Financial Law* (n 180) 67.
186 ibid.
187 *Westdeutsche Landesbank Girozentrale v Islington BC* [1996] 2 All E.R. 961 (H.L.), *per* Lord Browne- Wilkinson, 982.

In fact, under this assumption, the interest rate swap payments are as follows: Company *B* pays Company *A* periodic amounts equal to the variable interest rate of 100. Company *A* pays Company *B* periodic amounts to a fixed interest rate of 100, plus an additional amount representing the profit of Company *B*. Payments will be agreed upon for a specific date in a way that can be compensated.

The economic rationale of a transaction in this regard is that Company *A* is a bank that can lend money at a fixed rate, while Company *B* is less creditworthy, and therefore goes to the bond issue. Reciprocal payments are not self-interest, but sums equal to interest calculated on a single principal sum, which, for example, might be £100.

The creditors of Company *A* and Company *B* will not be affected, as they must comply with the payment of their obligations thereunder, regardless of whether the payments within the structure of the swap are made or not. So, if Company *B* becomes insolvent, Company *A* must also pay the rate of 10% to the bondholders and is not receiving payments from Company *B*.

Basic Structure of Interest Rate Swaps[188]

The example helps to illustrate how some types of derivatives serve functions like insurance, especially the possibility to enter a mirror transaction to hedge the risks of the first contract. However, there are some practices that allow special reductions of risk, and are exclusive of financial derivatives. For instance, compression in IRSs is a technique that

> enables swap dealers with substantial two-way (pay and receive) swap activity to terminate substantial amounts of swap contracts before they expire by their terms. The benefits of compression include reductions in counterparty credit exposure, operational risk and cost, as well as lower legal and administrative expenses in the event of a default of any participating dealer. Importantly, since contracts are actually eliminated, under some regimes capital costs can be reduced. Together with expanded clearing of IRS, compression produces tremendous reduction of risk in the derivatives marketplace.[189]

Although futures, options, and swaps are the basic transactions, called 'vanilla products',[190] there is an increasing variety of novel[191] and exotic products[192]

188 Graphic elaborated by the author.

189 International Swaps and Derivatives Association, 'Interest Rate Swaps Compression: A Progress Report', ISDA Study, 2012.

190 The most basic or standard version of a financial instrument, usually options, bonds, futures, and swaps. Jongho Kim, 'From Vanilla Swaps to Exotic Credit Derivatives: How to Approach the Interpretation of Credit Events', *FJCFL* 13 (2008): 705.

191 Robert Lenzner and William Heuslein, 'The Age of Digital Capitalism', *Forbes*, 29 March 1993, 62.

192 Randy Myers, *What Every CEO Needs to Know about Weather Risk Management* (n 85); See Ledyard Carter and L. L. P. Milburn, 'Client Advisory, Forward Freight Agreements'. www.clm.com/publication.cfm/ID/85. in Timothy Lynch, 'Derivatives: A Twenty-First Century Understanding' (n 78).

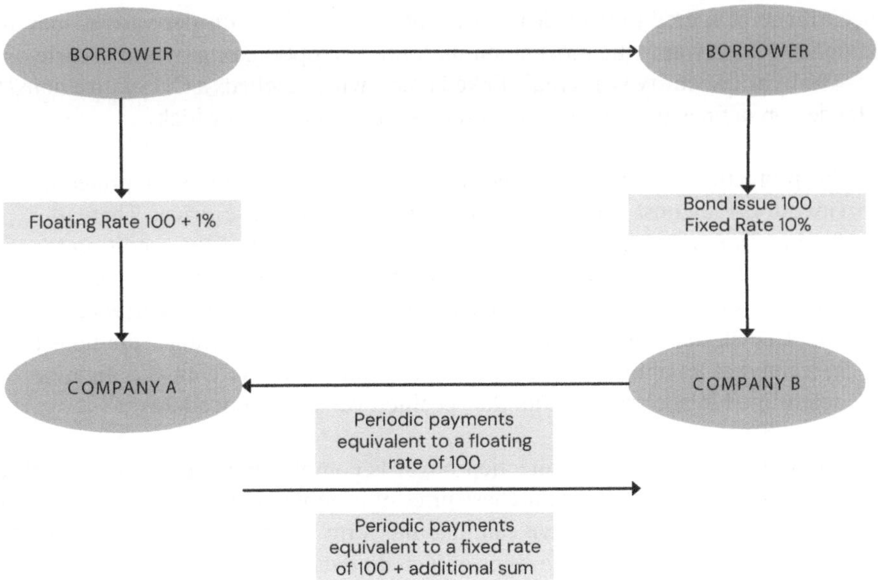

Figure 3.1 Basic Structure of an Interest Rate Swap

Source: Author

resulting from the combination of the basic forms. One form particularly relevant to the Global Financial Crisis is the credit default swap (CDS).[193] These are credit derivatives where a seller of protection, (the guarantor) agrees to pay to the buyer of protection (the creditor) an amount if, during an agreed period, a prescribed credit event occurs, signifying a problem in relation to a reference obligation (the guaranteed debt).[194] The credit event usually refers to default, bankruptcy, insolvency restructuring, or rating downgrade, depending on what the contractual parties agree.

Credit Derivatives

This category includes transactions that are intended to transfer credit exposure vis-à-vis specific obligors.[195] These products involve two parties – one is the protection buyer and the other is the protection seller.[196] When the transaction is linked to the

193 Rasiah Gengatharen, *Derivatives Law and Regulation* (Kluwer Law International, 2001) 59.
194 ibid.
195 Norman Menachem Feder, 'Deconstructing Over-the-Counter Derivatives' (n 108) 706.
196 John Kiff and Ron Morrow, 'Credit Derivatives', *Bank of Canada Review* 3 (2000): 7.

occurrence of a credit event, it is a default product.[197] Credit derivatives may be structured as a swap – the most common form – an option, or a hybrid security.[198]

The hybrid security is a 'credit-linked note', which embeds a CDS into a note.[199] Henderson defines the credit-linked note as an instrument in which

> the protection buyer (the issuer) issues notes to the sellers of protection (investors), against their payment of the note purchase price. Thereafter, the investors receive an agreed rate of return, the cost of the credit protection effectively being the margin (adjusted upwards for the credit risk of the issuer) over the floating rate of interest on the note. On the occurrence of a credit event and satisfaction of any other specified conditions, the note is redeemed at an amount equal to the then value of the reference obligation, determined in accordance with the specified valuation procedures.[200]

Within this transaction, the protection buyer is completely covered of credit risk, because the seller has paid the purchase price of the note, performing his obligation.

Moreover, a credit derivative can take the form of an option. In this case, the option is exercised on the occurrence of a credit event. The difference between the option and a CDS is that the 'premium is paid in full in advance and is non-refundable while in the swap the fixed amount is paid overtime until the occurrence of the credit event and satisfaction of any other conditions to settlement'.[201]

According to the CDS, a seller of protection, called the guarantor, agrees to pay to the protection buyer (the creditor) an amount during an agreed upon period if a prescribed *credit event*[202] occurs, signifying a problem in relation to a reference obligation (the guaranteed debt) of a reference entity, the principal debtor. Basically, it works as a guarantee and the instrument will be enforced only when the underlying obligation is in default – that is called a *credit event*. The protection payment results from the difference between the reference price (agreed at the beginning) and the final price of the reference obligation; it is a percentage applied to the notional amount (also called calculation amount).

In the words of Henderson, 'a reference obligation is an obligation which is usually but not necessarily issued or guaranteed by the reference entity, which may be a loan, debt security or other type of payment obligation'.[203] The uses of such reference obligations vary according to the parties' will. They are used either to determine the cash settlement amount, to determine the existence of a credit event,

197 Schuyler Henderson, *Henderson on Derivatives* (n 79) 106.

198 The term *hybrid securities* 'was originally conceived as securities with embedded derivatives which were hedged by the issuer through a swap with the dealer. The issuer's sole interest is generally in the reduced all-in borrowing cost it achieves through the combined cash flows of the derivative and the debt instrument', ibid., 189.

199 ibid., 200.

200 ibid.

201 ibid., 111.

202 Usually a credit event includes bankruptcy, insolvency restructuring, or rating downgrade.

203 Schuyler Henderson, *Henderson on Derivatives* (n 79) 107.

or 'in physical settlement, may be delivered on the occurrence of a credit event, on exercise or at the termination date'.[204] Particularly important is to point out the difference between a cash-settled and physically-settled CDS. In the first case, the delivery of a credit event notice is enough to require the protection payment from the buyer, while the second requires a notice of physical settlement by the buyer.

Finally, the definition of the credit event is left to the parties. It can be, but is not necessarily, linked to the insolvency of the counterparty.[205] Alternatively, it can include a credit rating downgrade or the default in the payment of a specific amount.

Understanding the Process of Financial Derivatives Trading

The study and the regulatory treatment of derivatives have been historically divided into two markets in which they are traded: Exchange and OTC. Traditionally, exchange-traded derivatives are standardised products traded on centralised trading platforms. Hence, users are obliged to accept the rules and requirements set by the exchange. OTC derivatives were often non-standardised and bespoke instruments; they were traded in a market that bestowed all participants with limitless flexibility and innovation. However, after the post-GFC regulatory reforms, a large part of the OTC derivatives transactions were expected to be standardised, and subject to a heavier regulatory burden.

On the one hand, stock exchanges control[206] all the transactions by imposing margin requirements, standard forms, transparency rules, settlement amounts, maturity dates, and strike prices,[207] and act as clearinghouses.[208] The benefits of this type of trading are mainly low credit risk, low transaction costs, a greater price transparency, and a higher degree of liquidity.[209] Since the contract is more easily sellable because the contracts are standardised, liquidity is increased. Regarding price transparency, exchanges must usually publish the price of trades immediately. As a result, the price is likely to be close to market price.

On the other hand, OTC[210] derivatives are individually tailored to meet the specific needs of counterparties.[211] This was traditionally a non-standardised market,

204 ibid.

205 Felix Salmon, 'Sovereign Market Awaits Court Verdicts', Euromoney, May 2002, 32 (in light of the Argentine crisis of 2001, sovereign credit derivatives market requires clear definition of what constitutes credit event).

206 They are called Self-Regulatory Organisations, or SROs.

207 Dan Awrey, 'The Dynamics of OTC Derivatives Regulation: Bridging the Public-Private Divide' (n 149) 11.

208 Council of Financial Regulators, 'OTC Derivatives Reform Considerations', March 2012, 4. www.treasury.gov.au/~/media/Treasury/Publications%20and%20Media/Publications/2012/CFR%20report%20on%20over%20the%20counter%20derivatives/Downloads/PDF/CFR%20Report.ashx accessed 16th September 2015.

209 ibid.

210 Edward Green, *United States Regulation of the International Securities and Derivatives Markets* (Aspen Law & Business, 2002) 21.

211 ibid., 21.

where private parties set out their own rules;[212] such flexibility hindered the surveillance and control of the market itself. End users enter into OTC derivatives, either through bilateral transactions or by participating in some structured instruments, such as CDOs and other securitisations.[213] The inherent risk in the OTC market is that the derivatives investor is exposed to the risk that his counterparty may default.[214] Besides this, there are concerns regarding the pricing of the derivatives; in these transactions counterparties freely agree upon the price, which facilitates speculation. Arguably, the post-GFC regulatory reforms have tackled some of these shortcomings.

The negotiation of most derivatives transactions follows a general course.[215] This consists of deciding to deal and document the transaction, usually using standard models;[216] the most used is the International Swaps and Derivatives Association (ISDA) Master Agreement.[217] The transaction is then executed according to the terms of the documentation. The content of the OTC derivatives documentation is changing to keep up with the new regulatory changes. During the life of the transaction, it is necessary to 'net' the transactions and to value them, usually using a mark-to-market procedure.[218] In the context of ESG derivatives, recognising that standardisation is a crucial factor in fostering the expansion and widespread adoption of these transactions, ISDA has been diligently advancing efforts to enhance standardisation.

These traditional differences between exchange and OTC markets have changed with the postcrisis regulatory reforms, mainly because the OTC derivatives market is progressively becoming more standardised, and now is regulated. The reason is that the new regulations are introducing changes to the OTC derivatives trading and post-trading. The postcrisis regulatory reforms – following the G20 statement – seek to ensure that all standardised OTC derivatives contracts should be traded on exchanges or electronic platforms, where appropriate, and cleared through CCPs.

Regulatory Context

One of the major changes in the OTC derivatives market after the GFC was the inclusion of new post-trading market infrastructures; these are CCPs and trade repositories (TRs).

The impact of the introduction of CCPs, as new intermediaries of the market, is reflected firstly in the structure of these transactions. The traditional bilateral

212 ibid., 19.
213 Dan Awrey, 'The Dynamics of OTC Derivatives Regulation: Bridging the Public-Private Divide' (n 149).
214 Richard Dale, *Risk and Regulation in Global Securities Market* (n 113) 153.
215 See Schuyler Henderson, *Henderson on Derivatives* (n 79).
216 Dan Awrey, 'The Dynamics of OTC Derivatives Regulation: Bridging the Public-Private Divide' (n 149).
217 See www2.isda.org.
218 See Schuyler Henderson, *Henderson on Derivatives* (n 79).

structure of OTC derivatives has been replaced by the intermediation of CCPs that will become the counterparty of each of the two initial parties. Similarly, the imposition of the mandatory clearing obligation for certain types of derivatives results in a higher standardisation of such products. In the initial stage of its implementation, regulators expected that mandatory clearing would become the general rule for OTC transactions. However, regulators and market participants rapidly recognised that an important portion of OTC derivatives transactions would not be subject to the clearing obligation. Thus, to regulate those uncleared products, regulators decided to increase the margin and liquidity requirements.

However, the task of making OTC derivatives markets safer and sounder did not stop there – and they have involved important changes in the trading of OTC derivatives. In Europe, two instruments that entered into force in 2017 are complementing the initial post-trading reform (EMIR). Markets in Financial Instruments Directive (MiFIR) and Markets in Financial Instruments Directive (MiFID) (especially MiFID II) seek to move OTC trading to organised trading venues. Indeed, Michel Barnier, EU Internal Markets Commissioner, stated that MiFID II sought to put 'an end to the rule of opaqueness, and an end to the reign of over the counter transactions'.[219] With this panorama, it might be anticipated that the foreseeable consequence of MiFID II forcing a reduction in OTC trading would be an OTC derivatives market with less liquid and more tailored products. In this context, the evolution of ESG derivatives has a competitive advantage to offer financial transactions that contribute to achieving a wide range of sustainability objectives.

The Capital Requirements Directive and Regulation (CRD/CRR)[220] outlined the regulations governing the capital treatment of non-centrally cleared derivatives. Under these regulatory provisions, financial institutions must maintain an adequate capital buffer to account for market and credit valuation adjustment (CVA) risks associated with derivative transactions. This requirement ensures that they have sufficient capital reserves to address adverse market movements, and potential declines in the market value of counterparty exposures. Some components of these reforms, such as the Fundamental Review of the Trading Book (FRTB),[221] revisions to the CVA framework, and the capital output floor, have yet to be fully implemented as part of the broader Basel III regulatory reform package.

The reform pertaining to central clearing of derivatives in the US is an integral part of the Dodd-Frank Wall Street Reform and Consumer Protection Act of 2010. Title VII of the Dodd-Frank Act laid down a comprehensive framework for the oversight of the OTC swaps market. Specifically, the Act designates the SEC to

219 Aisha Dudhia, '10 Significant Ways MiFID II will change our trading environment Part 1', RegTech, 21 July 2015. https://jwg-it.eu/article/10-significant-ways-mifid-ii-will-change-our-trading-environment-part-1/ accessed 13th June 2023.

220 Capital Requirements Directive (CRD): Directive 2013/36/EU (CRD).

221 ICMA, 'Fundamental Review of the Trading Book (FRTB)'. www.icmagroup.org/market-practice-and-regulatory-policy/secondary-markets/secondary-markets-regulation/fundamental-review-of-the-trading-book-frtb/#:~:text=The%20Fundamental%20Review%20of%20the,to%20banks%27%20wholesale%20trading%20activities accessed 10th October 2023.

regulate 'security-based swaps', the CFTC to oversee 'swaps', and establishes that 'mixed swaps' will be jointly regulated by both the SEC and CFTC. Title VIII of the Dodd-Frank Act introduces regulatory measures for central clearing, which are applicable to clearing agencies and designated clearing organisations (DCOs).[222] The overarching goal of these reforms is to align the swaps market more closely with the regulatory framework governing futures markets.[223] These reforms include mandatory central clearing for eligible contracts, reporting of transactions to swap data repositories (SDRs), real-time reporting and public disclosure of transaction details, and the trading of contracts designated as 'made available to trade' (MAT) on swap execution facilities (SEFs), which are electronic trading venues allowing for multilateral trading.[224]

EU Regulation Applicable to ESG Derivatives

Regarding the regulation adopted in the EU to rule green financial products, there are some instruments that are relevant in the context of ESG derivatives. The five milestones of the EU sustainable finance pillar are the (i) Taxonomy Regulation,[225] (ii) the Sustainable Finance Disclosure Regulation (SFDR),[226] (iii) the EU climate benchmarks in the Benchmark Regulation,[227] (iv) the European Green Bond Regulation,[228] and (v) the Corporate Sustainability Reporting Directive (CSRD).[229]

The first regulatory instrument to consider for the purpose of ESG derivatives is the EU taxonomy, as a central tool within the European Green Deal[230] and the Sustainable Finance Action Plan. This regulation introduces a classification system,

222 Arias Barrera and Ligia Catherine, *Regulation and Supervision of the OTC Derivatives Market* (Routledge, 2018) 15.

223 Karel Lannoo and Apostolos Thomadakis, 'Derivatives in Sustainable Finance', CEPS-ECMI Study, Centre for European Policy Studies, 2020, 22. www.ceps.eu/wp-content/uploads/2020/07/Derivatives-in-Sustainable-Finance.pdf accessed 10th October 2023.

224 ibid.

225 Regulation (EU) 2020/852 of the European Parliament and of the Council of 18 June 2020 on the establishment of a framework to facilitate sustainable investment, and amending Regulation (EU) 2019/2088.

226 Regulation (EU) 2019/2088 of the European Parliament and of the Council of 27 November 2019 on sustainability-related disclosures in the financial services sector, OJL 317, 9.12.2019.

227 Regulation (EU) 2019/2089 of the European Parliament and of the Council of 27 November 2019 amending Regulation (EU) 2016/1011 as regards EU Climate Transition Benchmarks, EU Paris-aligned Benchmarks and sustainability-related disclosures for benchmarks, OJL 317, 9.12.2019.

228 Proposal for a Regulation of the European Parliament and of the Council on European Green Bonds, COM/2021/391 final. Political agreement reached by co-legislators on 28 February 2023.

229 Directive (EU) 2022/2464 of the European Parliament and of the Council of 14 December 2022 amending Regulation (EU) No 537/2014, Directive 2004/109/EC, Directive 2006/43/EC and Directive 2013/34/EU, as regards corporate sustainability reporting, OJL 322, 16.12.2022.

230 Communication from the Commission to the European Parliament, the European Council, the Council, the European Economic and Social Committee and the Committee of the Regions, The European Green Deal, COM/2019/640 final, 11 December 2019. https://eur-lex.europa.eu/legal-content/EN/TXT/?qid=1588580774040&uri=CELEX%3A52019DC0640 accessed 10th October 2023.

often referred to as a 'taxonomy', which serves as a common language for businesses to determine whether a specific economic activity qualifies as 'environmentally sustainable'. This classification system empowers businesses to assess the extent to which their investments align with environmental sustainability criteria. Within this context, the framework of the EU taxonomy plays a pivotal role in pinpointing the most salient risks. This serves as the initial component of the risk-based approach that we employ as the methodological lens in this study. The environmental criteria set by the EU taxonomy allows us to clearly define the objectives from the outset – this is a task that is particularly important when dealing with ESG factors, which tend to be criticised by their over-comprehensive character. In turn, such regulatory objectives are closely linked to the risks that firms and individuals pose to its achievement.

The taxonomy is designed to be utilised by the EU, its member states, corporate issuers, and financial services firms, when evaluating and disclosing information related to environmental sustainability. To clarify the meaning of an economic activity that is environmentally sustainable, the EU taxonomy adopts a series of criteria. The adoption of these criteria reveals how the EU regulator, adopting a risk-based approach, prioritises those sources of risk that are considered most prominent in the sustainability policy. The criteria involve that: the activity makes a significant contribution to one of the six specified environmental objectives; it does not cause substantial harm to any of the environmental objectives; it adheres to a set of basic social safeguards; and that the activity meets specified performance thresholds, also referred to as 'technical screening criteria' (TSC). When these criteria are met, such activities will be referred to as 'taxonomy-aligned economic activities'. The TSC, as a tool to objectively define the prioritised risks, is further clarified by the Climate Delegated Act of December 2021. The Delegated Act established the criteria for determining when an economic activity qualifies as 'contributing substantially' to climate change mitigation or climate change adaptation. It also provides the basis for the assessment of whether the said economic activity avoids causing significant harm (referred to as 'does no significant harm' or DNSH) to any of the environmental objectives (i.e., climate change mitigation, climate change adaptation, the sustainable use and protection of water and marine resources, the transition to a circular economy, pollution prevention and control, and the protection and restoration of biodiversity and ecosystems).[231]

Following the structure of risk-based regulation, the EU taxonomy is in the process of continuously reassessing the content of the sustainability criteria. On 17 October 2023, in collaboration with the European Commission, the Platform on Sustainable Finance[232] unveiled the Stakeholder Request Mechanism for the EU

231 Article 9 EU Taxonomy.

232 EU Commission, 'Platform on Sustainable Finance: EU Taxonomy Stakeholder Request Mechanism', 17 October 2023. https://finance.ec.europa.eu/sustainable-finance/overview-sustainable-finance/platform-sustainable-finance/stakeholder-request-mechanism_en accessed 17th October 2023.

Taxonomy. This tool reveals how the risk-based regulation allows for a multi-actor construction of risk perceptions that are continuously reviewed to better reflect the content of regulated risks.[233] The mechanism empowers stakeholders to propose additions to the EU taxonomy or suggest potential modifications to existing economic activities, backed by scientific and technical evidence.[234]

Alongside the disclosure regulation, the taxonomy mandates that firms disclose the level of sustainability of financial products marketed as environmentally friendly, or provide disclaimers where they do not meet these criteria. The SFDR serves as a foundational framework compelling financial operators to disclose how their products align with the broader framework of the EU taxonomy for sustainable activities.[235] Within the SFDR, specific categories are delineated to classify financial products, ranging from those lacking in sustainability considerations, to those explicitly designed with a focused and identified sustainability objective.[236] This aspect of the SFDR aligns with the risk-based regulatory approach. Remarkably, it extends beyond the transference of risk-based considerations, from regulatory policies to the firm's operational level. Indeed, it goes a step further, mandating a thorough risk identification process during the development of each financial instrument comprising a company's sustainable finance strategy.

Financial products falling within the scope of Article 6 of the SFDR are characterised by the absence of explicit sustainability objectives. This approach aligns with what seems the current prevailing stance of regulators concerning ESG derivatives, since they have been regarded as 'neutral activities'. For such products, it is mandatory to provide 'transparency on the integration of sustainability risks', and to offer a clear rationale if the product does not take sustainability risks into consideration.

Nevertheless, there is an expectation that, as the ESG derivatives market expands, regulators will recognise the potential of these transactions in advancing sustainability goals. If this materialises, Articles 8 and 9 of the SFDR may become applicable to ESG derivatives, particularly to those transactions that inherently incorporate ESG factors, such as sustainable linked derivatives (SLDs) and voluntary carbon market derivatives (VCMD). Regarding financial products where sustainability plays a more distinct role, Article 8 outlines the requirement for 'transparency of the promotion of environmental or social characteristics in precontractual disclosures'. This entails product managers revealing how these characteristics are attained and the methodology employed for their measurement. Article

233 Julia Black, 'Risk-based Regulation: Choices, Practices and Lessons Being Learnt', *OECD* (2010): 185–224.

234 EU Commission, 'Platform on Sustainable Finance: EU Taxonomy Stakeholder Request Mechanism' (n 232).

235 F. Schütze and J. Stede, 'The EU Sustainable Finance Taxonomy and its Contribution to Climate Neutrality', *Journal of Sustainable Finance & Investment* (2021): 1–33.

236 Chiara Cremasco and Leonardo Boni, 'Is the European Union (EU) Sustainable Finance Disclosure Regulation (SFDR) Effective in Shaping Sustainability Objectives? An Analysis of Investment Funds' Behaviour', *Journal of Sustainable Finance & Investment* (2022): 1–19.

9 pertains to products explicitly devised with a sustainability objective. It requires 'transparency of sustainable investments in pre-contractual disclosures', calling for an explanation of how the investment contributes to the declared sustainability objective, and clarifying how this objective diverges from a conventional market-oriented objective. In the context of ESG derivatives, the requirement would oblige financial parties to clearly explain how the contractual terms and KPIs make the transaction different from a traditional financial derivative.

Considering the widespread use of derivatives, the proper disclosure of their function in the context of sustainable finance is of the utmost significance. The aim is to ensure that financial market participants elucidate and disclose whether their use of derivatives aligns with the environmental or social characteristics of the promoted financial product, or the pursued sustainable investment objective. Transparency regarding adverse impacts is also required. These proposed requirements would directly impact financial market participants, as they would be obligated to demonstrate how their use of derivatives aligns with the ESG characteristics of the respective product.

The third EU regulatory instrument that may be relevant for ESG market participants, but not for the transactions themselves, is the Corporate Sustainability Reporting Directive (CSRD), finalised in December 2022. The primary aim of the CSRD is to standardise sustainability reporting among companies and enhance the accessibility and quality of ESG disclosures. The Directive seeks to impact more entities than those obliged to report ESG data under the EU nonfinancial reporting directive (NFRD) of 2014, including certain US and other non-EU companies and subsidiaries. The CSRD amends four existing European legislations: the accounting directive, the transparency directive, the audit regulation, and the audit directive. It introduces several significant changes regarding the scope, encompassing specifically that all companies listed on regulated markets (excluding micro-undertakings) will now have new reporting obligations. Moreover, the CSRD introduces more rigorous and standardised reporting requirements. For instance, companies must report detailed information on their material sustainability risks, opportunities, and impacts in alignment with European Sustainability Reporting Standards (ESRS).[237] These standards cover environmental, social, and governance aspects, and will be established through delegated acts by the European Commission. Additionally, sustainability information must undergo mandatory assurance, which can be conducted by statutory auditors or independent assurance providers, at the discretion of EU member states. The CSRD initially calls for a 'limited assurance' level, with the possibility of transitioning to 'reasonable assurance', starting in 2028. A more in-depth examination of the exploitation of sustainability reporting

237 In April 2021, the European Commission adopted a legislative proposal for a Corporate Sustainability Reporting Directive (CSRD) that requires companies within its scope to report using a double materiality perspective in compliance with European Sustainability Reporting Standards (ESRS) adopted by the European Commission as delegated acts. The ESRS were adopted on 31 July 2023. https://ec.europa.eu/commission/presscorner/detail/en/mex_23_4044 accessed 10th October 2023.

standards, and the issue regarding their global harmonisation will be explored in Chapter 4.

As in any regulatory process, the adoption of the CSDR and the final version of the ESRS (approved on 19 October 2023, initially expected to enter into force in June 2024, now rescheduled to June 2026), have been widely debated, and reflect strong political conflict of interests and diverse perceptions of risk. The European Commission has proposed the so called 'SME Relief Package'[238] with the objective of narrowing the CSRD's scope by introducing new exemptions and curbing its downstream effects on the value chain. Proposed Action 9 states: 'Modifying the thresholds that define an SME under the Accounting Directive will reduce the number of companies currently subject to the sustainability reporting requirements of the Corporate Sustainability Reporting Directive (CSRD)'. In turn, Action 14 suggests 'establishing a legal boundary on the information that European Sustainability Reporting Standards can compel large companies to collect from SMEs in their value chain, thereby limiting the cascading effects'. The concern lies in the use of the SME Relief Package as a pretext to undermine the CSRD. Instead, it would be more beneficial to focus on assisting small businesses with tools and resources, enabling the collection of meaningful ESG information throughout the value chain.

Adopting more exceptions to the CSDR will end up limiting the core objectives of this regulation. The CSRD already only applies to a small portion of European businesses: in its current form, approximately just 50,000 firms will need to comply, while Europe boasts over 22 million businesses in total.[239] Rolling back the CSRD's scope further will limit its scope to primarily targeting large companies, which are already reporting. Moreover, the CSRD was established to standardise, benchmark, and facilitate comparisons of ESG information. If companies are continually excluded, and numerous exceptions created, such an endeavour loses significant value. Most companies that the proposal aims to exempt from the CSRD already face ESG disclosure requests from larger business partners. Therefore, as ESG information is already a business reality, there is no clear rationale behind excluding from the CSDR scope (in the form of a delayed implementation) 24 million SMEs, which represent 99% of business in the EU.[240]

The extent of modification in the process of implementation of EU regulation has been redesigned, according to the European Commission work programme for 2024.[241] In a prioritisation exercise, the EU Commission reiterated its intention to

238 European Commission, 'SME Relief Package', 12 September 2023. https://single-market-economy.ec.europa.eu/system/files/2023-09/COM_2023_535_1_EN_ACT_part1_v12.pdf accessed 17th October 2023.

239 Statista, 'Number of Enterprises in the Non-Financial Business Economy of the European Union (EU27) from 2008 to 2022', 28 February 2023. www.statista.com/statistics/1248775/number-of-businesses-eu/#:~:text=In%202022%2C%20the%20European%20Union,business%20enterprises%20during%20this%20period accessed 17th October 2023.

240 EU Commission, 'SME Relief Package' (n 238) 1.

241 EU Commission, '2024 Work Programme', 17 October 2023. https://commission.europa.eu/publications/2024-commission-work-programme-key-documents_en accessed 17th October 2023.

reduce EU companies' reporting burdens by 25%, which they hope to achieve by rationalising and streamlining existing reporting requirements,[242] postponing the deadline for the adoption of the sector-specific ESRS from June 2024 to June 2026, adjusting the thresholds for SMEs under the Accounting Directive to consider inflation, and supporting a 'proportionate' application of requirements under the Corporate Sustainability Due Diligence Directive (CSDDD).

In the context of our study, it is essential to highlight the investor community's demand for companies within the CSDDD's scope to establish and execute robust transition plans. These plans should integrate science-based climate targets,[243] aligning with the CSRD and the ESRS. They should also cover short-term, medium-term, and long-term emissions reduction targets, making these objectives practical and preventing the risk of greenwashing. Furthermore, there have been numerous proposals to broaden the directive's applicability to the financial sector, specifically encompassing investment services.[244] This expansion should be carefully structured to guarantee equitable due diligence requirements across different industries, while also aligning with global initiatives like the UN Guiding Principles[245] and OECD Guidelines.[246]

Although at the time of writing, the final version of the CSDDD is not available,[247] we emphasise the need to not only expand the scope of the directive to investment services and products – which could strengthen the use of ESG derivatives for social targets – but also to clarify how risk identification and management should be articulated. In particular, that – if and when the CSDDD applies to investment – the concepts of materiality and human rights salience assessments are coherently implemented.[248] Materiality is a fundamental concept that forms the basis of corporate disclosure, whereas salience is a foundational concept guiding a company's prioritisation of actions to address human rights impacts. Materiality is rooted in disclosure, encompassing all relevant ESG issues, while salience has been traditionally confined to human rights impacts.[249] Among the various definitions of

242 The EU Commission has adopted 15 proposals and initiatives since March 2023 regarding the revision of reporting requirements.

243 Article 15, paragraphs 1 and 2.

244 PRI, 'How to Make the CSDD Directive Practicable for the Investment Industry', 2 March 2023. www.unpri.org/policy-reports/how-to-make-the-csdd-directive-practicable-for-the-investment-industry/11228.article accessed 17th October 2023.

245 UN Guiding Principles on Business and Human Rights (UNGPs).

246 OECD, *Managing Climate Risks and Impacts Through Due Diligence for Responsible Business Conduct: A Tool for Institutional Investors* (OECD Publishing, 2023). https://doi.org/10.1787/8aee4fce-en.

247 EU Commission, 'Proposal for a Directive on Corporate Sustainability Due Diligence and Annex', 23 February 2022. https://commission.europa.eu/publications/proposal-directive-corporate-sustainability-due-diligence-and-annex_en accessed 17th October 2023.

248 BSR, 'Materiality and Salience'. www.bsr.org/en/prs/materiality-and-salience.

249 Samuel Moyn, 'Substance, Scale, and Salience: The Recent Historiography of Human Rights', *Annual Review of Law and Social Science* 8.1 (2012): 123–140.

materiality, the one proposed by the IFRS tends to illustrate regulators approach. Accordingly,

> information is material if omitting, misstating, or obscuring that information could reasonably be expected to influence decisions that the primary users of general-purpose financial reporting make on the basis of those reports, which include financial statements and sustainability-related financial disclosures and which provide information about a specific reporting entity.[250]

Thus, the convergence of materiality and salience would improve the consistency of a risk-based approach for the firm, and the relevant investment transactions. It allows the firm, and within it, the highest governance body, to determine the material topics or salient issues in the framework of their ESG targets and the design of investment contracts.

The importance of this call is to align the CSDDD with the international standards, such as the Global Reporting Initiative and ESRS. These instruments are narrowing the gap between these two concepts, by employing the same criteria (i.e., scope, scale, remediation potential, likelihood) and methodology (meaningful stakeholder engagement) to both materiality and salience assessments.

There are other regulatory instruments to consider when setting the framework of EU regulation for ESG derivatives. This is the prudential regime of green assets. The revised Capital Requirements Regulation (CRR) II/Capital Requirements Directive (CRD) V package contains a mandate[251] for the EBA to assess, by June 2025, whether dedicated prudential treatment of exposures linked to assets or activities substantially associated with environmental and social objectives would be justified. This assessment would be incorporated as a component of Pillar 1 capital requirements. The evaluation's key objectives include determining the relative riskiness of exposures linked to assets and activities connected with environmental and social objectives, compared to other exposures. It also considers the appropriate criteria for assessing physical risks and transition risks, along with their development, and the potential effects of dedicated prudential treatment of exposures linked to environmental and social objectives on financial stability and bank lending within the EU.[252] Following this call, on 17 October 2023, the EBA recommends accelerating integration of ESG Risks into the Capital Requirement Framework.[253] The EBA's report highlights the importance of encompassing

250 IFRS Sustainability Disclosure Standard General Requirements (IFRS S1), June 2023. www.ifrs.org/issued-standards/ifrs-sustainability-standards-navigator/ifrs-s1-general-requirements/# accessed 17th October 2023.

251 Article 501c of CRR 2.

252 EBA, 'EBA Action Plan on Sustainable Finance', European Banking Authority, 6 December 2019.

253 EBA, 'Report: On the Role of Environmental and Social Risks in the Prudential Framework', EBA/REP/2023/34, 17 October 2023. www.eba.europa.eu/sites/default/documents/files/document_library/Publications/Reports/2023/1062711/Report%20on%20the%20role%20of%20

the integration of environmental risks into stress-testing programmes, the promotion of environmental and social considerations in external credit assessments performed by credit rating agencies, as well as their inclusion in due diligence requirements, and the valuation of real estate collateral.[254] Additionally, near-term recommendations include mandates for financial institutions to evaluate whether environmental and social factors might act as triggers for operational risk losses. Institutions are also encouraged to formulate metrics addressing environmental concentration risks within their supervisory reports.[255] The report also suggests the introduction of metrics focused on environmental concentration risks under the Pillar 1 framework.[256]

Furthermore, on 27 June 2023, the Commission welcomed the political agreement on the EU banking package.[257] This package involves amendments to the CRR[258] and the CRD.[259] In the CRR III version of the regulation, additional measures have been adopted to incorporate ESG risks into prudential regulation. These measures mandate the systematic identification, disclosure, and management of ESG risks. The intervention in this regard encompasses routine climate stress-testing (both internal and supervisory), an assessment of ESG risks as a component of regular supervisory reviews, and the disclosure of the extent to which the institution is exposed to ESG risks.

To strengthen the prudential regulation around sustainable finance, the Renewed Sustainable Finance Strategy aims at implementing supplementary measures across four crucial domains: (i) enhancing the support for credible transition endeavours in the realm of financing; (ii) enhancing accessibility for citizens, SMEs, and public authorities to harness emerging opportunities; (iii) reinforcing the financial sector's ability to withstand risks associated with climate change and environmental degradation, while concurrently enhancing its sustainability; and (iv) establishing a lofty level of ambition and alignment within all international forums. The strategy expands the existing macroprudential policy toolbox for the EU financial sector, to

---

environmental%20and%20social%20risks%20in%20the%20prudential%20framework.pdf accessed 17th October 2023.

254 ibid.

255 Mark Seagal, 'EU Bank Regulator Recommends Accelerating Integration of ESG Risks into Capital Requirement Framework', *ESG Today*, 17 October 2023. www.esgtoday.com/eu-bank-regulator-recommends-accelerating-integration-of-esg-risks-into-capital-requirement-framework/ accessed 17th October 2023.

256 ibid.

257 EC, 'Commission Welcomes Political Agreement on EU Banking Package', 27 June 2023. https://finance.ec.europa.eu/news/commission-welcomes-political-agreement-eu-banking-package-2023-06-27_en accessed 10th October 2023.

258 The new rules amending the Capital Requirements Regulation (CRR) are expected to apply from 1 January 2025, with certain elements of the regulation phasing in over the coming years.

259 Changes related to the supervision of credit institutions are implemented via an amendment of the Capital Requirements Directive (CRD) and will have to be transposed by member states by mid-2025.

make it more adequate for identifying and addressing potential systemic financial stability risks associated with climate change.

In relation to sustainability-related obligations, there are some recent interventions applicable to derivatives transactions as a type of sustainable investment, in terms set by the European regulation.[260] The European Securities and Markets Authority (ESMA) announced in October 2023 the launch of a Common Supervisory Action (CSA) with national competent authorities (NCAs) on the integration of sustainability in firms' suitability assessment and product governance processes.[261] The goal is to understand how market intermediaries have been applying key sustainability requirements according to the amendments of the MiFID II Delegated Acts of 2018, and the final updated guidelines published in September 2022.[262] The revised Guidelines now permit companies to disclose their products with sustainability features to clients, only *after* the clients have explicitly expressed their intention to adjust their initial sustainability preferences. In the Delegated Regulation, sustainability preferences are defined in terms of a 'minimum proportion' invested in taxonomy-aligned or sustainable investments.[263] Unfortunately, the wording of the regulation permits intermediaries, when sustainability preferences are expressed in the profiling phase, to suggest or trade financial instruments that, although they align with the client's financial profile, do not align with the client's sustainability preferences.[264] This duality of financial profile and sustainability preferences might end up affecting the achievement of sustainability investment.

ESMA has also addressed queries about whether sustainability preferences apply to derivatives contracts used for hedging purposes, or profit from price movements without funding a specific economic activity.[265] ESMA has confirmed that a suitability assessment, including sustainability preferences, should always be conducted – regardless of the type of financial instrument in question.[266] Against this background, the purpose of the most recent announcement for a CSA is expected to provide more information about the relationship between firms, clients'

260 SFD Regulation (Regulation (EU) 2019/2088) and the Taxonomy Regulation (Regulation (EU) 2020/852) define sustainable investment as an investment in an economic activity that satisfies three key conditions: it contributes to achieving an environmental or social objective; it avoids causing significant harm to these objectives; and the entities conducting this activity adhere to sound governance practices (referred to as 'dark green' products).

261 ESMA, 'ESMA to Launch Common Supervisory Action on MiFID II Sustainability Requirements', 3 October 2023. www.esma.europa.eu/press-news/esma-news/esma-launch-common-supervisory-action-mifid-ii-sustainability-requirements.

262 ESMA, 'Final Report: Guidelines on Certain Aspects of the MiFID II Suitability Requirements', ESMA35-43-3172, 23 September 2022. www.esma.europa.eu/sites/default/files/library/esma35-43-3172_final_report_on_mifid_ii_guidelines_on_suitability.pdf accessed 4th October 2023.

263 Article 2 Regulation (EU) 2021/1253.

264 ESMA, 'ESMA to Launch Common Supervisory Action on MiFID II Sustainability Requirements' (n 261).

265 ibid.

266 ibid.

sustainability preferences, and the design and categorisation of products and portfolios with sustainability factors.

Besides the guidelines for sustainability preference, a second area of intervention of MiFID II is product governance.[267] With the regulatory objective of safeguarding the interests of investors, product governance standards are designed to ensure that all financial instruments are created and offered in the clients' best interests.[268] In this context, it is key to assess each financial instrument to ascertain its compatibility with the client's financial and sustainability profile. This assessment should cover the complete product lifecycle, including the stages of pre-distribution, marketing and distribution, and post-distribution.[269] During the pre-distribution phase, sustainability factors should be seamlessly integrated through information gathering. Subsequently, both manufacturers and distributors must maintain an ongoing review of the financial product's attributes, taking sustainability factors into consideration. Finally, in the post-distribution stage, this reassessment process should endure, to guarantee that financial products remain in harmony with sustainability objectives.[270]

Along with the guidelines for product governance, another regulatory instrument that could have the potential to complement the regime is the project, currently on hold, on the EU 'Ecolabel' framework for specific financial products.[271] The Ecolabel sets out the minimum environmental performance requirements for these products, and aims to encourage retail investors to invest in sustainable economic activities. The EU Ecolabel defines green thresholds at the portfolio level for funds, and assesses whether companies' green economic activities meet these thresholds.[272]

The draft report outlining the EU Ecolabel criteria introduces specific requirements for the use of derivatives by retail investment funds. It stipulates that undertakings for collective investment in transferable securities (UCITS) or retail alternative investment funds (AIFs) may employ derivatives, if they align with the fund's environmental investment objectives and are used for either hedging

267 These regulatory instrument collects the experience of the European Commission's Capital Markets Recovery Package and subsequent Amending Directive2; the sustainability-related amendments to the MiFID II Delegated Directive 3; the recommendations on the product governance guidelines by ESMA's Advisory Committee on Proportionality (ACP); and the findings of ESMA's 2021 Common Supervisory Action on product governance.

268 ESMA, 'Final Report: Guidelines on MiFID II Product Governance Requirements', 27 March 2023. www.esma.europa.eu/sites/default/files/2023-03/ESMA35-43-3448_Final_report_on_MiFID_II_guidelines_on_product_governance.pdf accessed 4th October 2023.

269 Maria Elena Salerno, 'Adding Sustainability Risks and Factors to the MiFID II Suitability and Product Governance Requirements', ITALJ 8.2 (2022): 816.

270 ibid.

271 This project will be based mainly on the requirements addressed in the Annex I of the Regulation (EC) No 66/2010 of the European Parliament and the council of 25 November 2009 on the EU Ecolabel. https://susproc.jrc.ec.europa.eu/product-bureau//product-groups/432/project-plan accessed 10th October 2023.

272 ibid.

or exposure management.[273] Additionally, the underlying assets must comply with EU Ecolabel criteria, including environmental and social exclusions and consumer information.

It is acknowledged, however, that evaluating and verifying criteria for derivative use could be complex and difficult,[274] as it may be challenging to link them directly to EU taxonomy-eligible activities or capital investment. On the other hand, excluding derivatives for which greenness verification is unnecessary from the total portfolio asset value would result in a portfolio with only a very small portion of qualifying green assets eligible for the EU Ecolabel.[275] Lannoo and Thomadakis argue that the proposed requirements permit the use of derivatives by retail funds to increase exposure to underlying assets, provided it is temporary, and in response to significant subscriptions.[276] This approach excludes synthetic replication through performance swaps by ESG funds in the context of passive management.[277]

UK Regulation for ESG Derivatives

The UK's framework for ESG comprises a collection of domestic and EU-derived laws and regulations, which cover a broad spectrum of areas, beyond just ESG. There are corporate governance and company law regulations; the UK Corporate Governance Code 2018 (UKCGC); and the Companies Act of 2006, that outlines directors' duties, including considerations related to ESG matters. For companies whose securities are traded on exchanges (e.g., the LSE) there are the Listing Rules, as well as the Disclosure Guidance and Transparency Rules (DTRs). Following the adoption of stewardship rules in 2010, the UK Stewardship Code 2020 (UKSC) establishes principles for asset owners and managers when engaging with investee companies.

Similarly, tackling some of the multiple issues at the core of the ESG, the UK has developed bodies of regulation, such as the Climate Change Act 2008 (CCA 2008), the Bribery Act 2010, the Corporate Manslaughter and Corporate Homicide Act 2007 (CMCHA 2007), and the Equality Act 2010, which is a legislation addressing equality and discrimination issues. Moreover, the Modern Slavery Act 2015 (MSA 2015) is focused on combating modern slavery and human trafficking. In 2022, the Companies (Strategic Report) on Climate-related Financial Disclosure Regulations[278] enhanced the requirements that private companies should follow to disclose material information. As may be anticipated, the UK's ESG regulatory

273 ibid.

274 Better Finance, 'Development of EU Ecolabel Criteria for Retail Financial Products', Better Finance Response, 6 May 2019, 3. https://betterfinance.eu/wp-content/uploads/BETTER-FINANCE-Ecolabels-Consultation.pdf accessed 10th October 2023.

275 Karel Lannoo and Apostolos Thomadakis, 'Derivatives in Sustainable Finance' (n 223).

276 ibid.

277 ibid.

278 The Companies (Strategic Report) (Climate-related Financial Disclosure) Regulations 2022.

landscape, therefore, consists of a diverse range of laws and regulations, applicable to businesses of all sizes.

In this context, the HM policy paper 'Greening Finance: A Roadmap to Sustainable Investing'[279] outlined the UK Government's vision of making the financial system environmentally responsible, and in harmony with the UK's globally pioneering net-zero pledge. As announced in 2021, the transformation would follow a three-stage process. It firstly guarantees the accessibility of meaningful sustainability information to financial decision-makers in the market. It then integrates this information into regular business and financial determinations. This in turn, will result in supporting the redirection of financial resources across the economy, to align with a net-zero and nature-friendly economic model.[280]

Although the roadmap consists of four primary pillars, the UK Green Taxonomy and SDRs have garnered the most attention. For the UK taxonomy, firms are seeking further clarity, as HM Treasury has confirmed its alignment with the structure of the EU taxonomy. However, the UK Government might diverge from the EU's approach concerning the Delegated Acts and Technical Screening Criteria. The government intends to initiate a consultation on this approach in Autumn 2024. The Green Technical Advisory Group (GTAG) has strongly advised prompt implementation of the UK Green Taxonomy to avoid further complexity. It is pivotal to align with existing taxonomies and to provide a definition for green, economically sustainable activities. Moreover, GTAG highlights that the UK has an opportunity to create 'a more efficient reporting framework' by addressing the usability challenges that emerged under the EU framework. This involves a re-evaluation of the KPIs pertinent to credit institutions and investors.

To tailor green financial products effectively, it is essential for the UK regime to underscore that reporting for investment funds should occur at the fund level, accompanied by the disclosure of taxonomy components for all funds, regardless of whether they possess a sustainability label.[281] This approach holds the promise of improving comparability between funds, reducing the risk of greenwashing, and creating a more equitable landscape concerning data costs for both sustainable and non-sustainable or non-designated financial products. This is important, because expenses may disproportionately impact management fees for sustainable products. This opportunity could enable the UK to address some of the limitations already encountered by the EU regulation, offering a substantial competitive

279 HM Treasury, 'Greening Finance: A Roadmap to Sustainable Investing', 18 October 2021. www.gov.uk/government/publications/greening-finance-a-roadmap-to-sustainable-investing accessed 17th October 2023.

280 ibid.

281 Elisabeth Overland, Anthea Bowater and Emily Smith, 'UK Green Taxonomy – GTAG Provides Further Technical Advice to the UK Government', 21 September 2023. www.freshfields.com/en-gb/our-thinking/knowledge/briefing/2023/09/uk-green-taxonomy-gtag-provides-further-technical-advice-to-the-uk-government/#:~:text=Aim%20of%20the%20UK%20Green%20Taxonomy&text=The%20aim%20is%20to%20improve,transition%20to%20a%20sustainable%20economy accessed 17th October 2023.

advantage to this market. Furthermore, GTAG believes that this strategy has the potential to encourage clients to express a preference for investments aligned with the UK Green Taxonomy.[282]

Regarding the UK SDRs, based on the International Sustainability Standards Board (ISSB) standards and transition planning disclosure requirements, the regulatory authority envisions a three-tier framework encompassing an investment product label, consumer-oriented product-level disclosures, and more comprehensive disclosures at both the entity and product levels.[283] The importance of disclosure is central to the further development of ESG financial products. The FCA considers the provision of additional requirements (for asset managers and for product-level disclosures) to be an effective regulatory tool. The objective is to enhance transparency and accountability about the sustainability performance and credentials of their investments.[284] Accessing this type of data will facilitate FCA's task of determining where a product is aligned to the UK Green Taxonomy. The FCA has also set its priorities regarding the SDRs by means of the supporting system for classifying investment labels.[285]

The framework for sustainable investment funds[286] comprises four labels, each with specific criteria. 'Sustainability Focus' requires a minimum 70% investment in environmentally or socially sustainable assets. 'Sustainability Improvers' is for assets not currently sustainable but aiming for improvement. 'Sustainability Impact' applies to products addressing societal or environmental challenges with measurable positive impacts. 'Sustainability Mixed Goals' is for funds with diverse sustainability objectives. Funds seeking these labels must adhere to strict guidelines, ensuring at least 70% of investments align with the labelled objective. The standard – an *absolute* measure of sustainability – undergoes independent assessment. The FCA mandates data-driven KPIs as evidence, demonstrating progress toward sustainability objectives.[287]

In the area of product labelling, the FCA acknowledges that many UK firms are subject to the EU's SFDR, and aims to explore how products categorised under SFDR can be integrated into the UK framework.[288] They propose a potential approach with three product labels: *sustainable*, *responsible*, and *not promoted as sustainable*. The sustainable product label would be applied to products that actively pursue specific sustainability characteristics, themes, or objectives while delivering a financial return. These products are further categorised into three types: 'impact', 'aligned' (corresponding to Article 9 funds under SFDR), and

282 ibid.

283 FCA, 'Sustainability Disclosure Requirements (SDR) and Investment Labels', CP22/20***, October 2022. www.fca.org.uk/publication/consultation/cp22-20.pdf accessed 17th October 2023.

284 ibid.

285 ibid.

286 FCA, 'Sustainability Disclosure Requirements and Investment Labels Policy Statement PS23/16', November 2023. www.fca.org.uk/publication/policy/ps23-16.pdf accessed 2nd November 2023.

287 ibid.

288 FCA, 'Sustainability Disclosure Requirements (SDR) and Investment Labels' (n 283).

'transitioning' (corresponding to Article 8 funds under SFDR). In this instance, we reiterate the need for regulators to look for types of ESG derivatives, such as SLDs and Carbon Market Derivatives – the inherent characteristics of a sustainable product. The second category, 'responsible' products, includes products in which the fund manager takes sustainability and stewardship issues into account when making investment decisions, even if there is not a specific sustainability objective. Then, for a broader range of investment products that are not offered in the market as sustainable, there is the 'not promoted as sustainable' label. This applies to products that do not consider any sustainability factors, even for risk management purposes.[289]

To the labelling regulation follow some questions regarding the legal certainty of how financial products will be treated under the UK Green Taxonomy. If the TSCs of the UK Green Taxonomy are expected to change, current taxonomy aligned products may no longer meet the criteria triggering legal uncertainty. To solve the potential legal risks this poses, the GTAG proposes the implementation of a 'grandfathering' clause, with parameters on how products will be treated.[290] The purpose is to ensure that current financial products keep being aligned with the taxonomy, even if the classification criteria changes. Therefore, alternatives such as granting transition periods to adjust the products or, in the case of green bonds and loans that were 'green' at the time of issuance, ensuring that they remain aligned until maturity,[291] are among the suggestions to enhance compliance with the taxonomy. The greater coherence in terms of labelling and treatment of financial products will also be beneficial to achieve greater development and standardisation of green financial products.

Along with the labelling approach, the FCA has also announced its intention to work towards more detailed disclosures for institutional investors.[292] This could include in-depth explanations of the methodologies used for assessing sustainability performance, details about data sources and limitations, alignment with taxonomy standards, and benchmarking information.[293]

The UK's strategy appears to be in line with a risk-based regulatory approach, as it tailors its requirements to specific investor groups with varying information needs. Likely, this approach means that regulators will require companies to implement new controls and processes to generate the disclosures under the SDRs

289 PWC, 'UK Sustainability Disclosure Requirements: How Can You Prepare?', August 2023. www.pwc.co.uk/industries/financial-services/understanding-regulatory-developments/uk-sustainability-disclosure-requirements-how-can-you-prepare.html accessed 17th October 2023.

290 GTAG, 'Treatment of Green Financial Products Under an Evolving UK Green Taxonomy', Green Finance Institute, September 2023. www.greenfinanceinstitute.com/wp-content/uploads/2023/09/GTAG-Final-Report-on-Treatment-of-Green-Financial-Products-Over-Time.pdf accessed 17th October 2023.

291 ibid.

292 ibid.

293 FCA, 'FCA Updates on Its Sustainability Disclosure Requirements (SDR) and Investment Labels Consultation', 29 March 2023. www.fca.org.uk/news/news-stories/fca-updates-sustainability-disclosure-requirements-and-investment-labels-consultation accessed 17th October 2023.

according to their level of risk.[294] The shortcoming, however, is that the approach might result in an increased workload for firms – both during the initial implementation phase, and on an ongoing basis.[295]

While the original and revised editions of the UK Green Finance Roadmap do not explicitly mention the promotion of new green financial products, one of the possible applications of the UK Green Taxonomy is to provide input for the creation of a regulated green label for UK financial products.[296] In this sense, we argue that, as the ESG derivatives market grows, regulators will recognise the opportunities brought by these type of transactions, especially those that have ESG targets at their core. This argument is in line with the interests of the FCA to broaden the spectrum for more sustainable investment products, to improve consumer and investor choices.[297]

In the area of ESG disclosures, the UK's primary ESG disclosure regulations are outlined in the Companies Act, the UKCGC, and the Taskforce on Climate-related Financial Disclosures (TCFD) framework. Section 172 of the Companies Act requires directors of UK companies to consider ESG factors (such as employee interests, community impact, and environmental effects) while primarily promoting the company's success for the benefit of shareholders. Moreover, large and medium-sized companies must publish an annual strategic report that includes ESG-related information, such as environmental impact, employee disclosures, social and human rights issues, and related policies. For companies with securities traded on certain exchanges or 'public interest entities', the report must contain a 'non-financial information statement' covering topics like human rights, anti-corruption, and anti-bribery. Regarding directors' duties, large companies must include a separate statement explaining how directors considered ESG matters while fulfilling their duties. In the annual directors' report, large companies must inform on GHG emissions and energy consumption, according to the rules of the Streamlined Energy and Carbon Reporting (SECR).[298]

The TCFD[299] recommendations are frequently adopted voluntarily by organisations. While not mandatory, these recommendations provide a structured

294 PWC, 'From Tactics To Strategy – How Firms Should Respond to Emerging UK Sustainable Finance Regulation', February 2022. www.pwc.co.uk/industries/financial-services/understanding-regulatory-developments/from-tactics-to-strategy-how-firms-should-respond-to-emerging-uk-sustainable-finance-regulation.html accessed 17th October 2023.

295 ibid.

296 GTAG, 'GTAG: Advice on the Development of a UK Green Taxonomy', October 2022. www.greenfinanceinstitute.com/wp-content/uploads/2022/10/GTAG-Advice-on-the-development-of-a-UK-Green-Taxonomy.pdf accessed 17th October 2023.

297 FCA, 'Sustainability Disclosure Requirements (SDR) and Investment Labels', Discussion Paper DP21/4, November 2021. www.fca.org.uk/publication/discussion/dp21-4.pdf accessed 17th October 2023.

298 The Companies (Directors' Report) and Limited Liability Partnerships (Energy and Carbon Report) Regulations 2018.

299 FSB, 'Task Force on Climate-related Financial Disclosures. Recommendations of the Task Force on Climate-related Financial Disclosures', June 2017. https://assets.bbhub.io/company/sites/60/2020/10/FINAL-2017-TCFD-Report-11052018.pdf accessed 17th October 2023.

framework for disclosing climate-related financial information. The framework encompasses four overarching themes around governance, strategy, risk management, and metrics and targets. As explained with the EU taxonomy, regulatory instruments such as the TCFD are meant to provide context and framework for the investment transactions designed to assist sustainability objectives. In this sense, the TCFD provides the baseline to understand climate-related risk and opportunities, which in turn, will inform the type of KPIs that companies and investors include in their financial contracts. We argue that disclosing the current and potential impacts of climate-related risks, on firms' operations, strategic planning, and financial considerations (when such information is of material significance), as well as risk management, metrics and targets is behaviour central to enhancing the coherence between the companies' sustainability strategies and the particular actions represented by KPIs included in financial contracts.

However, the overreliance on disclosure mechanisms is a latent failure of the UK Green Finance Strategy (announced in 2019, further developed in November 2020[300] and recently updated in March 2023).[301] The challenge in pinning down the effective execution of the UK Green Finance Strategy on disclosure mechanisms lies in their voluntary nature, and the need to incorporate them within the existing financial reporting obligations.[302] The extent to which companies comply will be influenced by factors such as the perceived relevance of these disclosures to investors, the ease of implementation for companies, and the actual and perceived legal responsibilities associated with including such information in financial reports.[303]

In this context, there are two primary considerations to address when accepting disclosure as the benchmark for adopting the UK Green Finance Strategy and shaping a company's sustainability strategy (which in turn, influences the inclusion of KPIs in ESG financial transactions). These concerns pertain to governance, materiality, and legal risks. On one hand, the incorporation of climate-related disclosures significantly impacts how materiality is perceived,[304] both within a company, and by investors and other stakeholders. On the other hand, legal risks come into play when increased information disclosure raises the potential for reporting errors or misrepresenting information. This heightened risk can lead to legal action, should someone experience substantial losses based on such information.

300 HM Treasury and Department for Business, Energy & Industrial Strategy (2019). 'Green finance strategy', 2019; HM Treasury (2020). 'Chancellor Sets Out Ambition for Future of UK Financial Services', November.

301 HM Government, 'Mobilising Green Investment: 2023 Green Finance Strategy', March 2023. https://assets.publishing.service.gov.uk/government/uploads/system/uploads/attachment_data/file/1149690/mobilising-green-investment-2023-green-finance-strategy.pdf accessed 17th October 2023.

302 R. G. Eccles and M. P. Krzus, 'Implementing the Task Force on Climate-related Financial Disclosures Recommendations: An Assessment of Corporate Readiness', *Schmalenbach Business Review* 71 (2019): 287–293.

303 ibid.

304 Climate Disclosure Standards Board (CDSB), 'Position Paper Materiality and Climate Related Financial Disclosures', 2018. www.cdsb.net/sites/default/files/materiality_and_tcfd_paper.pdf accessed 17th October 2023.

In 2022, the HM Treasury introduced the Transition Planning Taskforce (TPT)[305] within the context of climate-related disclosures. This taskforce was established to assist regulated entities in outlining how they intend to achieve climate targets, manage climate-related risks, and actively contribute to the broader climate transition, aligning with the Paris Agreement's commitment to limit global warming to 1.5°C above pre-industrial levels. This alignment also involves adapting to the adverse effects of climate change and enhancing resilience.[306] The TPT is anchored in this definition, and recommends that an effective transition plan should unequivocally express the entity's 'Strategic Ambition'. This includes delineating the entity's objectives and priorities for its role, in fostering low GHG emissions and a climate-resilient economy. Furthermore, it clarifies whether and how the entity is pursuing these objectives and priorities, in a manner that not only captures opportunities, but also avoids any detrimental effects on stakeholders and society, while safeguarding the natural environment. To foster good practice, the TPT framework is guided by three fundamental principles: ambition, action, and accountability.[307] In this scenario, one of the key contributions of the TPT for financial products is that the sustainability-related disclosures in general purpose financial reports become a reference point to the design of scalable and integrated products, directed towards financing transition.[308] Indeed, the further development of new financial instruments is included within the TPT implementation strategy.[309] It mandates regulated entities to disclose information or plans to change its portfolio of products and services, to achieve the Strategic Ambition of its transition plan.[310]

On 10 August 2023, the FCA indicated its intention to initiate consultations concerning transition plan disclosures for listed companies, aligning them with the TPT Disclosure Framework. These new obligations are projected to take effect for accounting periods starting in January 2025, with the inaugural reporting period commencing in 2026.[311] Furthermore, the UK Government is planning to solicit input on mandatory disclosure requirements for the largest public and private companies in the UK regarding their transition plans, if they have such plans in place.

305 TPT, 'Disclosure Framework', October 2023. https://transitiontaskforce.net/wp-content/uploads/2023/10/TPT_Disclosure-framework-2023.pdf accessed 17th October 2023.

306 UNFCCC, Paris Agreement, 2015.

307 TPT, 'Disclosure Framework' (n 305) 15.

308 ibid., 11.

309 Brendan Curran, Josie Murdoch, Oleksandra Plyska and Nick Robins, 'Response to the Transition Plan Taskforce Consultation on the TPT Disclosure Framework and Implementation Guidance', The Grantham Research Institute on Climate Change and the Environment, March 2023. www.lse.ac.uk/granthaminstitute/wp-content/uploads/2023/03/Response-to-Transition-Taskforce-Disclosure-Framework-and-Implementation-Guidance.pdf accessed 17th October 2023.

310 TPT, Implementation Strategy 2.2. Products and Services.

311 TPT, 'Summary of the TPT Recommendations', October 2023. https://transitiontaskforce.net/wp-content/uploads/2023/10/TPT-Summary-Recommendations.pdf accessed 17th October 2023.

Following the ample acceptance of the TCDF, the Taskforce for Nature-related Financial Disclosures (TNFD) was released in September 2023.[312] TNFD intentionally follows the structure of the TCFD framework. This approach aims to stimulate early adoption, and facilitate consistency with established risk-management methods. In formulating this new framework, the TNFD enables companies to channel investments towards fostering positive outcomes for the environment.[313] This contributes to the preservation of nature and its critical ecosystem services. The framework achieves this objective by requiring companies to divulge their engagements with the natural world, enabling investors to make well-informed choices and promoting sustainable investment practices. The TNFD considers the creation of financial products as a form of nature-related opportunities. These are activities that create positive outcomes for organisations and nature, by means of positive impact or mitigation of negative effects on nature.[314] These broad definitions would provide a baseline to develop and include more financial products that contribute to achieve such effects. Until now, the biodiversity finance reference guide has provided an indicative list of investment activities that contribute to the protection of biodiversity and ecosystem services.[315] Although the guide does not include financial derivatives in the list – because it uses as reference the principles for bond and green loans – we argue that the ESG derivatives have (in some instances) the potential to meet the criteria to be considered biodiversity finance. This might be the case for some types of ESG derivatives, because feasibility will depend completely on the areas tackled in the KPIs drafted in those transactions, and how they interact with SDGs in a particular context.

Another instrument key for the disclosure framework is the UK Stewardship Code (UKSC). This offers instructions for asset owners and managers regarding their engagement with investee companies, with a particular emphasis on managing environmental risks. This regulatory framework was originally introduced in the UK in 2010, and underwent a significant amendment that took effect in 2020. One of the key attributes of the UKSC is its comprehensive 'reporting expectations',[316] designed to provide extensive insights into the stewardship activities carried out by its signatories. The framework created by the UKSC clarifies the diverse techniques that go beyond engagement as an investment strategy, that entails diverse forms of direct communication between investors and companies

312 TNFD, 'Recommendations of the Taskforce on Nature-related Financial Disclosures', September 2023. https://tnfd.global/wp-content/uploads/2023/08/Recommendations_of_the_Taskforce_on_Nature-related_Financial_Disclosures_September_2023.pdf accessed 20th October 2023.

313 ibid.

314 ibid., 35.

315 IFC, 'Biodiversity Finance Reference Guide', May 2023. www.ifc.org/content/dam/ifc/doc/mgrt/biodiversity-finance-reference-guide.pdf accessed 20th October 2023.

316 Paul Davies, 'The UK Stewardship Code 2010–2020: From Saving the Company to Saving the Planet?', in Dionysisa Katelouzou and Dan W. Puchniak (eds), *Global Shareholder Stewardship* (Cambridge University Press, 2022) 44.

on ESG matters relevant to a company.[317] The UKSC includes as equally important strategies 'investment decision-making, monitoring assets and service providers, engaging with issuers and holding them to account on material issues, collaborating with others, and exercising rights and responsibilities'.[318] The rationale is that these strategies are a means to mainstream ESG factors into stewardship, where asset owners and managers are meant to play a central role in preserving market integrity and coherence in the investment portfolio.[319]

When considering the usefulness of the UKSC for the purpose of designing ESG-aligned financial transactions, there is the need to clarify the reasons to engage issuers with ESG topics. It might be argued that engagement has to do with informing proxy voting and voting guidelines, enhancing research capabilities, providing greater clarity on publicly available information, recognising parameters of management quality, identifying the best strategy for the company, uncovering investment opportunities, and enhancing reputation as an active and engaged shareholder, among others.[320] The questions are how the strategy serves the purposes outlined in the UKSC, and how this could enhance the use of financial products with ESG at its core. Professor Paul Davies explored the topic from the perspective of incentives for index and stock pickers funds. In his view, whilst the latter are likely to have greater incentives than the former, Davies concludes that financial reasons (such as low costs and short-term financial projections) are determinant in the form engagement takes place.[321] This would suggest that traditional engagement reasons are key to investment decisions and, at least intuitively, the 'ESG at core' approach is not as evident as we might expect. Therefore, ideas such as collectivising engagement[322] or planning a collaborative strategic planning[323] seem to offer potential ways to address incentive problems.

The rationale of collectivising engagement may solve the collective action problem. It follows the premise of overcoming the shortfalls related to high and non-spreadable costs that undermine a successful engagement strategy for institutional

317 Michelle Edkins, 'The Significance of Engagement', in *Engagement Strategies* (Harvard University). https://pcg.law.harvard.edu/wp-content/uploads/2015/12/esg-excerpt.pdf accessed 18th October 2023.

318 Financial Reporting Council, 'The UK Stewardship Code 2020', 2019. www.frc.org.uk/getattachment/5aae591d-d9d3-4cf4-814a-d14e156a1d87/Stewardship-Code_Dec-19-Final-Corrected.pdf accessed 18th October 2023.

319 ibid., 4.

320 Michelle Edkins, 'The Significance of Engagement' (n 317).

321 Paul Davies, 'The UK Stewardship Code 2010–2020: From Saving the Company to Saving the Planet?' (n 316) 50–54.

322 ibid., 55.

323 Anne Sheehan and Brian Rice, California State Teachers Retirement System (CalSTRS), *Laying the Foundation for Successful Engagement in Engagement Strategies* (Harvard University). https://pcg.law.harvard.edu/wp-content/uploads/2015/12/esg-excerpt.pdf accessed 18th October 2023.

investors.[324] Effective collective action by institutional investors provides a potentially attractive alternative to regulated solutions to governance concerns,[325] as is the integration of ESG factors into decision-making. However, as corporate dynamics and business models do not always capture all the relevant information required for an effective engagement, we would propose the activist hedge fund hypothesis as a solution.[326] Essentially, the appeal of hedge funds lies in their operational model, which enables them to identify companies where a change in strategy or management is probable. Although helpful, the reliance on the potential role of activist hedge funds was not considered by UK regulators as a lasting solution. Thus, the UKSC incorporates an obligation not only to report the engagement strategy,[327] but also its outcomes,[328] including those achieved by adopting collective engagement.

Against this background, the central query is to see how the UKSC integrates social and environmental issues into stewardship goals. Expressly, Article 7 requires a comprehensive integration of ESG factors into institutional investors' acquisition, monitoring and exit decisions. Understanding that institutional investors, by means of engagement and other strategies, can determine the path a company follows, their role is pivotal to strengthen the coherence between the broad company ESG strategy, and the way financial transactions are aligned with it. This is, however, a highly contended area – the link is not always clear between better financial performance for companies that adopt ESG strategies compared to those that do not. In the context of the UKSC, the responsible allocation and management of capital and the creation of sustainable value is, in the first instance, for the benefit of clients and investee companies. Then, such creation of value will, in turn, bring benefits for the economy, the environment, and society. In that sense, it seems that there is an 'action–reaction' effect – if we procure the creation of investor value, the result will naturally benefit other broader interests. We would praise this structure in that it seeks to abolish the traditional view of contending interests, instead, providing a prioritisation of diverse interests that could be easily embedded in a risk-based approach strategy.

The risk-based approach to regulation allows not only the identification of risks (in this case the risks to commit with an effective ESG policy), but takes the discretionary decision to prioritise the management of some risks above others. In this context, the level of discretion is aligned with the UKSC approach, whereby the normative structure for investment intermediaries follows the mandate to promote

324 Gaia Balp and Giovanni Strampelli, 'Institutional Investor Collective Engagements: Non-Activist Cooperation vs Activist Wolf Packs', *Ohio State Business Law Journal* 14.2 (2020): 135–209.

325 Craig Doidge, Alexander Dyck, Hamed Mahmudi and Aazam Virani, 'Can Institutional Investors Improve Corporate Governance Through Collective Action?', Rotman School of Management Working Paper 21, 2015. https://citeseerx.ist.psu.edu/document?repid=rep1&type=pdf&doi=b90b5f37d3eff512bd8be7190c5520b15222f3a0 accessed 20th October 2023.

326 Paul Davies, 'The UK Stewardship Code 2010–2020: From Saving the Company to Saving the Planet?' (n 316) 55.

327 Financial Reporting Council, 'The UK Stewardship Code 2020' (n 318) Principles 9–11.

328 ibid.

the success of the company, as described in Section 172 of the Companies Act 2006. The exercise of such discretion will be judged within the parameters of good faith. In this scenario, the UKSC plants the seed for ESG to be central to stewardship implementation. However, it anticipates that, realistically, this mandate does not ensure that in all events ESG factors will prevail over the creation of value for investors. Therefore, the dialogue is completed when investors find incentives to consider that the creation of value is enhanced when integrating ESG factors. This is to understand that investors are not purely guided by financial returns, but also have interests aligned with the economy, the environment, and society – and in that sense, they benefit from having high levels of commitment with ESG policies and good reputation in the market.

The ESG reputational risk becomes prominent, as it has a negative impact on a company's growth opportunities, thereby mitigating its long-term presence in the market.[329] Moreover, regulators have also expressed their intention to support the UKSC, when they announced that, if needed, the FCA will consider further actions to ensure effective stewardship.[330] This approach reinforces the importance of considering reputational risk in relation to regulatory intervention. If signatories of the UKSC behave in a way that demonstrates high levels of commitment and coherent policies, then regulatory action by means of sanctions will not be necessary. The regulatory dialogue that guides the investment community and companies is founded on a collaboration with the achievement of regulatory objectives, therefore the regulator chooses its primary areas of attention. Since 2021, the FCA has been focused on climate change and the policies of CO_2 emission reduction,[331] in line with the Paris Agreement commitments.

The TCFD Disclosure Requirements and voluntary ESG disclosures collectively create a framework for ESG disclosures and compliance in the UK. In addition to legal ESG disclosure requirements, UK organisations often engage in voluntary ESG-related initiatives, among them, the UN SDGs, the Principles for Responsible Investment (PRIs), the UK Stewardship Code (UKSC), and the Responsible Investment Framework (RIF). Along with these instruments, there are private sector initiatives related to ESG, primarily revolving around ESG reporting, responsible investment, and engagement efforts, for instance, the Climate Action 100+.[332] This is a five-year initiative, led by investors, that engages with major GHG emitters and

329 Irene Fafaliou, Maria Giaka, Dimitrios Konstantios and Michael Polemis, 'Firms' ESG Reputational Risk and Market Longevity: A Firm-Level Analysis for the United States', *Journal of Business Research* 149 (2022): 161–177.

330 FCA, 'Building a Regulatory Framework for Effective Stewardship, Feedback to DP 10/1', Feedback Statement, October 2019, paras 3.7 ff. www.fca.org.uk/publication/feedback/fs19-7.pdf accessed 20th October 2023. As cited in Paul Davies, 'The UK Stewardship Code 2010–2020: From Saving the Company to Saving the Planet?' (n 316) 62.

331 FCA, 'FCA Climate Change Adaptation Report', 1 October 2021. www.fca.org.uk/publication/corporate/fca-climate-change-adaptation-report.pdf accessed 20th October 2023.

332 Climate Action 100+. www.climateaction100.org accessed 17th October 2023.

other companies globally. Its aim is to drive the transition toward cleaner energy and align with the goals of the Paris Agreement on climate change.

These initiatives and voluntary disclosures reflect the private sector's commitment to ESG principles and sustainability, often going beyond regulatory requirements to address ESG challenges. As the rules for GHG emissions are closely related to carbon market derivatives, we will develop its incidence when exploring those transactions.

US Regulation Applicable to ESG Derivatives

Historically, ESG matters in the US have been tackled primarily through voluntary, market-driven initiatives, distinguishing this region from Europe and the UK, where dedicated ESG regulations are enforced. Nevertheless, the regulatory framework in the US has undergone significant changes in recent years. In February 2021, President Biden issued an executive order instructing the federal government to confront climate change and ESG-related risks in the economy.[333] Following this, the US SEC unveiled initiatives[334] aimed at tackling climate change and ESG concerns. These initiatives encompassed the establishment of a dedicated Climate and ESG Task Force within the Division of Enforcement. The SEC's first category of rules regarding climate change seek to make mandatory for regulated entities the reporting of information about management of climate-related-risks, and the measures to mitigate it. The identification of actual or potential material impacts of these risks on business and consolidated statements has influenced strategic decisions and business models. Lastly, the SEC requires firms to measure the effects of climate-related events and transition efforts on the specific aspects included in their consolidated financial statements.[335]

The second category of rules are focused on GHG emissions reductions. The rule would require reporting of audited emissions falling under both Scope 1 and Scope 2.[336] These emissions encompass those produced by a company's own operations, and those stemming from the energy it procures. Additionally, if Scope 3 emissions are either significant, or if the regulated entity has set specific targets, they would also need to be disclosed[337] according to the SEC proposed rules. Scope 3 emissions encompass upstream and downstream emissions across the entirety

333 The White House, 'Executive Order on Climate-Related Financial Risk', 20 May 2021. www.whitehouse.gov/briefing-room/presidential-actions/2021/05/20/executive-order-on-climate-related-financial-risk/ accessed 20th October 2023.

334 The SEC Proposal is based in part on the recommendations (the 'TCFD Recommendations') of the Task Force on Climate-related Disclosures (the 'TCFD').

335 SEC, 'The Enhancement and Standardization of Climate-Related Disclosures for Investors', 17 CFR 210, 229, 232, 239, and 249 [Release Nos. 33-11042; 34-94478; File No. S7-10-22]. www.sec.gov/files/rules/proposed/2022/33-11042.pdf.

336 Greenhouse Gas Protocol Sets Standards to Measure and Manage Emissions. https://ghgprotocol.org accessed 20th October 2023.

337 SEC, 'The Enhancement and Standardization of Climate-Related Disclosures for Investors' (n 335).

of the company's value chain.[338] When reporting emissions, companies would be required to provide the data in absolute terms, and in terms of intensity, considering both per unit of revenue (i.e., GHG per dollar in sales) and per unit of product (e.g., emissions per car manufactured).[339] Regulated entities must also outline the methodologies they used to derive these estimates, specify which GHGs the estimates encompass (e.g., methane, nitrous oxide, or CO_2), and describe the sources of these emissions. In response to the debate about the implications of requiring reporting on Scope 3, SEC Chair Gary Gensler anticipates a delay in implementation, to carefully consider the oppositions to the rule.[340] For our study, the accounting and reporting of GHG emissions on Scope 3 serve as a reference to help financial institutions develop climate-friendly financial products.[341] The Partnership for Carbon Accounting Financials (PCAF) provides guidance on the parameters to further develop certain financial products, such as bond and sustainability-linked loans. The Corporate Value Chain (Scope 3) Accounting and Reporting Standard[342] classifies Scope 3 emissions into 15 well-defined categories. These categories serve as a structured framework to assist companies in organising, comprehending, and reporting the various Scope 3 activities occurring within their corporate value chain.[343] The intention is to ensure that these categories do not overlap, preventing any double counting of emissions by a reporting company. The development of financial products is Category 15, named 'investments' – among them, financial derivatives are located as 'other investments' where accounting for emissions is optional. It is worth noting that this framework is primarily tailored for use by private financial institutions, such as commercial banks. However, it is also applicable to public financial institutions, including multilateral development banks and export credit agencies, as well as other entities with investments that fall outside the scope of Scope 1 and Scope 2 emissions.[344] Further development on carbon

338 Frédéric Ducoulombier, 'Understanding the Importance of Scope 3 Emissions and the Implications of Data Limitations', *The Journal of Impact and ESG Investing* 1.4 (Summer 2021).

339 Laura Corb, Kimberly Henderson, Tim Koller and Shally Venugopal, 'Understanding the SEC's Proposed Climate Risk Disclosure Rule', 3 June 2022. www.mckinsey.com/capabilities/strategy-and-corporate-finance/our-insights/understanding-the-secs-proposed-climate-risk-disclosure-rule accessed 20th October 2023.

340 Richard Vanderford, 'SEC's Climate-Disclosure Rule Isn't Here, But It May As Well Be, Many Businesses Say', *The Wall Street Journal*, 25 April 2023. www.wsj.com/articles/secs-climate-disclosure-rule-isnt-here-but-it-may-as-well-be-many-businesses-say-854789bd accessed 20th October 2023.

341 PCAF, *The Global GHG Accounting and Reporting Standard for the Financial Industry* (1st edn, 2020). https://ghgprotocol.org/sites/default/files/2023-03/The%20Global%20GHG%20Accounting%20and%20Reporting%20Standard%20for%20the%20Financial%20Industry.pdf accessed 20th October 2023.

342 GHG Protocol, 'Corporate Value Chain (Scope 3) Accounting and Reporting Standard, Supplement to the GHG Protocol Corporate Accounting and Reporting Standard'. https://ghgprotocol.org/sites/default/files/standards/Corporate-Value-Chain-Accounting-Reporing-Standard_041613_2.pdf accessed 20th October 2023.

343 ibid., 54.

344 ibid., 51.

emission reduction and carbon markets will be explored in the section devoted to carbon market derivatives.

The third SEC's category of rules is focused on the establishment of targets and transition plans.[345] As per the current rule, businesses would be required to reveal any pre-existing objectives related to emission reductions, energy consumption, nature preservation, or income derived from eco-friendly products. The SEC seeks comprehensive disclosure of the strategies, more stringent than the TCFD recommendations, designed to attain these goals, including specific details on the utilisation of offsets or renewable-energy credits. If a company employs an internal carbon-pricing mechanism, they will need to disclose this pricing structure, along with the methodology for its determination and the scope of its coverage.

The SEC proposals are uniformly applicable to all regulated entities, irrespective of their industry, and do not contain industry-specific provisions. In contrast, the TCFD has issued additional recommendations and guidance designed for distinct sectors, including the financial sector, as well as four nonfinancial sectors (energy; transportation; materials and buildings; and agriculture, food, and forest products).[346]

Along with the SEC rules, in June 2022, the CFTC released a request for information to seek public comment on climate-related financial risk, to better inform its understanding and oversight of these type of risks as pertinent to the derivatives markets and underlying commodities markets.[347] Some of the queries the CFTC sought to solve considered the type of data and data sources to evaluate the climate-related financial exposures of derivatives market participants.[348] In this context, one of the transversal questions is how to have better access to consistent and reliable data to assess climate-related financial risks, and to develop climate stress-test scenarios that are fit for purpose in the market. Similarly, the CFTC aim to identify the types of derivatives products being used to manage climate-related financial risk, and enhance price discovery or allocation of capital to climate projects.[349] The CFTC were also questioning whether they will have a role in enhancing the integrity of voluntary carbon markets[350] that – as we will study later – are becoming a great opportunity for financial derivatives.

345 SEC, 'The Enhancement and Standardization of Climate-Related Disclosures for Investors' (n 335).

346 Yaroslav Alekseyev, Rachel Barrett, Mike Bienenfeld and Aileen Buchanan, 'SEC's Climate Proposal vs. TCFD: What You Need To Know', *Linklaters*, 23 May 2022. www.linklaters.com/en/knowledge/publications/alerts-newsletters-and-guides/2022/may/19/secs-climate-proposal-vs-tcfd-what-you-need-to-know1 accessed 20th October 2023.

347 CFTC, 'Releases Request for Information on Climate-Related Financial Risk', 2 June 2022. www.cftc.gov/PressRoom/PressReleases/8541-22 accessed 20th October 2023.

348 CFTC, Request for Information on Climate-Related Financial Risk, Federal Register/Vol. 87, No. 110/Wednesday, 8 June 2022/Notices, 34858–34859. www.cftc.gov/sites/default/files/2022/06/2022-12302a.pdf accessed 20th October 2023.

349 ibid.

350 ibid.

Several responses to the CFTC information request agree that there is a growing trend in derivatives market participants in creating new products and financial market infrastructure services, such as the CME First Sustainable Clearing Service, created to provide better risk management to ESG risk. Likewise, there has been a steady growth in ESG futures, options, and swaps.[351] Regarding data quality and access concerns, market participants agree on the CFTC taking a soft approach, avoiding imposing additional reporting requirements, as such practices would hinder the growth of the market.[352] In general, a principles-based approach seems to be more fitting for the status of the market.

Interestingly, regarding the CFTC role in voluntary carbon markets, there are different views. Some respondents argue that the CFTC should oversee all VCM transactions under its comprehensive authority over derivatives. Verra clearly asserts, however, that numerous VCM contracts qualify as spot transactions for commodities. These transactions involve the direct exchange of a carbon credit for payment on a specified spot date, rather than dealing with derivative instruments.[353] Therefore, these transactions do not fall under the CFTC's jurisdiction for regulation. Nonetheless, the CFTC has the capability and the responsibility to initiate enforcement actions against instances of fraud or manipulation within the VCM;[354] such authority stems from its overarching statutory power to combat fraud and manipulation in commodities markets.

Following this ongoing discussion, Commissioner Goldsmith Romero[355] suggested establishing a distinct classification for derivatives products related to the environment and climate. This categorisation would enable the CFTC to collect information about these products and their associated markets, thereby fostering transparency in the market and facilitating price discovery.[356] We support this position, because recognising the particularities of ESG derivatives will promote greater use of these transactions, which in turn has the potential to strengthen risk-management tools and hedging in sustainable investment strategies.

351 CME Group Inc to the Request for Information on Climate-Related Financial Risk, 'Comment for Orders and Other Announcements 87 F.R. 34856', 5 October 2022. https://comments.cftc.gov/PublicComments/ViewComment.aspx?id=70809&SearchText= accessed 20th October 2023.

352 ibid.

353 Verra, 'Verra Comments on CFTC RFI on Climate-Related Financial Risk', 15 January 2023. https://verra.org/verra-comments-on-cftc-rfi-on-climate-related-financial-risk/ accessed 20th October 2023.

354 ibid.

355 Pamela T. Wu and Levi McAllister, 'CFTC Commissioner Proposes Framework for Environmental/Climate-Related Product Oversight', 10 March 2023. www.morganlewis.com/blogs/powerandpipes/2023/03/cftc-commissioner-proposes-framework-for-environmental-climate-related-product-oversight accessed 20th October 2023.

356 CFTC, 'Remarks of Commissioner Christy Goldsmith Romero at ISDA's ESG Forum on Promoting Market Resilience: A Thoughtful Approach to the Daunting Challenge of Climate Financial Risk', 7 March 2023. www.cftc.gov/PressRoom/SpeechesTestimony/oparomero7 accessed 20th October 2023.

The regulatory advancements of the CFTC are integrated to the efforts of the Financial Stability Oversight Council (FSOC). The FSOC has called for financial regulators to focus on capacity building, disclosure, data, and assessment of climate-related risks. As anticipated in the FSOC's report on climate-related financial risk,[357] the effect of the materialisation of climate risks can have a significant impact on financial stability, and on the functioning of the financial derivatives market. Both physical and transition risks can alter the stable functioning of the market. Physical events, like natural disasters or heatwaves, have the capacity to trigger extreme volatility in commodity and energy markets. This volatility is typically reflected in the re-evaluation of asset prices in securities markets, or adjustments in variation margin flows within derivatives markets.[358]

The FSOC warns of the importance of adopting more effective risk-management tools in derivatives markets to address highly volatile price shifts. Presently, derivatives market participants typically employ short-term horizon stress tests, usually spanning 1–5 days, known as 'stress period of risk' (or SPOR),[359] to assess their resilience to extreme price movements. However, events like the Lehman Brothers default and the COVID-19 crisis showed that future price movements, especially in a context of accelerated climate change, can surpass the predictive capacity of traditional stress tests.[360] Recognising the importance of tracking the market, and progressing towards providing more efficient risk management in the derivatives market and resilience to the unforeseen impact of climate-related risks, in 2021, the CFTC created the Climate Risk Unit (CRU).[361]

The CRU is tasked with encouraging an approach of enhancing risk management standards in CFTC-regulated markets through disclosures, stress testing, and other traditional financial risk-management techniques, adapted to improve the ability of financial institutions under CFTC regulation to withstand the challenges of climate change.[362] Furthermore, the CRU seeks to encourage the development of new financial instruments to assist in price discovery for climate-related financial risks and assist in capital allocation, such as water derivatives and voluntary carbon offset markets, and examine areas where adjustments or modifications could be made, either to climate-related products or to the CFTC's regulatory and supervisory approach.[363] The CRU will also further expand CFTC participation in domestic and international forums aimed at building consensus for consistent standards,

357 FSOC, 'Report on Climate Related Financial-Risk', 2021. https://home.treasury.gov/system/files/261/FSOC-Climate-Report.pdf accessed 23rd October 2023.

358 ibid.

359 CCP12 Primer on Credit Stress Testing – A CCP12 White Paper, August 2020, 10. https://ccp-global.org/wp-content/uploads/2020/08/20200803_CCP12_Primer_Credit_Stress_Testing.pdf accessed 23rd October 2023.

360 FSOC, 'Report on Climate Related Financial-Risk' (n 357).

361 CFTC, 'CFTC Acting Chairman Behnam Establishes New Climate Risk Unit', Release No. 8368-21, 17 March 2021. www.cftc.gov/PressRoom/PressReleases/8368-21 accessed 23rd October 2023.

362 ibid.

363 FSOC, 'Report on Climate Related Financial-Risk' (n 357).

definitions, disclosures, and practices across derivatives products and markets, and coordinate efforts to support the development of reliable data resources.[364] We welcome this clear approach of the CFTC's CRU, in terms of recognising the special role that the derivatives market has in supporting the transition to a more sustainable economy. Clarifying both types of ESG instruments and the role of the market supervisor will benefit the growth of these financial products. As may be anticipated, the openness of US regulators will become a competitive advantage for this market over the EU and, at least at the time of writing, the UK markets.

It is also worth mentioning developments on state-level regulations. Several US states have enacted or are considering requirements to enhance board diversity and promote sustainable investment. On 7 October 2023, California enacted its Climate Corporate Data Accountability Act (SB 253),[365] which directs the State Air Resources Board to develop regulations requiring corporations that do business in California, with annual revenues over USD 1 billion, to publicly disclose their GHG emissions. Reporting entities must provide annual disclosures for Scope 1 and Scope 2 emissions starting in 2026, and must report Scope 3 emissions starting in 2027.

The expanded scope of this regulation has three notable implications.[366] By explicitly mandating the disclosure of Scope 3 emissions, California's regulations can impact every aspect of a company's value chain, even if the SEC rules in this regard have been delayed. California's legislation also establishes the benchmark for climate-related disclosures in the US, marking the nation's inaugural mandatory climate disclosure regulation. Moreover, the legislation's jurisdiction extends to encompass many companies based outside California, both US and international corporations.[367] Because Californian regulations align with the GHG protocol, the TCFD recommendations, and the ISSB standards, investors can derive significant advantages from the extraterritorial applicability of these rules. This extension facilitates the availability of more uniform datasets, that encompass numerous companies globally. This represents a great leap forward for Californian regulation – in contrast with the highly questionable approach of the EU Commission, making corporate disclosures on Scope 1, 2, and 3 GHG emissions only voluntary, via the ESRS, subject to a materiality assessment.[368]

364 CFTC, 'Remarks of Chairman Rostin Behnam at the July 28, 2022 Financial Stability Oversight Council Meeting', 28 July 2022. www.cftc.gov/PressRoom/SpeechesTestimony/opabehnam25 accessed 23rd October 2023.

365 SB-253 Climate Corporate Data Accountability Act, Senate Bill No. 253 Chapter 382. https://leginfo.legislature.ca.gov/faces/billTextClient.xhtml?bill_id=202320240SB253 accessed 20th October 2023.

366 Isabel Verkes, 'How the New Emissions Disclosure Requirements in California and the EU will Apply to Companies Worldwide', in *Climate Disclosure Laws with Increasingly Long Arms ESG Book* (19 October 2023). www.esgbook.com/wp-content/uploads/2023/10/Climate-disclosure-Laws-1.pdf accessed 20th October 2023.

367 ibid.

368 Open Letter: Experts Plea for Advancement of the European Sustainability Reporting Standards. www.smurfitschool.ie/news/openletterexpertspleaforadvancementoftheeuropeansustainabilityreportingstandards.html accessed 23rd October 2023.

The praise for mandatory GHG emissions reduction disclosures is not just about favouring one regulatory approach over another. It has to do with ensuring real compliance with net-zero targets, which is pivotal when strengthening ESG policies and objectives. Mandatory disclosure in GHG emissions reduction contributes to a greater harmonisation of reporting requirements, higher quality of information, lower cost of capital,[369] and stricter control over what is assessed as material. All of this helps align incentives between market participants, investors, and managers.[370]

Regarding the US ESG disclosure regulations applicable to companies that trade derivatives, the SEC plays a crucial role in regulating ESG-related disclosures for public companies. The SEC mandates that public companies provide comprehensive information, encompassing ESG-related risks, deemed material for disclosure.[371] Recent updates to these regulations have homed in on human capital resources, including metrics linked to talent acquisition, retention, and professional growth. In this scenario, the objective seems to be to enhance investors protection, so they have enough information to compare companies on ESG factors.[372] It will also help to solve the problem of selective ESG disclosure as an instance of greenwashing. Despite these benefits, there are also some downfalls of imposing disclosure requirements. Those issues around jurisdiction and the query of whether a regulatory agency can legitimately exert influence to redirect the purpose of a company.[373]

Additionally, Nasdaq requires companies listed on its platform to adhere to specific diversity criteria,[374] considering it a pivotal governance factor for enhancing company performance. The mandate stipulates that these companies must have a minimum of two diverse directors on their boards. Nasdaq enforces transparency by requiring companies that do not meet these diversity criteria to provide a clear explanation for the shortfall. Another notable development involves amendments to Rule 14a-8 under the Exchange Act,[375] enabling shareholders to propose expanded ESG disclosures. These proposals often focus on topics such as climate risks, and aspects related to diversity, equity, and inclusion.

369 Jeremy Bertomeu, Anne Beyer and Ronald A. Dye, 'Capital Structure, Cost of Capital, and Voluntary Disclosures', *The Accounting Review* 86.3 (1 May 2011): 857–886.

370 John E. Core, Luzi Hail and Rodrigo S. Verdi, 'Mandatory Disclosure Quality, Inside Ownership, and Cost of Capital', *European Accounting Review* 24.1 (2015): 1–29.

371 See ESG Disclosure Simplification Act of 2019, H.R. 4329, 116th Cong. (2020); ESG Disclosure Simplification Act of 2021, H.R. 1187, 117th Cong. (2021).

372 Request for Rulemaking from Cynthia A. Williams, Jill E. Fisch and Brent J. Fields, 'Sec'y, SEC', 1 October 2018. www.sec.gov/files/rules/petitions/2018/petn4-730.pdf accessed 23rd October 2023.

373 Amanda M. Rose, 'A Response to Calls for SEC – Mandate ESG Disclosure', 8. www.sec.gov/comments/climate-disclosure/cll12-8785693-237729.pdf accessed 23rd October 2023.

374 Nasdaq, 'Board Diversity Matrix Disclosure Requirements and Examples', Last updated 6 June 2023. https://listingcenter.nasdaq.com/assets/Board%20Matrix%20Examples_Website.pdf accessed 23rd October 2023.

375 Securities and Exchange Commission, § 240.14a-8 Shareholder proposals. www.govinfo.gov/content/pkg/CFR-2011-title17-vol3/pdf/CFR-2011-title17-vol3-sec240-14a-8.pdf accessed 23rd October 2023.

In addition to mandatory disclosures, many US companies voluntarily adhere to various ESG disclosure frameworks, including the Global Reporting Initiative (GRI), the Sustainability Accounting Standards Board (SASB), which focuses on industry-specific ESG reporting, the TCFD, and the International Sustainability Standards Board (ISSB) standards. These voluntary frameworks allow companies to provide more comprehensive ESG information to stakeholders.

Final Remarks

In the context of sustainable finance, it is essential for the regulator to acknowledge the inherent limitations and challenges faced when adopting rules to promote changes of behaviour. Understanding that regulation is a dynamic process involving negotiation and strategic decision-making enables a clearer comprehension of the multiple tools to discipline market actors. Given that regulated entities' interests may frequently diverge, leading to conflicting collective and individual advantages, the use of the contract is key to supporting the adjustment of certain behaviours. However, the materialisation of sustainable development is frequently seen as a political concept closely linked to governance matters. We argue that translating the focus on sustainable development into tangible steps requires the participation of diverse societal stakeholders and legal institutions. Among these, the *contract* is a pivotal institution that wields considerable influence. It is widely recognised that contracts serve as governance mechanisms in modern economic and social interactions, therefore, the drafting of financial transactions can effectively serve the purpose of promoting greater and measurable ESG-related commitments.

We would underscore here that our position does not merely advocate for the inclusion of sustainability clauses in any financial or commercial contract. Instead, our argument endorses the concept that the central objective of the contract should align with particular and quantifiable sustainability metrics, known as KPIs. This is particularly relevant for the analysis that follows in Chapter 4 about the ESG derivatives being used in the market.

The traditional structure and operation of financial derivatives, as explained in this chapter, highlight the adaptability of these transactions to fulfil various objectives. Derivatives contracts are constructed by combining specific elements that provide counterparties with the means to raise capital and manage a range of risks. Consequently, many aspects of these transactions can be customised to meet the specific needs and interests of clients and investors. This inherent flexibility in the derivatives market enables the tailoring of transactions to address clients' unique requirements. We contend that this adaptability presents a significant opportunity for sustainable finance in this market. The high degree of flexibility, combined with the multifaceted variables influencing sustainability goals, aligns well with a market that is fundamentally founded on contractual freedom. Additionally, the characteristics of derivatives transactions can contribute to addressing certain issues in sustainable finance, such as price discovery, data collection in underlying markets, and enhanced transparency. In the next chapter, we will explore how each type of ESG derivative can achieve this objective.

The content of several regulatory reforms has been changing the landscape of the derivatives market, especially in the OTC – and with that, its traditional features as a non-standardised and self-regulated market. The reform has been clearly a huge step towards greater standardisation, increased transparency, and more regulated markets. The rules of MiFID II are designed to strengthen investor protection and to manage the risk of mis-selling, which is of relevance when trading ESG financial products. However, the derivatives market is still facing a high level of uncertainty as the treatment of ESG derivatives contracts is not uniform among the EU, UK, and the US. However, we may anticipate that, as the ESG derivatives market grows, regulators will increasingly acknowledge the potential of these transactions in promoting sustainability objectives.

The regulatory landscape discussed in this chapter is of great importance to market participants interested in ESG derivatives trading. Specifically, our analysis of regulatory instruments (such as the EU Taxonomy, the SFDR, the CSRD, ESRS, and the proposed CSDDD – all discussed earlier in the chapter) seeks to provide clarity regarding the fundamental disclosure and classification mechanisms adopted by the EU, which is at the forefront of these efforts.

These disclosure regimes encompass a wide range of rules designed to oversee the prudential framework for green assets. Notably, the revised CRR II and CRD V packages aim to establish a distinct treatment for exposures related to assets or activities significantly aligned with environmental and social objectives. Additionally, ESMA's call for the integration of sustainability assessments and product governance processes within firms' prudential measures is a significant development. This raises the important question of how to differentiate traditional derivatives used as hedging tools from transactions designed with ESG objectives at their core. Finally, we consider the potential implications of MiFID II product governance rules, assuming that regulators recognise ESG derivatives as sustainable finance products.

The UK framework for ESG comprises a comprehensive body of laws and regulations, drawing from both domestic and EU sources. These regulations span a wide range of areas that extend beyond ESG considerations. Notable components of this framework include corporate governance and company law regulations, such as the UKCGC, and the Companies Act of 2006, which delineates the responsibilities of directors, including their obligations related to ESG issues. Additionally, for companies whose securities are publicly traded on exchanges such as the LSE, the Listing Rules and DTRs apply. We highlight the increasing importance of stewardship practices, provoking the adoption of stewardship rules in 2010. These rules were further developed with the establishment of the UKSC 2020, which lay down principles guiding asset owners and managers in their interactions with companies in which they invest.

Finally, we explain how the US approach to addressing ESG concerns has largely relied on voluntary, market-led initiatives, setting it apart from Europe and the UK, where specific ESG regulations are mandated. However, such trends have witnessed noteworthy transformations in recent years, beginning with the initial set of regulations from the SEC. These rules focus on the obligation of regulated entities to disclose information about their management of climate-related risks and the steps they are taking to mitigate these risks. US regulators then established a common ground for the reporting of GHG emissions reductions, making the disclosure of audited emissions falling under both Scope 1 and Scope 2 mandatory, while Scope 3 emissions must be reported when considered significant (note that this regulatory decision opens the debate about conducting materiality assessments, and the potential shortcomings in the implementation of such requirement).

Furthermore, in a commendable approach, the CFTC's Climate Risk Unit has promoted the creation of new financial instruments to facilitate the determination of prices for climate-related financial risks and support capital allocation. These instruments include water derivatives and voluntary carbon offset markets. We believe this open approach to recognising the benefits of derivatives contracts in relation to sustainability objectives will provide the US market with a significant advantage over the EU and the UK.

Bibliography

Books

Arias-Barrera, L.C., *Regulation and Supervision of the OTC Derivatives Market* (Routledge 2018).

Black, F., 'Foreword: The Many Faces of Derivatives' in Francis, J.C., Toy, William W., and Whittaker, J.G. (eds.), *Handbook of Equity Derivatives* (Wiley Series on Financial Engineering 2000).

Culp, C., 'The Social Functions of Financial Derivatives' in Robert Kolb, R., and Overdahl, J. (eds.), *Financial Derivatives Pricing and Risk Management* (Kolb Series in Finance 2011).

Dale, R., *Risk and Regulation in Global Securities Market* (John Wiley & Sons Ltd 1996).

Davies, P., 'The UK Stewardship Code 2010–2020: From Saving the Company to Saving the Planet?' in Katelouzou, D., and Puchniak, Dan W. (eds.), *Global Shareholder Stewardship* (Cambridge University Press 2022).

Diamond, J., *Guns, Germs, and Steel: The Fates of Human Societies* (Norton 1997).

Hudson, A., *The Law on Financial Derivatives* (2nd edn, Sweet &Maxwell 1998).

Veljanovski, C., 'Strategic use of Regulation' in Baldwin, R., Cave, M., and Lodge, M. (eds.), *The Oxford Handbook of Regulation* (Oxford University Press 2010).

Articles

Awrey, D., 'The Dynamics of OTC Derivatives Regulation: Bridging the Public-Private Divide' *European Business Organization Law Review* (2010) 11.

Black, J., 'Risk and Regulatory Policy: Improving the Governance of Risk. Risk-based Regulation: Choices, Practices and Lessons Being Learnt' *OECD* (2010) 185.

Collins, H., 'Implied Terms: The Foundation in Good Faith and Fair Dealing' 67(1) *Current Legal Problems* (2014) 297.

Daugaard, D., and Ding, A., 'Global Drivers for ESG Performance: The Body of Knowledge' 14 *Sustainability* (2022) 2322.

Feder, N.M., 'Deconstructing Over-the-Counter Derivatives' *Columbia Business Law Review* (2002) 677.

Gardiner, S.M., and Hartzell-Nichols, L., 'Ethics and Global Climate Change' 3(10) *Nature Education Knowledge* (2012) 5.

Jackson, C.H., 'Have You Hedged Today? The Inevitable Advent of Consumer Derivatives' 67 *Fordham Law Review* (1999) 3206.

Johnson, C.A., 'At the Intersection of the Bank Finance and Derivatives: Who Has the Right Way?' 66 *Tennessee Law Review* (2008) 23.

Krawiec, K.D., 'Derivatives, Corporate Hedging, and Shareholder Wealth: Modigliani-Miller Forty Years Later?' *University of Illinois Law Review* (1998) 1039.

Kuprianov, A., 'The Role of Interest Rate Swaps in Corporate Finance' *Federal Reserve Bank of Richmond Economic Quarterly* (1994) 53.

Sangha, B., 'Financial Derivatives: Applications and Policy Issues' 95(1) *Business Economics January* (1995) 46.

Working Papers

Curran, B., Murdoch, J., Plyska, O., and Robins, N., 'Response to the Transition Plan Taskforce Consultation on the TPT Disclosure Framework and Implementation Guidance', The Grantham Research Institute on Climate Change and the Environment (March 2023).

ISDA, 'Interest Rate Swaps Compression: A Progress Report' (2012) <www.isda.org/a/BeiDE/irs-compression-progress-report-feb-2012.pdf > accessed 30th October 2023.

International Organizations Policy Documents and Reports

GHG Protocol, 'Corporate Value Chain (Scope 3) Accounting and Reporting Standard, Supplement to the GHG Protocol Corporate Accounting and Reporting Standard' (2011) <https://ghgprotocol.org/sites/default/files/standards/Corporate-Value-Chain-Accounting-Reporing-Standard_041613_2.pdf> accessed 20th October 2023.

IFRS, 'Sustainability Disclosure Standard General Requirements (IFRS S1)' (June 2023) <www.ifrs.org/issued-standards/ifrs-sustainability-standards-navigator/ifrs-s1-general-requirements/#> accessed 17th October 2023.

IOSCO, 'Recommendations on Sustainability-Related Practices, Policies, Procedures and Disclosure in Asset Management', Final Report, FR08/21 (November 2021) <www.iosco.org/library/pubdocs/pdf/IOSCOPD688.pdf> accessed 27th November 2023.

IPCC, '2001 Appendix II Glossary. IPCC Third Assessment Report – Climate Change 2001 Working Group III: Mitigation', Cambridge University Press (2001).

OECD, 'Managing Climate Risks and Impacts Through Due Diligence for Responsible Business Conduct: A Tool for Institutional Investors', OECD Publishing (2023) <https://doi.org/10.1787/8aee4fce-en> accessed 27th November 2023.

Paris Agreement to the United Nations Framework Convention on Climate Change, 12 December 2015, T.I.A.S. No. 16–1104.

Conference Papers

Mullins, D., 'Remarks on the Global Derivatives Study Sponsored by the Group of Thirty' (1993) ISDA Summer Conference.

US Legislation and Policy Documents

CFTC, 'CFTC Acting Chairman Behnam Establishes New Climate Risk Unit' (17 March 2021). Release Number 8368–21 <www.cftc.gov/PressRoom/PressReleases/8368-21> accessed 23rd October 2023.

CFTC, 'Releases Request for Information on Climate-Related Financial Risk' (2 June 2022) <www.cftc.gov/PressRoom/PressReleases/8541-22> accessed 20th October 2023.

CFTC, 'Remarks of Chairman Rostin Behnam at the July 28, 2022 Financial Stability Oversight Council Meeting' (28 July 2022) <www.cftc.gov/PressRoom/SpeechesTestimony/opabehnam25> accessed 23rd October 2023.

CFTC, 'Request for Information on Climate- Related Financial Risk, Federal Register/Vol. 87, No. 110/Wednesday' (8 June 2022) Notices., p. 34858–59 <www.cftc.gov/sites/default/files/2022/06/2022-12302a.pdf> accessed 20th October 2023.

FSOC, 'Report on Climate Related Financial-Risk' (2021) <https://home.treasury.gov/system/files/261/FSOC-Climate-Report.pdf>accessed 23rd October 2023.

SB-253 Climate Corporate Data Accountability Act, Senate Bill No. 253 Chapter 382 <https://leginfo.legislature.ca.gov/faces/billTextClient.xhtml?bill_id=202320240SB253> accessed 20th October 2023.

SEC, § 240.14a–8 Shareholder proposals <www.govinfo.gov/content/pkg/CFR-2011-title17-vol3/pdf/CFR-2011-title17-vol3-sec240-14a-8.pdf> accessed 23rd October 2023.

The White House, 'Executive Order on Climate-Related Financial Risk' (20 May 2021) <www.whitehouse.gov/briefing-room/presidential-actions/2021/05/20/executive-order-on-climate-related-financial-risk/> accessed 20th October 2023.

UK Legislation and Policy Documents

Companies (Directors' Report) and Limited Liability Partnerships (Energy and Carbon Report) Regulations 2018 (SI 2018/1155).

FCA, *Building a Regulatory Framework for Effective Stewardship*, Feedback to DP 10/1 (Feedback Statement, October 2019) paras 3.7 ff.

FCA, *Climate Change and Green Finance*, Discussion Paper DP18/8 (October 2018).

FCA, *FCA Climate Change Adaptation Report* (1 October 2021).

FCA, *FCA Updates on Its Sustainability Disclosure Requirements (SDR) and Investment Labels Consultation* (29 March 2023).

FCA, *Sustainability Disclosure Requirements (SDR) and Investment Labels*, CP22/20*** (October 2022).

FCA, *Sustainability Disclosure Requirements (SDR) and Investment Labels*, Discussion Paper.DP21/4 (November 2021).

FCA, *Sustainability Disclosure Requirements and Investment Labels*, Policy Statement, PS23/16 (November 2023).

GTAG, *GTAG: Advice on the Development of a UK Green Taxonomy* (October 2022).

GTAG, *Treatment of Green Financial Products Under an Evolving UK Green Taxonomy*, Green Finance Institute (September 2023).

HM Government, *Mobilising Green Investment: 2023 Green Finance Strategy* (March 2023).

HM Treasury, *Chancellor Sets Out Ambition for Future of UK Financial Services* (November 2020).

HM Treasury, *Green Finance Strategy* (London 2019).

HM Treasury, *Greening Finance: A Roadmap to Sustainable Investing* (18 October 2021).

PS23/16 (November 2023).
TPT, *Disclosure Framework* (October 2023).

EU Legislation

Directive (EU) 2022/2464 of the European Parliament and of the Council of 14 December 2022 amending Regulation (EU) No 537/2014, Directive 2004/109/EC, Directive 2006/43/EC and Directive 2013/34/EU, as regards corporate sustainability reporting.

Directive (EU) 2022/2464 of the European Parliament and of the Council of 14 December 2022 amending Regulation (EU) No 537/2014, Directive 2004/109/EC, Directive 2006/43/EC and Directive 2013/34/EU, as regards corporate sustainability reporting, [2022] OJ L 322.

Directive 2013/34/EU of the European Parliament and of the Council of 26 June 2013 on the annual financial statements, consolidated financial statements and related reports of certain types of undertakings, amending Directive 2006/43/EC of the European Parliament and of the Council and repealing Council Directives 78/660/EEC and 83/349/EEC.

Directive 2014/65/EU of the European Parliament and of the Council of 15 May 2014 on markets in financial instruments and amending Directive 2002/92/EC and Directive 2011/61/EU (recast) Text with EEA relevance.

Directive 2014/95/EU of 22 October 2014 as regards disclosure of non-financial and diversity information by certain large undertakings and groups.

EBA, 'Report: On the role of Environmental and Social Risks in the Prudential Framework', EBA/REP/2023/34 (17 October 2023) <www.eba.europa.eu/sites/default/documents/files/document_library/Publications/Reports/2023/1062711/Report%20on%20the%20role%20of%20environmental%20and%20social%20risks%20in%20the%20prudential%20framework.pdf> accessed 17th October 2023.

EU Climate Transition Benchmark (EU CTB) and the EU Paris-Aligned Benchmark (EU PAB), 'EU Technical Expert Group on Sustainable Finance, Report on Benchmarks: On Climate Benchmarks and Benchmarks: ESG Disclosures' (September 2019) <https://finance.ec.europa.eu/system/files/2019-09/190930-sustainable-finance-teg-final-report-climate-benchmarks-and-disclosures_en.pdf> accessed 17th October 2023.

EU Commission, 'Proposal for a Directive on Corporate Sustainability Due Diligence and Annex' (23 February 2022) <https://commission.europa.eu/publications/proposal-directive-corporate-sustainability-due-diligence-and-annex_en> accessed 17th October 2023.

EU Sustainable Finance Taxonomy Regulation (EU) 2020/852.

Proposal for a regulation of the European Parliament and of the Council on European green bonds, COM/2021/391 final. Political agreement reached by co-legislators on 28 February 2023.

Regulation (EU) 2019/2088 of the European Parliament and of the Council of 27 November 2019 on sustainability-related disclosures in the financial services sector, [2019] OJ L 317.

Regulation (EU) 2019/2089 of the European Parliament and of the Council of 27 November 2019 amending Regulation (EU) 2016/1011 as regards EU Climate Transition Benchmarks, EU Paris-aligned Benchmarks and sustainability-related disclosures for benchmarks, [2019] OJL 317.

Regulation (EU) 2020/852 of the European Parliament and of the Council of 18 June 2020 on the establishment of a framework to facilitate sustainable investment, and amending Regulation (EU) 2019/2088.

Regulation on OTC Derivatives, Central Counterparties and Trade Repositories known as EMIR Regulation (EU) No 648/2012.

4 What If Financial Derivatives Are Effective Tools to Hedge ESG Risks?

Introduction

This chapter is designed to explore the critical role that financial derivatives perform in any economic activity considering meeting sustainability objectives. The two main functions of financial derivatives to hedge ESG risks are: (i) risk management and aligning exposures with risk tolerance and risk management requirements; and (ii) enhancing transparency through the provision of forward information on the underlying assets. In the case of ESG investment, this is key to identifying and assessing the level of commitment and compliance towards SDGs. Here we consider whether the rising appetite for ESG investment strategies would be better served by the moderating force of regulation. Having access to a wider range of financial instruments – besides bonds, equities, and loans – complements ESG strategies for businesses. An additional area of demand for listed futures is expected from ETF market makers,[1] a strategy that will certainly have positive effects on pricing. Also, diverse market participants will seek considerable growth for structured products linked to ESG indices. For instance, clients are keen to invest in ESG products, because they think such an investment will lead to long-term investment returns, as well as creating a positive impact on their reputation. We argue that ESG derivatives ought to be regarded as *part of the process*, not as an outcome. This chapter examines various ESG derivatives available in the market at the time of writing. We analyse their terms and the relevant regulations applicable to each category. The risk-based approach aids in identifying the most significant characteristics of these transactions, as well as the challenges for the market's expansion.

To avoid confusion between real positive ESG impact and mere intentionality, financial derivatives are called to address two key fallbacks affecting current developments in sustainable finance. These are the lack of standardisation, and inconsistent levels of disclosure. This means that, through the provision of forward information on the underlying assets, financial derivatives might become a means

1 A 'market maker' is a broker that facilitates the trading of an ETF. They maintain efficient exchange of securities between buyers and sellers. This involves offering liquidity to the market, by selling units to investors and acquiring units when investors choose to sell.

DOI: 10.4324/9781003365242-4

to clarify definitions of green and brown assets, and inadequate environmental and climate data. Similarly, through the aligning of exposures with risk-tolerance and risk-management requirements, it would be possible to map how environmental risks, both physical and transitional, are transmitted to financial risk.

Having revisited the fundamentals of derivatives contracts in the previous chapter, our purpose here is to introduce the ESG derivatives transactions known at the time of writing. We explore the potential for existing derivatives to address the hedging of ESG risks, and thoroughly examine the role of sustainability-linked derivatives in driving the transition to a more sustainable economy. The chapter also emphasises the significance of voluntary carbon credits derivatives markets, and highlights the need to bolster the underlying primary market, to ensure its effectiveness in promoting sustainability. Overall, this chapter aims to shed light on the potential of financial derivatives contracts in advancing sustainability goals, and fostering a more responsible and environmentally conscious financial landscape.

Typology of ESG Derivatives

When delimiting the role of derivatives in hedging ESG-related risks, a categorisation of contracts has been generally accepted by the industry:[2] firstly, traditional derivatives (that add an ESG-related KPI); second, those that fall within the new category of sustainability-linked derivatives; and a third growing market of contracts in carbon markets, where derivatives are traded to hedge the risk associated to net-zero-carbon targets. Among this last category we may find derivatives transactions that allow companies to trade carbon allowances.[3] In this section, our purpose is to understand how these different transactions are designed to meet diverse ESG targets, and what are the opportunities and the potential downfalls they present to the use of derivatives transactions as effective tools to manage ESG risks.

Traditional Derivatives With an Added ESG KPI

There are some potential critiques to proposing traditional derivatives with additional ESG KPIs as being a standalone type of ESG derivatives. However, we bring this first category to the study to clarify how the role of derivatives in sustainability is, in general terms, in the provision of risk management. Clearly, this is not a novel or completely different type of hedging. Instead, we refer in this category to typical derivatives playing their fundamental role of supporting good practices in

2 Regulation Asia Interview: Scott O'Malia, 'Derivatives Will Help Drive Net Zero Transition', April 2023. https://youtu.be/f8fdntra95E?si=akQKTU4xDD35y_nR accessed 3rd October 2023.

3 Dean Naumowicz and Delyth Hughes, 'The Role of Sustainability-Linked Derivatives in Meeting Global ESG Goals', *Butterworths Journal of International Banking and Financial Law* (October 2021): 628.

risk management. As massive amounts of money are needed to finance transition, derivatives – as hedging tools – are key to managing interest rate risks, foreign exchange risk, credit risk, and liquidity risk.

The concept of ESG derivatives has been recognised for several years, aiming to encompass the various transactions drafted to hedge ESG risks. Standard & Poor reports that more than 1,000 of their credit rating decisions in the 2015–2017 period were linked to ESG concerns.[4] The expansion of this market is evident in the evolution of ESG indices,[5] the introduction of corresponding equity index futures and option contracts,[6] and the acceptance of CDS indices derived from ESG criteria[7] (e.g., iTraxx MSCI ESG Screened Europe CDS). This is not surprising, since CDSs are a common credit derivative in debt financing. Despite some critics,[8] the CDS indices are praised as tools that lower the cost of capital for companies compliant with ESG targets,[9] and as widely used high-liquid fixed-income instruments.[10]

Credit Default Swaps and ESG

There is still considerable debate when analysing the relationship between firms' risks (mainly credit risk) and ESG factors. Barth, Hübel, and Scholz[11] summarise the existing contradictory positions: while some argue that ESG considerations may mitigate firm risks, by potentially leading to increased and less volatile cash flows, others see that investments in ESG could be inefficiently using limited resources,

4 Standard & Poor's, 'How Environmental and Climate Risks and Opportunities Factor into Global Corporate Ratings – An Update', 2017. www.spglobal.com/ratings/en/research/pdf-articles/171109-how-environmental-and-climate-risks-and-opportunities-factor-into-global-corporate-ratings-an-update accessed 3rd October 2023.

5 Euronext, ESG Indices. https://live.euronext.com/en/products/indices/esg-indices accessed 3rd October 2023.

6 *See* Eurex, 'Product Coverage ESG Futures & Options', August 2023. www.eurex.com/resource/blob/2665714/e772e787f0997c11ca08372ee321dc65/data/presentation_ESG_product_coverage.pdf accessed 3rd October 2023.

7 Dean Naumowicz and Delyth Hughes, 'The Role of Sustainability-Linked Derivatives in Meeting Global ESG Goals' (n 3) 628.

8 Nikou Asgari, 'Slow Start for CDS Index Reveals Challenge for Sustainable Investment', *Financial Times*, 6 August 2020. www.ft.com/content/7a987c0c-9b5f-4daf-8b1d-2c265ea91fce accessed 3rd October 2023.

9 Ulf Erlandsson, 'ESG in CDS Indices – A Practitioner Perspective'. https://img1.wsimg.com/blobby/go/946d6aac-e6cc-430a-8898-520cf90f5d3e/downloads/AFIIQN_ESGCDSIndex.pdf?ver=1633964330185.

10 Oscar Britse Johan Jarnmo, 'Greenhouse Gas Footprint Minimisation of Credit Default Swap Baskets', Master Thesis, 30 ECTS Master of Science in Industrial Engineering and Management Department of Mathematics and Mathematical Statistics Ume ̊a University, Spring 2018, 8. http://umu.diva-portal.org/smash/get/diva2:1220081/FULLTEXT01.pdf accessed 3rd October 2023.

11 Florian Barth, Benjamin Hübel and Hendrik Scholz, 'ESG and Corporate Credit Spreads', *Journal of Risk Finance* 23.2 (May 2019): 1. https://joint-research-centre.ec.europa.eu/system/files/2019-07/3_1benjamin_hubel_paper.pdf accessed 3rd October 2023.

which will result in lower cash flows and elevated firm risk.[12] In this scenario, most of the literature is focused on investigating the influence of ESG factors on credit risks.[13] Such studies tend to follow either market-traded debt instruments, such as corporate bonds and credit ratings, or nonmarket traded debt, which includes interest rates on bank loans or cost of capital estimates. Within this context, identifying the relationship between ESG factors and the spreads of CDSs[14] is particularly helpful, to understand the benefits and shortcomings of adopting hedging strategies that involve CDSs and the performance of CDS spreads.

Exploring the risk-mitigation perspective of ESG factors concerning credit risk[15] reveals a correlation between higher ESG ratings and reduced CDS spreads.[16] This indicates lower credit risk for companies.[17] The existing literature also tends to agree on how corporate sustainability positively affects CDS spread.[18] The baseline for this assertion relies heavily on the type of data available to assess corporate sustainability. This is the publicly reported data reflected in common ESG scores (i.e., data on emissions, use of resources, human rights, product liability, innovation, workforce, management, corporate social responsibility, and shareholders).[19]

In this context, aligned with the rationale of risk and uncertainty followed in this book, we argue that the potential of CDSs as a hedging tool to manage ESG risks might be affected by two shortcomings: issues regarding nonfinancial data reporting, and endogeneity.

It has been widely debated that there are certain concerns regarding the trustworthiness of the data and the methodologies employed in ESG scores.[20] Common criticisms often revolve around data quality, comprehensiveness, and comparability. Both market participants and ESG credit rating agencies acknowledge the substantial challenges posed by the quality of nonfinancial data, which often do

12 A. Goss and G. S. Roberts, 'The Impact of Corporate Social Responsibility on the Cost of Bank Loans', *Journal of Banking and Finance* 35 (2011): 1794–1810, cited in Florian Barth, Benjamin Hübel and Hendrik Scholz, 'ESG and Corporate Credit Spreads' (n 11) 169–190. Emerald Group Publishing Limited.

13 See S. Kim and Z. Li (Frank), 'Understanding the Impact of ESG Practices in Corporate Finance', *Sustainability* 13 (2021). 3746.

14 Florian Barth, Benjamin Hübel and Hendrik Scholz, 'ESG and Corporate Credit Spreads' (n 11) 2.

15 A. Goss and G. S. Roberts, 'The Impact of Corporate Social Responsibility on the Cost of Bank Loans' (n 12) 3.

16 See G. Inderst and F. Stewart, *Incorporating Environmental, Social and Governance Factors into Fixed Income Investment* (World Bank, 2018).

17 See Mitch Reznick and Michael Viehs, 'Pricing ESG Risk in Credit Markets', Hermes Credit and Hermes EOS Research Paper Q2 2017; E. Landry and M. Castillo-Lazaro.

18 Stefano Caiazza, Giuseppe Galloppo and Giovanni La Rosa, 'The Mitigation Role of Corporate Sustainability: Evidence from the CDS Spread', *Finance Research Letters* 52 (2023): 103561.

19 G. Capelle-Blancard, P. Crifo, M. A. Diaye, R. Oueghlissi and B. Scholtens, 'Sovereign Bond Yield Spreads and Sustainability: An Empirical Analysis of OECD Countries', *Journal of Banking & Finance* 98 (2019): 156–169.

20 Alexandre Clément, Élisabeth Robinot and Léo Trespeuch, 'The Use of ESG Scores in Academic Literature: A Systematic Literature Review', *Journal of Enterprising Communities: People and Places in the Global Economy* (2023).

not align seamlessly with measurement methodologies for evaluating corporate sustainability performance.

In this context, there is an anticipation that regulators should intervene to address these concerns. Regulatory tools (like the European CSRD and the SEC's Climate Disclosure Rule Proposal, along with the ultimate version of the standards released by the ISSB) had the intention – but fell short – of establishing a global standard for corporate sustainability and climate-related disclosures. De Arriba-Sellier[21] foresees limitations in the ISSB's ability to deliver comprehensive, trustworthy, and universally comparable sustainability information. Additionally, he argues that, due to differing approaches adopted by the SEC and the CSRD, the ISSB struggles to establish itself as a global standard-setting instrument.[22]

Against this background, we argue that the positive correlation between corporate sustainability and CDS spread will only be completely reliable when advancement in ESG reporting truly enhances transparency and delivers its transformative potential for fostering corporate sustainability practices, in line with the SDGs and the Paris Agreement.[23]

Along with the rising concerns around data quality and reporting, the integration of corporate sustainability and CDSs should also consider the endogeneity issue.[24] Albuquerque et al.[25] explain that endogeneity exists when sustainability and risks are influenced by unobservable firm-related factors. These are factors that can be understood as potential future events (i.e., risks or uncertainties) that might affect the sustainability–risk relationship. Such factors suggest there may be concomitant unknown determinants of credit risk and ESG performance. Likewise, companies with lower risks face fewer impediments to invest in sustainable activities, whilst investments in such activities may lead to a reduction in company risks, including credit risk.[26]

Hence, acknowledging the potential impact of the endogeneity problem, the development of hedging strategies tilizing CDSs could be swayed by unobservable firm-specific variables. This implies that, while CDSs related to ESG risks might appear to demonstrate how corporate sustainability positively impacts

21 Nathan de Arriba-Sellier, 'The ISSB's New Standards: Breaking Ground or Low Hanging Fruits?', The ECGI Blog, 13 July 2023. www.ecgi.global/blog/issb%E2%80%99s-new-standards-breaking-ground-or-low-hanging-fruits?mc_cid=073f3c5cd3&mc_eid=3b6627f4d6 accessed 3rd October 2023.

22 ibid.

23 See Paulo Câmara, 'ESG Disclosure Rules: New Developments as Potential Catalysts of the "Cascade Effect"', The ECGI Blog, 26 September 2023. www.ecgi.global/blog/esg-disclosure-rules-new-developments-potential-catalysts-%E2%80%98cascade-effect%E2%80%99 accessed 3rd October 2023.

24 Stefano Caiazza, Giuseppe Galloppo and Giovanni La Rosa, 'The Mitigation Role of Corporate Sustainability: Evidence from the CDS Spread' (n 18).

25 R. Albuquerque, Y. Koskinen and C. Zhang, 'Corporate Social Responsibility and Firm Risk: Theory and Empirical Evidence', *Management Science* 65.10 (2019): 4451–4469 cited in Stefano Caiazza, Giuseppe Galloppo and Giovanni La Rosa, 'The Mitigation Role of Corporate Sustainability: Evidence from the CDS Spread' (n 18).

26 ibid.

CDS spreads, there could be additional hidden factors influencing this correlation. These factors, being inherently unidentified, are nearly impossible to quantify. Being aware of this potential distortion within the CDS market enables us to assert that CDSs play a contributory role in the alignment of corporate sustainability and investment strategies and ESG goals – though they do not guarantee alignment.

Despite these challenges, there is also a shared recognition of how poor ESG practices can result in the deterioration of a company's enterprise value.[27] This, in turn, adversely affects both equity and credit investors.[28] This discussion centres around the measurement of ESG risks, and it is precisely here where CDS transactions contribute to provide a source of greater transparency to the market. While there are correlations between the scores employed to gauge ESG risks and credit risk, there is also a significant variability in these scores within each rating category adopted by credit rating agencies. Consequently, the market cannot rely on ESG ratings with certainty. Some market participants[29] have addressed this, by developing pricing models capable of quantifying the impact of ESG risks on credit spreads. Their foundation is the observed positive connection between ESG scores and CDS spreads. The importance of solving this issue is critical in understanding the role of CDS transactions in promoting ESG goals.

Reznick and Viehs[30] explain that, in the context of CDSs, the pricing of ESG risks operates differently than in other types of securities, such as equity or cash bonds. This is because in the latter, features such as coupons, maturity structure, and interest rates make it difficult to separate the real impact of ESG risks. In the case of CDS, data is properly divided to clearly identify issue-level and external events, which, in turn, provides greater discoverability of credit risk across CDS indices. This shows the importance of CDS transactions, to measure not only the closest-to-real price of ESG risks, but also in accurately measuring a company's current level of ESG-risk exposure, as well as the direction that said company is likely to follow. Likewise, the measurement of ESG risk by means of structuring CDSs helps investors to analyse the stability of expected returns;[31] companies with lower ESG scores tend to produce more unpredictable returns.[32]

Within the numerous studies supporting the positive relationship between the adoption of ESG factors and the reduction of a company's CDS spreads, there is the recognition that the material effect of ESG is different, according to

27 Rob Bauer and Daniel Hann, 'Corporate Environmental Management and Credit Risk', ECCE Working Paper, University Maastricht, The European Centre for Corporate Engagement, 2010.

28 Mitch Reznick and Michael Viehs, 'Pricing ESG Risk in Credit Markets', Hermes Credit and Hermes EOS Research Paper Q2, 2017, 2. www.hermes-investment.com/uploads/2021/11/3fde0f24c45f95b3b633bd66ecda3805/hermes-credit-esg-paper-april-2017.pdf accessed 4th October 2023.

29 ibid.

30 ibid., 3.

31 ibid.

32 Rob Bauer and Daniel Hann, 'Corporate Environmental Management and Credit Risk' (n 27).

the size of the company and the market. Billio et al.[33] affirm that the impact of sustainability seems to be robust for companies with low leverage and substantial market capitalisation, but it does not yield significant benefits for smaller, debt-laden companies. Additionally, the risk-reduction effect of ESG tends to be most pronounced at moderate levels of ESG efforts, with less noticeable effects at both very high and very low ESG levels. Lastly, they note that the existing literature agrees that the risk-mitigating impact of ESG practices is more apparent in the EU[34] than in the US.[35] Using these patterns, we would contend that employing CDSs for mitigating ESG risks offers advantages that extend beyond the primary risk-management role. Nevertheless, both the regulatory environment and the company's specific characteristics have a part in determining the extent to which CDSs can enhance the tangible impact pursued by these ESG investment strategies.

Although there have been some discrepancies in the market, the adoption of the ITraxx main index from 22 June 2020 reflected the opportunities that CDS transactions bring to the promotion of sustainability objectives. The rationale of the index is to provide investors with the opportunity to gain exposure (either long or short) to the risk and return characteristics of a portfolio consisting of 125 highly liquid CDSs referencing European investment-grade bonds. It was designed to attract trading volumes of approximately EUR 1.5 trillion annually. One of the key features of the ITraxx main index is the mechanism of exclusion, which is expected to contribute to a better selection of issuers. The first step consists of applying a values-based screen, seeking to exclude any issuer that exceeds given thresholds of revenue coming from activities including alcohol, weapons, and thermal coal. Then, in the second step, any company exposed to major controversies regarding certain international sustainability and social responsibility principles is excluded. Finally, the process ends with an assessment of issuers' management of long-term, financially material ESG risks.

Options and Futures and ESG

Equity index futures and options contracts linked to ESG benchmarks offer managers valuable tools for hedging their ESG investments, executing their investment strategies, and optimising the management of cash flows into and out of their ESG funds. These types of transactions are useful, as they provide greater information about market dynamics and enhance transparency.[36] One central feature of index

33 Monica Billio, Michele Costola, Iva Hristova, Carmelo Latino and Loriana Pelizzon, 'Sustainable Finance: A Journey Toward ESG and Climate Risk', SAFE Working Paper No. 349, April 2022.

34 See D. Drago, C. Carnevale and R. Gallo, 'Do Corporate Social Responsibility Ratings Affect Credit Default Swap Spreads?', *Corporate Social Responsibility and Environmental Management* 26.3 (2019): 644–652.

35 Florian Barth, Benjamin Hübel and Hendrik Scholz, 'ESG and Corporate Credit Spreads' (n 11).

36 Colleen Baker, 'Derivatives and ESG', *American Business Law Journal* 59. 4 (Winter 2022): 745.

derivatives is how these transactions help to enhance price discovery[37] and information flow between correlated markets.[38] Within these transactions, there has been a consistent expansion of ESG indices monitoring various facets of listed companies' ESG performance. The popularity of current ESG indices stems from the fact that investment managers can gain deeper insights into investment choices when employing sustainable indices, compared to traditional conventional ones.[39] Since the investment approach aims for optimal diversification, considering both types of indices could be the most effective strategy. Furthermore, corporate executives should use ESG indices to benchmark their performance against other market participants, and stay up to date on industry developments.[40]

Prominent derivative exchanges currently provide futures and options linked to numerous ESG indices. The introduction of new futures and options based on well-established ESG indices has provided asset managers with cost-effective and highly precise execution strategies.[41] In October 2018, Nasdaq launched its OMXS30 ESG futures, which excluded a tobacco company from the flagship Stockholm 30 index. However, Eurex has emerged as a leader in the development of listed ESG futures and options. In February 2019, the German exchange commenced trading in several ESG indices, including the Euro Stoxx 50 low-carbon ESG index, the Stoxx 600 ESG-X index, and the Stoxx Europe Climate Impact index. Currently, Eurex offers trading in 12 ESG-linked futures and options contracts, with plans in the pipeline for additional launches. Several other exchanges have also entered the ESG derivatives arena, including CME, ICE, Japan Exchange, Euronext, CBOE, and TMX – all of which now provide ESG-linked futures or options contracts.[42]

One downfall of the negotiation of these types of derivatives transactions may come from the 'home bias' phenomenon. Home bias has been largely studied in the context of equity and bond ETFs under the context of ESG schemes;[43] it occurs when investors are discouraged to diversify their portfolio by including foreign financial instruments. Although home bias used to be attributed to barriers created by market dynamics or regulatory burdens, there is another prominent cause that is

37 Wei Peng Chen, Huimin Chung, Donald Lien, 'Price Discovery in the S&P 500 Index Derivatives Markets', *International Review of Economics & Finance* 45 (2016): 438–452.

38 Doojin Ryu, Heejin Yang, 'Price Disagreements and Adjustments in Index Derivatives Markets', *Economics Letters* 151 (2017): 104–106.

39 M. Jain, G. D. Sharma and M. Srivastava, 'Can Sustainable Investment Yield Better Financial Returns: A Comparative Study of ESG Indices and MSCI Indices', *Risks* 7 (2019): 15.

40 Antonio Vives and Baljit Wadhwa, 'Sustainability Indices in Emerging Markets: Impact on Responsible Practices and Financial Market Development', *Journal of Sustainable Finance and Investment* 2 (2012): 318–337.

41 Auciti, 'Special Report ESG: The Opportunity for the Sell-Side', December 2020. www.acuiti.io/wp-content/uploads/2020/12/ESG-the-opportunity-for-the-sell-side.pdf accessed 5th October 2023.

42 ibid.

43 Jasper Chan and Minchan Kim, 'ESG Performance in Exchange Traded Funds (ETFs) and Fixed Income in the Context of Home Bias', School of Economics and Management, Lund University, 29 May 2020, 5. https://lup.lub.lu.se/luur/download?func=downloadFile&recordOId=9014478&fileOId=9014487 accessed 4th October 2023.

especially relevant in the case of ESG investments. The information asymmetries between domestic and foreign investors affect large and small firms to different degrees.[44] We argue that the lack of consistency surrounding the nonfinancial data needed for ESG investments and the inadequate information on foreign investments are potential causes of home bias.[45] The baseline of this assertion comes from the divergent and noncomparable sources of sustainability-related data in different markets worldwide.[46] As a company's environment disclosures translate into higher ESG scores,[47] the lack of consistent and comparable sources of nonfinancial data may reduce investor appetite to trade foreign financial instruments – this, in turn, leaves most of these products being traded in large and more regulated international markets. Indeed, when investors are inclined to hedge against unforeseen changes in their investment opportunities, home bias might be accentuated.[48]

Attending to the growing interest in financing renewable energy, options and futures are also being used to hedge for price risk related to renewable energy production and related projects.[49] Baker identifies the types of contracts included in this category: 'power purchase agreements (PPAs), renewable energy certificates (RECs) futures, wind index futures, renewable identification numbers (RINs) futures and low carbon fuel standard futures'.[50]

One common feature of these products is to provide a competitive environment in which market participants face new challenges, due to risks and uncertainties triggered by the future prices. For instance, the price of electricity is characterised by high volatility. To mitigate market participant exposure, energy derivatives allow trading (e.g., futures) that commits the parties to fulfil their buying or selling obligations on a future date at a strike price. In this market, one of the challenges is how to accurately value futures contracts,[51] as this market exhibits high complexity regarding energy price series.[52] Arango suggests a potential solution that involves

44 Jun-Koo Kang and Rene M. Stulz, 'Why is there a Home Bias? An Analysis of Foreign Portfolio Equity Ownership in Japan', Working Paper Series Center on Japanese Economy and Business Graduate School of Business, Columbia University, February 1996, 5. https://academiccommons.columbia.edu/doi/10.7916/D8697B17/download accessed 4th October 2023.

45 Alan Greenspan, 'Global Finance – is it Slowing?', Chairman of the Board of Governors of the US Federal Reserve System, at the Bank of France International Symposium on Monetary Policy, Economic Cycle, and Financial Dynamics, Paris, France, (via Satellite), 7 March 2003. www.bis.org/review/r030311b.pdf accessed 4th October 2023.

46 Tarun Kumar Soni, 'Demystifying the Relationship Between ESG and SDG Performance: Study of Emerging Economies', *Investment Management and Financial Innovations* 20.3 (2023): 1–12. www.businessperspectives.org/images/pdf/applications/publishing/templates/article/assets/18424/IMFI_2023_03_Soni.pdf accessed 4th October 2023.

47 ibid.

48 R. M. Stulz, 'A Model of International Asset Pricing', *Journal of Financial Economics* 9 (1981): 383–406.

49 Colleen Baker, 'Derivatives and ESG' (n 36) 746.

50 ibid.

51 A. Arango-Londoño, 'Modelo de valoración de contratos en Derivex *[Contract Valuation Model on Derivatives]*'. Universidad Nacional de Colombia, 2023.

52 ibid.

adopting a decision model comprising a decision tree and a price evolution simulation model. This model accounts for different scenarios that can arise in electricity market operations, and incorporates probabilities associated with hydrology and demand factors.[53]

Examining the recent upheaval in the European energy market, due to the Russian invasion of Ukraine, provides insights into how price dynamics differ among energy products. These variations depend on factors such as ease of storage, transportation, and substitutability.[54] Any form of energy market shock is immediately transmitted to the derivatives market, where margin requirements on futures and swap contracts heighten counterparty credit risk; that's why the use of central clearing is perceived as a moderating solution to better risk management in this market. Likewise, the challenges related to liquidity highlight the need to assess the ability of collateral methodologies to respond to market stress, and enhance the liquidity readiness of all participants in the derivatives market.[55]

In the context of renewable energy, the PPAs are useful contracts. In a PPA, an energy consumer (buyer) agrees to a lengthy electricity supply contract with a plant operator (seller). The agreement governs the provision of electricity at a fixed priced, or a corresponding financial compensation.[56] The specific quantity of energy may not be known at the time of the agreement; both parties are protecting themselves against price fluctuations. Plant operators view PPAs as an opportunity to safeguard their revenue generation from renewable energy facilities. These agreements not only provide access to various financing sources for both current and future investments, but also ensure a stable power supply, consequently bolstering the creditworthiness of plant operators.

In the renewable electricity segment, solutions can be achieved either by directly constructing a renewable energy asset,[57] or by procuring green power from a third-party project.[58] In both instances, parties acquire renewable energy certificates. PPAs are part of the strategy to secure power from a renewable energy asset, and

53 ibid.

54 Oana Furtuna, Alberto Grassi, Annalaura Ianiro, Kristina Kallage, Robert Koci, Francesca Lenoci, Andrzej Sowiński and Francesco Vacirca, 'Financial Stability Risks from Energy Derivatives Markets', *Financial Stability Review*, November 2022. www.ecb.europa.eu/pub/financial-stability/fsr/special/html/ecb.fsrart202211_01~173476301a.en.html#toc8 accessed 4th October 2023.

55 ibid.

56 F. Huneke, S. Göß, J. Österreicher and O. Dahroug, 'Power Purchase Agreements: Financial Model for Renewable Energies', Energy Brainpool, Whitepaper, Berlin, 16 February 2018. https://enb-cs.e-fork.net/sites/default/files/2023-01/ppa-energy_brainpool-02_2018.pdf accessed 5th October 2023.

57 See IFC, 'Concessions for Infrastructure: A Guide to Their Design and Award', World Bank Technical Paper No. 399 Finance, Private Sector, and Infrastructure Network Annex 2: 'A Guide to Power Purchase Agreements', 1998, 160. https://ppp.worldbank.org/public-private-partnership/sites/ppp.worldbank.org/files/ppp_testdumb/documents/concessions_fulltoolkit.pdf accessed 5th October 2023.

58 M. Stanitsas, K. Kirytopoulos and E. Vareilles, 'Facilitating Sustainability Transition Through Serious Games: A Systematic Literature Review', *Journal of Cleaner Production* 208 (2019): 924–936.

in this context, they are regarded as effective instruments to mitigate development risks and capitalise on financial opportunities for market actors.[59]

The PPA market has developed two types of agreements: physical PPA and virtual PPA (VPPA). While the first type of agreement requires the corporate buyer to take ownership of the electrons produced by the renewable energy project (with the subsequent responsibility to sell the electrons in the wholesale electricity market), in the VPPA, the buyer neither owns nor is responsible for the physical electrons. Instead, the agreement gives a fixed cash flow to the energy project developer, while providing the energy consumer with a floating cash flow that varies according to the project energy production and sales in the market[60] and RECs.[61] An REC (also known as a 'green tag,' 'green certificate,' or 'renewable energy credit') is a certificate that signifies the production of one megawatt-hour (MWh) of electricity from a qualified renewable energy source.[62] Each REC provides details about the source of generation, its location, and the year of generation (often called 'vintage'). RECs are commonly viewed as a representation of the environmental attributes associated with renewable energy production.

PPAs hold appeal for power projects involving a public sector purchaser. In such scenarios, negotiating PPAs serves several crucial purposes, such as ensuring predictable revenues, managing competitive pressures, addressing major customer needs, and ensuring reliable supply.[63] Although PPAs are especially attractive vehicles for corporates – as they offer the opportunity to reduce energy cost by greening their operations and taking a more strategic approach to procuring renewable power – there are also risks triggered by this market.

The first risk is the complexity of the agreement for new or inexperienced participants, which we could locate as a form of information asymmetry. For companies new to this market, there is a need for a change of mindset.[64] Firms are accustomed to a market where they purchase electricity for 1–3 years ahead, and the key factor in purchasing choice is the supplier that offers lower prices.

59 M. Stanitsas and K. Kirytopoulos, 'Sustainable Energy Strategies for Power Purchase Agreements (PPAs)', *Sustainability* 15 (2023): 6638.

60 Gabriel Chan, 'Assessing a Solar Project and a Virtual Power Purchase Agreement Between the Red Lake Nation and the Minnesota Department of Transportation', Office of Research and Innovation, Final Report 2023-12, March 2023. https://cts-d8resmod-prd.oit.umn.edu/pdf/mndot-2023-12.pdf accessed 6th December 2023.

61 Rachit Kansal, 'Virtual Power Purchase Agreement: Introduction to the Virtual Power Purchase Agreement', Rocky Mountain Institute, November 2018, 3. https://rmi.org/wp-content/uploads/2018/12/rmi-brc-intro-vppa.pdf accessed 5th October 2023.

62 World Resources Institute, 'Bottom Line on Renewable Energy Certificates', 20 November 2008. www.wri.org/research/bottom-line-renewable-energy-certificates accessed 5th October 2023.

63 World Bank, 'Power Purchase Agreements (PPAs) and Energy Purchase Agreements (EPAs)', October 2021. https://ppp.worldbank.org/public-private-partnership/sector/energy/energy-power-agreements/power-purchase-agreements accessed 5th October 2023.

64 Kasper Walet, 'Challenges and Risks of Corporate PPAs' (Part 3 of PPA Series)', 2 March 2016. www.linkedin.com/pulse/challenges-risks-corporate-ppas-part-3-ppa-series-kasper-walet/ accessed 5th October 2023.

In the PPA market, by contrast, buyers have to accept a lengthy agreement (e.g., 10–15 years) with a renewable project. Additionally, the greater complexity of the PPA market may represent a barrier for smaller companies that have insufficient resources to access it.

Another downside of the PPA market is aggravated in times of extreme volatility.[65] As was noted in 2022, an increase in commodity market prices leads to higher expenses for developers of renewable energy projects. As a result, these additional costs end up being transferred to buyers, causing significant disruptions in the PPA markets. The push-up of PPA prices is also fuelled by the rising cost of financing the construction of new projects.[66] Additionally, experts anticipate insufficient hedging scope of PPAs. Understanding that major infrastructure projects carried out to promote renewable projects triggered a wide range of risks (e.g., price, liquidity, volume, credit, and profile risk), the PPA hedging market is relatively small.[67] We argue the need to integrate this instrument to new forms of hedging, to achieve the best protection possible for companies.

Future markets to trade RECs allow developers to raise funds by entering contracts to sell the certificates. The buyer, however, will not actually receive them until after the power is produced.[68] Companies with exposure to electricity and renewable energy markets use futures to better manage their risks.

As with PPAs, despite the benefits of the RECs futures market, there are some shortcomings that should be considered before negotiating contracts.[69] The mere creation or promotion of the RECs market does not automatically ensure environmental benefits. This is because, as long as the demand for RECs does not surpass the supply of fossil fuel generation, the latter will still be utilised elsewhere, resulting in no real change unless overall consumption decreases.[70] Moreover, as REC markets are delimited by jurisdictions, the conditions regarding prices and incentives will vary across markets.[71] As a result, the market fails to provide a real global solution to pollution and environmental goals. Besides this, the structure of the market may also pose some further challenges – as RECs can only be sold once, there is restricted liquidity, and little to no opportunity for speculation. Added to

65 Carolyn Addi and Paul Hill, 'Navigating the Ups and Downs of the Power Purchase Agreement (PPA) Market: How to Set Your Company Up for Success', South Pole, 3 February 2023. www.southpole.com/blog/ppa-markets-challenges-success accessed 5th October 2023.

66 ibid.

67 Jakub Pilc, 'Corporate PPAs: Are You Covering All the Risks?', *DNV*. www.dnv.com/article/corporate-ppas-are-you-covering-all-the-risks-179426 accessed 5th October 2023.

68 https://hejc.environment.harvard.edu/files/hejc/files/clark_renewable_energy_certificates.pdf.

69 E. Holt, J. Sumner and L. Bird, *Role of Renewable Energy Certificates in Developing New Renewable Energy Projects* (N. P., 2011). www.osti.gov/biblio/1018490 accessed 5th October 2023.

70 J. L. Holechek, 'A Global Assessment: Can Renewable Energy Replace Fossil Fuels by 2050?', *Sustainability* 14 (2022): 4792.

71 Inês Campos, Guilherme Pontes Luz, Esther Marín-González, Swantje Gährs, Stephen Hall and Lars Holstenkamp, 'Regulatory Challenges and Opportunities for Collective Renewable Energy Prosumers in the EU', *Energy Policy*, 138 (2020): 111212.

high risk and volatility, these constraints may deter market participants embarking on long-term investments.[72]

Catastrophe Weather Derivatives

There is also the category of catastrophe weather derivatives – which must be differentiated from its predecessor, weather derivatives.[73] Whilst the latter is conceived to hedge weather risks such as temperature, humidity, rainfall, snowfall, stream flow, and wind,[74] catastrophe weather derivatives are meant to assist the management of risks caused by hurricanes, tornadoes, and windstorms, among other extreme weather events.[75]

Following the notion of risk and uncertainty as methodological lenses to understand the role of ESG derivatives, it is first important to elucidate the meaning of 'catastrophe risks'. Posner[76] classifies catastrophe risks into three groups: scientific accidents, other unintended man-made catastrophes, and intentional catastrophes. For our study, we understand that the ESG factors may encompass all of these kinds of catastrophe risks. Therefore, it is pivotal to see how the assessment process begins with the collection of essential technical data, to estimate (to the extent possible) the likelihood of occurrence of certain ESG risks.[77] The aim is to anticipate and measure physical and monetary outcomes, as well as assessing the viability of different financial instruments to mitigate the effects of such risks.

The origins of catastrophe derivatives can be traced back to products such as Catastrophe Swaps (CAT swaps),[78] as a type of insurance-linked securities (ILS),[79] which are structured around catastrophic events as the underlying assets. Reinsurers

72 Christopher B. Berendt, 'A State-Based Approach to Building a Liquid National Market for Renewable Energy Certificates: The REC-EX Model', *The Electricity Journal* 19.5 (2006): 54–68.

73 Patrick L. Brockett, Mulong Wang and Chuanhou Yang, 'Weather Derivatives and Weather Risk Management', *Risk Management and Insurance Review* 8 (2005): 127–140.

74 ibid.

75 Ivana Stulec, Kristina Petljak and Tomislav Bakovic, 'Effectiveness of Weather Derivatives as a Hedge Against the Weather Risk in Agriculture', *Agricultural Economics – Czech* 62.8 (2016): 356–362. www.old-aj.cz/publicFiles/188_2015-AGRICECON.pdf accessed 14th September 2023.

76 Richard A. Posner, 'What are the Catastrophic Risks, and How Catastrophic Are They?', *Catastrophe: Risk and Response* (Oxford University Press, 2004; online edn, Oxford Academic, 12 November 2020) 21.

77 Richard A. Posner, 'How to Evaluate the Catastrophic Risks and the Possible Responses to Them', *Catastrophe: Risk and Response* (Oxford University Press, 2004; online edn, Oxford Academic, 12 November 2020). https://doi-org.basesbiblioteca.uexternado.edu.co/10.1093/oso/9780195178135.003.0006 accessed 3rd October 2023.

78 Carsten Kretzler and Fred Wagner, 'The Catastrophe Risk Exchange (Catex) in New York: An Exchange and Electronic Processing System for Reinsurance Business', *The Geneva Papers on Risk and Insurance. Issues and Practice* 25.1 (2000): 136–153. www.jstor.org/stable/41952517 accessed 14th September 2023.

79 E. Michel-Kerjan and F. Morlaye, 'Extreme Events, Global Warming, and Insurance-Linked Securities: How to Trigger the "Tipping Point"', *Geneva Papers on Risk and Insurance. Issues and Practice* 33 (2008): 153–176.

engage in these agreements as a means to effectively manage such risks. CAT Swaps come in two primary forms: portfolio CAT swaps and financial CAT swaps.[80] Portfolio CAT Swaps are typically traded among reinsurers and insurers to exchange portfolios of catastrophe risk exposures, which may or may not be correlated. If the exchanged risk materialises, the party assuming that risk would be obligated to make a contingent payment to the other party. One illustrative example of a CAT swap is the one agreed between Swiss Re and Mitsui Sumitomo Insurance Company in 2003. The CAT swap arranged a USD 100 million catastrophe risk swap,[81] structured in two risk exchanges of USD 50 million each: Japan typhoon for North Atlantic hurricane, and Japan typhoon for European windstorm. The swap agreement entailed two high-risk scenarios for both parties, as Swiss Re aimed to exchange a portion of its North Atlantic hurricane and European windstorm risks for Mitsui Sumitomo's Japanese typhoon exposure. This arrangement enabled Mitsui Sumitomo and Swiss Re to enhance the diversification of their risk portfolios by trading segments of Japanese catastrophe event exposure for North Atlantic and European catastrophe risks. The advantages of employing CAT swaps for insurers and reinsurers lie in hedging and diversification. Through the exchange of risk, the correlation among the portfolios of policies held by participating insurers decreases. This enables them to bolster portfolio diversification, reduce their overall risk exposure, and increase their ability to take on new risks.[82]

These swaps are facilitated through either through the Catastrophic Risk Exchange (CATEX), an online platform where insurers and reinsurers can arrange reinsurance contracts and conduct swap transactions,[83] or OTC markets.

In financial CAT swaps, one party (the cedant) enters a swap contract with a counterparty (investor) for the exchange of a series of contingent payments, for claims that occur in the event of a catastrophic loss and a premium payment. As in reinsurance contracts, the cedant seeks to secure capacity from the investor, assuming the cost of the reinsurance premium. However, in financial CAT swaps, the losses are determined differently than in reinsurance, as they are measured based on a market loss index, and do not consider the cost-effectiveness of the reinsurance arrangement. The Deutsche Bank Event Loss Swaps (ELSs)[84] exemplify this type of CAT swap. ELSs were designed for US windstorms, hurricanes, and

80 Joseph Iranya, Dip CII, 'Understanding Catastrophe Derivative Contracts (CAT Swaps)', 7 January 2018. www.linkedin.com/pulse/understanding-catastrophe-derivative-contracts-cat-swaps-joseph/ accessed 19th September 2023.

81 Swiss Re, 'Mitsui Sumitomo Arrange $100M Catastrophe Risk Swap'. www.insurancejournal.com/news/international/2003/08/06/31232.htm accessed 19th September 2023.

82 María José Pérez-Fructuoso, 'Diversificación de los grandes riesgos asegurados a través de los mercados de capital: análisis de los swaps de catástrofes', *RIS, Bogotá (Colombia)* 36. 21 (enero-junio de 2012): 201–217. https://revistas.javeriana.edu.co/index.php/iberoseguros/article/download/12103/9958/0 accessed 19th September 2023.

83 Carsten Kretzler and Fred Wagner, 'The Catastrophe Risk Exchange (Catex) in New York: An Exchange and Electronic Processing System for Reinsurance Business' (n 78).

84 Maritime Insights & Intelligence Limited, 'Alternative Insurance Capital', 2006. www.i-law.com/ilaw/doc/view.htm?id=55582 accessed 5th October 2023.

tornadoes, offering threshold options of USD 20, 30, or 50 billion. For earthquake-based contracts, the protection level was USD 10–15 billion. These types of contracts have a standard maturity period of one year, and notional amounts are usually structured in increments of USD 5 million.[85]

In 2009, ISDA unveiled a comprehensive documentation template designed for catastrophe swap transactions that reference US windstorm events.[86] The primary objective was to mitigate uncertainty, enhance market liquidity and transparency, and foster growth within this market segment. Further standardisation is meant to promote the evolution of this market, and broaden the access – not only to insurance and reinsurance companies, but also to investment banks, hedge funds, and other institutional investors. Despite this progress, the lack of sufficient liquidity remains a central challenge for the growth of this type of transaction.

As the risk of catastrophe keeps increasing, so does the opportunity for these types of transactions to provide both financing and hedging. For instance, in March 2023, the World Bank structured a dual catastrophe bond and swap transaction to Chile, with USD 630 million for earthquakes, including tsunamis.[87] To this end, the World Bank simultaneously initiated and executed a USD 350 million CAT bond and USD 280 million in CAT swaps. Both the bond and swaps adhered to identical financial terms, with the CAT bond involving bond investors and the CAT swaps involving (re)insurance companies.[88] According to the agreement, Chile pays a fixed insurance premium, which the World Bank redirects to the investors of the CAT bond and counterparties in the CAT swaps. This fixed premium remains constant throughout the three-year coverage term. In the event of a qualifying incident, the World Bank will provide insurance pay-outs to Chile, based on specific earthquake parameters which have been established according to Chile's requirements.[89]

Should a qualifying event occur, Chile will notify the independent calculation agent (AIR Worldwide). This agent will determine the pay-out amount, considering the earthquake's location, magnitude, and depth. Once a calculation report is available (typically within one month after an earthquake), the World Bank will transfer the payouts to Chile.[90]

In the context of catastrophe risk, there has also been a growing market for other types of plain vanilla derivatives, such as options and futures. The key function

85 Alexander Braun, 'Pricing Catastrophe Swaps: A Contingent Claims Approach', *Insurance: Mathematics and Economics* 49.3 (2011): 520–536.

86 ISDA, 'US Wind Event Confirmation', 19 May 2009. www.isda.org/book/isda-us-wind-event-confirmation/ accessed 5th October 2023.

87 The World Bank, 'World Bank Executes its Largest Single Country Catastrophe Bond and Swap Transaction to Provide Chile $630 Million in Financial Protection Against Earthquakes', Press Release, 17 March 2023. www.worldbank.org/en/news/press-release/2023/03/17/world-bank-executes-its-largest-single-country-catastrophe-bond-and-swap-transaction-to-provide-chile-630-million-in-fin accessed 5th October 2023.

88 ibid.

89 ibid.

90 ibid.

of these types of contracts is to facilitate the exchange of risk by transferring it to investors, who take positions on the occurrence and cost of catastrophe.[91] 'Catastrophe Equity Put Options' are a type of option that grants their holders the privilege to sell a specific quantity of stocks to investors at a strike price. The holder can exercise the option when cumulative losses exceed a designated trigger point.[92] These types of contracts allow insurance companies to secure additional equity capital by selling their stocks precisely when the need arises, to cover expenses resulting from catastrophic losses. Hence, insurance companies can effectively manage and offset substantial losses stemming from catastrophic events. Although the Catastrophe Equity Put Options market has been reported as extinct, the reasons for its disappearance (i.e., low issue size, basis risk,[93] and low trading volumes[94]) should be considered in the market, to see whether a revival is possible and useful.

Sustainability-linked Derivatives (SLDs)

One of the fundamental aspects of SLDs lies in their anticipated role in bolstering the flow of capital towards financing ESG objectives. Their remarkable degree of flexibility allows for tailoring contracts to cater to the diverse array of ESG-related purposes. The emergence of SLDs as a nascent market began to reveal its potential when the first SLDs were negotiated in 2019. While the SLDs negotiated thus far have predominantly centred around environmental goals,[95] it is crucial to recognise their potential to also contribute to the attainment of social and governance targets. As in other instances, the maturation of this market hinges on adopting more established market practices and strengthening the requisite documentation.[96] In this context, ISDA highlights market priorities being understanding issues in commercial, operational, regulatory, and legal areas.[97]

Against this background, some might start calling for greater levels of standardisation. However, the most prominent challenge is triggered by the lack of commonality in the SLDs market. The commonality in liquidity reflects the impact of

91 Sara Borden and Asani Sarkar, 'Securitising Property Catastrophe Risk', *Current Issues in Economics and Finance Federal Reserve Bank of New York* 2.9 (August 1996): 1. https://citeseerx.ist.psu.edu/document?repid=rep1&type=pdf&doi=7d276ec52759abb5ff74c46083a27b381e9d8d7b accessed 3rd October 2023.

92 Guanying Wang, Xingchun Wang, Xinjian Shao, 'Exchange Options for Catastrophe Risk Management', *The North American Journal of Economics and Finance* 59 (2022): 101580.

93 Sara Borden and Asani Sarkar, 'Securitising Property Catastrophe Risk', *Current Issues in Economics and Finance, Federal Reserve Bank of New York* 2.9 (August 1996). https://citeseerx.ist.psu.edu/document?repid=rep1&type=pdf&doi=7d276ec52759abb5ff74c46083a27b381e9d8d7b accessed 5th October 2023.

94 ibid.

95 ISDA, 'Sustainability-linked Derivatives: Where to Begin?', ISDA Future Leaders in Derivatives, May 2022, 3. www.isda.org/a/ZfVgE/Sustainability-linked-Derivatives-Where-to-Begin.pdf accessed 4th September.

96 ibid.

97 ibid.

a common liquidity factor on an individual firm, both in terms of bid–ask spreads and depths.[98] Understanding that SLDs will likely be classified as OTC derivatives, the existing regulatory requirements summarised in the beginning of this chapter will need to be considered when trading SLDs.

The ISDA has been working on providing a common framework for SLD trade life cycle, to include the features of pre-trade, trade execution, post-trade, and trade termination.[99] Across this examination, the purpose is to identify regulatory and risk considerations, the role of documentation, KPI disclosure, and data management.[100] For the purpose of this book, we will follow the rationale of having risk and uncertainty as methodological lenses, to explain the relevance and challenges of each of these areas in the development of the SLD market.

The rationality of a risk society provides insight into the various reasons driving market participants – both buy side and sell side – to opt for SLDs. On the buy side, counterparties have several motivations for engaging in SLD negotiations. Firstly, it serves as a means to implement a 'self-control mechanism' for all their ESG objectives, and effectively communicate these objectives to the market, reaping the benefits of an enhanced reputation. Secondly, SLDs offer an alternative for participants who are beginning to contemplate adopting a more concrete ESG strategy. Engaging in dialogue with their SLD counterparts can facilitate the refinement and improvement of the ESG strategy, along with the corresponding KPIs. Moreover, achieving these KPIs may unlock preferential rates compared to traditional transactions, and SLDs can also incentivise greater efficiency across various products when KPIs are applied to multiple transactions. On the sell side, counterparties may view SLDs as a credible strategy to enhance their ESG market profile, while supporting their clients in their sustainability endeavours.[101] It represents an opportunity to gain a competitive advantage across a broader spectrum of asset classes, including interest rates, foreign exchange, commodities, and more. As expected, the interplay and convergence between buy-side and sell-side counterparty interests is the baseline for the trading of SLDs, and fits into one of the fundamental principles of the risk society – only the creation of a common understanding of certain risks can bring a change in society's perceptions and reactions. In this context, 'society' is represented by market participants, who must establish a consensus on common perceptions of ESG risks, to inform the drafting of key provisions in SLDs.

We argue that the very nature of SLDs must be understood from a risk perspective. SLDs are transactions that, in line with the definition of risk as an effect of a future event on a particular objective, facilitate the integration of the typical features of risk management into a contract, putting ESG at the centre. We refer

98 Paul Brockman, Dennis Y. Chung and Christophe Pérignon, 'Commonality in Liquidity: A Global Perspective', *The Journal of Financial and Quantitative Analysis* 44.4 (August 2009): 851.

99 ISDA, 'Sustainability-Linked Derivatives: Where to Begin?' (n 95).

100 ibid.

101 Auciti, 'Special Report ESG: The Opportunity for the Sell-Side' (n 41) 7.

to a methodology of risk management where the adoption of a clear strategy and forecasting, the incorporation of elements of governance, and the definition of risk appetite allow for the orderly identification, evaluation, and prioritisation of sustainability risks, to minimise the probability of occurrence and negative impact. In this context, the drafting of strict and clear KPIs is key to using the rationale of the risk management chart into the negotiation and drafting of SLDs. This is why ESG KPIs[102] should clearly set a correlation to risk factors for each type of corporate business, as well as being significant for investment decisions, and allow for the activities they involve being quantifiable, comparable, and benchmarkable for each company and its peers.[103]

The underlying reasoning behind risk, KPIs, and SLDs is evident in the objectives these transactions aim to achieve. These objectives range from motivating one party to fulfil and maintain specific sustainability objectives, or attain and uphold a particular ESG rating, to obliging either party to allocate investments towards specific sustainability initiatives.[104] The adoption of a risk strategy provides the baseline to understand the level of tolerance and management of risk accepted by each counterparty. Each KPI included in SLDs should contribute to achieving short-, medium-, and long-term sustainability targets, consistent with the risk strategy.

ESG components of most SLDs expressed in KPIs show how the risk governance and risk appetite of each counterparty determines the drafting of these contracts. The consequences of meeting or failing to meet KPIs strengthen the control, monitoring, and accountability of counterparty behaviours. Ranging from the addition of requirements to pay either a positive spread when the KPIs have not been met, or a negative spread otherwise, to making donations to sustainable or charitable organisations or initiatives (payable by the bank where a KPI has been met or by the corporate or borrower when a KPI has not been satisfied) is evidence that the financial incentives included in SLDs *will* enhance ESG-target compliance.[105] Other various incentives have been implemented, including discounted or favourable FX rates, rate/spread adjustments based on the number of KPIs met, and reinvestment of any surplus premium into predetermined sustainability projects when KPIs are achieved.[106] All these potential outcomes based on the fulfilment or nonfulfilment of KPIs, while highly customisable, enable counterparties to employ their risk management tools to define their individual risk preferences for each transaction.

102 EFFAS, 'KPIs for ESG: A Guideline for the Integration of ESG into Key Performance Indicators for Environmental, Social & Governance Issues', *Financial Analysis and Corporate Valuation* (2009). https://ec.europa.eu/docsroom/documents/1547/attachments/1/translations/en/renditions/native accessed 5th October 2023.

103 ibid.

104 Dean Naumowicz and Delyth Hughes, 'The Role of Sustainability-Linked Derivatives In Meeting Global ESG Goals' (n 3) 628.

105 ibid.

106 ibid.

One could argue that the high level of customisation of SLDs might be seen as an opportunity for parties always to adopt the best-fit-for-purpose ESG risk strategy. However, from the perspective of market growth and expansion, a certain level of standardisation is desirable.[107] The adoption of further common benchmarks for the addition of amounts to schedule payments under SLDs would provide clear understanding about the characterisation of such incentives. Naumowicz and Hughes[108] anticipate the need to address questions about whether an increase in payments could be deemed a penalty, its potential impact on the reputation of one or both parties, or if the receiving counterparty should utilise these proceeds in a manner aligned with ESG principles.

SLDs traded in the market tend to consider either an adjustment to an interest rate or cross-currency transaction tied to an underlying financial arrangement, or being an independent product not tied to an underlying arrangement. Both instances of SLDs are effective to incentivise counterparties to work towards and improve their ESG targets. There is, however, a looming challenge concerning the regulation applied to those transactions. According to the classification of the EU taxonomy, SLDs (and derivatives transactions in general) are considered to do 'no significant harm' to specified environmental objectives. The EU Taxonomy has introduced a 'do no significant harm' principle, which dictates that taxonomy-aligned investments should not inflict significant harm on EU taxonomy objectives; it is accompanied by precise EU criteria. The 'do no significant harm' principle is applicable solely to those investments that form the basis of the financial product, and adhere to the EU criteria for environmentally sustainable economic activities. Whilst this provides an initial understanding of how regulators see ESG derivatives, as the market develops, there is the need to recognise that SLDs are products that inherently promote specific sustainable targets.

SLD Regulatory Treatment

The ISDA has developed guidance to explore the regulatory challenges that may affect the growth of the SLDs market.[109] In doing so, they propose to classify SLDs into two categories: SLD1 refers to a scenario in which the KPI and its associated impact on cash flows are integrated within the underlying derivatives transaction. For instance, this can involve a cross-currency interest rate swap that incorporates additional payments, spread adjustments, or a favourable exchange rate when the KPI is achieved.[110] In SLD2, the KPIs and cashflows related to them are set out in a separate agreement that references underlying (generally vanilla) derivatives

107 Regulation Asia Interview: Scott O'Malia, 'Derivatives Will Help Drive Net Zero Transition' (n 2).

108 Dean Naumowicz and Delyth Hughes, 'The Role of Sustainability-Linked Derivatives in Meeting Global ESG Goals' (n 3) 628.

109 ISDA, 'Regulatory Considerations for Sustainability-linked Derivatives', December 2021. www.isda.org/a/58ngE/Regulatory-Considerations-for-Sustainability-linked-Derivatives.pdf accessed 7th October 2023.

110 ibid.

transactions for setting the reference amount to calculate the KPI-linked cash flow. This type of arrangement generally does not impact the terms, including pricing, of the underlying transactions. An example might be an agreement to make a payment based on a counterparty meeting its KPIs, with the payment calculated as a percentage of the notional amount, from unrelated, separately documented derivatives transactions.[111] The ISDA clarifies that the purpose of this categorisation is to provide clarity regarding the classification of SLDs as either swaps or security-based swaps. This determination is crucial in establishing whether the applicable derivatives market regulations in the US, the UK, and the EU are relevant to them. In simpler terms, SLDs will only be subject to derivatives regulation in these three jurisdictions if they can be categorised as swaps or security-based swaps under the US regulatory framework.[112]

The US SLD Regime. In general terms, a swap is a transaction that features three elements. First is a put, call, cap, floor, collar, or similar option related to the purchase or sale (or based on the value) of one or more commodities, securities, quantitative measures, or other financial interests. Second, it provides any purchase, sale, payment, or delivery contingent upon the occurrence, nonoccurrence, or a specified degree of occurrence of an event linked to potential financial, economic, or commercial consequences. Third, a swap facilitates payment exchanges based on the value or level of one or more commodities (in a broad sense), while simultaneously involving the transfer of financial risk associated with a future change in value or level (without entailing ownership or liabilities associated with the corresponding underlying asset).[113]

A security-based swap is typically defined as any agreement, contract, or transaction that qualifies as a 'swap', and has references to a narrow-based security index, a single security or loan, and to the occurrence, nonoccurrence, or extent of an event related to a single issuer of a security or issuers of securities in a narrow-based security index – provided that this event directly impacts the financial statement, condition, or obligation of the issuer.[114]

In the context of the US regulation, the ISDA explains that if the derivative underlying a SLD1 is already classified as a swap, the introduction of KPI-linked cash flows is unlikely to alter this classification. Therefore, the instrument is likely to remain subject to all relevant US derivatives regulations. However, the inclusion of KPI-related cash flows may raise other regulatory considerations. Parties involved will need to assess whether valuation and margin models are appropriately adjusted to accommodate the additional cash flow(s), ensure proper disclosure to counterparties, and meet the internal risk-management requirements stipulated by regulators.

111 ibid.
112 ibid.
113 7 U.S.C. §1a (47).
114 7 U.S.C. §1a (47)(A)(iv).

Another important question pertains to whether the inclusion of KPI-linked payment terms might transform what would otherwise be a security-based swap (SBS) into a mixed swap. As of now, there is not enough data on equity- or credit-related SLDs to identify any prevailing trends in these products. The term 'mixed swap' pertains to a type of security-based swap that derives its value from one or more factors, such as interest rates, currencies, commodities, debt instruments, indices, quantitative measures, financial or economic interests, or any form of property (excluding single securities or narrowly defined security indices). It also considers events or contingencies associated with potential financial, economic, or commercial outcomes, with specific exceptions.[115]

Determining whether SLD2 should be classified as swaps under US regulation is a more intricate matter. ISDA's assessment involves an examination of the three aspects of the swap regulatory definition.[116] Regarding the first aspect (that a swap involves a put, call, cap, floor, collar, or similar option related to the purchase or sale of one or more underlying assets), ISDA suggests that SLD2 are unlikely to be categorised as options, because none of the parties involved in these transactions pay a premium to obtain the right (without an obligation) to buy or sell an asset.

Regarding the fact that a swap provides any purchase, sale, payment, or delivery contingent upon the occurrence, nonoccurrence, or a specified degree of occurrence of an event linked to potential financial, economic, or commercial consequences, the ISDA's perspective is that KPI payments in SLD2, as they are currently structured, are not tied to those potential consequences, and, as a result, they do not qualify as swaps in a strict sense. Indeed, a KPI payment might only become due when a counterparty achieves a sustainability target, rather than being based on a hedge or a speculative investment.

In terms of the third element of swap definition, the ISDA acknowledges that SLD2 may involve an exchange of payments, but these payments are not rooted in the transfer of financial risk. Therefore, the ISDA suggests that such payments are unlikely to be characterised as hedging or insurance against the failure to meet a KPI target. Instead, these payments are more aptly viewed as incentives to motivate the parties to attain their sustainability objectives. Based on this analysis alone, it can be inferred that ISDA does not consider SLD2 as falling within the definition of swaps as outlined in US regulations.[117]

As we discussed in the earlier book, *Regulation and Supervision of the OTC Derivatives Market*,[118] US derivatives regulation includes exemptions from clearing, on-platform trade execution, and margin requirements for swaps involving

115 7 U.S.C. §1a (47).

116 ISDA, 'Regulatory Considerations for Sustainability-linked Derivatives' (n 109) 8.

117 Deanna Reitman, Glenn Reitman, Claire Hall, Marc Horwitz and Jesse Medlong, 'Are SLDs Swaps Under US Regulation? A Look at ISDA's Analysis', 14 March 2022. www.dlapiper.com/en/insights/publications/2022/03/are-slds-swaps-under-us-regulation accessed 6th October 2023.

118 See Arias-Barrera and Ligia Catherine, *Regulation and Supervision of the OTC Derivatives Market* (Routledge, 2018) ch. 6.

certain market participants that are primarily nonfinancial, and use swaps for hedging or mitigating commercial risk.[119] For instance, when parties engage in a cross-currency IRS, they should evaluate whether the nonfinancial counterparty still qualifies as using the swap 'to hedge or mitigate commercial risk' if it has access to features like a spread ratchet, improved exchange rate, or an additional payment contingent on meeting its KPI target.[120]

SLD1 may be considered to fulfil hedging purposes in line with the US clearing exception when the KPIs affect or create cash flows within standard or vanilla derivatives, which may have originally been employed for hedging purposes. In such cases, the primary objective of the overall transaction typically remains the hedging of the initial risk, and does not shift to hedging the KPI-linked risk. For instance, it is improbable that either party would primarily use the transaction to hedge the KPI-linked risk associated with a sustainability-linked loan or bond.

Likewise, in the absence of unusual or added payment structures, the ISDA affirms that it may be reasonable to conclude that the swap continues to meet the exemption requirement that it is 'economically appropriate for the reduction of risks in the conduct and management of a commercial enterprise' stemming from the relevant exposure.[121] Consequently, counterparties may want to clarify that the inclusion of KPI-linked payment terms is not for speculative, investment, or other trading purposes, but is intended to enhance the sustainability of the nonfinancial entity's operations. The ISDA recommends the inclusion of these types of investments in the SLD documentation, and to be reinforced by selecting meaningful and ambitious KPI targets for the SLD.[122]

The US regime also considers an additional exemption for a list of commercial transactions that – although they technically fall within the definition of swaps – are not considered as such. The CFTC and the SEC have indicated that, for an agreement or transaction to qualify for the Commercial Agreement Exemption, it should not involve separate and distinct payment obligations, not be traded OTC or on an organised market, not be entered into by commercial or nonprofit entities for the purpose of serving an independent commercial, business, or nonprofit objective, and not be entered into for speculative, hedging, or investment purposes. Against this definition, the ISDA observes that most SLD2 meet these criteria. Therefore, it could be safely concluded that SLD2 are likely to be subject to the commercial agreement exemption. The definitive answer, however, will only be made certain on a case-by-case basis.

The EU and UK SLD Regimes. The use of SLDs may be influenced by two significant regulatory bodies: regulations pertaining to ESG products as a whole and regulations associated with OTC derivatives. In the first category, we find

119 Section 2(h)(1) Dodd-Frank Act.

120 ISDA, 'Regulatory Considerations for Sustainability-Linked Derivatives' (n 109) 6.

121 ibid.

122 ibid.

regulations such as the EU Taxonomy Regulation and the Sustainable Finance Disclosure Regulation (SFDR). These regulations establish specific criteria to assess whether economic activities qualify as environmentally sustainable, and mandate market participants to furnish information, including details on how their operations align with these criteria.

When the underlying derivative is already categorised as such under EU/UK law, and the incorporation of SLD KPIs does not significantly modify the fundamental rights and obligations of that transaction, it is probable that the inclusion of features consistent with SLD1 will not change this classification. In such cases, the transaction will continue to be considered an OTC derivative and, as such, the contracts should comply with clearing, reporting, portfolio reconciliation, and margin requirements as set out in EMIR and MiFID I and II.[123] Nonetheless, depending on the legal status of the parties involved in the transaction, the precise nature of these regulatory obligations could potentially be influenced by the KPIs.

As for SLD2, the question arises of whether they should be classified as derivatives under EU law. Under EU law, the definition of a derivative is based on a subset of financial instruments outlined in MIFID II. This directive is a piece of EU legislation that establishes, among other things, the regulatory requirements for market participants engaged in derivatives trading. While these transactions are unlikely to be categorised under the primary types of derivatives outlined in MIFID II, they could conceivably fall under the expansive category of 'other derivative contracts that exhibit the traits of other derivative financial instruments', as per EU law. Article 8 of the delegated regulation provides more specific criteria for determining which instruments fall under this broad category of 'other derivatives'. According to these regulations, a derivative will be encompassed by this provision if it meets both of the following conditions: (i) the derivative contract is settled in cash, and (ii) it pertains to at least one of a designated set of underlying assets or variables. This includes items such as allowances, credits, permits, rights, or similar assets directly associated with renewable-energy-derived energy supply, geological or environmental factors, physical assets, or rights of a fungible nature (excluding service rights) that can be transferred, and an index or measure linked to the price, value, or volume of transactions involving any asset, right, service, or obligation.[124] Whether these criteria apply to a particular SLD2 depends on the specific details of the KPI.

More recent regulatory developments in the EU should also be considered to complete the current regulatory treatment for SLDs. The Delegated Regulation 2021/1253[125] came into force on August 2, 2022; this pertains to the integration of sustainability factors, sustainability risks, and preferences into specific

123 See Arias-Barrera and Ligia Catherine, *Regulation and Supervision of the OTC Derivatives Market* (n 118).

124 Article 7(3) of the delegated regulation.

125 Commission Delegated Regulation (EU) 2021/1253 of 21 April 2021 amending Delegated Regulation (EU) 2017/565 as regards the integration of sustainability factors, risks and preferences into certain organisational requirements and operating conditions for investment firms.

organisational requirements and operational conditions applicable to investment firms and credit institutions. According to these provisions, regulated entities are obliged to take sustainability risks into account, especially when establishing and implementing decision-making processes, risk management, internal control mechanisms, and internal reporting. Additionally, they must consider sustainability factors when documenting their activities and internal organisation.[126] In line with the MiFID II aim to strengthen investor protection, regulatees must also ensure they have a comprehensive understanding of the nature and characteristics of the investment services and financial instruments they select for their clients, including any relevant sustainability factors. Moreover, in terms of providing investment advice, there is an obligation for regulated entities to give clients specific information, including all matters related to sustainability, when deciding the best financial instrument. Therefore, the previous considerations about the way KPIs should be drafted play a crucial role in delineating the sustainability commitments of investment firms and credit institutions for each transaction.

Entities offering investment advice or portfolio management services[127] must ensure that recommended or executed transactions align with the client's potential sustainability preferences. In this context, our previous reflection on the coherence between SLDs, ESG, and risk strategy will serve as the baseline to structure such clients' preferences. The regulation also provides that, in this context, investment advice implies avoiding transaction recommendations that do not do not align with the client's sustainability preferences.

In the context of product governance, Delegated Directive 2021/1269 focuses on incorporating sustainability factors into product governance obligations.[128] When manufacturing financial instruments, it is essential to consider the sustainability-related objectives associated with these instruments while defining their potential target market.[129] This information should be conveyed clearly to the distributors of these financial instruments. Moreover, the regulation underscores the significance of providing products and services that are in line with the sustainability objectives set for the defined target market, and aligned to the

126 Vivian Walry, Benjamin Bada, Aurélia Viémont, Sarah Hantscher, Mélanie Poirrier and Anne Picot-Guillot, 'New Requirements in Governance Policy and Product Distribution Policy for Credit Institutions, Investment Firms, Insurance and Reinsurance Undertakings Regarding ESG', *Lexology*, 5 July 2022. www.lexology.com/library/detail.aspx?g=0671aa1f-4ab8-4415-87a0-66c1ae56a8f7 accessed 7th October 2023.

127 ESMA, 'Guidelines on Certain Aspects of the MiFID II Suitability Requirements', 3 April 2023. www.esma.europa.eu/sites/default/files/2023-04/ESMA35-43-3172_Guidelines_on_certain_aspects_of_the_MiFID_II_suitability_requirements.pdf accessed 7th October 2023.

128 Commission Delegated Directive (EU) 2021/1269 of 21 April 2021 amending Delegated Directive (EU) 2017/593 as regards the integration of sustainability factors into the product governance obligations.

129 ESMA, 'Final Report: Guidelines on MiFID II Product Governance Requirements', 27 March 2023. www.esma.europa.eu/sites/default/files/2023-03/ESMA35-43-3448_Final_report_on_MiFID_II_guidelines_on_product_governance.pdf accessed 7th October 2023.

client's preferences.[130] These guidelines offer further clarity regarding the terms and conditions that should be considered when negotiating and drafting SLDs and their corresponding KPIs.

Under UK law, there exists a specific category of contracts for differences as defined in the FSMA (Regulated Activities) Order 2001.[131] These contracts pertain to agreements whose value is contingent upon fluctuations in a reference factor.[132] It is conceivable that this category could encompass SLD2. The determination of whether a SLD2 falls within the scope of these classifications (and consequently qualifies as a derivative for regulatory purposes) hinges on the specific details inherent to each transaction. Therefore, market participants who engage in this type of SLD should carefully assess the structure of the relevant KPIs and cash flow adjustments, if they intend to avoid additional regulatory obligations.[133]

Wu, Barber, and Hart[134] argue that there are some concerns that only the further development of the market will solve. Firstly, how KPI-related cash flow adjustments might impact the valuation and potential margin requirements for the underlying derivative? For instance, there is an ongoing debate regarding whether margin calculation methodologies (such as ISDA's Standard Initial Margin Model) should encompass risks associated with KPIs. The question remains whether these KPI-related risks should be factored in. We would argue that, since the primary purpose of an initial margin is to play a role in minimising contagion, preventing spillover effects, and mitigating counterparty credit and systemic risks,[135] KPI-related risks should be included. In the end, what this means is the attractiveness of SLDs will be determined solely by market dynamics, and how the increase in initial margin is perceived.

Secondly, a technical question arises concerning the categorisation of SLD1. The query is whether SLD1 should be viewed as interest rate or foreign exchange derivatives with an ESG layer, or should they be considered an entirely new class of underlying asset (referred to as the 'ESG' underlying variable) within OTC derivatives?[136] This distinction may hold significance for various reasons, including EMIR reporting and the application of the hedging test, as well as the

130 ibid.

131 The Financial Services and Markets Act 2000 (Regulated Activities) Order 2001.

132 See Part II of Schedule 2 FSMA 2000 and FSMA 2000 Regulated Activities Order (SI2001/544) defines particular types of investments, including instruments which are derivative products; HM, 'CFM13120 – Understanding Corporate Finance: Derivatives: Types of Derivative: Regulatory Definitions', HMRC Internal Manual: Corporate Finance Manual, 16 April 2016. www.gov.uk/hmrc-internal-manuals/corporate-finance-manual/cfm13120 accessed 7th October 2023.

133 Jia Wu, Edmund Barber and Richard Hart, 'Part 3: Sustainability-linked Derivatives – Regulation', *Lexology*, 4 October 2022. www.lexology.com/library/detail.aspx?g=357454d1-ad27-43fb-9eac-aab09884d248 accessed 7th October 2023.

134 ibid.

135 V. Acharya, and A Bisin (2014), 'Counterparty Risk Externality: Centralized versus Over-The-Counter Markets', *Journal of Economic Theory*, 149: 153–182.

136 Jia Wu, Edmund Barber and Richard Hart, 'Part 3: Sustainability-linked Derivatives – Regulation' (n 133).

classification of nonfinancial counterparties (NFCs) based on asset class categories. As these products evolve, market participants will need to engage in nuanced assessments and seek consensus on these matters, which will depend on the specific terms of individual transactions.

Risk Considerations in SLDs

A wide range of SLDs have emerged since the first transaction in August 2019. Although these transactions are meant to enhance the flow of capital to achieve sustainability objectives in general, the most recent SLDs are related to the most prominent risk among climate issues: *reaching GHG emission targets*.

In March 2023, ING announced the successful negotiation of an SLD for Ant Group, a Chinese technology provider, with a total value of USD 400 million.[137] This SLD is structured as an interest rate swap, to hedge the interest rate risk associated with a floating-rate credit facility that includes sustainability components. The SLD incorporates a unique two-way incentive mechanism, directly tied to Ant Group's sustainability performance. Specifically, the selected KPIs focus on critical environmental and social objectives outlined in Ant Group's broader ESG strategy.[138] In pursuit of its environmental KPI, Ant Group is actively implementing green computing algorithms – a set of proprietary technologies – to enhance server efficiency within its leased data centres, and reduce the emissions intensity associated with Scope 3 emissions. Many of these algorithms have been made open source, enabling carbon innovators worldwide to utilise them free of charge. Additionally, social impact KPIs are integrated into the structure, leveraging the expansive Alipay user base and ecosystem maintained by Ant Group, to encourage greener practices across communities and industries.[139] These predefined targets will undergo thorough verification by an impartial third-party entity. Upon the successful attainment of these targets, Ant Group becomes eligible for a rebate from ING. Conversely, if none of these targets are achieved, Ant Group has committed to making a predetermined payment to ING.[140]

Similarly, in May 2023, Bell Canada (Bell) revealed its inaugural SLD with several financial institutions.[141] The transaction introduces a pricing-adjustment mechanism that influences the cost of the derivative based on Bell's progress towards achieving its science-based target. This target entails a substantial 58% reduction in operational GHG emissions (Scope 1 and 2) by the year 2030,

137 ING Wholesale Banking APAC, Press Release, Singapore/Hong Kong, 10 March 2023. www.ingwb.com/binaries/content/assets/ingwb.com/network/singapore/press-release-ing-closes-landmark-sustainability-linked-derivative-for-ant-group.pdf accessed 9th October 2023.

138 ibid.

139 ibid.

140 ibid.

141 CIBC Capital Markets, Desjardins Securities, National Bank Financial Markets, RBC Capital Markets and Wells Fargo.

measured from a 2020 baseline year, in alignment with the Science Based Targets initiative (SBTi).[142] Bell has specifically chosen this Sustainability Performance Target (SPT) – with the same function of a KPI – to bolster its commitment to realising science-based GHG emission reduction goals. The SPT's evaluation will take place in 2030, subject to a review conducted by an independent third party.[143]

As the market develops and more SLDs are being traded in the market, one of the most prominent risks is how to ensure that market participants delimit and choose the right KPIs. A KPI should not only be relevant to a company's operations, but also challenging enough to encourage growth, all while remaining attainable. Striking the right balance can be a complex endeavour. The ISDA has provided some guidance in this regard, by featuring the five overarching principles that KPIs should follow. To ensure the credibility, KPIs should be specific, measurable, verifiable, transparent, and suitable.[144]

The specific character of KPIs is set to avoid the potential risk of disputes arising between the counterparties when ESG targets are met. According to traditional definitions of risk,[145] it is advisable that targets count with a form of measurement that can be objectively verified by either the counterparty or a third independent expert. For instance, if there is a clear quantity of emissions to be reduced, the verification process will be set from the beginning so the actions taken by the counterparty are adequately certified. It is important to highlight that general promises that cannot be measured or that are open to interpretation (e.g., reasonableness or materiality) should be avoided in KPIs, as they do not provide sufficient certainty; the specificity of a KPI should *not* allow for divergent interpretations. In this context, referring to business lines or market practices could be useful to reach a common understanding of the actions to be displayed by the counterparty. For instance, indicating the type of nature-based[146] (e.g., conservation and restoration of forests) or technology-based[147] (e.g., renewable energies or carbon capture projects) solution to be adopted; the timeline to reach the specified goal; and the methodologies to measure the outcome. As these

142 Bell Announces First sustainability-Linked Derivatives, 24 May 2023. www.bce.ca/news-and-media/releases/show/bell-announces-first-sustainability-linked-derivatives accessed 9th October 2023.

143 ibid.

144 ISDA, 'Sustainability-linked Derivatives: KPI Guidelines', September 2021. www.isda.org/a/xvTgE/Sustainability-linked-Derivatives-KPI-Guidelines-Sept-2021.pdf accessed 23rd October 2023.

145 D. Lupton (ed), *Risk and Sociocultural Theory: New Directions and Perspectives.* (Cambridge University Press, 1999).

146 UNFCCC, 'Innovative Approaches for Strengthening Coastal and Ocean Adaptation – Integrating Technology and Nature-Based Solutions', 13 June 2022. https://unfccc.int/documents/510426 accessed 23rd October 2023.

147 UNFCCC, 'Technology and the UNFCCC Building the Foundation for Sustainable Development', 2016. https://unfccc.int/ttclear/misc_/StaticFiles/gnwoerk_static/NAD_EBG/54b3b39e25b84f96aeada52180215ade/b8ce50e79b574690886602169f4f479b.pdf accessed 23rd October 2023.

KPI Guidelines

SPECIFIC	MEASURABLE	VERIFIABLE	TRANSPARENT	SUITABLE
Documentation	Quantifiable	By counterparties	Type of information	KPIs material and significant
Scope	Objective	Third party	Who	Consistent
Timeline	Benchmarked (SDGs)	Available data	Frequency	Outcomes
Methodology calculation	Key to address greenwashing			Ambitious
Consequences				Meaningful

Figure 4.1 KPI Guidelines

Source: Author

KPIs are the first step at which data points are comparable,[148] another feature of their specificity is the adoption of a reference point or source, so that progress can be clearly established and verified.[149]

As the current adoption of ESG KPIs is not well standardised, KPI methodology calculation should be chosen by counterparties. The paramount consideration is to understand what is being assessed and managed, with a crucial focus on ensuring that these metrics contribute value to both the company and its stakeholders.[150] The ESG KPIs are established, monitored, and eventually disclosed by a company, and will therefore be shaped by its strategic corporate objectives, mirroring the distinct characteristics of that organisation.[151]

Equally important is to agree on the consequences of achieving or failing to meet an ESG target.[152] We can acknowledge that this component serves as the primary rationale for incorporating KPIs in SLDs, given that these KPIs are designed to underpin transactions with ESG considerations at their core. The consequences involve the counterparties' incentives to take and commit themselves to specific actions.

148 Blank Herb, Gregg Sgambati and Zack Truelson, 'Best Practices in ESG Investing', *The Journal of Investing* 25.2 (2016): 103–112. www.academia.edu/download/48183190/Best_Practices_in_ESG_Investing.pdf accessed 23rd October 2023.

149 ISDA, 'Sustainability-Linked Derivatives: KPI Guidelines' (n 144).

150 Alena Kocmanová and Marie Dočekalová, 'Construction of the Economic Indicators of Performance in Relation to Environmental, Social and Corporate Governance (ESG) Factors', *Acta Universitatis Agriculturae et Silviculturae Mendelianae Brunensis* 60.4 (2012): 195–206.

151 A. Redlein, C. Baretschneider and L. Thrainer, 'ESG Monitoring and Optimisation Solutions and Their Return on Investment: Results of Several Case Studies', *IOP Conference Series: Earth and Environmental Science* 1176 (2023): 012029. https://iopscience.iop.org/article/10.1088/1755-1315/1176/1/012029/pdf accessed 23rd October 2023.

152 ISDA, 'Sustainability-Linked Derivatives: KPI Guidelines' (n 144).

As a general rule, KPIs should be quantifiable, and within the counterparty's control in terms of achievement. As a quantifiable metric, a KPI serves as a gauge of a company's success in accomplishing its business goals, and they are instrumental in tracking the advancement of the organisation's strategic initiatives.[153] These indicators can encompass a diverse array of measurement units, encompassing both financial and non-financial aspects, and are sometimes presented as a combination of these elements. The UN SDGs are the most widely accepted benchmarks for the measurement of ESG-KPIs.[154] The advantage of using the SDGs is that they are broad enough to provide market participants with a framework for building and measuring the compliance of their sustainability strategy. It is also possible to use the large range of regulatory instruments to understand the context in which the ESG targets are designed. Likewise, a counterparty may choose to measure its progress against its own performance.[155]

The debate about the measurement and credibility of ESG-KPIs causes some authors[156] to assert that there is a considerable risk of disparity between the drafting of the KPIs and the actual actions deployed by counterparties. It is essential to tackle such lack of coherence to avoid the risk of greenwashing. Companies may engage in making partial, deceptive, or untrue environmental assertions to mitigate potential damage to their reputation and maintain legitimacy, thereby heightening information asymmetries with their stakeholders.[157] In this context, the impact of greenwashing is reflected in the deterioration of firm value, which in turn, leads to financial markets and investors discern when a company fails to align its ESG claims with its actual performance. Empirical evidence shows that investors, on average, can identify and penalise firms that do not genuinely uphold their environmental commitments, irrespective of the ESG ratings' assessments.[158] Thus, the strict and credible use of KPIs becomes pivotal in encouraging the further development of the SLD market.

The verifiable and transparent character of KPIs is also emphasised by the ISDA. The availability and quality of the information, as well as the adoption of feasible mechanisms of verification (including third-party auditing) are of paramount importance. Insufficient transparency in KPIs may lead to a scarcity

153 Federica dal Bello, 'The Role of KPIs in the Integrated Report: An Empirical Analysis', Università degli Studi di Padova, 2017–2018, 33. https://thesis.unipd.it/bitstream/20.500.12608/25467/1/Federica_Dal_Bello.pdf accessed 23rd October 2023.

154 N. Fallah Shayan, N. Mohabbati-Kalejahi, S. Alavi and M. A. Zahed, 'Sustainable Development Goals (SDGs) as a Framework for Corporate Social Responsibility (CSR)', *Sustainability* 14.3 (2022): 1222.

155 ISDA, 'Sustainability-linked Derivatives: KPI Guidelines' (n 144).

156 F. Testa, I. Miroshnychenko, R. Barontini and M. Frey, 'Does It Pay to Be A Greenwasher or a Brownwasher?', *Business Strategy and the Environment* 27.7 (2018): 1104–1116.

157 F. Bowen and J. A. Aragon-Correa, 'Greenwashing in Corporate Environmentalism Research and Practice: The Importance of What We Say and Do', *Organisation & Environment* 27 (2014): 107–112.

158 Marco Ghitti, Gianfranco Gianfrate and Lorenza Palma, 'The Agency of Greenwashing', *Journal of Management and Governance* (2023): 1–37.

of readily accessible market data, potentially giving rise to accounting-related complications.[159] Hence, the involved parties must explicitly specify the nature of the information to be disclosed throughout the transaction's duration, the methods for sharing this information, and determine which parties will be granted access.[160]

Finally, KPIs must be suitable for the relevant counterparties and the derivatives structure.[161] The relevance will be determined on a case-by-case basis. However, in general, KPIs should be material and strategically significant to the counterparties' businesses.[162] In this scenario and in line with the recently approved ESRS, we argue that ESG-KPIs should be coherent with the company's general sustainability strategy, its business model and value chain, whilst contributing to manage the impacts, risks, and opportunities relevant to the counterparties.[163] This means bringing the concept of double materiality[164] to the drafting of consistent and feasible KPIs. The double materiality perspective allows the adoption of a risk-based approach to the design of KPIs, as it prioritises actions based on the probability and significance of the counterparty actions to address meaningful sustainability issues.

The rationale of risk that supports the drafting of SLDs is expected to be embedded in the future forms of standardisation that the market expects. In terms of further clarifying how SLDs are designed, ISDA suggests including key provisions in SLD documentation. They recommend a comprehensive description of the ESG targets, accompanied by objective measurement methodologies, and the inclusion of KPIs with the above-mentioned features.[165] Moreover, there is a recommendation that could be framed as a typical element of a risk-based approach: to consider the potential fallbacks when the agreed upon KPI verification method cannot be used (the ISDA advises counterparties to consider the inclusion of an alternative method to overcome potential disputes).

As verification and disclosure may be designated to a third party, the suggestion is for the counterparties to clearly identify the practicalities of the process. One of the challenges in this area is the reliance on inadequate and inconsistent data, as well as contradictory ESG rating and data providers. The extent of the debate about the inconsistency of ESG ratings has been deeply studied by experts like Daniel Cash. Following a judicious study of ESG rating agencies, he draws attention to a

159 ISDA, 'Accounting Analysis for ESG-related Transactions and the Impact on Derivatives', September 2021. www.isda.org/2021/09/07/accounting-analysis-for-esg-related-transactions-and-the-impact-on-derivatives accessed 23rd October 2023.

160 ISDA, 'Sustainability-linked Derivatives: KPI Guidelines' (n 144).

161 ibid.

162 ibid.

163 ibid.

164 Christian Nielsen, 'ESG Reporting and Metrics: From Double Materiality to Key Performance Indicators', *Preprints*, 19 October 2023. www.preprints.org/manuscript/202310.1191/v1 accessed 23rd October 2023.

165 That is: quantifiable, measurable, credible, verifiable, transparent, and suitable.

lack of transparency[166] and varying stakeholder preferences[167] as main the pitfalls[168] in full stakeholder acceptance of ESG assessments.

Likewise, regulators have expressed their concern about the quality of ESG ratings and the divergent methodologies adopted by ESG rating agencies. Japan's Financial Services Agency[169] was first regulator to adopt a regime for these agencies. In 2022, The Japanese FSA issued a groundbreaking Code of Conduct, comprising six fundamental principles, focusing on transparency regarding methodologies and data sources, and adopting a comply-or-explain approach.[170] On 13 June 2023, the European Commission announced a proposal on establishing a regulatory framework for ESG rating agencies, as part of the sustainable finance package.[171] The overarching goal of this initiative is to enhance the quality of ESG ratings, enabling investors to make more informed decisions regarding sustainability objectives and combating the practice of greenwashing. Similarly, in the UK, the HM Treasury[172] announced its intention to promote a regulation for ESG rating agencies that enhances transparency, good governance, clear management of conflict of interest, and robust systems and controls on processes and methodologies. Such regulation would require that these agencies become FCA-authorised entities.[173]

Another crucial aspect to address when documenting SLDs is the anticipation of unforeseen events related to ESG factors. Such unpredicted events are of particular significance in the context of climate change. The inherent nature of uncertainty poses challenges in assessing both the likelihood of these events happening, and the extent of their impacts. Notably, climate experts contend that over recent decades, the uncertainties surrounding future climate change projections have not notably decreased.[174] Climate models and real-world observations

166 Daniel Cash, 'The Sustainability Rating Industry', in *Sustainability Rating Agencies vs Credit Rating Agencies* (Palgrave Studies in Impact Finance, Palgrave Macmillan, 2021) 3.

167 Kenza Bryan, 'ESG Ratings: Whose Interests Do They Serve?', *FT*, 3 October 2023. www.ft.com/content/fbe10867-fea1-4887-b404-9f9e301e102e accessed 23rd October 2023.

168 See Daniel Cash, *ESG Rating Agencies and Financial Regulation: A Signalling Theory Approach* (Edward Elgar Publishing, 2024).

169 ESG Investor, 'Japan Finalises Code of Conduct for ESG Data Providers', 19 December 2022. www.esginvestor.net/japan-finalises-code-of-conduct-for-esg-data-providers/ accessed 23rd October 2023.

170 ibid.

171 EC, 'Sustainable Finance Package', 13 June 2023. https://finance.ec.europa.eu/publications/sustainable-finance-package-2023_en accessed 23rd October 2023.

172 HM Treasury, 'Future Regulatory Regime for Environmental, Social, and Governance (ESG) Ratings Providers Consultation', March 2023. https://assets.publishing.service.gov.uk/government/uploads/system/uploads/attachment_data/file/1147458/ESG_Ratings_Consultation_.pdf accessed 23rd October 2023.

173 FCA, 'Enhancing Climate-Related Disclosures by Standard Listed Companies and Seeking Views on ESG Topics in Capital Markets', Consultation Paper CP21/18, June 2021. www.fca.org.uk/publication/consultation/cp21-18.pdf accessed 23rd October 2023.

174 Gerard H. Roe and Marcia B. Baker, 'Why Is Climate Sensitivity So Unpredictable?', *Science* 318 (2007): 629–632.

consistently yield a broad range of probability distributions, when forecasting long-term global mean temperature increases, resulting from a doubling of atmospheric carbon dioxide.[175] This substantial level of uncertainty can also influence the commitments that counterparties make when incorporating KPIs into their financial agreements. Therefore, within the framework of considering the key provisions of SLDs, counterparties are expected to strategise how to mitigate the adverse consequences that may arise from the occurrence of such events on counterparty performance.[176]

The ISDA aims to underscore the importance of implementing a set of provisions that provide clarity regarding the nature and classification of SLDs. This structuring is intended to help establish connections between SLDs, the underlying products, and the asset class to which the transaction is associated.[177] Coherence is needed between the SLD and the underlying debt instrument terms, to ensure that all key provisions are integrated and designated for the successful completion of the SLD. Furthermore, in cases where there is potential for debate regarding the SLD structure and the asset class to which the transaction belongs, it is essential for counterparties to agree on the appropriate classification from the outset. Failure to do so may lead to the risk of recharacterisation.[178] For the SLDs based on existing products, such as interest rate swaps, it is important to differentiate them to ensure the proper characterisation of the transaction. In this context, the ISDA advises counterparties to consider and document whether the SLD can be justified as a standalone type of transaction, or as a secondary classification.

Finally, to avoid costly and lengthy proceedings arising from KPI compliance issues, it is advisable that the counterparties establish an alternative mechanism for resolving and preventing disputes.[179] Potential disagreements can be better solved by a tailored proceeding to disclose and verify KPIs and corresponding valuation. A customised dispute resolution mechanism (such as Alternative Dispute Resolution (ADR) or Online Dispute Resolution (ODR)) can help establish a step-by-step process for resolving KPI-related disputes, starting with negotiation, progressing to mediation, and potentially culminating in arbitration.[180] We argue that such a system should adopt a pre-emptive approach, where the event-monitoring tool captures not only a historical perspective of the initial terms, but also the current status of data relevant to each KPI. The system would also facilitate the collection of data related to the frequency, outcomes, and objectives of ESG-specific events.[181]

175 ibid.

176 ISDA, 'Sustainability-Linked Derivatives: KPI Guidelines' (n 144).

177 ibid.

178 Paul U. Ali, 'Credit Derivatives and Synthetic Securitisations: Innovation and Fragility', *Banking & Finance Law Review*; *Toronto* 20.3 (2004/2005): 293–317.

179 Patrick Leonard and Hayley O'Donnell, 'Arbitration in Derivatives Contracts', *Journal of International Arbitration* 39.1 (2022): 61–78.

180 Nicolás Lozada-Pimiento, 'AI Systems and Technology in Dispute Resolution', *Uniform Law Review* 24.2 (June 2019): 348–366.

181 ISDA, 'Sustainability-Linked Derivatives: KPI Guidelines' (n 144).

Integrating this system within the conventional framework of ADR/ODR would further improve the handling of potential contractual disputes.

The system should be linked to several data points to ensure the proper functioning of valuation, cash flows, and transaction processing. The valuation, which is required for collateral management and other operational features of the transaction, should clearly reflect a risk-free blend of the underlying asset and the derivative, resulting in a distinct derivative valuation that reduces any potential for arbitrage.[182] Regarding cash flows, when a derivative is classified as a cash flow hedge, the effective portion of the derivative's fair value change is recorded as part of accumulated other comprehensive income (i.e., loss), until the hedged item is included in earnings or the expected transaction is no longer likely to happen. If a derivative does not meet the criteria for a highly effective hedge, any fair value change is promptly reflected in earnings.[183] Regarding transaction processing, there is the need to engage in the management of trade life cycle events (e.g., the quarterly payments that occur over the contractual lifetime of a CDS).[184] These processes depend on the availability of data concerning the ESG overlay of an SLD, which must be collected and retained to produce precise results.[185] Therefore, parties should ensure the interoperability of different data sources that reflect ESG event performance, when those sources are available.

In sum, SLDs provide a mechanism for companies to align their financial incentives with their sustainability objectives. These derivatives transactions promote responsible practices and encourage companies to adopt sustainable strategies. Moreover, SLDs offer a means to manage financial risks associated with sustainability factors. By incorporating sustainability metrics into derivative contracts, investors can better assess and manage the potential impact of ESG risks on their portfolios. However, a critical challenge in the implementation of SLDs lies in developing reliable and standardised sustainability metrics. The enhancement of confidence in the market and in the role of SLDs requires robust verification mechanisms, and independent audits of each transaction's KPIs. This will help to reduce the risk of greenwashing, and the potential for companies to misrepresent their sustainability performance to access favourable financial terms.

Likewise, obtaining high-quality ESG data continues to pose a challenge within the sustainable finance arena. The dependability and comparability of data are pivotal for the valuation and assessment of SLD instruments. There is a pressing

182 IMF, 'Classification of Financial Derivatives Involving Affiliated Enterprises in the Balance of Payments Statistics and the International Investment Position (IIP) Statement', June 2002. www.imf.org/external/np/sta/fd/index.htm#:~:text=The%20value%20of%20a%20financial,and%20no%20investment%20income%20accrues accessed 26th October 2023.

183 SEC, 'Note 14 – Derivative Instruments and Hedging Activities', 30 September 2019. www.sec.gov/Archives/edgar/data/26076/000155837019011159/R22.htm accessed 26th October 2023.

184 BIS, 'IFC Bulletin No. 35, Data Requirements for Monitoring Derivative Transactions', February 2012. www.bis.org/ifc/publ/ifcb35.pdf accessed 26th October 2023.

185 ISDA, 'Sustainability-Liked Derivatives: Where to Begin? ISDA Future Leaders in Derivatives', 3 May 2022. https://www.isda.org/a/ZfVgE/Sustainability-linked-Derivatives-Where-to-Begin.pdf.

need for initiatives aimed at enhancing data transparency, reliability, and reporting standards to ensure precise valuation of these financial products. Collaborative efforts involving market participants, regulatory bodies, and standards-setting organisations are essential for addressing concerns related to metrics, data quality, and the potential for greenwashing. We recognise that the future of SLDs hinges on bolstering the reliability of their applications, reinforcing the legal framework governing these instruments in various regulatory environments, and advancing investor education and awareness about the potential of SLDs. Investors and companies must grasp the advantages, risks, and intricacies linked to these instruments to make well-informed decisions.

Voluntary Carbon Credit Derivatives

As the urgency to combat climate change intensifies, carbon markets have gained significant prominence as a key policy tool for reducing GHG emissions. The regulation of carbon markets plays a pivotal role in ensuring the integrity, transparency, and effectiveness of these markets. To understand the role of financial derivatives in zero-emissions targets, we now explore the concept, importance, challenges, and prospects of regulating carbon markets to foster climate action, promote sustainable development, and facilitate the transition to a low-carbon economy.

Carbon markets provide a market-based approach to tackle climate change, by putting a price on carbon emissions. We refer, in general, to GHG emissions that comprise carbon dioxide (CO_2), methane (CH_4), nitrous oxide (N_2O), and fluorinated gases.[186] Among those gases, CO_2 is the most emitted by multiple factors, especially by human activity.[187] The goal of net zero was conceived to keep global warming to no more than 1.5°C – as called for in the Paris Agreement. To that end, emissions need to be reduced by 45% by 2030, and reach net zero by 2050.[188] Despite the critical importance of reaching this goal for our planet, the latest Emissions Gap Report for 2022[189] reveals that we are significantly off track from the Paris Agreement's objective of restricting global warming to well below 2°C. Current policies suggest a temperature increase of 2.8°C by the end of the century.[190] The rationale we all must bear in mind is that 'net zero' is fundamentally a scientific concept – not a policy one. Scientifically speaking, when

186 EPA, 'Overview of Greenhouse Gases', US Environmental Protection Agency. www.epa.gov/ghgemissions/overview-greenhouse-gases accessed 23rd October 2023.

187 EPA, 'Sources of Greenhouse Gas Emissions', US Environmental Protection Agency. www.epa.gov/ghgemissions/sources-greenhouse-gas-emissions accessed 23rd October 2023.

188 UN, 'For a Livable Climate: Net-Zero Commitments Must Be Backed by Credible Action'. www.un.org/en/climatechange/net-zero-coalition#:~:text=To%20keep%20global%20warming%20to,reach%20net%20zero%20by%202050 accessed 23rd October 2023.

189 UN Environment Program, 'The Closing Window: Climate Crisis Calls for Rapid Transformation of Societies', Emissions Gap Report, 2022. www.unep.org/resources/emissions-gap-report-2022 accessed 23rd October 2023.

190 ibid.

the goal is to constrain the increase in global average temperatures to specific limits, the laws of physics dictate that there exists a finite carbon dioxide budget that can be released into the atmosphere, along with other GHGs.[191] Once this budget is exceeded, any additional emissions *must* be counterbalanced by removal or sequestration into sinks.[192] In this context, policy instruments, global commitments, and market developments are intended to serve as mechanisms to prevent the crossing of planetary boundaries.[193]

Carbon markets have emerged as a critical tool to address climate change and advance sustainable development. By facilitating carbon offsetting and supporting certified projects, these markets contribute to global emissions reductions and provide co-benefits to communities. In the process of adopting international policies, the Kyoto Protocol introduced a milestone in the fight against climate change,[194] establishing the world's first global compliance carbon market mechanism. Under the Kyoto Protocol, three notable approaches came forth: the Clean Development Mechanism (CDM), International Emissions Trading (IET), and Joint Implementation (JI).[195] Among these, the CDM emerged as a central hub for compliance carbon market activities.[196] There are also successful mechanisms for carbon trading in the form of the EU's Emissions Trading System (ETS) and the northeastern US's Regional Greenhouse Gas Initiative.

The CDM is widely recognised, as it facilitated the implementation of nearly 8,000 projects in more than 100 countries, resulting in an impressive 1.9 billion certified emissions reductions.[197] These reductions played a pivotal role in global initiatives to combat carbon emissions. All CDM projects are registered with the UNFCCC, and carbon financing is usually directed through private sector entities or World Bank carbon funds. These entities subsequently provide funding for offset projects in the developing world.[198]

In 2003, the World Wildlife Fund (WWF) and other INGOs joined forces to create the Gold Standard, a voluntary carbon offset programme and registry designed to maximise the impact of carbon projects and provide value to developers

191 S. Fankhauser et al., 'The Meaning of Net Zero and How to Get It Right', *Nature Climate Change* 12 (2022): 15–21.

192 ibid.

193 See Katherine Richardson et al., 'Earth Beyond Six of Nine Planetary Boundaries', *Science Advances* 9 (2023): eadh2458.

194 Kyoto Protocol to the United Nations Framework Convention on Climate Change, 'FCCC/CP/1997/L.7/Add.1', 10 December 1997. https://unfccc.int/documents/2409 accessed 26th October 2023.

195 UNFCCC, 'Mechanisms Under the Kyoto Protocol'. https://unfccc.int/process/the-kyoto-protocol/mechanisms accessed 26th October 2023.

196 Michael Gillenwater and Stephen Seres, 'The Clean Development Mechanism: A Review of the First International Offset Programme', *Greenhouse Gas Measurement and Management* 1.3–4 (2011): 179–203.

197 UNFCCC, 'The Clean Development Mechanism'. https://unfccc.int/process-and-meetings/the-kyoto-protocol/mechanisms-under-the-kyoto-protocol/the-clean-development-mechanism accessed 30th October 2023.

198 A. Bumpus and D. Liverman, 'Accumulation by Decarbonisation and the Governance of Carbon Offsets', *Economic Geography* 84.2 (2008): 127–156.

worldwide.[199] The promise of the Gold Standard Certified Emission Reductions is to provide a more trustworthy certification of the projects that have this label. This means that the process to obtain the Gold Standard label is far more rigorous, as it is designed to ensure that labelled projects meet the highest levels of compliance.[200] The assessment is built based on the CDM, but it involves a three-screening stage. The first two stages are the 'project type screen', which delimits and restricts the types of projects focused on renewable energy and use-efficiency. Then, the third screen seeks to ensure that the project contributes to local sustainable development objectives. Hence, embracing the Gold Standard assists us in grasping a fundamental characteristic of carbon markets: the greater the confidence in a project's actual impact on reducing carbon emissions, the greater the advantages for both the project itself and the associated financial instruments.

We argue that a risk-based strategy rationale aids in comprehending the dynamics of the carbon market. Carbon emissions constitute the ultimate risk to diminish, mitigate, and eradicate, as they pose a significant threat to global climate stability. The establishment and expansion of carbon markets represent a means to effectively address these escalating risks. In this context, the adoption of market systems and labelling mechanisms that offer trustworthy risk management gains confidence. This approach can materialise the anticipated advantages of carbon markets as an efficient route towards achieving net-zero emissions. The risk-based strategy contributes to delimiting attainable targets according to the diverse levels of commitment across markets, and across jurisdictions. Indeed, the fact that net-zero targets have been constantly reviewed reveals the complexities associated with the interaction between risk and uncertainty. The risk of carbon emissions clashes with the uncertainties triggered by conflicting interests and market forces behind the adoption of actual emission reduction actions. In this context, any regulatory or self-regulatory mechanism designed to strengthen the rigor of carbon emission reduction assessment is welcome, as it directly tackles the adverse impact of uncertainties over risks.

The rationale of risk and uncertainty also helps to clarify the different perceptions of risks that are central to understand the meaning of net zero: in essence, the crucial distinction between gross zero and net zero.[201] Whilst a gross-zero emissions target aims to reduce all emissions in all sectors uniformly to zero, a net-zero target allows for some residual emissions in specific sectors. This is to recognise that there are sectors where emission reduction is not feasible, either because it is excessively expensive or because there are no available technological solutions to achieve it. In this instance, regulators, industry, and the corporate sector act under the assumption

199 Gold Standard, 'Environmental Markets: Carbon Markets'. www.goldstandard.org/impact-quantification/carbon-markets accessed 30th October 2023.

200 Moritz A. Drupp, 'Does the Gold Standard Label Hold its Promise in Delivering Higher Sustainable Development benefits? A Multi-Criteria Comparison of CDM Projects', *Energy Policy* 39.3 (2011): 1213–1227.

201 Joshua Burke and Ajay Gambhir, 'Policy Incentives for Greenhouse Gas Removal Techniques: The Risks of Premature Inclusion in Carbon Markets and the Need for a Multi-Pronged Policy Framework', *Energy and Climate Change* 3 (2022): 100074.

that these emissions are compensated for by more substantial reductions or removals of emissions elsewhere.[202] Achieving the latter can involve the use of natural or engineered carbon sinks. Likewise, there is a context for reaching the target of 'net negative'. Net-negative emissions occur when the amount of gross negative emissions matches or exceeds the amount of gross positive emissions.[203]

In this scenario, policies, and plans around net zero are dealing with the typical problem of the prioritisation of risks. This involves the selection of attainable targets and the consideration of various tools, including regulatory instruments or processes that offer a more effective roadmap for managing these risks. The prioritisation of risks comes from the clear reliance of the Paris Agreement commitments on seeing emission reductions as the first of the solutions to be implemented worldwide.[204] Along with emission reductions, there are the complementary solutions of carbon dioxide removal[205] and the broad category of net-negative emissions techniques.[206] However, the complete adoption of these solutions may be affected by certain perceptions that countries and business have, regarding the manufactured risks[207] created by these remedies. There is a perception that integrating carbon dioxide removal into net-zero strategies carries risks for successful mitigation.[208] As a result, the idea of distinguishing between targets for emission reduction and carbon dioxide removal has been proposed to mitigate these risks.[209] This concept has gained rapid acceptance and has been supported in an increasing number of

202 C. Stark et al., 'Net Zero: The UK's Contribution to Stopping Global Warming', UK Committee on Climate Change, 2019. https://research.tees.ac.uk/ws/portalfiles/portal/43823540/227721345.pdf accessed 30th October 2023.

203 Joshua Burke and Ajay Gambhir, 'Policy Incentives for Greenhouse Gas Removal Techniques: The Risks of Premature Inclusion in Carbon Markets and the Need for a Multi-Pronged Policy Framework' (n 201).

204 IPCC, *Summary for Policymakers in Global Warming of 1.5 °C. An IPCC Special Report on the Impacts of Global Warming of 1.5 °C Above Pre-Industrial Levels and Related Global Greenhouse Gas Emission Pathways, in the Context of Strengthening the Global Response to the Threat of Climate Change, Sustainable Development, and Efforts to Eradicate Poverty* (World Meteorological Organisation, 2018).

205 Among them: 'afforestation, soil carbon sequestration, enhanced weathering, biochar, bioenergy with carbon capture and storage, and direct air carbon capture and storage'. National Academies of Sciences, Engineering & Medicine, *Negative Emissions Technologies and Reliable Sequestration: A Research Agenda* (The National Academies Press, 2019).

206 'Some of the technologies designed to achieve negative emissions are based the encouragement of natural processes that uptake and store atmospheric carbon, such as afforestation (AF), and soil carbon sequestration (SCS). Other negative emission technologies (NETs) rely on human engineering, such as capture and storage of CO_2 from the combustion of biomass for energy (bioenergy with carbon capture and storage, BECCS), or the chemical removal of CO_2 directly from air, and subsequent storage (direct air capture with storage, DAC-S)'. Samantha Eleanor Tanzer and Andrea Ramírez, 'When are Negative Emissions Negative Emissions?', *Energy & Environmental Science* 12 (2019): 1210–1218. https://pubs.rsc.org/en/content/articlehtml/2019/ee/c8ee03338b accessed 30th October 2023.

207 Anthony Giddens, 'Risk and Responsibility', *The Modern Law Review* 69 (1999): 4.

208 Stephen Smith, 'A Case for Transparent Net-Zero Carbon Targets', *Communications Earth & Environment* 2 (2021): 24.

209 ibid.

policy-focused briefings,[210] making it an emerging issue in the EU's updated 2030 climate package.[211]

As the global community grapples with the pressing challenges related to the adoption of diverse market and industry solutions to achieve net zero, along with the compliance carbon markets, voluntary carbon markets (VCMs) have emerged as a powerful mechanism to drive climate action and sustainable development. Both markets are conceived to facilitate emissions trading. Under the compliance or mandatory markets, there is the cap-and-trade system.[212] Here, a regulatory authority sets a limit (cap) on the total amount of GHG emissions allowed within a specific jurisdiction. Emitters are then allocated or must purchase emission allowances or permits, which can be traded among participants.[213] Along with compliance markets, VCMs provide an alternative venue for companies and individuals to voluntarily offset their carbon emissions by purchasing and retiring carbon credits generated through certified projects. Despite the differences in the functioning of these markets,[214] both aim to incentivise emission reductions and facilitate the transition to a low-carbon economy. While the compliance market is strictly regulated, as it includes mechanisms to define credits and establish standards for projects' designs and methodologies,[215] the voluntary market is considerably less regulated. It operates with several competing voluntary standards, diverse carbon calculators, and with different definitions of credits.[216]

VCMs operate on the principle of carbon offsetting, whereby organisations, businesses, or individuals voluntarily compensate for their own GHG emissions by supporting projects that reduce or remove emissions elsewhere.[217] These projects generate carbon credits, which represent the reduction or removal of one metric ton of carbon dioxide equivalent (CO_2e) from the atmosphere. Nonetheless, the concept of carbon offsetting often faces harsh criticism, because of its fragmented and constrained impact. It is often alleged that these practices may inadvertently perpetuate certain narratives that do not align with actual emissions reduction efforts.[218] Furthermore, there is a significant ongoing debate about whether current offset

210 K. Levin, D. Rich, K. Ross, T. Fransen and C. Elliott, *Designing and Communicating Net-Zero Targets* (World Resources Institute, 2020).

211 F. Simon, 'Commission under Fire for Including "Carbon Sinks" into EU Climate Goals', 2020. www.euractiv.comwww.euractiv.com/section/climate-environment/news/commission-under-fire-for-including-carbon-sinks-into-eu-climate-goals/ accessed 30th October 2023.

212 Robert N. Stavins, 'Addressing Climate Change with a Comprehensive US Cap-and-Trade System', *Oxford Review of Economic Policy* 24 (2008): 298–321.

213 ibid.

214 Heather Lovell and Diana Liverman, 'Understanding Carbon Offset Technologies', *New Political Economy* 15.2 (2010): 255–273.

215 A. Bumpus and D. Liverman, 'Accumulation by Decarbonisation and the Governance of Carbon Offsets' (n 198).

216 Nadaa Taiyab, *Exploring the Market for Voluntary Carbon Offsets* (International Institute for Environment and Development (IIED), 2006).

217 House of Commons Environmental Audit Committee, *The Voluntary Carbon Offset Market: Sixth Report of Session 2006*, vol. 7 (The Stationery Office, 2007).

218 Heather C. Lovell, 'Governing the Carbon Offset Market', *WIREs Climate Change* 1.3 (2010): 353–362.

markets effectively involve developing countries and promote prudent investments in cost-effective emission control strategies.[219] Moreover, the nonuniform nature of carbon credits in the voluntary offset market, and the relatively limited oversight for their verification, measurement, and auditing give rise to substantial information asymmetries and increased transaction costs.[220]

Notwithstanding the critiques of VCMs, in 2007, environmental leaders and businesses established the Verified Carbon Standard, or VERRA, which currently maintains the most active registry within the VCMs, having issued nearly 1 billion credits to date.[221] VERRA and the Gold Standard aim to foster integrity and quality into carbon markets, while providing user-friendly yet secure registries. The VCMs have grown alongside the CDM framework, creating a more functional and transparent market. Considering the downfalls of the Kyoto Protocol implementation, VCMs have gained considerable interest. According to the Taskforce on Scaling Voluntary Carbon Markets, the demand for voluntary carbon credits is expected to grow by 15% by 2030.[222] By contrast, with the conclusion of the 2012 'first commitment period' of the Kyoto Protocol, activity in the CDM markets decreased, and a noticeable transition towards VCMs took place.

As VCMs continued to evolve, the UNFCCC introduced the Reducing Emissions from Deforestation and Forest Degradation (REDD+) framework in 2015.[223] This initiative brought land-based voluntary carbon projects to the forefront of global discussions on carbon reduction. In the same year, during COP21, parties to the annual UN Climate Change Conference adopted the historic Paris Agreement. Within the scope of VCMs, the Paris Agreement plays a pivotal role in determining the market's functioning and the eligibility of carbon mechanisms for inclusion under the agreement. The introduction of guidelines for Article 6 of the Paris Agreement, along with the initiation of the first Nationally Determined Contributions (NDCs), established a new global framework within which the VCM operates. According to Article 6.2, a host government holds the authority to approve emission reductions or removals, referred to as 'mitigation outcomes' within Article 6, for utilisation in their NDCs, or by public and private entities for other global mitigation endeavours.

Negotiators completed the Paris Rulebook at COP26 in Glasgow,[224] providing guidance on how each country establishes and updates their own emissions targets

219 Heather Lovell and Diana Liverman, 'Understanding Carbon Offset Technologies' (n 214).

220 H. Lovell, H. Bulkeley and D. Liverman, 'Carbon Offsetting: Sustaining Consumption?', *Environment and Planning A* 41.10 (2009): 2357–2379.

221 VERRA, 'VCCs' Program Overview'. https://verra.org/programs/verified-carbon-standard/vcs-program-details/ accessed 30th October 2023.

222 Nick Ferris, 'The Mission to Mend the Voluntary Carbon Offset Market', *Energy Monitor*, 19 August 2022. www.energymonitor.ai/policy/carbon-markets/the-mission-to-mend-the-voluntary-carbon-offset-market/#?cf-view&cf-closed accessed 30th October 2023.

223 UNFCCC, 'What is REDD+?', 2015. https://unfccc.int/topics/land-use/workstreams/redd/what-is-redd accessed 30th October 2023.

224 UNFCCC, 'Report of the Conference of the Parties Serving as the Meeting of the Parties to the Paris Agreement on its Third Session, Held in Glasgow from 31 October to 13 November 2021'. https://unfccc.int/sites/default/files/resource/cma2021_10_add1_adv.pdf accessed 30th October 2023.

(NDCs). The rule book also outlines transparency safeguards, ensuring parties accurately report their financial contributions, emission baselines, and progress towards emissions reduction targets. The Paris Agreement explicitly recognises the significance of carbon markets as a central tool for international cooperation in reducing emissions. It calls for the trading of Internationally Transferred Mitigation Outcomes (ITMOs) while ensuring such exchanges promote sustainable development.

According to the Paris Agreement, the country acquiring ITMOs under Article 6.2 is referred to as the 'host country', where the project or activity generating GHG emission reductions or removals is situated.[225] For host countries procuring ITMOs, often located in the Global South, ITMO transactions serve as an innovative avenue to direct investments into low-carbon projects that contribute to their sustainable development. For the receiving country, ITMO transactions provide the opportunity to enhance ambition for its NDCs, by financing projects or activities in regions where GHG emissions reductions or removals can be achieved in a more cost-effective manner. Alternatively, receiving countries may choose not to include ITMOs in their NDCs, but may opt to use them as a supplementary measure.[226]

Despite the benefits expected from the adoption of VCMs, one of the recurring concerns in these markets is how to maintain the integrity and credibility of emission reductions. Robust regulatory frameworks are meant to ensure that emission allowances or carbon credits represent real, measurable, and additional emission reductions. The effectiveness of such regulations should be reflected in the prevention of fraud, double counting, and other malpractices, instilling confidence in market participants and investors. Indeed, due to the complexity of the Paris Agreement, measures are in place to prevent double counting of carbon credits as they are traded between entities. Article 6 negotiations during COP26 introduced the concept of Corresponding Adjustments (CAs) to address this issue. Under the CA mechanism, a project's host country must make accounting adjustments to its NDC when offset credits are transferred internationally, ensuring that carbon emission reductions are only counted once. Articles 6.2. and 6.4 of the Paris Agreement also require the use of CAs, when granted, for 'other international mitigation purposes' by the host country. This encompasses both 'global mitigation objectives unrelated to achieving an NDC', such as CORSIA,[227] and 'other objectives determined by the initial transferring participating Party', as seen in the VCMs. Therefore, Article 6 units can be globally traded for utilisation in the VCMs without necessitating a

225 Frequently Asked Questions on Article 6 of the Paris Agreement and Internationally Transferred Mitigation Options (ITMOs), 'United Nations Development Programme'. www.undp.org/kazakhstan/news/how-article-6-powers-global-climate-cooperation accessed 30th October 2023.

226 'Ghana, Vanuatu, and Switzerland Launch World's First Projects Under New Carbon Market Mechanism Set Out in Article 6.2 of the Paris Agreement', United Nations Development Programme, 12 November 2022. www.whitecase.com/insight-alert/emerging-fundamentals-climate-mitigation-through-itmo-transactions-under-paris accessed 30th October 2023.

227 Carbon Offsetting and Reduction Scheme for International Aviation (CORSIA). www.icao.int/environmental-protection/CORSIA/Pages/default.aspx accessed 30th October 2023.

country authorisation, and they will not entail a CA.[228] However, having a CA may be deemed more valuable by certain buyers, as it mitigates the risk of double claiming, and we may witness a premium being offered for units that come with the CA.

As parties to the Paris Agreement continue the implementation processes for CAs, centralised marketplaces will continue to provide data and transparency, assisting governments and corporations in avoiding double counting and ensuring the integrity of the carbon market.

Types of rights conferred by carbon credits. These must be understood before exploring how derivatives complement VCM. The first is the right to *generate*.[229] This is the right of a project developer to carry out an undertaking that will ultimately result in the generation of carbon credits or prompt the relevant carbon registry to issue them. In this instance, there is an obligation of governments to provide a registry and an approval proceeding according to Article 6.4 of the Paris Agreement. However, governments are not mandated to provide similar approvals for activities registered with other programmes, such as those typically associated with the VCMs. Regarding this right, the adoption of compliance carbon markets regulation might help countries to rule registration[230] and approval processes.

The second is a *property* right.[231] This entails the project developer's entitlement to possess and assert legal ownership of carbon assets, typically in the form of credits, that can be attributed to the emission reductions or removals stemming from a specific activity. The exercise of this right is usually contingent upon agreements among the parties involved in the relevant activity and the legal, regulatory, and customary framework of the country where the activity is carried out. The relevant regulation for this type of right in VCMs can be found in international standards, such as VERRA and the Gold Standard. For instance, in the latter it is required to prove 'full and uncontested legal ownership of any Products that are generated under Gold Standard Certification'.[232]

The third type of right encompasses *the use of carbon credits*.[233] This refers to the entitlement of an entity to utilise carbon credits for a particular purpose, be it for corporate claims, achieving NDC targets, or fulfilling compliance obligations. Although

228 The Nature Conservancy, 'Article 6 Q&A on What Was Decided and Next Steps after COP26'. www.nature.org/content/dam/tnc/nature/en/documents/Article_6_Common_Questions_V2.pdf accessed 30th October 2023.

229 EY, 'Carbon Credit Rights under the Paris Agreement: How Article 6 and the Implementation of NDCs May Shape Government Approaches to the Carbon Market, and What This Mean for Rights Related to Carbon Credits', November 2022. www.goldstandard.org/sites/default/files/documents/carbon_credit_rights_under_the_paris_agreement_november_2022.pdf accessed 30th October 2023.

230 In Colombia certain activities are required to register on RENARE, the National Registry of Reduction of Greenhouse Gas Emissions. Law 1753 2015. Article 175, Resolution 1447 2018.

231 ibid.

232 Gold Standard for the Global Goals, Principles and Requirements Version 1.2, October 2019. https://globalgoals.goldstandard.org/standards/101_V1.2_PAR_Principles-Requirements.pdf accessed 30th October 2023.

233 ibid.

there is no international definition of carbon credits, the regulatory recognition as a commodity, financial instrument, tangible, or intangible asset, or as a set of contractual rights,[234] is key to understanding carbon credit functionality. For instance, to define carbon assets as intangible assets categorises them as a provision of services. This is the case of the Colombian regulatory definition of voluntary carbon credits (VCCs),[235] and the interpretation of the English Courts.[236] The LSE's VCM[237] considers VCCs a tradeable certificate that represents a certified removal or avoidance of one ton of CO2 equivalent. Alternatively, the ISDA identifies the possibility of characterising VCCs as a bundle of rights, therefore identifying the claimed reductions as a 'contractual right to benefit from the verification process performed by the project developer'.[238] This legal nature of VCCs requires clarity regarding express and implied contractual rights, as well as the liability regime for project developers, verifiers, carbon standard and registrar.[239] As we explained earlier in this book, implied terms allow for judicial intervention, while maintaining the appearance of respecting the parties' self-determination. This is a trend adopted in the UK, the EU, and the US, that seeks to recognise parties' commitments to sustainability-related clauses.

There is also the possibility of categorising VCCs as financial instruments. In the EU, financial derivatives associated with VCCs, excluding those involving emission allowances, are classified as financial instruments if they meet the criteria outlined in Section C of Annex I of MIFID II.[240] In general, all transactions other than spot contracts will be regulated as financial instruments. Therefore, they will also be subject to EMIR.[241] In the UK, the question would be whether derivatives on VCCs would classify as 'specified investments' under the Financial Services and Markets Act 2000 rules for Regulated Activities.[242] The FCA Handbook clearly identifies that the trade of emission allowances is considered financial instrument, whether negotiated on the spot or as an underlying for an option, a future, or a contract for differences.[243]

In the US, if VCCs are the underlying asset in a derivatives transaction, it is probable that it would be categorised as a swap. In such a scenario, the extent of regulatory supervision varies depending on whether it is traded on a designated contract market (DCM)[244] or executed directly between eligible contract

234 ISDA, 'Legal Implications of Voluntary Carbon Credits', December 2021. www.isda.org/a/38ngE/Legal-Implications-of-Voluntary-Carbon-Credits.pdf accessed 30th October 2023.

235 Colombian Nacional Tax Law (Estatuto Tributario). Article 420.

236 *Armstrong v Winnington* [2012] EWHC 10, [2013] ch. 156.

237 London Stock Exchange, Market Notice, N12/22 – Consultation on the Creation of London Stock Exchange's Voluntary Carbon Market and Amendments to the Admission and Disclosure Standards, 2022, 6. https://docs.londonstockexchange.com/sites/default/files/documents/n1222_2.pdf accessed 30th October 2023.

238 ISDA, 'Legal Implications of Voluntary Carbon Credits' (n 234) 10.

239 ibid.

240 Directive 2014/65/EU (as amended).

241 Regulation (EU) No. 648/2012 (as amended).

242 FSMA 2002, Order 2001/544.

243 FCA Handbook, PERG 2.6.19D, 'Specified Investments: A Broad Outline – Emission Allowances'.

244 Section 5 of the Commodity Exchange Act (CEA).

participants.[245] Futures contracts traded on a DCM are subject to CFTC oversight, which encompasses activities like trade practice monitoring and enforcement measures. On the other hand, bilateral derivatives might potentially fall under the purview of the CFTC's regulations governing trading, clearing, and reporting, in addition to obligatory margin rules.[246]

The VCM, with its intricate network of registries, standards, and frameworks, provides a solid foundation for the development of a robust secondary market for VCM units (e.g., VCCs). This burgeoning secondary market now incorporates financial derivative products that play crucial roles in supporting the market's growth and stability.

Types of derivatives in the carbon markets. Derivatives have become a significant component in compliance markets for carbon emissions, with the EU ETS leading the way as the world's most developed carbon market.[247] In 2021, the EU ETS accounted for a substantial portion of carbon trading, reflecting the success of futures and options contracts related to compliance products. Compliance products, such as emission certificates, are ideal for futures markets, due to their standardised nature, ensuring perfect fungibility and ease of trade on exchanges and OTC markets.

In the context of the EU, the compliance market is ruled by an ample cap-and-trade system. The regulation includes the EU ETS Directive, European Climate Law, Regulation (EU) 2018/84216, and Regulation (EU) 2018/841. The EU ETS Directive mandates that member states compel companies involved in specific regulated activities and emitting designated GHGs during those activities to obtain Emission Allowances (EAs) for engagement in those activities.[248]

To clarify the market structure, the ISDA explains that carbon markets are also divided into primary and secondary markets. The first allows the selling of allowances by parties in compliance carbon schemes, and the purchasing of carbon credits generated by emission reduction projects by entities in compliance and voluntary markets.[249] Secondary markets exist for the subsequent trading of EAs and offset credits. In these markets, counterparties can trade on the spot or through derivatives contracts, whereby the most traded are futures and options.[250]

According to ESMA,[251] secondary market trading in EAs occurs through both trading venues authorised under MiFID II and OTC transactions. These are derivatives related to EAs: contracts with a daily expiration or 'daily futures' (futures with varying maturities), and options on futures. In practice, numerous regulated

245 Dodd-Frank Act 2010.

246 CFTC, '17 CFR Parts 39 and 140 RIN 3038-AF12 Reporting and Information Requirements for Derivatives Clearing Organisations', Latest Reform 8 August 2023. www.cftc.gov/sites/default/files/2023/08/2023-16591a.pdf accessed 30th October 2023.

247 ISDA, 'Role of Derivatives in Carbon Markets', September 2021. www.isda.org/a/soigE/Role-of-Derivatives-in-Carbon-Markets.pdf accessed 30th October 2023.

248 Annex I EU ETS Directive.

249 ibid.

250 ibid.

251 ESMA, 'Final Report on Emission Allowances and Associated Derivatives', ESMA70-445-48 (hereafter: 'ESMA Report 2022'), 28 March 2022, paras 16–18.

entities opt to enter long future positions with investment firms to obtain EAs, rather than acquiring them directly from the spot market.[252]

Along with the MiFID II provisions (that understand that EAs and derivatives with EAs as underlying assets are financial instruments), the Market Abuse Regulation[253] is also applicable to these transactions. When EAs and related derivatives are negotiated on a trading venue, counterparties must comply with provisions to prevent and detect abusive behaviour.

Also, as the categorisation of financial instruments of MiFID II mandates the adoption of the Central Securities Depositories Regulation,[254] such regulation also governs EAs and related derivatives. Hence, transactions involving EAs are required to be settled no later than the second business day following the trading (T+2), except in the case of private negotiations.[255] The Central Securities Depositories Regulation mandates that trading venues and central securities depositories implement measures to prevent and address settlement failures. Settlement discipline encompasses three key components: reporting requirements, cash penalties, and mandatory buy-ins. The first two elements became effective only in February 2022, while the implementation of mandatory buy-ins was suspended.[256] Moreover, under EMIR, counterparties to derivative transactions involving EAs must report these trades to a trade repository.[257]

EAs and related derivatives can also be traded on the OTC market. Although these transactions can be freely negotiated, the delivery of the allowances always takes place through the Union Registry.[258] According to EMIR, OTC derivatives transactions should be reported to a trade repository.[259]

In addition to the EU ETS, derivatives markets have emerged for the UK ETS,[260] Regional Greenhouse Gas Initiative,[261] and California Carbon allowances in North

252 Melvin Tjon Akon, 'The Role of Market Operators in Scaling Up Voluntary Carbon Markets', *Capital Markets Law Journal* 18.2 (2023): 259–275.

253 Regulation (EU) No. 596/2014 of 16 April 2014 on market abuse.

254 Art 2.1.8 CSDR (referring to art 4.1.15 MiFID II).

255 Melvin Tjon Akon, 'The Role of Market Operators in Scaling Up Voluntary Carbon Markets' (n 252).

256 EC, 'Reviewing the Central Securities Depositories Regulation to boost the EU's Capital Markets Union', 16 March 2022. https://ec.europa.eu/commission/presscorner/detail/en/qanda_22_1730 accessed 1st November 2023.

257 Art 9.1 EMIR.

258 ESMA Report 2022, para 20; Art 4 Auctioning Regulation, Commission Regulation (EU) No. 1031/2010 of 12 November 2010 on the timing, administration and other aspects of auctioning of greenhouse gas emission allowances.

259 See Arias-Barrera and Ligia Catherine, *Regulation and Supervision of the OTC Derivatives Market* (n 118).

260 The UK Emissions Trading Scheme (UK ETS) replaced the UK's participation in the European Union Emissions Trading Scheme (EU ETS) on 1 January 2021. See UK Government, 'Policy Paper.UK Emissions Trading Scheme Markets', 5 September 2023. www.gov.uk/government/publications/uk-emissions-trading-scheme-markets/uk-emissions-trading-scheme-markets accessed 31st October 2023.

261 Regional Greenhouse Gas Initiative (RGGI): An Initiative of Eastern States of the US. www.rggi.org/program-overview-and-design/elements accessed 31st October 2023.

America.[262] The UK ETS[263] was designed to replace the EU ETS market after Brexit, and applies to energy-intensive industries, the power generation sector, and aviation. The Regional Greenhouse Gas Initiative is a collaborative endeavour, involving Connecticut, Delaware, Maine, Maryland, Massachusetts, New Hampshire, New Jersey, New York, Rhode Island, and Vermont. Its primary goal is to limit and decrease CO_2 emissions from the power sector, by setting a regional cap on the quantity of carbon dioxide emissions generated by power plants and issuing a restricted quantity of tradable carbon dioxide allowances.[264] The programme is praised for reducing fossil fuel energy sources for electricity generation;[265] however, its classification as a subregional programme entails the risk of emissions leakage, as it allows for emissions reductions in the regulated regions to be potentially counteracted by an increase in emissions in the unregulated regions.[266] In this scenario, the risks created by the functioning of compliance markets illustrates, once again, the difficulties that carbon markets face as an effective solution to achieve net zero.

By contrast, in the VCM, the development of derivatives has been slower.[267] Unlike compliance markets, where a central entity issues compliance instruments, VCMs rely on certified carbon projects.[268] These carbon offset credits, once certified, become freely tradable – but possess unique characteristics defined by factors such as project type, geography, vintage year, certifying entity, and associated co-benefits. This diversity makes standardisation challenging, leading to a wide range of prices in the VCM space. In this context, it is essential to make a conceptual distinction. Carbon offsetting represents the actionable process responsible for generating the carbon credit, whereas a carbon credit serves as the tangible metric demonstrating the amount of GHG extracted from the atmosphere via a designated carbon-offset project. This implies that carbon offsets do not necessarily need to be retired after purchase, whereas carbon credits, once purchased, can be retired. When a carbon credit is retired, it is taken out of the market – making it non-negotiable – as an entity has confirmed the fulfilment of the emission reductions promised.[269]

262 ICE Environmental Markets. www.theice.com/energy/environmental accessed 30th October 2023.

263 The Greenhouse Gas Emissions Trading Scheme Order 2020. www.legislation.gov.uk/uksi/2020/1265/contents/made accessed 1st November 2023.

264 Jingchi Yan, 'The Impact of Climate Policy on Fossil Fuel Consumption: Evidence from the Regional Greenhouse Gas Initiative (RGGI)', *Energy Economics* 100 (2021): 105333.

265 ibid.

266 ibid.

267 Gregor Spilker and Nick Nugent, 'Voluntary Carbon Market Derivatives: Growth, Innovation & Usage', *Borsa Istanbul Review* 22.Supplement 2 (2022): s109–s118.

268 Allegra Dawes, Cy McGeady and Joseph Majkut, 'Voluntary Carbon Markets: A Review of Global Initiatives and Evolving Models', CSIS Briefs, May 2023. https://csis-website-prod.s3.amazonaws.com/s3fs-public/2023-05/230531_Dawes_Voluntary_CarbonMarkets.pdf?VersionId=Ji7fxv9DiPwRUJekj.0SJ14GCdstvZh8 accessed 31st October 2023.

269 McKinsey, 'A Blueprint for Scaling Voluntary Carbon Markets to Meet the Climate Challenge', 29 January, 2023. www.mckinsey.com/capabilities/sustainability/our-insights/a-blueprint-for-scaling-voluntary-carbon-markets-to-meet-the-climate-challenge accessed 1st November 2023.

In terms of market development, some actors such as CME Group, and exchanges such as ICE and Nodal/EEX, have been offering standardised VCM futures. This new offer responds to market participants' needs. Seeking to provide a solution for managing price risks associated with carbon markets in different regions, the CME Group created the Global Emissions Offset futures (GEO) contract.[270] The contract is a physically settled agreement, that enables the delivery of CORSIA-eligible voluntary carbon offset credits sourced from three registries: Verified Carbon Standard,[271] American Carbon Registry,[272] and Climate Action Reserve (CAR).[273] The facilitation of deliveries is managed by CBL.[274]

Furthermore, the CME Group introduced CBL Nature-based Global Emissions Offset (N-GEO) futures, featuring offset credits from Verra AFOLU projects,[275] which must conform to Verra's Climate, Community, and Biodiversity (CCB) standards to capture co-benefits. This agreement extends the achievements of CBL GEO futures, providing an additional risk management instrument for addressing carbon footprints in the expanding voluntary emissions offset market.[276] The CME Group also launched CBL Core GEO Global Emissions Offset (C-GEO) futures, aiming to align with the Core Carbon Principles (CCPs),[277] an emerging set of transparent standards overseen by the Integrity Council for the Voluntary Carbon Market. This contract enhances and further leverages the achievements of both CBL GEO futures and CBL N-GEO (Nature-based) futures, offering greater flexibility to industries that are proactively managing their carbon footprints in the voluntary emissions offset market.[278]

As the market evolves, these derivatives help connect physical and financial markets, facilitating the growth and scalability of voluntary carbon projects

270 CME Group, 'CBL Global Emissions Offset futures (GEO)'. www.cmegroup.com/education/articles-and-reports/cbl-global-emissions-offset-futures-faq.html accessed 31st October 2023.

271 Verra, 'The World's Leading Greenhouse Gas Crediting Program'. https://verra.org/programs/verified-carbon-standard/ accessed 1st November 2023.

272 American Carbon Registry Standard was Founded in 1996 as the GHG Registry. www.offsetguide.org/understanding-carbon-offsets/carbon-offset-programs/voluntary-offset-programs/american-carbon-registry/ accessed 1st November 2023.

273 Climate Action Reserve – Voluntary Offset Program. www.climateactionreserve.org/how/voluntary-offset-program/ accessed 1st November 2023.

274 CBL is an Xpansiv company that offers access to the global energy and environmental commodity markets, enabling the safe and smooth trading of various commodities, including carbon, renewable energy, water, and natural gas. https://xpansiv.com accessed 31st October 2023.

275 Verra, 'Area of Focus – Agriculture, Forestry, and Other Land Use (AFOLU)'. https://verra.org/programs/verified-carbon-standard/area-of-focus-agriculture-forestry-land-use/ accessed 1st November 2023.

276 CME Group, 'CBL Nature-Based Global Emissions Offset', Last updated 31 October 2023. www.cmegroup.com/markets/energy/emissions/cbl-nature-based-global-emissions-offset.html# accessed 31st October 2023.

277 ICVCM, 'The Core Carbon Principles', March 2023. https://icvcm.org/wp-content/uploads/2023/07/CCP-Foreword-R2-FINAL-26Jul23.pdf accessed 31st October 2023.

278 CME Group, 'CBL Core Global Emissions Offset Futures', Last updated 31 October 2023. www.cmegroup.com/markets/energy/emissions/cbl-core-global-emissions-offset-c-geo.html# accessed 31st October 2023.

worldwide.[279] Indeed, there are several initiatives that see – in the blockchain tokenisation – an opportunity to integrate innovation and the benefits of the VCM. With the promise of a more transparent, secure, and immutable ledger system, the adoption of blockchain based systems may help overcome some of the VCM's shortfalls. As enhanced monitoring and reporting mechanisms are essential to track emissions, verify reductions, and ensure compliance, blockchain-based solutions may provide greater levels of transparency and traceability.[280]

Blockchain enables the creation of an unalterable ledger that records the complete life cycle of carbon credits.[281] Every transaction, from credit issuance to retirement, is meticulously documented in a transparent and publicly accessible manner. This transparency fosters trust among participants and enables buyers to trace the origin and legitimacy of carbon credits. Similarly, blockchain-based platforms can provide real-time reporting of emissions reductions, enabling buyers to track the impact of their investments almost immediately. This level of accountability enhances the credibility of carbon credits.

The emergence of blockchain tokenisation and exchange-traded funds holding futures contracts has further diversified market participation and trading practices. While these developments bring opportunities for liquidity and innovation, they have also raised concerns about potential value erosion, and the need to maintain the integrity and reputation of the VCM. As the market matures, striking a balance between standardisation and innovation remains crucial for building a VCM market that is sustainable and effective.

The rise of reference prices and associated derivatives represents a significant milestone for the VCM sector.[282] In the past, price transparency was a challenge, and there were concerns that project developers, especially in the Global South, were disadvantaged by intermediaries who obtained low-cost offset credits and resold them at high margins.[283] However, the introduction of futures contracts with publicly available settlement prices now offers project developers the means to observe benchmark carbon offset values for both immediate and future delivery

279 Gregor Spilker and Nick Nugent, 'Voluntary Carbon Market Derivatives: Growth, Innovation & Usage' (n 267).

280 UNFCCC, 'UN Supports Blockchain Technology for Climate Action', 2018. https://unfccc.int/news/un-supports-blockchain-technology-for-climate-action accessed 31st October 2023.

281 Adam Sipthorpe, Sabine Brink, Tyler Van Leeuwen and Iain Staffel, 'Blockchain Solutions for Carbon Markets Are Nearing Maturity', Centre for Environmental Policy, Imperial College London, One Earth 5, 15 July 2022, 779–791. www.cell.com/one-earth/pdf/S2590-3322(22)00325-6.pdf accessed 31st October 2023.

282 Karel Lannoo and Apostolos Thomadakis, 'Derivatives in Sustainable Finance', Centre for European Policy Studies (CEPS) and the European Capital Markets Institute (ECMI), 2020. www.ceps.eu/wp-content/uploads/2020/07/Derivatives-in-Sustainable-Finance.pdf accessed 1st November 2023.

283 Betz Regina, Axel Michaelowa, Paula Castro, Raphaela Kotsch, Michael Mehling, Katharina Michaelowa and Andrea Baranzini, *The Carbon Market Challenge: Preventing Abuse Through Effective Governance (Elements in Earth System Governance)* (Cambridge University Press, 2022).

periods.[284] This newfound price transparency is immensely valuable to project developers,[285] empowering them with a reference point to budget, negotiate, and execute carbon offset projects.

Though these reference prices might not exactly match the unique attributes of each project, they can serve as a foundation for price negotiations. Project-specific qualities can be accounted for, through premiums or discounts attached to the reference prices. As Spilker and Nugent highlight,[286] leading exchanges like CME Group, among others, are listing various futures contracts to establish distinct reference prices for different sectors within the VCM. These sectors encompass CORSIA-aligned projects, nature-based solutions, natural climate solutions, and IVSCM-aligned projects.[287] This approach mirrors the path taken by oil derivatives markets, where physically deliverable futures contracts for WTI and Brent serve as global reference prices for crude oil,[288] with regional quality differences reflected in premiums or discounts compared to those global benchmarks.[289] By adopting this trajectory of futurisation, and embracing standardised reference prices, the VCM is moving towards greater clarity and efficiency in its pricing mechanisms, providing a stable foundation for the market's continued growth and success.

Regulations in carbon markets facilitate efficient allocation of emission allowances or carbon credits, by establishing clear rules and market mechanisms. Transparent and well-functioning markets enable price discovery, helping to internalise the cost of carbon and guide investment decisions. Projects in VCMs encompass a wide range of activities, including renewable energy installations, energy efficiency initiatives, afforestation and reforestation projects, methane capture and destruction projects, and community-based sustainable development projects. These projects are typically certified according to recognised standards, such as the Verified Carbon Standard or the Gold Standard, ensuring their environmental integrity and contribution to sustainable development. Despite these positive features of the VCM, there are also shortcomings that affect the development of the market.

Unsolved challenges of the VCM. There are multiple features that build credibility in pricing accuracy and trustworthiness. However, some challenges remain, such as an opaque trading environment and related quality concerns.

284 OPIS Carbon Team, 'Price Transparency and Growth in the Voluntary Carbon Market', 10 February 2022. www.opisnet.com/blog/price-transparency-growth-vcm/ accessed 2nd November 2023.

285 See Aki Kachi and Michel Frerk, *Carbon Market Oversight Primer* (International Carbon Action Partnership (ICAP), 2013).

286 Gregor Spilker and Nick Nugent, 'Voluntary Carbon Market Derivatives: Growth, Innovation & Usage' (n 267).

287 ibid.

288 Pavel Katyukha and Angela Mottaeva, 'Evolution of Global Oil Benchmarks: New Trends in Pricing in the International Oil Market', *E3S Web of Conferences* 284 (2021): 01008. www.e3s-conferences.org/articles/e3sconf/pdf/2021/60/e3sconf_tpacee2021_01008.pdf accessed 2nd November 2023.

289 ICE, 'Global Crude Benchmarks: Brent Sets the Standard', 2020. www.ice.com/global-crude-benchmarks-brent-sets-the-standard accessed 2nd November 2023.

Even though VCMs offer a market signal and establish a carbon price, which, in turn, encourages businesses and investors to incorporate the cost of carbon emissions and sustainability considerations into their decision-making processes, the varied scope of available projects presents pricing challenges, ultimately resulting in issues related to information asymmetry.[290] To understand the value of credits under negotiation, project developers and buyers must keep track of competitors' bilateral agreements and consider differences between projects in terms of type, technology, geography, and methodology.[291] This ad hoc, bilateral carbon sales system creates an opaque trading environment, causing prolonged negotiations and high transaction costs for both parties.[292] Unfortunately, this burden tends to fall disproportionately on project developers, who rely on financing and are eager to secure deals, while well-capitalised buyers can take their time to accumulate carbon project inventory.

In the past, the opacity and evolving nature of the VCM led to quality concerns with certain credits.[293] Projects verified under less rigorous monitoring and verification requirements, as well as early iterations of methodologies, may not accurately represent actual reductions or avoidance in CO_2 emissions. This situation allowed savvy traders to sell these credits, generating revenue without significant emissions impact.[294] As a result, credits of older vintage slipped into purchase agreements, leading to public criticism and accusations of a fraudulent and poorly functioning market.

To address these issues, exchanges have emerged to facilitate and optimise price discovery in the VCM.[295] By establishing standard trading terms, exchanges seek to improve transparency in the VCM space. For example, the LSE VCM[296] was created with three primary goals in mind: boosting funding for emissions reduction initiatives; enhancing transparency and regulatory structures within the global VCM; and providing companies and investors with access to a marketplace for acquiring carbon credits. Similarly, there has been a surge of private multi-actor

290 Allegra Dawes, Cy McGeady and Joseph Majkut, 'Voluntary Carbon Markets: A Review of Global Initiatives and Evolving Models', 21 May 2023. www.csis.org/analysis/voluntary-carbon-markets-review-global-initiatives-and-evolving-models accessed 2nd November 2023.

291 Gregor Spilker and Nick Nugent, 'Voluntary Carbon Market Derivatives: Growth, Innovation & Usage' (n 267).

292 A. Bose, J. Cohen, B. Fattouh, O. Johnson and G. Spilker, 'Voluntary Markets for Carbon Offsets: Evolution and Lessons for the LNG Market', 2021. www.oxfordenergy.org/wpcms/wp-content/uploads/2021/10/Voluntary-markets-for-carbon-offsets-Evolution-features-and-lessons-for-the-LNG-market-ET03.pdf accessed 2nd November 2023.

293 Allegra Dawes, Cy McGeady and Joseph Majkut, 'Voluntary Carbon Markets: A Review of Global Initiatives and Evolving Models' (n 290).

294 A. Bose, J. Cohen, B. Fattouh, O. Johnson and G Spilker, 'Voluntary Markets for Carbon Offsets: Evolution and Lessons for the LNG Market' (n 292).

295 Allegra Dawes, Cy McGeady and Joseph Majkut, 'Voluntary Carbon Markets: A Review of Global Initiatives and Evolving Models' (n 290).

296 LSE, 'London Stock Exchange's Voluntary Carbon Market'. www.londonstockexchange.com/raise-finance/sustainable-finance/voluntary-carbon-market accessed 2nd November 2023.

initiatives as the GX League. This initiative is a system for voluntary emissions reduction and trading, attracting participation from Japanese corporations. While joining the GX League is voluntary, adherence to the rules and meeting emissions reduction targets is compulsory for companies to maintain their position in the league. The GX League carbon credit market will be facilitated by the Japan Exchange Group, and accessible to both GX League participants and other organisations looking to engage in credit trading. The Ministry of Economy, Trade, and Industry (METI)[297] intends to establish annual price floors and ceilings for carbon, with gradual increments in these price limits over time.

The development of the CCPs is regarded as an important step towards greater transparency and reliability of the VCM and for the financial contracts within it. These CCPs are based on previous and well recognised regulatory instruments, such as: the TSVCM, the IPCC, the UNFCC Paris Agreement and Cancun Safeguards, the International Civil Aviation Organisation CORSIA, and the work of Calyx Global and the Carbon Credit Quality Initiative.[298] This integration is key, to see the broad structure that guides the development of the VCM. Although the CCPs are praised for being comprehensive in terms of governance, emissions impact, and sustainable development, real corporate commitment is still required.[299] A recent principal study challenges the common notion that most projects aimed at reducing emissions from deforestation and forest degradation are as beneficial as they are frequently portrayed to be.[300] It is argued that the methodologies employed to establish deforestation baselines for carbon offset initiatives require prompt revisions, to accurately attribute reduced deforestation to these projects.[301]

The CCPs are under continuous review, seeking to become a tool for the growth of the VCM in both developed and developing countries. The Integrity Council[302] has initiated evaluations of carbon-crediting programmes and credit categories using the CCPs Assessment Framework. Following the completion of these assessments, programmes meeting the CCP eligibility criteria will gain the ability to issue credits labelled as CCP-compliant, provided they are from CCP-approved credit categories. The purpose of the CCP label is to facilitate access to essential private

297 METI, 'Making Progress toward Social Transformation and New Market Creation for Carbon Neutrality with the 440 Companies Endorsing the GX League!', Second Segment Held, 1 April 2022. www.meti.go.jp/english/press/2022/0401_001.html accessed 2nd November 2023.

298 ICVCM, 'Section 2: Core Carbon Principles – Core Carbon Principles 2023', July 2023. https://icvcm.org/wp-content/uploads/2023/07/CCP-Section-2-R2-FINAL-26Jul23.pdf accessed 31st October 2023.

299 Melodie Michel, 'Voluntary Carbon Market Integrity Initiative: "We Need Corporates to Take Action"', 10 October 2023. www.csofutures.com/news/voluntary-carbon-market-integrity-initiative-we-need-corporates-to-take-action/ accessed 1st November 2023.

300 Thales A. P. West et al., 'Action Needed to Make Carbon Offsets From Forest Conservation Work for Climate Change Mitigation', *Science* 381 (2023): 873–877.

301 ibid.

302 ICVCM, 'Core Carbon Principles Assessments and Working Groups Now Underway', 1 November 2023. https://icvcm.org/core-carbon-principles-assessments-and-working-groups-now-underway/ accessed 2nd November 2023.

sector investments in climate solutions, that might not otherwise be economically viable. This, in turn, is expected to benefit the flow of financial resources to nations in the Global South, supporting the development of robust green economies.[303]

The projects' assessment against the CCPs establishes the criteria that carbon-crediting programmes and categories need to satisfy to be eligible for the CCP label.[304] These criteria require that credits must support projects aimed at alignment with a transition to net zero. Projects must be designed to compensate for any reversals that might occur within a 40-year timeframe. Regarding additionality, the emissions reductions and removals should be a direct result of the revenue generated from carbon credits, meaning they would not have occurred otherwise.[305] Moreover, the emissions impact should be strictly measured to minimise the risk of overestimation. Once the assessment has been conducted, it can yield one of three outcomes: the programme is granted CCP-eligibility status, or it receives approval but with specified remedial actions to be addressed within a two-month period, or the programme is not approved, and the reasons for rejection will be communicated to the programme. There is then the option to reapply after a six-month interval.[306]

Evaluating the quality of a carbon project hinges significantly on the concept of additionality. This concept ensures that emission reductions or removals are *additional* to business-as-usual scenarios[307] – crucial in carbon market regulation. Additionality is a critical requirement, because if non-additional projects are eligible for carbon finance, it could lead to a continued increase in net GHG emissions. This would, in turn, raise doubts about the environmental integrity of carbon reduction projects.[308] There has been an extensive debate on how to better approach the additionality issue of carbon markets, as it is a constant risk that undermines the confidence in the market. One proposal suggests adopting the notion of legal or regulatory additionality.[309] If there is an existing law regulating a specific activity, it is highly likely that the project associated with it will not qualify for carbon finance. Consequently, for a project to satisfy the legal additionality standard, it must deliver carbon reductions that surpass the legally mandated requirements.[310] Although helpful to measure the level of compliance with emission reduction targets, legal additionality may exacerbate the risk of negative incentives in the carbon market. Seen through the lens of the risk-based approach, regulatory additionality may manufacture new risks triggered by a

303 ibid.

304 ICVCM, 'The Core Carbon Principles Assessment Framework', July 2023. https://icvcm.org/assessment-framework/ accessed 2nd November 2023.

305 ibid.

306 ICVCM, 'CCPs' Assessment Procedure', July 2023. https://icvcm.org/wp-content/uploads/2023/07/CCP-Section-6-R2-FINAL-26Jul23.pdf accessed 2nd November 2023.

307 See World Bus, 'Council for Sustainable Development', *CDM Project Developers Workshop* 6 (2005). www.wbcsd.org accessed 1st November 2023.

308 Brian Joseph McFarland, 'Carbon Reduction Projects and the Concept of Additionality', *Sustainable Development Law & Policy* 11 (2011): 15.

309 ibid.

310 ibid.

merely formalistic compliance of the law. Likewise, legal additionality might not always be welcomed. In cases where projects offer crucial financing in countries with pre-existing corrupt infrastructures, there might be a reluctance to enhance legal frameworks that could potentially reduce the quantity of carbon reduction projects.[311]

The risk of corruption and the malfunctioning of carbon markets is intertwined with another risk stemming from the underlying rationale of these markets. This revolves around the dual purpose of carbon markets: reducing emissions to combat climate change, while also serving as a financial mechanism to facilitate the 'internalisation' of costs for carbon-emitting entities and maintaining their competitiveness.[312] This risk was acknowledged by the Clean Development Mechanism (CDM) through the concept of financial additionality. Within this category, entities should assess whether the project would have been financially viable, even in the absence of income generated from carbon reduction credits.[313] The problem of considering financial additionality is that the metrics used (i.e., discount rates and benchmarks) are not always uniformly adopted. There are also some other arbitrary variables that certain types of projects take into consideration (e.g., company size, geographical location, time in business, and so on). Against this background, alternative conceptions of additionality have been discussed, mainly those suggesting a project-by-project or performance-by-sector approach. These approaches, adopted by the Verified Carbon Standard, seek to provide a more accurate instance of how additionality should be measured.

Within the UNFCCC, sectoral concepts are typically considered as subcategories of Nationally Appropriate Mitigation Actions, designed for developing countries. The introduction of new mechanisms aimed at encouraging emission reductions in developing countries is likely to intensify the demand for assessing additionality in various endeavours, whether they involve financing or emission reduction efforts. Streck[314] asserts that, in cases where emission reductions are credited at the policy or programme level, the additionality test would need to be conducted at policy level, rather than at the level of the individual units implementing the policy or programme. We contend that, to guarantee the consistent adoption of a risk-based approach to additionality, it is essential to establish robust verification mechanisms, and conduct independent and tailored audits. These measures are crucial to ensure the environmental integrity of emission reductions and carbon credits. Stringent and risk-based oversight is required to prevent the issuance of credits for projects that would have transpired regardless, thereby upholding the integrity of the market.

311 U4 Expert Answer, 'Carbon Market Corruption Risks and Mitigation Strategies', Anti-Corruption Resource Centre, 24 September 2015. www.u4.no/publications/carbon-market-corruption-risks-and-mitigation-strategies# accessed 1st November 2023.

312 ibid.

313 Brian Joseph McFarland, 'Carbon Reduction Projects and the Concept of Additionality' (n 308).

314 Charlotte Streck, 'Ensuring New Finance and Real Emission Reduction: A Critical Review of the Additionality Concept', *Carbon & Climate Law Review* 5 (2011): 158.

There is also the risk of double counting, where the same emission reduction is claimed and sold as carbon credits in multiple markets. In the simplest terms, double counting occurs when a carbon credit (along with its associated climate impact) is claimed by multiple entities.[315] Developing robust accounting methodologies and transparent registries is crucial to prevent double counting, and maintain the environmental integrity of VCMs. Collaboration between governments, market participants, and standard-setting bodies is essential to establish internationally recognised accounting rules and mechanisms. The Gold Standard, for instance, issued some guidelines to manage this risk. It gives the project developer the opportunity to collect evidence to show the Gold Standard that there is no risk of double counting. Alternatively, the project developer may choose to cancel a valid or eligible unit, in accordance with the rules of the host country or the international accounting mechanism.[316] The guideline minimises the risk of double counting, by implementing a safeguard against the potential of a second claim through the cancellation of a second unit.[317]

Despite the efforts to prevent double counting, this practice is not eliminated, and it can manifest in various ways. The most significant manifestations of double counting are double issuance, which involves the issuance of two units for the same reductions, and double claiming, where the same reductions are accounted for both in a GHG inventory and as units toward achieving a mitigation pledge.[318] These occurrences can take place not only directly but also through more intricate means that can be difficult to detect.[319] If we bring the risk-based approach to effectively addressing double counting, the adoption of clear measures regarding unit accounting, the formulation of mechanisms that issue units, and the uniform tracking and reporting of units, must be at the core of the analysis. Moreover, along with stricter market governance, which the CCPs intend to provide, the adoption of new technologies can help to mitigate these risks. By employing blockchain technology, it is possible to reduce the risk of double counting and address similar concerns, all while streamlining the processes of reporting, tracking, and managing corresponding adjustments.[320]

The adoption of VCM instruments for corporate offset strategies is another area of interest. This is of particular significance, since 2023 marks the first time in at

315 Lambert Schneider et al., 'Double Counting and the Paris Agreement Rulebook', *Science* 366 (2019): 180–183.

316 Gold Standard, 'Double Counting Guideline', November 2015. www.goldstandard.org/sites/default/files/documents/2015_12_double_counting_guideline_published_v1.pdf accessed 1st November 2023.

317 ibid.

318 Lambert Schneider, Anja Kollmuss and Michael Lazarus, 'Addressing the Risk of Double Counting Emission Reductions under the UNFCCC', *Climatic Change* 131 (2015): 473–486.

319 ibid.

320 Henrique Schneider, 'Blockchain, Double Counting, and the Paris Agreement', First International Conference on Carbon Pricing, World Bank Working Paper Series, November 2019. www.researchgate.net/profile/Shiran-Shen/publication/338393718_Pricing_Carbon_to_Contain_Violence/links/5e11d1b5a6fdcc28375844e6/Pricing-Carbon-to-Contain-Violence.pdf#page=100 accessed 1st December 2023.

least seven years when the VCMs have shown a decrease in size.[321] This raises questions about how companies integrate VCM projects into their overall sustainability and environmental strategies, how they select offset projects, and the impact of these choices on their brand, reputation, and financial performance.

Recent recommendations on scaling up VCM[322] identify four areas of attention. The first area of focus is to *establish the role of carbon credits in achieving net-zero emissions*. In this regard, it is essential to factor in five aspects: (i) precisely define how they fit within the broader net-zero strategy of the company; (ii) emphasise their complementary nature in conjunction with direct emissions reduction efforts; (iii) ensure that this role is in line with science-based targets;[323] (iv) adhere to the mitigation hierarchy; and (v) take into consideration technological, financial, and other constraints that affect the decarbonisation process.[324]

This foundational task should start with a well-defined reference point, serving as the baseline for mapping the company's emissions footprint, including Scopes 1, 2, and 3 emissions, across its operations and the entire value chain. While the Scope 1 encompasses the direct GHG emissions produced by the company, Scope 2 covers the indirect emissions associated with the company, for instance, when the electricity or energy used for heating and cooling in its buildings is generated on its behalf.[325] The category of Scope 3 includes all emissions that are not directly generated by the company itself, but for which the organisation holds indirect responsibility along its entire value chain.[326] This includes emissions stemming from purchasing products from suppliers and emissions arising when customers use the company's products. In this context, developing a net-zero strategy with science-based targets entails a strong commitment to prioritising emissions reductions over reliance on carbon offsets. The company should transparently outline its plans for reducing emissions and establish pathways to replicate and disseminate successful practices throughout the value chain.

The second of the four areas is concerned with *how the VCM will benefit from companies demonstrating value and gaining recognition*. This requires following a process where multiple risks and interests are in play, to identify and communicate the tangible benefits resulting from carbon market activities to both internal and external stakeholders. This approach enhances risk management, strengthens reputation, and engages employees in the company's sustainability efforts. Moreover, the

321 Susanna Twidale and Sarah McFarlane, 'Carbon Credit Market Confidence Ebbs as Big Names Retreat', 1 September 2023. www.reuters.com/sustainability/carbon-credit-market-confidence-ebbs-big-names-retreat-2023-09-01/ accessed 2nd November 2023.

322 WEF, 'Scaling Voluntary Carbon Markets: A Playbook for Corporate Action', Whitepaper, September 2023. https://www3.weforum.org/docs/WEF_Scaling_Voluntary_Carbon_Markets_2023.pdf accessed 2nd November 2023.

323 See SBTi, 'SBTi Corporate Net-Zero Standard', Version 1.1, April 2023. https://sciencebasedtargets.org/resources/files/Net-Zero-Standard.pdf accessed 2nd November 2023.

324 WEF, 'Scaling Voluntary Carbon Markets: A Playbook for Corporate Action' (n 322) 4.

325 GHG, 'GHG Protocol Corporate Standard', 1998. https://ghgprotocol.org/sites/default/files/standards_supporting/FAQ.pdf accessed 2nd November 2023.

326 ibid.

creation of shareholder value is also benefited, at least in the short term, when carbon-related instruments are embedded in corporate strategies.[327] However, involving stakeholders in the conversation and publicising the benefits of a corporate carbon strategy should be done with rigour. A corporate strategy that aligns effectively with tangible and measurable targets is essential for ensuring the alignment between green marketing initiatives and the preservation of corporate reputation.[328]

Thirdly, *companies need to customise their portfolio* to prioritise the development of high-quality, high-impact carbon credit portfolios,[329] and to recognise the importance of avoidance credits, especially in the initial stages, while gradually increasing the focus on permanent carbon removal outcomes. In this scenario, it is central to analyse how corporate strategies encompass the use of VCM projects and derivatives into their sustainability and carbon reduction efforts. The element of measuring financial performance against carbon related targets is pivotal. Some research[330] argues that companies tend to achieve their best financial performance when their carbon performance falls within an intermediate range, neither exceptionally low nor high. Furthermore, environmental processes seem to play a moderating role in this relationship, strengthening a firm's financial performance by enhancing their stakeholder management.[331] Moreover, investment strategies that incorporate carbon offsets tend to yield higher than those that do not.[332] Thus, despite investor uncertainties due to the shortfalls affecting the VCM, portfolios that include emissions products (versus those that do not) perform better, and allow investors flexibility and scale in implementing their carbon strategy.

Finally, *the company's carbon credit strategy should be integrated into its broader net-zero approach and organisational structure*, ensuring coherence and accountability.[333] This means ensuring that carbon credits are seamlessly linked to the overall decarbonisation path and sustainability strategy. Within the corporate strategy the adoption of a risk-based approach can be beneficial, allowing understanding of how VCM derivatives are used for risk management and price discovery. As part of the assessment of the company´s financial performance and

327 Bin Zhang, Kee-hung Lai, Bo Wang and Zhaohua Wang, 'Shareholder Value Effects of Corporate Carbon Trading: Empirical Evidence from Market Reaction Towards Clean Development Mechanism in China', *Energy Policy* 110 (2017): 410–421.

328 Ugur Bati, 'Green Marketing Activities to Support Corporate Reputation on a Sample from Turkey', 26 May 2016. http://ugurbati.com/upload/A2%20(1).pdf accessed 2nd November 2023.

329 WEF, 'Scaling Voluntary Carbon Markets: A Playbook for Corporate Action' (n 322) 4.

330 Nicola Misani and Stefano Pogutz, 'Unravelling the Effects of Environmental Outcomes and Processes on Financial Performance: A Non-Linear Approach', Bocconi University, 21 November 2014. https://mpra.ub.uni-muenchen.de/60359/1/MPRA_paper_60359.pdf accessed 2nd November 2023.

331 ibid.

332 Carsten Mueller, Papa Orgen and Patrick Behr, 'Portfolio Allocation and Optimisation with Carbon Offsets: Is it Worth the While?', *Journal of Climate Finance* 5 (2023): 100019.

333 C. Blaufelder and C. Levy, 'A Blueprint for Scaling Voluntary Carbon Markets', McKinsey, 29 January 2021. www.mckinsey.com/capabilities/sustainability/our-insights/a-blueprint-for-scaling-voluntary-carbon-markets-to-meet-the-climate-challenge accessed 2nd November 2023.

profitability of VCM projects, the cost-effective analysis and returns from derivatives transactions should be revealed. In this context, it is important to recognise the role of retail providers in VCM.[334] They help structure deals and connect project developers with corporate buyers. They offer advisory services and market expertise to buyers who may not be familiar with the VCM's intricacies. These firms also hold inventory of offset credits; while some large corporate buyers may directly produce carbon offsets with project developers, retail providers and brokers remain instrumental in the market.[335] They often assist in financing projects at an early stage by committing to purchase a minimum number of credits at a fixed price, agreed upon in the present.[336]

Conclusion

While there may be potential criticisms regarding the introduction of traditional derivatives with specific ESG KPIs as a distinct category of ESG derivatives, we include this initial category in our study to elucidate the general role of derivatives in sustainability, which primarily revolves around risk management. In this category, we refer to CDS, futures, options, and catastrophe weather derivatives as conventional transactions fulfilling their core function of facilitating effective risk-management practices. The issues related to poor quality of ESG data and endogeneity should be considered when including these derivatives, especially CDSs, into an investment or corporate strategy. Indeed, we argue that the strong connection between corporate sustainability and CDS spreads will only be entirely dependable when progress in ESG reporting significantly improves transparency, and fully realises its potential for driving corporate sustainability initiatives in alignment with the SDGs.

In the context of negotiating options and futures linked to an underlying ESG target, one significant concern is the potential presence of home bias. As we elaborated on in Chapter 2, the availability of ESG data is not uniform across different jurisdictions, with developed economies having a clear advantage over emerging and frontier markets. This situation could exacerbate the existing home bias issue in ESG futures and options markets, further excluding developing markets and depriving them of the opportunity to engage in these types of derivative transactions.

The emergence of SLDs stands out as a prominent example of the significant potential of financial derivatives in advancing well-defined sustainability and ESG objectives. In our examination, these transactions are constructed with the goal of carefully identifying specific KPIs. These KPIs must be integrated into each counterparty's sustainability strategy, to ensure consistency and a systematic approach, making derivatives instrumental in translating sustainable objectives into reality.

334 Camilla Hodgson, 'Surge of Investment into Carbon Credits Creates Boom Time for Brokers', *Financial Times*, 2 May 2022. www.ft.com/content/739a5517-4de6-43f7-ae47-1ce8d4774d50 accessed 2nd November 2023.

335 Gregor Spilker and Nick Nugent, 'Voluntary Carbon Market Derivatives: Growth, Innovation & Usage' (n 267).

336 ibid.

The ISDA recommendations on key provisions and core elements for drafting KPIs serve as the foundation for market participants to ensure that their SLDs achieve the desired outcomes. A key characteristic of SLDs is their adaptability, allowing contracts to be tailored to a wide range of ESG-related objectives.

Carbon markets have witnessed significant growth in recent years, but their potential remains largely untapped. To unlock their full potential, there is a need to scale up the market by increasing demand, enhancing transparency, and streamlining certification processes. Governments, businesses, and civil society must collaborate to create an enabling environment that encourages participation and drives market expansion. VCMs offer a mechanism to simultaneously address climate change and contribute to SDGs. Many offset projects prioritise co-benefits, such as poverty alleviation, biodiversity conservation, clean energy access, and improved livelihoods for local communities. By supporting these projects, VCM participants can actively contribute to the social, economic, and environmental well-being of communities around the world. However, challenges related to additionality, standardisation, and double counting must be addressed through collaborative efforts. With increased market transparency, harmonised standards, and technological advancements, derivatives negotiated in VCMs can play a transformative role in the transition to a low-carbon economy, foster sustainable development, and create a more resilient future for generations to come.

The regulation of carbon markets is crucial for driving climate action, fostering sustainable development, and transitioning to a low-carbon economy. Effective derivatives market regulations and standardised practices ensure market integrity, facilitate emission reductions, and provide price signals to guide investment decisions. By continually adapting and improving the design of carbon credit derivatives, carbon markets can play a transformative role in mitigating climate change and building a more sustainable future.

Bibliography

Books

Betz, R., Michaelowa, A., Castro, P., Kotsch, R., Mehling, M., Michaelowa, K., and Baranzini, A., *The Carbon Market Challenge: Preventing Abuse Through Effective Governance* (Cambridge University Press 2022).

Cash, D., *ESG Rating Agencies and Financial Regulation: A Signalling Theory Approach* (Edward Elgar Publishing 2024).

Cash, D., 'The Sustainability Rating Industry' in *Sustainability Rating Agencies vs Credit Rating Agencies* (Palgrave Macmillan 2021).

Articles

Acharya, V., and Bisin, A., 'Counterparty Risk Externality: Centralized Versus Over-The-Counter Markets' 149 *Journal of Economic Theory* (2014) 153.

Akon, M.T., 'The Role of Market Operators in Scaling Up Voluntary Carbon Markets' 18(2) *Capital Markets Law Journal* (2023) 259.

Albuquerque, R., Koskinen, Y., and Zhang, C., 'Corporate Social Responsibility and Firm Risk: Theory And Empirical Evidence' 65(10) *Management Science* (2019) 4451.

Baker, C., 'Derivatives and ESG' 59(4) *American Business Law Journal* (2022) 745.

Blank, H., Sgambati, G., and Truelson, Z., 'Best Practices in ESG Investing' 25(2) *The Journal of Investing* (2016) 103.

Chan J., and Kim, M., 'ESG Performance in Exchange Traded Funds (ETFs) and Fixed Income in the Context of Home Bias' *School of Economics and Management, Lund University* (2020) 5.

Fankhauser, S., Smith, S.M., Allen, M. *et al.*, 'The Meaning of Net Zero and How to Get It Right' 12 *Nature Climate Change* (2022) 15.

Gardiner, S.M., and Hartzell-Nichols, L., 'Ethics and Global Climate Change' 3(10) *Nature Education Knowledge* (2012) 5.

Gillenwater, M., and Seres., S., 'The Clean Development Mechanism: A Review of the First International Offset Programme' 1(3) *Greenhouse Gas Measurement and Management* (2011) 179.

Lannoo, K., and Thomadakis, A., 'Derivatives in Sustainable Finance', *CEPS-ECMI Study, Centre for European Policy Studies* (2020) 8.

Naumowicz, D., and Hughes, D., 'The Role of Sustainability-Linked Derivatives in Meeting Global ESG Goals' *Butterworths Journal of International Banking and Financial Law* (2021) 628.

Spilker, G., and Nugent, N., 'Voluntary Carbon Market Derivatives: Growth, Innovation & Usage' 22(2) *Borsa Istanbul Review* (2022) S109.

Working Papers

Dawes, A., Cy McGeady, C., and Majkut, J., 'Voluntary Carbon Markets: A Review of Global Initiatives and Evolving Models', CSIS Briefs (May 2023).

Eurex, 'The Changing Shape of Derivatives Markets: A Deep Dive into ESG Investing'(2020) <www.eurexchange.com/resource/blob/1680460/2aa48304dc6662065a81e880e720bd9d/data/A_Deep_dive_into_ESG.pdf>accessed 29th November 2023.

Eurex, 'Product Coverage ESG Futures & Options' (August 2023) <www.eurex.com/resource/blob/2665714/e772e787f0997c11ca08372ee321dc65/data/presentation_ESG_product_coverage.pdf>accessed 3rd October 2023.

ISDA, 'Accounting Analysis for ESG-related Transactions and the Impact on Derivatives' (September 2021) <www.isda.org/2021/09/07/accounting-analysis-for-esg-related-transactions-and-the-impact-on-derivatives> accessed 23rd October 2023.

ISDA, 'Consultation Response ESAs Call for Evidence on Greenwashing' (10 January 2023) <www.isda.org/a/GYxgE/ISDA-response-to-ESAs-greenwashing-CfE.pdf> accessed 19th November 2023.

ISDA, 'Legal Implications of Voluntary Carbon Credits' (December 2021) <www.isda.org/a/38ngE/Legal-Implications-of-Voluntary-Carbon-Credits.pdf> accessed 30th October 2023.

ISDA, 'Overview of ESG-related Derivatives Products and Transactions' (January 2021) <www.isda.org/a/qRpTE/Overview-ofESG-related-Derivatives-Products-and-Transactions.pdf > accessed 18th November 2023.

ISDA, 'Regulatory Considerations for Sustainability-linked Derivatives' (5 December 2021) <www.isda.org/a/58ngE/Regulatory-Considerations-for-Sustainability-linked-Derivatives.pdf> accessed 7th October 2023.

ISDA, 'Role of Derivatives in Carbon Markets' (September 2021) <www.isda.org/a/soigE/Role-of-Derivatives-in-Carbon-Markets.pdf> accessed 30th October 2023.

ISDA, 'Sustainability-linked Derivatives: KPI Guidelines' (September 2021) <www.isda.org/a/xvTgE/Sustainability-linked-Derivatives-KPI-Guidelines-Sept-2021.pdf> accessed 23rd October 2023.

ISDA, 'Sustainability-linked Derivatives: Where to Begin?, ISDA Future Leaders in Derivatives' (3 May 2022) <www.isda.org/a/ZfVgE/Sustainability-linked-Derivatives-Where-to-Begin.pdf> accessed 4th September 2023.

International Organizations Policy Documents and Reports

GHG Protocol, Corporate Value Chain (Scope 3) Accounting and Reporting Standard, Supplement to the GHG Protocol Corporate Accounting and Reporting Standard (2011) <https://ghgprotocol.org/sites/default/files/standards/Corporate-Value-Chain-Accounting-Reporing-Standard_041613_2.pdf> accessed 20th October 2023.

ICVCM, 'The Core Carbon Principles' (March 2023) <https://icvcm.org/wp-content/uploads/2023/07/CCP-Foreword-R2-FINAL-26Jul23.pdf> accessed 31st October 2023.

Kyoto Protocol to the United Nations Framework Convention on Climate Change, 10 December 1997, 2303 U.N.T.S. 162.

Paris Agreement to the United Nations Framework Convention on Climate Change, 12 December 2015, T.I.A.S. No. 16–1104.

UNFCCC, 'Innovative Approaches for Strengthening Coastal and Ocean Adaptation – Integrating Technology and Nature-based Solutions' (13 June 2022) <https://unfccc.int/documents/510426> accessed 23rd October 2023.

UNFCCC, 'Technology and the UNFCCC: Building the Foundation for Sustainable Development' (2016) <https://unfccc.int/ttclear/misc_/StaticFiles/gnwoerk_static/NAD_EBG/54b3b39e25b84f96aeada52180215ade/b8ce50e79b574690886602169f4f479b.pdf> accessed 2nd November 2023.

Conference Papers

Collins, J., 'Unlocking Private Climate Finance for Emerging Markets', Panel Discussion Vice Chairman, Banking, Capital Markets and Advisory, Citi, Online (2 October 2023).

Katyukha, P., and Mottaeva, A., 'Evolution of Global Oil Benchmarks: New Trends in Pricing in the International Oil Market', E3S Web of Conferences (2021).

Mullins, D., 'Remarks on the Global Derivatives Study Sponsored by the Group of Thirty' (1993) ISDA Summer Conference.

US Legislation and Policy Documents

CFTC, '17 CFR Parts 39 and 140 RIN 3038–AF12 Reporting and Information Requirements for Derivatives Clearing Organisations', Latest Reform (8 August 2023) <www.cftc.gov/sites/default/files/2023/08/2023-16591a.pdf> accessed 30th October 2023.

CFTC, 'Releases Request for Information on Climate-Related Financial Risk' (2 June 2022) <www.cftc.gov/PressRoom/PressReleases/8541-22> accessed 20th October 2023.

Commodity Exchange Act 1936.

Dodd-Frank Wall Street Reform and Consumer Protection Act 2010.

UK Legislation and Policy Documents

FCA, 'Enhancing Climate-Related Disclosures by Standard Listed Companies and Seeking Views On ESG Topics In Capital Markets', Consultation Paper CP21 (18 June 2021).

FCA Handbook, PERG 2.6.19D Specified Investments: A Broad Outline – Emission Allowances.

Financial Services and Markets Act 2000 (Regulated Activities) Order 2001.

TPT, *Disclosure Framework* (October 2023).

EU Legislation

Commission Delegated Directive (EU) 2021/1269 of 21 April 2021 Amending Delegated Directive (EU) 2017/593 as Regards the Integration of Sustainability Factors into the Product Governance Obligations.

Directive (EU) 2022/2464 of the European Parliament and of the Council of 14 December 2022 Amending Regulation (EU) No 537/2014, Directive 2004/109/EC, Directive 2006/43/EC and Directive 2013/34/EU, as Regards Corporate Sustainability Reporting.

Directive (EU) 2022/2464 of the European Parliament and of the Council of 14 December 2022 Amending Regulation (EU) No 537/2014, Directive 2004/109/EC, Directive 2006/43/EC and Directive 2013/34/EU, as Regards Corporate Sustainability Reporting, [2022] OJ L 322.

EU Sustainable Finance Taxonomy Regulation (EU) 2020/852.

Regulation (EU) 2019/2089 of the European Parliament and of the Council of 27 November 2019 amending Regulation (EU) 2016/1011 as regards EU Climate Transition Benchmarks, EU Paris-Aligned Benchmarks and Sustainability-Related Disclosures For Benchmarks, [2019] OJL 317.

Regulation (EU) 2020/852 of the European Parliament and of the Council of 18 June 2020 on the Establishment of a Framework to Facilitate Sustainable Investment, and Amending Regulation (EU) 2019/2088.

5 The Problem of Environmental Risks and Uncertainties in ESG Derivatives

This fifth chapter defends the importance of understanding the differences between risks and uncertainties when approaching environmental factors within ESG derivatives. Our purpose in this chapter is to explore how the environmental issues can be articulated with the categories of risk and uncertainty – and by so doing, to establish the impact that such differentiation should have in the dialogue among society, regulators, and financial institutions, and taken into consideration when designing ESG derivatives. This approach allows us, from the outset, to set realistic expectations surrounding sustainable finance, in pursuing a more sustainable world in the long term. We bring to the discussion Power's call for more explicit politics of uncertainty[1] to inject a note of realism into what he argues is a misplaced belief in risk-management methodologies to deliver desired regulatory outcomes – in this context, environment-related objectives.

Introduction

By borrowing key concepts of *risk* and *uncertainty*, coined in sociological theory, we argue that risks mean the anticipation of a positive or negative situation in the future. Risks are by nature objective, measurable, and identifiable. According to risk society theorists, however, there is not always social awareness about the risks faced by a particular social group. Indeed, the wide variety of areas encompassed by the term 'ESG' is challenging, when determining the risks that should be prioritised. Only the creation of a common understanding of those risks can bring a change in society's perception and reaction towards the matter. Hence, a development of ESG derivatives that are drafted either to hedge those risks, or to provide the means to achieve measurable sustainability-linked KPIs will contribute to enhance the recognition of ESG risks, whilst providing efficient risk-management mechanisms. However, not all future events are necessarily foreseeable or measurable. This feature is especially relevant when dealing with environmental risks.

1 Michael Power, *The Risk Management of Everything: Rethinking the Politics of Uncertainty* (Demos, 2004).

DOI: 10.4324/9781003365242-5

Unlike risk, uncertainty cannot be measured and thereby cannot be controlled, because its outcomes cannot always be predicted. Besides, there is an intermediate category of 'unknown risks' that challenges the modernisation of society. Such a category requires the identification of potential unintended effects or unknown risks, and the delimitation of what is tolerable about them.

In the context of the ESG derivatives' role in dealing with environmental risks, to articulate the language of risk and uncertainties, we follow the structure of the risk-based approach to regulation. Despite the increasing reporting standards focused on environmental risk-related data available to investors, a persistent challenge in this arena is accurately quantifying the benefits and the risks that would result from investments in natural resources.[2] The challenge not only involves the clear identification of environmental risks, but also understanding how the market utilises environmental sustainability as a criterion for creating new financial products aligned with ESG targets. In this scenario, risk-based regulation[3] facilitates the prioritisation of actions based on an evaluation of the relevant risks.[4] In the area of environmental risks, the world is confronted with unparalleled and interconnected challenges, spanning areas such as climate change, clean water, ocean health, and biodiversity.[5] These issues are continually evolving, necessitating a dynamic approach that can adapt to the pace of these changes. Thus, the risk-based approach offers ample opportunity to build a dynamic strategy to deal with environmental risks.

The emergence of risk-based regulation in the 1980s was a response to the 'regulatory crisis' and the rise of the term 'regulatory state'.[6] It aimed to address issues of inflexibility and overregulation, with a focus on cost-benefit analysis[7] for more objective and transparent regulation.[8] We argue that the risk-based approach demonstrates ample flexibility and dynamism, enabling a more accurate and timely identification and assessment of environmental risks, along with the subsequent evolution of ESG derivatives transactions. The regulatory state involved a shift

2 Judith Rodin and Saadia Madsbjerg, *Making Money Moral: How a New Wave of Visionaries is Linking Purpose and Profit* (Wharton School Press, 2021) 53.

3 Julia Black, 'The Emergence of Risk-Based Regulation and the New Public Risk Management in the United Kingdom', *Public Law* 2005 (Autumn 2005): 512–549.

4 Julia Black, Martin Lodge and Marck Thatcher, *Regulatory Innovation a Comparative Analysis* (Edward Elgar Publishing, 1999). Julia Black, 'The Development of Risk-Based Regulation in Financial Services: Just "Modelling Through"?', *ESRC Centre for the Analysis of Risk and Regulation* (2005): 156.

5 UNGC, 'Address Environmental Risks and Leverage Opportunities'. https://unglobalcompact.org/what-is-gc/our-work/environment accessed 13th November 2023.

6 Julia Black, *Tensions in the Regulatory State* (Public Law, 2007) 1.

7 Christopher Hood, Henry Rothstein and Robert Baldwin, *The Government of Risk: Understanding Risk Regulation Regimes* (Oxford University Press, 11 March 2004).

8 Bridget M. Hutter, 'The Attractions of Risk-Based Regulation: Accounting for the Emergence of Risk Ideas in Regulation', Discussion Paper No. 33 ESCR Centre for Analysis of Risk and Regulation, March 2005, 1. www.lse.ac.uk/accounting/CARR/pdf/DPs/Disspaper33.pdf accessed 13th November 2023.

from centralised control to privatised institutions,[9] leading to a fragmented regulatory space and new forms of state regulation. In this context, the design and implementation of an effective risk-based approach can help organise and address the uncertainties arising from the sudden proliferation of private and public regulatory reporting standards related to environmental risks.

A risk-based approach becomes a strategy to manage institutional risk, rationalising resource allocation, and addressing the limitations of traditional command and control regimes.[10] It introduces a matrix of assessments focusing on uncertainties, impacts, and probabilities,[11] offering a formalised and systematic regulatory policy based on risk conceptions and the new politics of accountability.[12] This rationale is particularly valuable for managing the risks and uncertainties inherent in changing environmental conditions. It is widely acknowledged that environmental science evolves with the emergence of changes in nature. Therefore, a risk-based approach serves as a foundation for continually updating and reviewing environmental risk assessments. Moreover, the traditional lines dividing regulators and regulated entities also require re-evaluation, as the construction of the approach benefits from public and private perceptions of risks.[13] In the area of environmental risks, diverse perspectives and assessments are crucial in establishing a shared language and a unified understanding of the priorities to be established.

Additionally, the introduction of risk-based approach is seen by some as a form of 'regulatory innovation',[14] involving subjective decisions by regulators and regulated entities to adopt new organisational and decision-making processes.[15] In the context of environmental risk, the novelty should be reflected in the collaboration required to achieve the regulatory goals. The integrated frameworks implemented to objectively assess environmental risks across regulated firms are pivotal in achieving environmental objectives in a timely manner. Indeed, regulators adopt risk-based approaches to overcome limitations in administering traditional command and control regimes,[16] expecting greater effectiveness from such intervention.

The emergence of the risk-based approach is part of the broader movement known as 'New Public Risk Management' (NPRM), encompassing internal risk-management practices and risk-based regulation to address risks within and outside

9 John Braithwaite, 'Accountability and Governance Under the New Regulatory State', *Australian Journal of Public Administration* 58.1 (1999): 90.

10 ibid.

11 Julia Black, 'The Emergence of Risk-Based Regulation and the New Public Risk Management in the United Kingdom' (n 3).

12 Julia Black, *Tensions in the Regulatory State* (n 6) 2.

13 Julia Black, 'Critical Reflections on Regulation (27 Australian Journal of Legal Philosophy 1 and CARR Discussion Paper, 2002)'. www.lse.ac.uk/accounting/CARR/pdf/dps/disspaper4.pdf accessed 13th November 2023.

14 Julia Black, 'The Development of Risk-Based Regulation in Financial Services: Just "Modelling Through"?', in Julia Black, Martin Lodge and Mark Thatcher (eds), *Regulatory Innovation* (Edward Elgar Publishing, 2005) ch. 8.

15 ibid.

16 ibid.

regulatory agencies.[17] The NPRM consists of two interconnected strands: internal risk management practices and the risk-based regulation. The former involves applying private sector risk-management methods to central government, encompassing activities like risk identification, assessment, management, and evaluation. The latter, the risk-based regulation approach, addresses two dimensions – the regulation of risks to society and general well-being, and the institutional risk, referring to the risk faced by the regulatory agency in achieving its objectives. Although these strands are interrelated, they pertain to distinct sources of risk: internal organisational factors and external risks beyond the regulatory agency's control. We argue that the NPRM has the potential to streamline the adoption of rational, objective, and transparent methodologies for prioritising environmental risks, acknowledging the inherent challenge of anticipating and managing all negative effects.[18] This underscores the vital role of the risk-based approach in addressing environmental risks and prompts a deeper exploration of the regulatory and mitigative aspects – examining both the extent and manner in which risks can be effectively regulated and reduced.

Features of the Risk-based Approach for Environmental Matters

Risk-based regulation necessitates regulators to establish clear objectives from the outset. These statutory objectives are closely tied to the risks posed by firms and individuals in relation to achieving those objectives. As a result, regulatory agencies engage in a decision-making process to determine which risks to address and prioritise. However, it is highly probable that this process is influenced by biases and prone to errors or diverse perception in judgment. To shed light on this situation, scholars have drawn upon a theory developed in the field of societal risk regulation known as *the theory of the two types of errors*.[19] This theory encompasses Type I errors, which involve erring on the side of caution by perceiving something as risky when it is not, and Type II errors, which involve erring on the side of risk by perceiving something as safe when it is not. When applied to the risk selection process, this theory demonstrates how regulators' judgments are significantly subjective, and susceptible to both internal perceptions and external factors.[20]

17 Jeroen van der Heijden, 'Risk Governance and Risk-Based Regulation: A Review of the International Academic Literature', State of the Art in Regulatory Governance Research Paper Series, 2019. https://papers.ssrn.com/sol3/papers.cfm?abstract_id=3406998 accessed 14th November 2023.

18 Arjen Boin, 'Preparing for Future Crises: Lessons from Research', in B. M. Hutter (ed), *Creating Space for Engagement? Lay Membership in Contemporary Risk Governance* (Cambridge University Press, 2010) 231–248.

19 K. S. Schrader-Frechette, *Risk and Rationality* (University of California Press, 1991).

20 Julia Black, 'Risk and Regulatory Policy: Improving the Governance of Risk', in *Risk-Based Regulation: Choices, Practices and Lessons Being Learnt* (OECD, 2010) 185–224. www.keepeek.com/Digital-Asset-Management/oecd/governance/risk-and-regulatory-policy/risk-based-regulation_9789264082939-11-en#page6 accessed 14th November 2023.

In the context of environmental risks, the accurate identification of relevant risks and uncertainties serves as a decision-making tool that enables a thoughtful response to potential harm or gain in situations where there is a deficiency of knowledge, whether qualitatively or quantitatively.[21] The risk selection of environmental impacts typically includes energy efficiency, emissions, waste, climate change, as well as various environmental programmes.[22] Hence, the design of a risk management strategy examines past liabilities, current challenges, and future risk scenarios.[23]

The assessment of environmental risks has been strongly determined by the content of regulation that requires companies, financial institutions, and other market participants to report relevant nonfinancial information. Like financial reporting, sustainability reports should prioritise providing meaningful information that is relevant and assessable to the target audience – a concept known as 'materiality'. In this scenario, companies grapple with the challenge of narrowing down their reporting to focus on topics that are material to them, given the diverse aspects encompassed by ESG areas.

The Double Materiality Principle (DMP), introduced by the CSDR,[24] represents an evolving concept in sustainability reporting, urging companies to consider materiality from two distinct perspectives: the *inside-out perspective* (impact materiality) and the *outside-in perspective* (financial materiality).[25] The first (inside-out) perspective helps companies identify the actual and potential positive and negative impacts of their business activities on various sustainability topics. The latter (outside-in) scrutinises the opportunities and risks of sustainability topics for a company's financial position and the future viability of its business model. When employing the DMP for materiality analysis, a topic is considered material either if it generates risks and opportunities for business success, or if it holds significance based on the impact of business activities on the environment and people. Consequently, a topic becomes subject to reporting obligations if it is classified as material from either of these perspectives.

In this context, the CSDR provides the basis to assess and identify how certain risks are material and to what extent. It involves engaging stakeholders, identifying a comprehensive list of potentially relevant sustainability issues, defining impacts, risks, and opportunities, conducting impact assessments, evaluating financial opportunities and risks, and compiling the materiality overview.[26] When a topic

21 See Jenny Steele, *Risk and Legal Theory* (Hart Publishing, 2004).

22 Hanna Silvola and Tina Landaw, *Sustainable Investing: Beating the Market with ESG* (Springer Nature, 2021) 5.

23 ibid.

24 Directive (EU) 2022/2464 of 14 December 2022 in (29) Article 19a(1) and Article 29a(1) of Directive 2013/34/EU.

25 Jörg Plass, 'Road to Corporate Sustainability Reporting Directive (CSRD)', Wolters Kluwer, 30 October 2023. www.wolterskluwer.com/en/expert-insights/esg-corporate-sustainability-reporting-directive accessed 18th November 2023.

26 Femke Helgers and Stuti Sethi, 'CSDR – Double Materiality Assessment', PWC, 2023. www.pwc.nl/en/topics/sustainability/esg/corporate-sustainability-reporting-directive/csrd-double-materiality-assessment.html accessed 18th November 2023.

meets these criteria, the company is obligated to report on it, in accordance with the specific ESRS standard for that topic. This reporting encompasses details about the strategy and governance related to the topic, information about implemented measures, as well as targets and KPIs.

The innovative DMP introduces a new paradigm that could inundate the market with extensive data. This change has the potential to shift the focus of companies and investors away from sustainability information that is specifically relevant to individual companies.[27] There is a concern that information crucial to stakeholders may not receive the attention it merits under the upcoming reporting regime,[28] and the abundance of information does *not* guarantee greater accuracy in identifying relevant risks and uncertainties. In this context, the adoption of a risk-based approach becomes valuable. This approach can help mitigate errors in judgment, and simultaneously contribute to prioritising the most pressing risks. By organising risks into levels, the corporate strategy can be systematically designed to address material risks in a structured manner.

Additionally, we believe that the discourse surrounding materiality and the associated reporting requirements of Scope 1, 2, and 3 in GHG emissions could benefit from the framework of risk-based regulation. By integrating a materiality assessment – which is a strategic methodology empowering companies to comprehensively understand and prioritise their sustainability issues – a risk-based approach can enhance the identification of ESG issues crucial for the company. In the context of GHG emissions, materiality refers to identifying and prioritising emissions that are most relevant for disclosure. This, in turn, can facilitate the development of ESG derivatives specifically tailored to address those issues. The rationale is that a company can ensure the complete coherence of its sustainability strategy, aligning the drafting of ESG derivatives with the broader spectrum of corporate strategy and regulatory objectives, as explained in Chapter 3. This process involves incorporating stakeholder perspectives on their products or services, ensuring a holistic and informed approach to identifying and addressing key sustainability concerns.

The integration of multiple perceptions in the risk and materiality assessments enhances the accuracy of the sustainability corporate strategy.[29] One often underestimated aspect of emissions reporting, which we would locate as a typical Type II error, lies in not recognising them as a tool to identify areas in need of substantial improvement. Emissions reporting functions not only as a means of disclosure, but also as a diagnostic tool. By discerning which activities significantly contribute to

27 Carol A. Adams and Subhash Abhayawansa, 'Connecting the COVID-19 Pandemic, Environmental, Social and Governance (ESG) Investing and Calls for "Harmonisation" of Sustainability Reporting', *Critical Perspectives on Accounting* 82 (2022): 102309.

28 Josef Baumüller and Karina Sopp, 'Double Materiality and the Shift from Non-Financial to European Sustainability Reporting: Review, Outlook and Implications', *Journal of Applied Accounting Research* 23.1 (February 2022): 8–28.

29 Kevin Dancey and Maria Mendiluce, 'Demystifying Emissions Reporting', *Harvard Business Review* (7 August 2023). https://hbr.org/2023/08/demystifying-emissions-reporting accessed 18th November 2023.

total emissions, entities can pinpoint their most critical areas for enhancement, and subsequently devise focused reduction strategies.[30] Focusing on activities with a material impact on total emissions provides companies with valuable insights into their operations. It is also an opportunity to open the spectrum of financial transactions that contribute to creating real change. The insights of materiality assessments go beyond mere numerical values for inclusion in sustainability reports. They represent actionable data points that can inform the development of targeted reduction strategies, which in turn can illustrate the type of KPIs that a company may incorporate in its ESG derivative transactions. The emphasis is not solely on reporting to comply with specific regulatory mandates, but on utilising the reported data as a strategic asset for the organisation, the market, and other stakeholders.

Along with the purpose of providing a diagnostic about the level of commitment with GHG emission reduction targets, the progress on emission disclosure and the correlated identification of clear risks is also beneficial for company reputation and investor relationships.[31] To guide and standardise the emission-reduction reporting, regulators have set the tone of what is expected in relation to emissions disclosure. The ISSB released in June 2023 its inaugural standards – IFRS S1 and IFRS S2 – marking the commencement of a new phase in sustainability-related disclosures across global capital markets.[32] These standards apply to annual reporting periods started as early as 1 January 2024. Additionally, the European Commission's European Sustainability Reporting Standards (ESRS), developed under the EU's Corporate Sustainability Reporting Directive, are set to take effect in 2024.

Given this context, the widespread adoption of a global standard for sustainability-related disclosures reflects a universal demand for a consistent understanding of how sustainability factors influence companies' prospects. This adoption aids in more accurately assessing the impact of materiality assessments within the spectrum of Scope 1, 2, and 3 emissions. The heightened clarity contributes to companies developing financial transactions that more effectively and consistently manage material environmental risks. Notably, this data assessment is crucial when incorporating ESG derivatives into an investment strategy. Therefore, constructing a cohesive sustainability strategy with real impact is more effectively facilitated by the structure provided by the risk-based approach.

Another area that could benefit from the adoption of a risk-based approach, regarding the accurate identification of risk, is the design of financial instruments with broader environmental objectives, such as debt-for-nature swaps for conservation and other 'green' projects.[33] In the process of identifying the most prominent

30 Yann Ferrat, 'Carbon Emissions and Firm Performance: A Matter of Horizon, Materiality and Regional Specificities', *Journal of Cleaner Production* 329 (2021).

31 Ian Stannard, 'ICE Sustainable Finance Impact Briefing: Disclosure Delight', December 2022. www.ice.com/insights/sustainable-finance/disclosure-delight accessed 17th November 2023.

32 Ramona Dzinkowski, 'A Baseline for Sustainability Standards', *Strategic Finance; Montvale* 103.3 (September 2021): 38–43.

33 Brijesh Thapa, 'Debt-for-Nature Swaps: An Overview', *International Journal of Sustainable Development & World Ecology* 5.4 (1998): 249–262.

environmental risks of highly indebted developing countries, the design of effective debt swaps can prove effective in a dual manner. Risk identification, prior to the drafting of the swap, should consider both the *level of debt* of a specific country (that affects its capacity to finance environmental projects), and *the country's environmental priorities*. Thus, debt swaps can become a considerably helpful mechanism for debt relief and more equitable distribution of capital for sustainability purposes.

Debt swaps involve the sale of foreign-currency-denominated debt by a creditor nation to an investor, such as a nonprofit organisation or a central bank.[34] The investor purchases the debt at a price that allows for a profit margin.[35] Subsequently, the investor can exchange this debt with the debtor nation, receiving payment in local currency. This payment may take the form of shares in a national company, or contribute to a diverse array of development projects.[36] Specifically, debt-for-environment swaps target initiatives related to conservation and other environmentally friendly projects, with recent expansions incorporating climate change programs.[37] Moreover, swaps have the potential to generate additional revenue for countries with valuable biodiversity. This instrument enables these nations to charge others for safeguarding their biodiversity, essentially transforming it into a global public good.

As can be seen, the risk-based approach functions as a framework for a thorough and systematic identification of environmental risks. Both regulatory standards and market practices play a role in delineating these risks. However, the precise evaluation of material risks is contingent on the unique characteristics of the actors involved. The outcomes of risk management methodologies are also shaped by two essential pillars: the adoption of sustainable investing methods, and the development of financial products aligned with corporate sustainability strategies. While commonly acknowledged methods encompass exclusion, active ownership, and the integration of ESG factors into investment decisions, the formulation of ESG financial products is notably influenced by prevalent transaction types in the market. Our argument aims to highlight the potential role of ESG derivatives in the context of environmental risks. As we will explain in the next sections, these transactions can address certain challenges in the accurate identification, measurement, and management of environmental risks.

34 IMF, 'Regional Economic Outlook, West Hemisphere, Online Annex 5. Debt-for-Nature Swaps in Latin America and the Caribbean', October 2023. www.imf.org/-/media/Files/Publications/REO/WHD/2023/October/English/onlineannex-5-en.ashx accessed 18th November 2023.

35 Robert Deacon and Paul Murphy, 'The Structure of an Environmental Transaction: The Debt-for-Nature Swap', *Land Economics* 73.1 (1997): 1–24.

36 Kristalina Georgieva, Marcos Chamon and Vimal Thakoor, 'Swapping Debt for Climate or Nature Pledges Can Help Fund Resilience', 14 December 2022. www.imf.org/en/Blogs/Articles/2022/12/14/swapping-debt-for-climate-or-nature-pledges-can-help-fund-resilience accessed 18th November 2023.

37 OCDE, 'Debt-for-Environment Swaps'. www.oecd.org/env/outreach/debt-for-environmentswaps.htm accessed 18th November 2023.

Risk Prioritisation

In applying the theoretical framework of prioritisation to environmental risks, it is crucial to recognise that risk prioritisation stems primarily from policy and regulatory decisions grounded in scientific findings. For example, the specific emphasis on climate change mitigation and adaptation is informed by the scientific evidence supporting the Paris Agreement.[38] Research on climate change spans a broad spectrum of topics, encompassing earth sciences, climate modelling, prediction adaptation, mitigation, financial flows, and social implications. The outcomes of such research offer valuable insights applicable to diverse sectors, including society, economies, ecosystems, and financial services.

However, it is crucial to acknowledge the significance of evaluating environmental risks at company level. The design and implementation of Environmental Risk Assessment (ERA) methodologies play a critical role in identifying relevant risks on a case-by-case basis. This approach ensures a nuanced understanding of how a specific company's operations may contribute to or be affected by environmental risks, allowing for more targeted and tailored risk-management strategies. Common frameworks for the design of ERAs include risk identification, risk exposure, risk assessment, and risk mitigation.[39] Along these stages of risk evaluation, different models are used for assessing either physical or transition risks.

The models used to assess physical risks are designed to encapsulate their impact on company financials. In this context, variables such as declining revenues or escalating costs are commonly employed for assessment. Additionally, the potential for business interruption and disruption of economic activities is considered a secondary impact. The anticipation of changes in financial performance, measured through stress-test analysis, is an integral component of ERA models assessing physical risks.[40] Similarly, models for assessing transition risks focus on the financial impact of policies and technological changes implemented at the company level to address various environmental risk scenarios. Climate-related transition-risk analysis is a widely used tool in this context.[41] It involves the creation of temperature-based or event-based scenarios using underlying models, such as Integrated Assessment Models (IAM).[42] The temperature-based scenarios are formulated in accordance with the recommendations of the Task Force on Climate-related Financial

38 UNFCCC, 'Science in the UNFCCC Negotiations? How Does Science Connect to Policy Under the UNFCCC?'. https://unfccc.int/topics/science/the-big-picture/science-in-the-unfccc-negotiations accessed 13th November 2023.

39 Network for Greening the Financial System, 'Overview of Environmental Risk Analysis by Financial Institutions', Technical Document, September 2020. www.ngfs.net/sites/default/files/medias/documents/overview_of_environmental_risk_analysis_by_financial_institutions.pdf accessed 13th November 2023.

40 ibid.

41 ibid.

42 Stefanno Battiston, Antoine Mandel, Irene Monasterolo, Franziska Schütze and Gabriele Visentin, 'A Climate Stress-Test of The Financial System', *Nature Climate Change* 7.4 (2017): 283–288.

Disclosures (TCFD), which suggests that organisations utilise a scenario with a temperature increase of 2°C or lower.[43]

The adoption of ERA models helps financial institutions and corporates to estimate the changes in the valuation of securities and assets. For instance, the Carbon Risk Management CARIMA[44] aims at quantifying risks for the values of financial assets (and their respective portfolios) affected by climate change scenarios.[45] Its methodology creates 'carbon betas', which are climate-adjusted metrics assessing price volatility in comparison to the market, considering various scenarios across the economy.[46] The Transition Pathways Initiative evaluates the quality of management, carbon performance, and the preparedness for transition of issuers; it was developed in partnership with PRI and FTSE Russell.

In addition to policy-driven environmental risk priorities and the establishment of ERAs, ESG-scoring methodologies play a crucial role in evaluating ESG risk management. These scores are incorporated into investment management practices to select securities and effectively manage financial risk exposure. Leading rating agencies have integrated 'material' ESG factors into their credit analysis, focusing on factors that heighten the risk of default and credit loss.[47] Note that the market faced a setback when S&P decided to drop ESG scores from credit ratings.[48] Moreover, due to the increasing demand for reliable ESG data,[49] there has been increased scrutiny regarding the reliability of assessments provided by ESG rating agencies.[50] The notable deficiencies in their methodologies and incentives – diminishing the informativeness of their assessments[51] – affects the ability of ESG scores to serve as a valuable initial screening. The considerable lack of confidence affecting ESG ratings undermines its potential for fighting the risk of greenwashing.

43 See Financial Stability Board, 'Task Force on Climate-Related Financial Disclosures 2023 Status Report', October 2023. www.fsb.org/wp-content/uploads/P121023-2.pdf accessed 13th November 2023.

44 Siddhartha Chakrabarty and Suryadeepto Nag, 'Risk Measures and Portfolio Analysis in the Paradigm of Climate Finance: A Review', *SN Business & Economics* 3 (2023); 69.

45 See Théo Roncalli, Théo Le Guenedal, Frederic Lepetit, Thierry Roncalli and Takaya Sekine, 'Measuring and Managing Carbon Risk in Investment Portfolios', 26 August 2020.

46 See Transition Pathway Initiative. www.transitionpathwayinitiative.org accessed 13th November 2023.

47 Network for Greening the Financial System, 'Overview of Environmental Risk Analysis by Financial Institutions' (n 39).

48 Ahren Lester, 'Surprise as S&P drop ESG Scores from Credit Ratings', Environmental Finance, 9 August 2023. www.environmental-finance.com/content/analysis/surprise-as-s-and-p-drop-esg-scores-from-credit-ratings.html accessed 13th November 2023.

49 Kenza Bryan, 'ESG Ratings: Whose Interests Do They Serve?', *FT*, 3 October 2023. www.ft.com/content/fbe10867-fea1-4887-b404-9f9e301e102e accessed 13th November 2023.

50 Brian Tayan, 'ESG Ratings: A Compass without Direction', Harvard Law School Forum on Corporate Governance, 24 August 2022. https://corpgov.law.harvard.edu/2022/08/24/esg-ratings-a-compass-without-direction/ accessed 13th November 2023.

51 Daniel Cash, 'Can Regulatory Intervention Save the Sustainability Rating Industry?', *Business Law Review* 42.1 (8 September 2020/2021).

Among the solutions proposed by experts in credit ratings functioning is the recommendation of disclosing methodologies. Cash argues that such methodological transparency could be assessed by evaluating whether a third party could replicate the ESG rating based on the information provided.[52] Additionally, introducing ESG signifiers (similar to the 'sf' signifier used in structured finance ratings) could enhance market clarity. For ESG ratings, these signifiers could indicate whether the rating is 'inward', 'outward', or 'circular' looking. The 'inward' category reflects the impact of the outside world on the rated entity, 'outward' reflects the impact of the rated entity on the outside world, and 'circular' indicates a co-dependent, circular, nonbinary nature of a metric.[53] Experts also advise breaking down each of the ESG factors, providing the market with a clear and detailed perspective on the specific issues under assessment.

Risk-based Strategies

Risk-based regulation demands a regulatory strategy that prioritises the effectiveness of a firm's internal controls. The fundamental rationale is to strengthen a firm's regulatory framework, allowing regulators to allocate fewer resources to future monitoring.[54] To attain this goal, a collaborative arrangement between regulators and regulated firms is imperative, with firms assuming the primary responsibility for self-regulation, ensuring their rules align with and support the regulators' objectives. However, successful cooperation hinges on regulators possessing enforceable instruments of discretion for rule implementation.[55]

In a broader context, risk regulation extends beyond the technical implementation of risk assessment and management techniques.[56] It involves adopting a risk-based regulatory approach, and establishing a corresponding operational framework.[57] Specifically, in the context of environmental risk, it is crucial to underscore that the risk-based approach empowers corporations and financial institutions to comprehensively address three key areas in the design of financial instruments aligned with sustainability.

Firstly, it is essential to *establish the foundations for creating ESG-aligned transactions*. This involves defining the principles and criteria that underpin the transaction's alignment with ESG targets. Secondly, there is a need to *evaluate the*

52 Marilyn Waite, Daniel Cash and Bill Harrington, 'The Wild West of Regulating ESG investments', *The Hill*, 7 December 2022. https://thehill.com/opinion/energy-environment/3556053-the-wild-west-of-regulating-esg-investments/ accessed 13th November 2023.

53 ibid.

54 Robert Baldwin, Martin Cave and Martin Lodge, *Understanding Regulation: Theory, Strategy, and Practice* (2nd edn, Oxford University Press, 2011; online edn, Oxford Academic, 20 April 2015) 105.

55 Julia Black and Robert Baldwin, 'When Risk-Based Regulation Aims Low: Approaches and Challenges', *Regulation and Governance* 6 (2012): 2.

56 Joanna Gray and Jenny Hamilton, *Implementing Financial Regulation* (John Wiley & Sons, Ltd, 2011) 15.

57 Her Majesty's Treasury, *Reforming Financial Markets* (HM Treasury, 2009).

methodologies that provide a comprehensive framework for designing such instruments.[58] This step involves assessing the tools and techniques used to structure ESG financial products. Finally, the risk-based approach requires the *collection of information, encompassing both quantitative and qualitative data*. This information is instrumental in addressing issues related to measurement, analysis, and comparability, all of which are integral components of investment decisions made with the use of ESG financial instruments.[59]

Furthermore, the design of ESG financial products – especially ESG derivatives – should be informed by the categories of environmental risks explained in Chapter 2: physical and transition risks. An innovative demand introduced by the sustainability discourse is necessity to comprehend the transmission mechanisms between these environmental risks and financial risks. The outcome of designing ESG derivatives is to address the prevailing issue of the pricing and inadequate recognition of environmental risks. Essentially, the growth of the market relies on both financial institutions and corporates gaining an understanding of the potential magnitude of the financial impact when environmental risks materialise. As we discussed in Chapter 4, ESG derivatives are expected to play a crucial role in enhancing transparency and the pricing of underlying markets, fostering a more comprehensive and informed approach to managing environmental risks within the financial market.

The Politics of Uncertainty

Given that not all forthcoming environmental events are foreseeable and quantifiable, it becomes imperative to acknowledge the role of uncertainties when drafting financial contracts aimed at addressing the consequences of their occurrence. In this context, uncertainties serve as both a parameter of choice and an object of choice. Different types and levels of uncertainty impose constraints on actors, compelling them to respond. Simultaneously, actors actively influence the existing levels of uncertainty, either reducing, renewing, or amplifying them.[60] We adopt Schedler's conceptualisation of uncertainties,[61] recognising them as both constraints and targets. The former necessitates adaptive responses in the face of incomplete information, while the latter underscores uncertainties as creative responses to imperfect communication about specific situations. Within this framework, our argument revolves around viewing the evolution of ESG derivatives as a solution

58 Jón Daníelsson, 'On the Feasibility of Risk Based Regulation', *Institute for Economic Research, CESifo Economic Studies* 49.2 (2003): 1.

59 Malgorzata Tarczynska-Luniewska and Sebastian Majewski, 'Designing Sustainable Financial Instruments', in Magdalena Ziolo (ed), *Finance and Sustainable Development: Designing Sustainable Financial Systems* (Taylor & Francis, 2020) 61.

60 Andreas Schedler, 'The Politics of Uncertainty', in Andreas Schedler (ed), *The Politics of Uncertainty: Sustaining and Subverting Electoral Authoritarianism, Oxford Studies in Democratization* (Oxford University Press, 2013; online edn, Oxford Academic, 26 September 2013) 21.

61 ibid.

to information and data shortcomings in the context of environmental issues. Consequently, the imperfect market data related to environmental matters finds in ESG derivatives a tool to augment transparency, and facilitate price discovery in underlying markets and assets. This is to understand the use of ESG derivatives as a mechanism to help solve the information asymmetry affecting the management of environmental risks.

The hypothesis of information asymmetry as a market failure is a foundational concept in regulatory design. The regulatory approach, based on market failures, assumes that regulators can identify entities and market participants best suited to compile and reproduce information about market risks, ensuring that both regulated entities and regulators are adequately informed about potential positive and negative effects. However, viewing market failure as a starting point for regulatory reform reveals challenges related to information costs and exclusion costs.[62] Regulated entities must bear information costs for assessing their exposure to risks, while exclusion costs involve efforts to avoid specific risks. If these challenges are not effectively addressed, regulation becomes sufficient only when exclusion and information costs are significantly high, limited to the affected area with these elevated costs. While the market failure hypothesis is valuable for understanding a risk-based approach in dealing with environmental uncertainties, it is not absolute. Market failures alone do not dictate the content of regulation and the dynamic of a market. Even though the initial motivation may be the occurrence of these failures, other factors can influence the design of potential solutions. Additionally, not all aspects of regulatory control can be explained solely from the perspective of market failures.

Alternatively, accepting the role of uncertainties as sources of creative solutions in the context of imperfect communication opens up the possibility of the adoption of a risk-based approach to two central hypotheses: (i) the public-perception hypothesis, and (ii) the industry/trade influence hypothesis.

According to the first hypothesis, in which the perception of the public shapes regulation content, the perception or opinion of the public can help explain how responsive regulators and regulated entities design and implement the risk-based approach. The premise is that regulated entities that have been affected by the materialisation of risks or uncertainties and their consequent costs are in a better position to inform regulators about the best way to control those types of events. Thus, cooperation between regulators and regulated entities shapes public expectations regarding the content of regulation. The limitation of using public perception as a regulator content shaper is how to reconcile differences between different opinions within the social group. Furthermore, the interpretation that regulators make of public perceptions can be influenced by factors that change their initial meaning, and all of this will be reflected in the design and implementation of the risk-based approach. As a result, the public perception hypothesis informs more about the

62 Christopher Hood, Henry Rothstein and Robert Baldwin, *The Government of Risk: Understanding Risk Regulation Regimes* (n 7).

structure and extent of regulation than its content. The main reason for this is that public opinion and the regulators perception thereof can be distorted and affected by information asymmetry, which, in any case, prevents it from being the sole starting point in the decision-making and regulatory design process.

On the other hand, the influence of industry interests, trade associations, and regulated entities in the adoption of the risk-based approach should be thoroughly examined. Organised groups of regulatory targets provide visibility into their interests and preferences regarding regulation. (e.g., the leading voice of ISDA identifying the potential of ESG derivatives). However, these groups may have conflicting interests at times, and their stance may not fully represent the entirety of the risk-based approach. Embracing this perspective offers the advantage of facilitating the identification of specific elements related to the approach concerning risks and uncertainties shaped by regulated groups. This approach seems to lay the groundwork for a more comprehensive understanding of the interplay between the content of the risk-based approach – such as the identification and assessment of risks and uncertainties – and the organised interests of regulated entities. It is a scenario in which a contingent reality is denoted to the task of every regulator, consisting of constant negotiation between the different interests that shape the regulation.[63] This is to identify the public interests, which are the ones that should prevail in the construction of the environmental-risk management, and the private interests, whose influence will depend on the degree of pressure exerted by interest groups. The negotiation process leads to the creation of regimes aimed at solving specific problems judged as urgent. In addition, it is perfectly possible that certain regulatory instruments end up favouring the interests of groups with a higher degree of organisation and power over the regulator (e.g., industry associations).

To mitigate the undue influence of specific market participants' interests over others, incorporating the elements of the risk-based approach can help pinpoint ESG risks that are to be managed through ESG derivatives.

Elements of the Risk-based Approach

The objective of this section is to underscore the advantages, drawbacks, and intricacies tied to the adoption of a risk-based approach in the context of environmental risk management, also considering the role of uncertainties. Despite occasional critiques for its perceived inadequacy, and sluggishness in promptly identifying and managing systemic risks during times of reform, the risk-based strategy boasts notable breadth and flexibility. As we explained before, the risk-based approach reveals an inescapable reality: the perpetual constraints on resources available for overseeing specific risk types and, consequently, the imperative to prioritise both risks and the utilisation of available resources. Moreover, it enables an assessment of the alignment between regulatory frameworks, corporate sustainability

63 Malcolm Sparrow, *The Regulatory Craft: Controlling Risks, Solving Problems, and Managing Compliance* (Brooking Institution Press, 2000) 549.

strategies, and expectations surrounding transparency and the allocation of responsibility. This evaluation is particularly pertinent for those involved in the utilisation of ESG derivatives within the context of a sustainable finance strategy.

In this context, we contend that a comprehensive risk-based approach serves as the foundation for ESG derivatives, fostering alignment with the SDGs. Integrating the elements of a risk-based approach can address obstacles impeding the growth of sustainable finance. Overcoming challenges tied to a slow and fragmented understanding of sustainability themes, and their linkage to company valuation, is achievable by reinforcing the integration of ESG derivatives. These transactions not only complement financing, but also provide hedging for relevant risks. Furthermore, issues related to inconsistent and noncomparable sustainability reporting, impacting sustainability analysis, can be alleviated through market research associated with the underlying assets of financial derivatives. Claims regarding the extent and reconfiguration of fiduciary duty for institutional investors and asset managers may find greater clarity through enhanced transparency surrounding ESG risks and their impact on asset profitability. Lastly, the expansion of ESG derivatives tailored to effectively address ESG risks and uncertainties has the potential to diversify the range of sustainable investment products adhering to standardised benchmarks. This, in turn, mitigates the risk of greenwashing within the market.

While the specifics of the risk-based approach may vary depending on the area and jurisdiction of implementation, certain common elements can be identified.

Risk Tolerance

At the core of the risk-based approach is the concept of risk tolerance,[64] signifying the discretionary power wielded by regulatory authorities to assess which risks are deemed acceptable and to what degree. A notable characteristic of the risk-based approach is the considerable latitude granted to regulators in determining the prioritisation of risks – deciding which risks to emphasise, and which to potentially disregard. In the context of environmental risk, this discretionary authority, while affording flexibility, introduces a potential challenge. Prioritising certain risks inherently circumscribes the regulator's intervention scope from the outset, presenting a delicate balance between flexibility and the potential limitation of regulatory oversight.

It is crucial to emphasise that regulators do not adhere to a policy of eliminating all sources of crises, or ensuring an infallible 'non-zero-failure' stance.[65] Even with the urgency of environmental risk, regulators accept that there are certain risks that will be successfully controlled only if regulated entities progress in a consistent manner.[66] Hence, the focus lies in establishing early risk-identification and crisis-

64 Julia Black, 'Risk and Regulatory Policy: Improving the Governance of Risk' (n 20).

65 Financial Services Authority, *Reasonable Expectations* (FSA, 2003). www.fsa.gov.uk/pubs/other/regulation_non-zero.pdf accessed 14th November 2023.

66 See UNEP, 'Environmental Rule of Law: First Global Report', 24 January 2019. www.unep.org/news-and-stories/press-release/dramatic-growth-laws-protect-environment-widespread-failure-enforce accessed 19th November 2023.

management systems, acknowledging that the objective is not to eradicate future crises, but to adeptly utilise available regulatory tools in efficiently managing risks, and when they materialise, mitigating their adverse impacts. This highlights the significant impact of public expectations[67] and political dynamics on the areas of focus for regulators, especially during the risk identification phase.

Risk Identification

The second integral element of risk-based approach is risk identification,[68] where regulators are tasked with pinpointing risks that could impede the attainment of regulatory objectives. During this phase, the regulator relies on collected information to select the most pertinent risks, focusing on those with which it is familiar and confident it can effectively manage. Ensuring regulators have access to comprehensive, accurate, and current information is crucial in mitigating challenges related to information asymmetry, and ensuring a thorough assessment of current and future risks.

Following risk identification, the regulator proceeds to establish risk indicators,[69] which encompass a series of activities and events indicative of the realisation of identified risks. The selection of risk indicators is influenced by the regulator's analysis of past crises or failures and its tacit knowledge of warning signals for risk materialisation. In environmental risks, the identification encompasses a wide spectrum of sophisticated spatial decision-making systems, designed to study the effects of air, water, and soil pollution, ecological imbalances, and natural disasters on both the natural and man-made environment.[70] This includes an analysis of their impact on living beings, properties, infrastructure, vegetation, and ecology.[71]

Risk Assessment

At the stage of risk assessment, financial regulators refer to impact and probability;[72] these two features are at the core of any risk-assessment model. Besides impact and probability, weighting is also an important element in designing a risk-based regime. 'Weighting' gives more importance to certain risks than others; it reveals the risk appetite of the regulator, and, in turn, the amount of resources that it is

67 Bridget M. Hutter, 'The Attractions of Risk-Based Regulation: Accounting for the Emergence of Risk Ideas in Regulation', CARR Discussion Paper No. 33 (DP 33). ESRC Centre for Analysis of Risk and Regulation.

68 Julia Black, 'Risk and Regulatory Policy: Improving the Governance of Risk' (n 20) 193.

69 ibid., 195.

70 Iyyanki V. Muralikrishna and Valli Manickam, 'Environmental Risk Assessment', in Iyyanki V. Muralikrishna and Valli Manickam (eds), *Environmental Management* (Butterworth-Heinemann, 2017) 135–152.

71 ibid.

72 ibid., 196.

willing to devote to manage the relevant risks. The weighting shows the level of risk the regulator is prepared to accept.

Such a model usually uses as a starting point the 'risk to objectives' approach; this is the risk posed by regulated firms to the achieving of regulator's statutory objectives[73] (i.e., environmental risk objectives). The clarity of such statutory objectives is paramount to understanding the selection of risks regulators make when designing the model to be adopted into the corporate sustainability strategy, that in turn will guide the drafting of the terms in ESG derivatives.

During the stage of identifying and evaluating environmental risks, risk regulators are expected to establish those risks that can potentially affect the achievement of its objectives. Once they are clearly identified, regulators will seek to create mechanisms of control.[74]

We would emphasise that one of the distinctive features of risk-based approach is the need to prioritise resources to induce a change in behaviour in some types of regulated entities more than others. We should recognise that all regulators, regardless of the regulatory strategy they adopt, are required to allocate their resources – therefore, the novel element of the risk-based approach is that it clearly defines the risks that the regulator is called upon to prevent and those it is not.[75] In this process, challenges arise related to the justification and legitimation in decision-making, regarding which risks are important and which are not.

The process of justifying risk selection in the risk-based approach raises significant questions regarding accountability, particularly in the context of ongoing debates around climate change science.[76] The dynamic implementation of this approach involves two perspectives: *managerial accountability*, rooted in the organisation and structure of the regulators, and *political accountability*, derived from public expectations. In both scenarios, the regulator shapes the content and extent of responsibility from the outset of their intervention. Essentially, the regulator determines the most significant risks, and allocates resources accordingly, directing regulatory intervention towards the most urgent challenges. Consequently, other risks are acknowledged but considered less important, and the exercise of discretion precisely delineates the regulator's responsibility.[77] This highlights the necessity for new criteria and policies, to ensure that regulator accountability effectively aligns with the evolving landscape of risk-based regulatory strategies.

73 One example of this 'risk to objectives' approach was the FSA in the UK.

74 Robert Baldwin, Martin Cave and Martin Lodge, *Understanding Regulation* (n 54) 283.

75 See Michael Power, *The Risk Management of Everything: Rethinking the Politics of Uncertainty* (Demos, 2004); Julia Black, 'The Emergence of Risk-Based Regulation and the New Public Risk Management in the United Kingdom' (n 3).

76 Jeff Tollefson, 'Top Climate Scientists are Sceptical That Nations Will Rein in Global Warming', *Nature* (1 November 2021). www.nature.com/articles/d41586-021-02990-w accessed 19th November 2023.

77 Julia Black, 'The Emergence of Risk-Based Regulation and the New Public Risk Management in the United Kingdom', (n 2).

Additionally, when defining responsibility parameters, it is necessary to shape the respective public and policy expectations regarding the management of environmental risks. The benefit of implementing a system in these conditions is reflected in the fact that both regulators and regulated entities are aware of the 'rules of the game' from the outset. However, difficulties arise when it is assumed that certain regulated entities and their activities are *not* risky even though they are, or vice versa, and such a decision ends up affecting the public. For this reason, Power argues that the new responsibility policies and parameters associated with a risk-based approach require new policies of certainty and security. As we explained before, the goal is to ensure that the regulator and the regulated entities have the tools to review their risk assessments, and include future categories of risk types. In the final section of this chapter, we propose a structure to conduct a risk-impact analysis.

Limits of Risk-based Regulation

Despite the extensive and celebrated benefits of a risk-based approach, this strategy presents some significant conceptual challenges for those who adopt it. Baldwin explains the need for regulators to clearly identify their goals and the risks that regulated entities present for their achievement – a determination that adds complexity to the regulatory process.[78] Furthermore, the adverse effects associated with the development of a risk identification and assessment system involve a clear distinction between the intrinsic risks of the activity, and how efficient the internal control system of regulated entities is in mitigating these risks.[79] Therefore, risk-based regulation entails a complex process of choices and evaluations. The budget for this process is based on ensuring that regulated entities have risk assessment systems with a forward-looking approach,[80] thereby ensuring constant review and updating of the process to include both known present risks and future potential risks.

Julia Black particularly emphasises the importance of looking beyond the individual regulated entity when conducting a risk analysis or assessment.[81] This involves integrating the risks of regulated entities with the risk-assessment systems of the industry or market to which they belong. However, the difficulty arises when trying to reconcile individual risk assessments (with their various activities) and the parameters of market analysis adopted.

Another limitation of risk-based regulation is associated with its implementation. This stage requires clarity regarding how risk assessments inform and guide regulatory actions. It's not about trying to reconcile public expectations with the real needs of regulation, but about identifying the most rational and defensible

78 Robert Baldwin, Martin Cave and Martin Lodge, *Understanding Regulation* (n 54) 281.

79 ibid.

80 Julia Black, 'Risk and Regulatory Policy: Improving the Governance of Risk' (n 20).

81 ibid.

intervention tools for making decisions.[82] This is about implementing a risk-based system that responds adequately to the institutional and political context faced by regulators. The goal is to avoid multiple regulatory strategies running counter to each other, and affecting the primary purpose of the risk-based approach.[83]

In this sense, the interaction between risk assessments of regulators and a specific compliance or enforcement system depends on the design of the strategy, and whether it includes systems for assessing the compliance and enforcement actions or not.[84] Each regulator has the discretion to integrate enforcement and compliance components into risk-assessment systems. There are different mechanisms to do this; for example, creating teams that integrate inspection and compliance functions, or designing intervention strategies for each type and level of risk. In the context of ESG derivatives, we advocate for a *comprehensive risk-impact assessment*. This assessment is designed to evaluate and validate the alignment between the corporate sustainability strategy, the identified material environmental risks that underpin this strategy, and the specific terms and KPIs incorporated into ESG derivatives. The objective is to ensure a robust and coherent integration of these elements, providing a thorough understanding of how ESG derivatives contribute to addressing and mitigating the identified environmental risks, within the overarching framework of the corporate sustainability strategy.

The risk-based approach, when employed as a control strategy,[85] requires complementarity with other mechanisms to address inherent limitations. Julia Black emphasises that the successful implementation of a risk-based approach should transcend a purely diagnostic role, and avoid being exclusively curative. It is crucial to recognise that the risk-based approach may introduce new risks, prompting the need for a nuanced understanding of its potential drawbacks. Achieving clarity on regulatory priorities is equally essential, to prevent the dissemination of inaccurate or conflicting messages to the public.[86]

Greenwashing as a Regulatory Risk

We argue that one of the primary imperatives of a risk-based approach concerning environmental issues is the management of the risk of greenwashing. As elucidated in Chapter 1, greenwashing manifests in various forms. Nevertheless, we assert that the concept of regulatory risk contributes to a better understanding of the role that ESG derivatives can play as a tool against greenwashing practices.

Regulatory risk primarily arises in the context of regulatory and government policy transitions.[87] Its primary effect is the imposition of gains and/or losses on

82 Julia Black and Robert Baldwin, 'When Risk-Based Regulation Aims Low: A Strategic Framework', *Regulation and Governance* 6 (2012): 131.

83 Robert Baldwin, Martin Cave and Martin Lodge, *Understanding Regulation* (n 54) 287.

84 Julia Black, 'Risk and Regulatory Policy: Improving the Governance of Risk' (n 20) 215.

85 Robert Baldwin, Martin Cave and Martin Lodge, *Understanding Regulation* (n 54) 105.

86 ibid., 5.

87 Louis Kaplow, 'An Economic Analysis of Legal Transitions', *HLR* 99.3 (Enero 1986): 509–617.

the recipients of regulation. In the context of environmental risk regulation, the dynamic nature of environmental threats has the potential to swiftly escalate regulatory burdens and elevate market expectations. This environment, in turn, can inadvertently provide fertile ground for the emergence of greenwashing practices.

In the context of regulatory changes, it is crucial to understand that – instead of being an objectively measurable risk – what precedes the regulator's action is *uncertainty*. This transition is not always accompanied by a clearly defined regime or an adaptation period to the emerging conditions. In the case of environmental risk, the ever-changing and accelerated nature of risks and uncertainties makes it difficult to concede long adaptation periods. In this regard, the varying adaptability of regulated entities becomes a determining factor in terms of the extent of the impact they are expected to endure. For example, in the field of investment instruments or vehicles,[88] deregulation trends, changes in monetary and fiscal policies, reforms in corporate and insolvency regulations, and reforms in investor protection regulations, among others, can affect the realisation of projected returns. Regarding environmental risks, challenges arise when corporations, failing to align their business practices with sustainable norms, resort to deceptive 'environmentally friendly' campaigns, or issue misleading statements about their progress toward environmental targets.

One trend involves a heightened awareness of environmental issues,[89] while the other is characterised by increasingly stringent regulatory demands[90] for corporations to demonstrate their commitment to sustainability targets. Contrary to assertions from European regulators,[91] ESG derivatives should not be viewed as instruments facilitating greenwashing. Instead, these transactions hold the potential to enhance transparency regarding ESG data and foster more accurate pricing methodologies. ESG derivatives, in essence, serve as valuable tools for addressing various challenges within sustainable finance regulations.

Regulatory transition can be due to an intentional redistribution of burdens or as an incidental effect of regulation.[92] In the first case, the regulator has identified that existing regulation is insufficient, or that it inefficiently distributes burdens among the regulated entities. The changes will be aimed at correcting errors and adjusting the regulation to make it more balanced. In the second case, the action of the regulatory authority is directed at achieving specific objectives, and the generation of contingent gains or losses for the regulated entities is accepted as an inevitable

88 See Robert Hale, 'Value and Vested Rights', *Columbia Law Review* 27 (1927): 523.

89 Y. Chen and C. Chang, 'Enhance Green Purchase Intentions', *Management Decision* 50.3 (2012): 502–520.

90 Ziyuan Sun and Weiwei Zhang, 'Do Government Regulations Prevent Greenwashing? An Evolutionary Game Analysis of Heterogeneous Enterprises', *Journal of Cleaner Production* 231 (2019): 1489–1502.

91 ISDA, 'Consultation Response ESAs Call for Evidence on Greenwashing', 10 January 2023. www.isda.org/a/GYxgE/ISDA-response-to-ESAs-greenwashing-CfE.pdf accessed 19th November 2023.

92 Schwartz, 'New Products, Old Products, Evolving Law, Retroactive Law', *NYU Law Review* 58 (1983): 796.

effect. In the context of environmental risk regulation, the formulation of specific targets, exemplified by those articulated in the Paris Agreement, acknowledges the need to create new regulatory tools, the intricacy of achieving these goals, and the implications of emerging transition risks.[93] There is a prevailing recognition, however, that the benefits resulting from the transition will surpass both the costs and the inherent risks manufactured with the transitional process.[94]

The generation of risks and uncertainties typical of regulatory transition periods is often combined with the adoption of incentive systems. However, the adoption of such systems must be based on the existence of a comprehensive framework for regulation and supervision, efficient mechanisms for control, and information disclosure.[95] As we have explained in this work, the broad range of regulatory disclosure mechanisms about nonfinancial information is crafted to foster widespread compliance across various sectors. Nonetheless, the efficacy of these regimes should be complemented by an incentive structure aligned with regulatory objectives. The adoption of clear regulatory incentives could help with issues related to agency problems that affect the achievement of regulatory objectives.

The agency theory presupposes that the agent, tasked with responsibilities, inherently prioritizes their own interests over those of the principal who assigns the task. Consequently, the agent may not consistently act in the best interest of the principal, often safeguarding their personal interests instead. In this context – considering the regulator as the principal and the regulated entity as the agent – the regulator's challenges regarding greenwashing can be analysed through the lens of agency theory. Firstly, there is a perpetual risk that regulated entities may adopt practices aimed at maximising profits, even if they only superficially comply with regulations – common to various greenwashing strategies. Secondly, challenges arise due to information asymmetry between regulated entities and regulators, impacting the regulators' ability to intervene promptly and effectively. The manifestation of the risk of greenwashing is not always readily discernible to regulators and control authorities. Consequently, delayed responses to greenwashing practices could lead to the unfortunate proliferation of such corporate behaviour.

Managing the risks arising from regulatory transition is a priority for regulated entities. However, some authors claim that, regardless of the characteristics of this type of risk, it does not much differ from other risks generated in the market.[96] As such, the mechanisms for addressing it created by the regulated entities can become more efficient than those proposed by the regulators. In line with this reasoning,

93 Gregor Semieniuk, Emanuele Campiglio, Jean-Francois Mercure, Ulrich Volz and Neil Edwards, 'Low-Carbon Transition Risks for Finance', *WIREs Climate Change* 12 (2021): e678.

94 Juan C. Reboredo and Andrea Ugolini, 'Climate Transition Risk, Profitability and Stock Prices', *International Review of Financial Analysis* 83 (2022).

95 Rahul Dhumale, 'An Incentive Based Regulatory System: Bridge too Far', ESRC Centre for Business Research, University of Cambridge. Working Paper No. 170, Junio 2000, 2. www.cbr.cam.ac.uk/fileadmin/user_upload/centre-for-business-research/downloads/working-papers/wp170.pdf accessed 18th November 2023.

96 Louis Kaplow, 'An Economic Analysis of Legal Transitions' (n 87).

ESG derivatives possess the potential to address issues in sustainable finance arising from regulatory uncertainty and inconsistent regulatory approaches, and market deficiencies related to transparency and price discovery. In other words, ESG derivatives, created by market participants, can play a role in managing greenwashing risk that may elude the oversight of regulators.

Regardless of the stance taken, it is acceptable to assume that regulatory change risk is inherent in the development of regulated activities. According to Bittker,[97] regulatory changes are predictable when deciding to start a business or engage in an activity. The focus then shifts to the tools available to the regulated entities to identify, assess, and control this risk. Some of the available tools include cost-benefit analysis, regulatory-impact analysis, and the design and implementation of a risk-based approach. We assert that the adoption of a risk-based approach is the most flexible and comprehensive tool to ensure that the corporate sustainability strategy serves as the foundation for utilising ESG derivatives that facilitate the management of environmental risks.

Although these tools generate high expectations of objectivity, the decision-making process regarding what is considered a risk and what is not often considers nature, political, ethical, and business considerations.[98] This is why the risk-based approach is perceived as a sufficiently broad strategy to take a holistic approach to environmental risk management.[99] It allows for the integration of multiple and changing risk perceptions, which is pivotal regarding environmental risks. Indeed, climate scientists identify the changing nature of these risks by introducing novel dimensions in two key aspects. Firstly, there is a global scale to the potential changes under consideration, encompassing alterations in the Earth's atmosphere. Secondly, these changes seem to be influenced by human activities, which have escalated to a point where they can impact the worldwide climate.[100] While climate has historically been unpredictable, the addition of these two elements has heightened uncertainty, both qualitatively and quantitatively.[101] In light of such a dynamic nature of environmental risks, the risk-based approach provides a framework for ongoing assessment and timely adjustments to the strategy for managing these risks.

Against this background, ESG derivatives play a crucial role in reinforcing the achievement of regulatory objectives related to environmental risk management, making them effective instruments in the fight against greenwashing. However, as we argued in Chapter 4, more clear and consistent regulatory treatment is necessary.

97 Boris Bittker, *Federal Taxation of Income, Estates and Gifts* (Thomson Reuters, 1981) 3.3.4 en 3.28.

98 Mary Douglas and Aaron Wildavsky, *Risk and Culture: An Essay on the Selection of Technological and Environmental Dangers* (University of California Press, 1983) 64.

99 Bridget M. Hutter, 'Risk, Regulation, and Management', in Peter Taylor-Gooby and Jens Zinn (eds), *Risk in Social Science* (OUP, 2006).

100 Graciela Chichilnisky and Geoffrey Heal, 'Global Environmental Risks', *Journal of Economic Perspectives* 7.4 (Fall 1993): 65–86.

101 ibid.

Derivatives play a pivotal role in economic activities, by facilitating the mobilisation and allocation of capital for green finance. They assist businesses and investors in effectively managing their exposure to risks, aligning exposures with risk tolerance, and meeting risk management requirements.[102] Additionally, the derivatives market contributes significantly to transparency, by providing information about underlying markets (i.e., commodities, securities, or assets).[103] We argue that increased transparency empowers market participants with additional information to structure sustainability-related transactions in line with higher environmental targets. The advantage of having access to more substantial information enables investors to make more impactful contributions to green transition.

As we explained in Chapter 3, financial services are a crucial facilitator of economic activity. The development of financial instruments, such as ESG derivatives, holds a key role in propelling the transition to a low-carbon and sustainable economy. Achieving this transition requires substantial long-term funding – and ESG investments, coupled with derivative instruments to mitigate associated risks, are indispensable in this journey.[104] They play a crucial role in helping companies efficiently meet their sustainability goals, contributing to an effective transition to a green economy.[105] Furthermore, derivatives contribute to positive market outcomes through the exercise of voting rights and investor engagement, the sharing of business risk and economic exposure, and the provision of cash for specific needs.[106] Therefore, we defend that the design of ESG derivatives with specific environmental goals in mind can yield similar benefits for achieving environmental targets.

It is noteworthy that derivatives linked to equity and corporate bonds play a pivotal role in determining a company's cost of capital, by mitigating business risks.[107] Consequently, they influence the financing and refinancing costs, similar to the impact made when activist investors divest from specific companies or sectors. In such cases, these assets or sectors face a higher cost of capital. Derivatives of this nature convey a clear signal to the market, indicating which sector is likely to experience a higher or lower cost of funding.[108]

The expansion of ESG markets in recent years underscores the necessity for forward prices related to these assets and their corresponding indices.[109] Derivatives markets are integral to mature secondary markets, and the surging demand for both listed and OTC ESG derivatives highlights their pivotal role in sustainable

102 ISDA, 'Consultation Response ESAs Call for Evidence on Greenwashing' (n 91).

103 ibid.

104 ibid.

105 Eugene Fama and Kenneth R. French, 'Disagreement, Tastes, and Asset Prices', CRSP Working Paper No. 552, Tuck Business School Working Paper No. 2004-03, November 2005.

106 ibid.

107 ISDA, 'Consultation Response ESAs Call for Evidence on Greenwashing' (n 91) 5.

108 ibid.

109 ISDA, 'Overview of ESG-related Derivatives Products and Transactions'. www.isda.org/a/qRpTE/Overview-ofESG-related-Derivatives-Products-and-Transactions.pdf accessed 18th November 2023.

investment strategies. The availability of liquid and transparent derivatives, in particular, has the potential to significantly reduce funding and financing costs for share and bond issuers in primary markets.

As ESG investment markets evolve, and substantial funds are required to fuel the transition to a sustainable economy, the derivatives market becomes crucial for facilitating the financing of green investments.[110] As we explained in detail in Chapter 4, ESG derivatives serve not only as hedging tools to manage associated ESG risks, but also play a critical role in supporting sustainability objectives. As ISDA asserts,[111] financial market participants should have the freedom to utilise derivatives to advance these goals.

Recognising the need for the integration of a risk-based approach with other regulatory tools to enhance performance and enforcement, the next section delves into the essential elements of regulatory-impact analysis.[112] This exploration aims to improve regulatory decision-making and practices concerning environmental risks.

Regulatory Impact Analysis From the Risk-based Approach Perspective

The risk-based approach necessitates regulators and regulated entities possess a toolkit for identifying and assessing risks, in alignment with regulatory objectives. In the context of environmental risks, the primary causes of concern are climate change, clean water, ocean health, and biodiversity. Consequently, the analysis should strive to align the perception of these risks for market participants, financial institutions, consumers, and investors with that of the regulator. This involves acknowledging that future events or situations stemming from the activity can either be objectively measurable risks, or fall within the area of uncertainty. Moreover, these events may originate directly from the activity, or result from the activities and the market in which regulated entities are engaged. In line with this reasoning, the formulation of a corporate strategy and the development of ESG derivatives should encompass a thorough consideration of material risks and associated uncertainties that can influence corporate behaviour. Thus, we argue that the methodology of regulatory-impact analysis can help to more accurately assess the progress in relation to specific ESG targets.

The categorisation and differentiation between risk and uncertainty[113] are influenced by both scientific–rationalist trends[114] (which define risk as an objectively quantifiable event with a certain probability and severity), and socio-constructivist

110 Ibid.

111 ibid.

112 Claudio Radaelli and Fabrizio de Francesco, 'Regulatory Impact Assessment' in Robert Baldwin, Martin Cave and Martin Lodge (eds), *The Oxford Handbook of Regulation* (online edn, Oxford Academic, 2 September 2010).

113 See C. Hood and D. K. C. Jones (eds), *Accident and Design. Contemporary Debates in Risk Management* (UCL Press, 1996).

114 D. Lupton, *Risk* (Routledge, 1999) 6.

movements (which recognise that future events can be either risks or uncertainties and may not always be quantifiable). Both risk and uncertainty carry potential positive and negative outcomes, with the common element being the anticipation[115] of their potential effects. Apart from the measurability aspect, a key distinction between these two categories is that risks, unlike uncertainties, enjoy social recognition and legitimacy. This legitimacy is exemplified through two dimensions: the willingness to expose oneself to risk and the asymmetry of information,[116] encompassing moral hazard, adverse selection, and limited information transfer, known as 'signalling'.[117]

Given the broad range of regulatory expectations related to environmental risk management outlined in various regulatory instruments, the following structure aims to establish the foundation for crafting an assessment that encompasses both the overarching corporate sustainability strategy, and its alignment with the parameters governing the negotiation and execution of ESG derivatives.

In this context, regulatory-impact analysis and regulatory improvement processes can rely on two premises:[118] (i) the initial premises of regulatory-impact analysis, and (ii) the premises for regulatory analysis from the risk-based approach perspective.

i. The initial premises of regulatory-impact analysis:

   The initial premises encompass the consideration of the materiality assessment that helps to determine specific environmental problems to be solved, as well as the regulatory tools that guide the corporate's action to manage the relevant risks. Within this framework, the risk assessment serves to delineate corporate strategies regarding the most effective implementation mechanisms, the selection of which is contingent on the nature of the risk. In this context, the strategic choice of financial instruments assumes a pivotal role, ensuring that the adopted solutions are adequately financed and hedged against the associated risks. Integrating the analysis of these variables contributes to the formulation of KPIs within ESG derivatives, intricately linked to the broader objectives of the company.

   Following the evaluation and adjustment of the initial premises, the subsequent steps in the process should incorporate the principles of regulatory analysis within the risk-based approach framework.

ii. Premises for regulatory analysis from the risk-based approach perspective:

The premises for regulatory analysis within the risk-based approach contemplate distinct stages and content in systematically examining each of the material

115 Ulrich Bech, *Risk Society: Towards a New Modernity* (Sage Publications, 1992) 33.

116 Martin Lodge and Kai Wegrich, *Managing Regulation: Regulatory Analysis, Politics and Policy. The Public Management and Leadership Series* (Utrecht University and Netherlands School of Government Springer Nature Limited, 2019) 223.

117 Claudio Radaelli and Fabrizio de Francesco, 'Regulatory Impact Assessment' (n 112) 283.

118 Martin Lodge and Kai Wegrich, *Managing Regulation: Regulatory Analysis, Politics and Policy* (n 116).

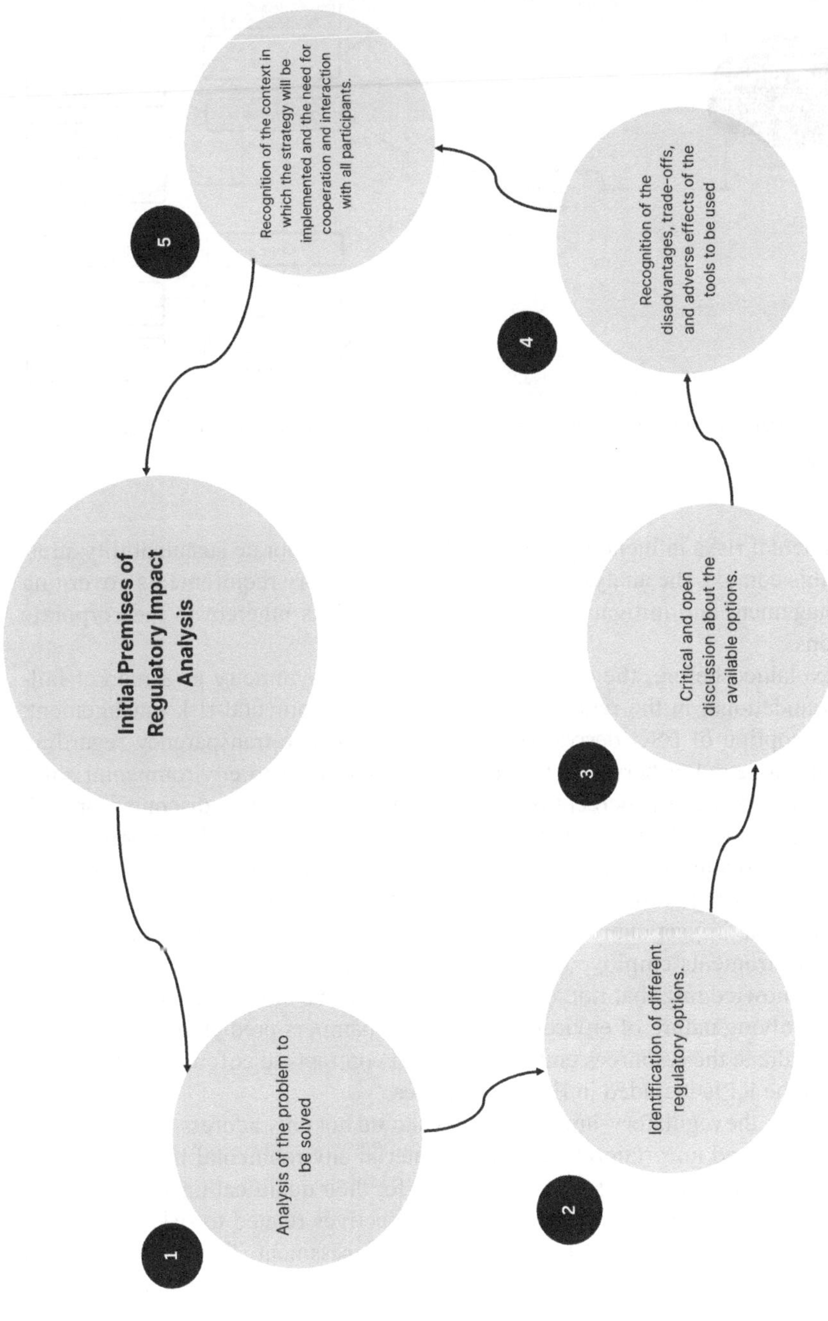

Figure 5.1 Initial Premises of Regulatory Impact Analysis

Source: Author

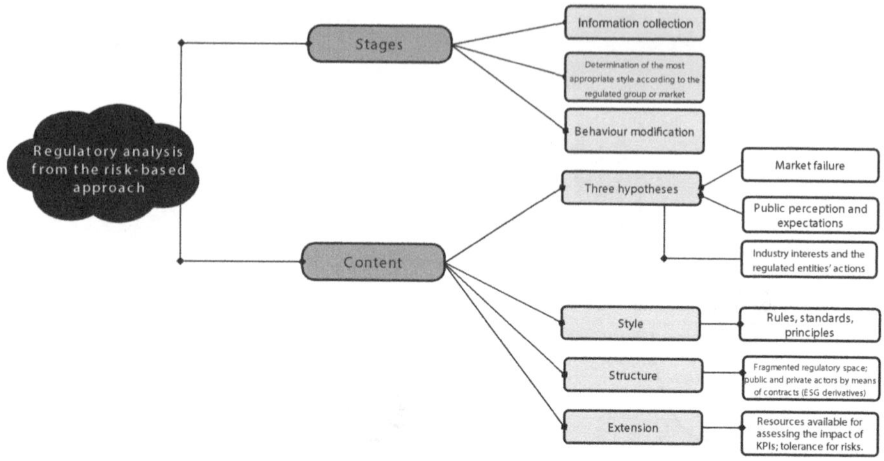

Figure 5.2 Premises for Regulatory Analysis From the Risk-based Approach Perspective

Source: Author

environmental risks influencing the formulation of a corporate sustainability strategy. In this context, the analysis delves into the regulatory requirements governing the management and mitigation of environmental risks inherent to the corporate operations.

As explained before, the concept of information asymmetry as a market failure is foundational in the regulatory design for environmental-risk management, and the adoption of ESG derivatives as tools to enhance transparency regarding underlying assets. Furthermore, the level of commitment to environmental solutions hinges on the risk perceptions of regulated entities. The discourse on risk must integrate these diverse risk perceptions to formulate a set of regulatory tools fostering behaviour aligned with explicit environmental objectives. However, recognising that regulatory compliance and enforcement mechanisms may prove insufficient, the impact analysis structure must encompass an examination of the financial instruments employed to ensure the attainment of specific ESG targets. Lastly, acknowledging that not all types of risks can be effectively managed, and that the evolving nature of environmental issues hampers predictability, there is a need to evaluate the resources embedded within contracts to enforce strict compliance with the KPIs included in ESG derivatives.

Moreover, the regulatory-impact analysis should not only address the distinction between risks and uncertainties related to material environmental issues, but also establish both objective and subjective criteria for their qualification and classification. It is imperative to explicitly define the objectives related to risks, creating a comprehensive framework for regulatory impact assessment. This crucial element serves as a means to test the KPIs embedded in ESG derivatives against potential changes in corporate behaviour. The alignment between the corporate sustainability strategy and the formulation of KPIs in ESG derivatives must undergo scrutiny for adaptability mechanisms, considering contingencies arising from inherent, activity-related, market-driven, and regulatory-induced risks and uncertainties. Furthermore, objective criteria must be set for evaluating the effectiveness of KPIs, in ensuring regulatory compliance and the attainment of specific ESG goals. Central to this context is the development of mechanisms for the early identification and containment of risks, facilitating proactive risk-management strategies.

Conclusion

The adoption of a risk-based approach enables the implementation of a versatile strategy, capable of adapting to the evolving dynamics of any regulated environment. By defining categories for risk and uncertainty, it facilitates a clear delineation of the true scope of regulation, and the objectives that regulatory authorities need to accomplish. This approach provides regulators with a strategic 'roadmap' that guides the design and implementation of their regulatory framework. The ongoing integration of risk and uncertainty perceptions from both regulators and regulated entities creates an environment conducive to fostering voluntary compliance with proposed rules, principles, and standards. The risk-based approach serves as a valuable starting point for identifying areas requiring immediate attention, while ensuring that all regulated entities operate within a regulatory framework aligned with their risk profile.

In the scenario of environmental risks, precise identification of pertinent risks and uncertainties functions as a decision-making tool, facilitating a thoughtful response to potential consequences in situations marked by knowledge deficiencies related to environmental issues. The evaluation of environmental risks is significantly influenced by regulatory content that compels companies, financial institutions, and other market participants to report material nonfinancial information. However, the complex regulatory landscape makes companies face the daunting task of identifying and selecting the risks that hold material significance for them, navigating a multitude of factors within the broad spectrum of ESG areas.

In navigating this intricate landscape, regulatory tools like the CSRD introduce the concept of double materiality, to provide clarity on the expected reporting concerning environmental and social impacts. While regulatory benchmarks and market practices play roles in delineating relevant environmental risks, the risk-based approach functions as a framework for the thorough and systematic identification of such risks. The comprehensive assessment of environmental risk management is further shaped by the choice of sustainable investing methods, and the crafting of financial products aligned with corporate sustainability strategies. Within this context, ESG derivatives emerge as valuable instruments for addressing specific challenges in the precise identification, measurement, and management of environmental risks.

Recognising the inherent unpredictability and difficulty quantifying future environmental events, it is crucial to acknowledge the presence of uncertainties when formulating financial contracts to address their potential consequences. We argue that ESG derivatives emerge as a remedy to information and data deficiencies within the area of environmental issues. These transactions have the potential to enhance transparency and streamline the process of price discovery in underlying markets and assets.

Despite the structural foundation offered by the risk-based approach, the identification of material environmental risks may be susceptible to the predominant interests of specific market participants. To address this potential shortcoming, we advocate for a comprehensive risk-based approach that includes risk tolerance, identification, and assessment, as the bedrock of ESG derivatives aligning with the SDGs. Additionally, integrating elements from this approach can adeptly overcome challenges impeding the growth of sustainable finance.

No analysis of environmental risk in finance is complete without considering the phenomenon of greenwashing. We argue that such practices can be effectively managed as a subset of regulatory risk. Regulatory risk primarily manifests during periods of regulatory transitions, imposing additional burdens on regulated entities. In the context of environmental risk regulation, the dynamic evolution of nature threats can rapidly escalate regulatory burdens and elevate market expectations, creating an environment conducive to the proliferation of greenwashing practices. In this context, ESG derivatives emerge as crucial tools, playing a pivotal role in bolstering the achievement of regulatory objectives related to environmental risk management, and establishing themselves as potent instruments in the battle against greenwashing.

Nevertheless, it is crucial to recognise certain limitations that necessitate ongoing evaluation of the risk-based approach strategy, post-implementation. This includes a focused examination of the direct correlation between regulatory objectives and the risks emanating from regulated entities, along with a thorough assessment of how the risk-based approach influences the modification of these entities' behaviours, regarding environmental issues. Considering these constraints, a judicious approach involves complementing the risk-based strategy with other regulatory methodologies, such as regulatory-impact analysis. This integrated approach ensures a comprehensive and effective regulatory framework that addresses both the risks and behavioural dynamics of the regulated entities.

Bibliography

Books

Bech, U., *Risk Society: Towards a New Modernity* (Sage Publications 1992).

Hood, C., Rothstein, H., and Baldwin, R., *The Government of Risk: Understanding Risk Regulation Regimes* (Oxford University Press 2004).

Magdalena Ziolo, M. (ed.), *Finance and Sustainable Development: Designing Sustainable Financial Systems* (Taylor & Francis 2020).

Muralikrishna, I.V., and Manickam, V. (eds.), *Environmental Management* (Butterworth-Heinemann 2017).

Power, M., *The Risk Management of Everything: Rethinking the Politics of Uncertainty* (Demos 2004).

Radaelli, C, and de Francesco, F., 'Regulatory Impact Assessment' in Baldwin, R., Cave, M., and Lodge, M. (eds.), *The Oxford Handbook of Regulation* (Oxford University Press 2010).

Schedler, A., *The Politics of Uncertainty: Sustaining and Subverting Electoral Authoritarianism* (Oxford University Press 2013).

Silvola, H., and Landau, T., *Sustainable Investing: Beating the Market with ESG* (Palgrave Macmillan 2021).

Articles

Black, J., 'The Emergence of Risk-Based Regulation and the New Public Risk Management in the United Kingdom' 512 *Public Law* (2005) 535.

Cash, D., 'Can Regulatory Intervention Save the Sustainability Rating Industry?' 42(1) *Business Law Review* (2021) 5.

Chakrabarty, S., and Nag, S., 'Risk Measures and Portfolio Analysis in the Paradigm of Climate Finance: A Review' 3 *SN Business & Economics* (2023) 69.

Chen, Y., and Chang, C., 'Enhance Green Purchase Intentions' 50(3) *Management Decision* (2012) 502.

Chichilnisky, G., and Heal, G., 'Global Environmental Risks' 7(4) *Journal of Economic Perspectives* (Fall 1993) 65.

Deacon, R., and Murphy, P., 'The Structure of an Environmental Transaction: The Debt-for-Nature Swap' 73(1) *Land Economics* (1997) 24.

Dzinkowski, R., 'A Baseline for Sustainability Standards' 103(3) *Strategic Finance* (2021) 38.

Reboredo, J., and Ugolini, A., 'Climate Transition Risk, Profitability and Stock Prices' 83 *International Review of Financial Analysis* (2022) 6.

Tollefson, J., 'Top Climate Scientists Are Sceptical That Nations Will Rein In Global Warming' *Nature* (1 November 2021) 2.

Ziyuan, S., and Zhang, W., 'Do Government Regulations Prevent Greenwashing? An Evolutionary Game Analysis Of Heterogeneous Enterprises' 231 *Journal of Cleaner Production* (2019) 1489.

Working Papers

Dhumale, R., 'An Incentive Based Regulatory System: A Bridge Too Far' ESRC Centre for Business Research, University of Cambridge. Working Paper N. 170 (2 Junio 2000) <www.cbr.cam.ac.uk/fileadmin/user_upload/centre-for-business-research/downloads/working-papers/wp170.pdf> accessed 18th November 2023.

Fama E., and French, K., 'Disagreement, Tastes, and Asset Prices', CRSP Working Paper No. 552, Tuck Business School Working Paper No. 2004–03 (November 2005) <www.evidenceinvestor.com/evidence/disagreement-tastes-asset-prices/> accessed 18th November 2023.

ISDA, 'Consultation Response ESAs Call for Evidence on Greenwashing' (10 January 2023) <www.isda.org/a/GYxgE/ISDA-response-to-ESAs-greenwashing-CfE.pdf> accessed 19th November 2023.

ISDA, 'Overview of ESG-Related Derivatives Products and Transactions' (January 2021) <www.isda.org/a/qRpTE/Overview-ofESG-related-Derivatives-Products-and-Transactions.pdf > accessed 18th November 2023.

International Organizations Policy Documents and Reports

Financial Stability Board, 'Task Force on Climate-related Financial Disclosures 2023 Status Report' (October 2023) <www.fsb.org/wp-content/uploads/P121023-2.pdf> accessed 13th November 2023.

IFRS, 'Sustainability Disclosure Standard General Requirements (IFRS S1)' (June 2023) <www.ifrs.org/issued-standards/ifrs-sustainability-standards-navigator/ifrs-s1-general-requirements/#> accessed 17th October 2023.

Network for Greening the Financial System, 'Overview of Environmental Risk Analysis by Financial Institutions', Technical Document (September 2020) <www.ngfs.net/sites/default/files/medias/documents/overview_of_environmental_risk_analysis_by_financial_institutions.pdf> accessed 13th November 2023.

OCDE, 'Debt-for-environment Swaps' (2022) <www.oecd.org/env/outreach/debt-for-environmentswaps.htm> accessed 18th November 2023.

Paris Agreement to the United Nations Framework Convention on Climate Change, 12 December 2015, T.I.A.S. No. 16–1104.

UNEP, 'Environmental Rule of Law: First Global Report' (24 January 2019).

UNFCCC, 'Science in the UNFCCC negotiations? How Does Science Connect to Policy under the UNFCCC?' (2023) <https://unfccc.int/topics/science/the-big-picture/science-in-the-unfccc-negotiations> accessed 13th November 2023.

UK Legislation and Policy Documents

Bank of England, *Our Response to Climate Change* (London 2023).

HM Treasury, *Green Finance Strategy* (London 2019).

HM Treasury, *Reforming Financial Markets* (London 2009).

EU Legislation and Policy Documents

Directive (EU) 2022/2464 of the European Parliament and of the Council of 14 December 2022 amending Regulation (EU) No 537/2014, Directive 2004/109/EC, Directive 2006/43/EC and Directive 2013/34/EU, As Regards Corporate Sustainability Reporting.

Directive (EU) 2022/2464 of the European Parliament and of the Council of 14 December 2022 amending Regulation (EU) No 537/2014, Directive 2004/109/EC, Directive 2006/43/EC and Directive 2013/34/EU, As Regards Corporate Sustainability Reporting, [2022] OJ L 322.

EU Sustainable Finance Taxonomy Regulation (EU) 2020/852.

Regulation (EU) 2019/2089 of the European Parliament and of the Council of 27 November 2019 amending Regulation (EU) 2016/1011 As Regards EU Climate Transition Benchmarks, EU Paris-Aligned Benchmarks And Sustainability-Related Disclosures For Benchmarks, [2019] OJL 317.

6 Profile

ESG Derivatives as a Social Licence

This chapter promotes a provocative double-edged hypothesis: to defend that sustainability makes real the social licence of finance, and that financial derivatives play a central role in making that happen.

To effectively articulate this argument, it is pivotal to elucidate the social dimension inherent in using financial derivatives. A derivative, in essence, represents a mode of value production subject to trade, in a market oriented by accumulation, within a capitalist framework. Subsequently, to explore the potential of these instruments – often overlooked in financial perspectives – entails the construction of a *social licence for financial services*. This contends that, while the derivatives market serves as a venue for attributing value to capital exposed to risk, there exists an opportunity for the market to evolve into a catalyst for multiplying social wealth. Therefore, the definition of what is social should be set to encompass *all the ways in which concrete human actions are the product of the organisation and involve all dimensions of contemporary life*. Embedding these notions in a consistent argument will lead us to argue how multiple perceptions of social risk and uncertainty enact a socio-structure of the derivatives market. This is to understand that ESG derivatives can be rethought to harness and redirect wealth created for socially productive purposes.

To develop this argument, we first define what the generation of wealth means, from a risk-based perspective. What wealth is, and the way is crafted, states the content of the *social factor* within ESG considerations. The creation of a positive social impact from a financial system is closely linked to the movement to strengthen environmental, social, and governance sustainability – the ESG factors. The purpose of this chapter is to contribute to the debate on the construction of a social factor through the determination of the elements that make up a social licence; the role of conduct regulation; and the way in which financial contracts can contribute to the strengthening of such a licence. We argue that that the construction of a social licence uses various sources of regulation that interact with mechanisms created by individuals to rule their own economic interests. The arguments defended in this chapter are built upon the discussion in Chapter 3, concerning the teleology of regulation and its relationship with the contract as an instrument. We explore the building blocks for the construction of a social licence in the financial system, setting out the issuers and the recipients, as well as the benchmarks of such

DOI: 10.4324/9781003365242-6

a licence. To the extent that the construction of a social licence for the financial system is based on regimes created by regulatory agencies, we explain how the regulation of conduct for institutions and individuals fits into this discourse. Lastly, we argue the need to reconfigure financial derivatives – transforming them from activities centred on value extraction to instruments focused on value creation.

Introduction

Gapponshugi is a Japanese principle involving virtue and moral values in economic activities, and, in that sense, it can serve to open a discussion about the interests involved in carrying out market activities.[1] The regulation of economic activities, including those in the financial sector, is divided between regulation created by state agencies, and regulation emanating from individuals through self-regulatory instruments, as well as the disposition of individual interests through contracts. We propose the construction of a 'social licence' for the financial system and its consolidation through financial contracts, in particular, by means of ESG derivatives.

Our argument recognises that the concept of a social licence is grounded in specific criteria: financial, stock market, and insurance activities – which all involve the management, use, and investment of collective resources – are considered to be activities of public interest. Within this framework, financial services are inherently rooted in the social sphere, and not just merely an effect of social processes.[2] Likewise, it is accepted that national governments have the responsibility of intervening in this activity, in search of promoting and democratising equal access to financial services. Although a social licence for the financial system draws on concepts such as authorisation, administration of public resources, and the tacit acceptance of the need for regulation and supervision, our purpose is to argue how financial contracts and, in particular, ESG derivatives are called upon to complement and strengthen the construction of such a social licence. Let us understand that the behaviour of market participants is framed by structural factors, such as law, regulation, and contracts – these generate a system of incentives that evolves as they do.[3] The transformation required in financial services is the creation of a positive social impact, underpinned by fundamental principles of justice, equality, efficient resource distribution, and the generation of shared wealth in the execution of financial activities. The generation of positive social impact from the activities of the financial system is closely linked to strengthening ESG criteria. Our purpose is to contribute to the debate on the construction of social criteria, through determining the elements that make up a financial social licence, as well as the role that

1 Patrick Fridenson, 'The Father of Japanese Capitalism: Shibusawa Eiichi's Vision of the Ethical Corporation', in Patrick Fridenson and Kikkawa Takeo (eds), *Ethical Capitalism: Shibusawa and Business Leadership in Global Perspective* (University of Toronto Press, 2017).

2 Edward LiPuma, *The Social Life of Financial Derivatives: Markets, Risk, and Time* (Duke University Press, 2017) 348.

3 J. C. de Swaan, *Seeking Virtue in Finance: Contributing to Society in a Conflicted Industry* (Cambridge University Press, 2020) 5.

behaviour regulation plays, and how ESG derivatives can contribute to strengthening such a license.

One crucial idea for rethinking financial derivatives' purpose in this way, and the market generally, is the adoption of a broad definition of wealth. The concept formulated by Adam Smith in *The Wealth of Nations* assists in shaping this study. Smith argues that wealth is reflected in how well people can live with what they have[4] and, as such, money is only the 'wheel' that facilitates the functioning of an economy. The smoother the circulation of money, the more prosperous a nation can become. Following this argument, Smith explains that the development of banking – and, we would say, of financial services – is meant to benefit all of society. Some other authors[5] consider that wealth should be seen as the overall value of economically significant private and public assets, encompassing physical/natural, financial, human, and social capital. Such wealth is meant to be distributed equally among society. Therefore, wealth is featured as both a stock and a flow. Though it is a *stock* – because it represents an economically significant quantity at a particular point in time – it is also a *flow* that involves increasing and decreasing quantities over a specified period. Both aspects of wealth are influenced by market dynamics and price mechanisms.[6] Thus, the creation of wealth possesses intrinsic value and instrumental value, of which the latter may be used for consumption or investment.[7] Investment is essential for both preserving and expanding wealth.

There is, however, an ever-growing irresponsible use of resources, closely tied to excessive consumption that affects investment. This is why the notion of wealth should be encompassed within that of sustainability. This means a concept of wealth that fulfils the demand to meet 'the needs of the present without compromising the ability of future generations to meet their own needs'.[8] The prioritisation of needs and interests inherent in the concept of sustainability necessitates an understanding of the role that financial services, particularly financial derivatives, should play in contributing to the achievement of sustainable wealth for all. In this scenario, our approach entails that financial derivatives, as instruments for the multiplication and distribution of wealth, should be designed to ensure such wealth is equally distributed among market participants. This means a reconsideration of derivatives as value-*extracting* activities, towards value-*creation* activities.

One of the transversal elements of the use of regulation as a tool for economic development relates to the notion of *contract*, and its role as an instrument for

4 Adam Smith and A. Skinner (eds), *The Wealth of Nations* (Penguin, 1776/1999).

5 Georges Enderle, 'A Rich Concept of Wealth Creation, Beyond Profit Maximization and Adding Value', *Journal of Business Ethics* 84 (2009): 281–295.

6 ibid.

7 David Landes, *The Wealth and Poverty of Nations: Why Some are so Rich and Some are so Poor* (Norton, 1999).

8 World Commission on Environment, Development, *Our Common Future* (Oxford University Press, 1987).

regulating private interests. However, as argued in Chapter 3, our purpose is to formulate a path that allows the function of financial contracts, not only to attend to the individual interests of the parties, but also to integrate and at the same time become a tool for reconfiguring the larger interests involved in the provision of financial services. With this objective in mind, in the following section we will explain the formulation of a social licence for the financial system, defining what it is, who is called upon to grant it, and what regulatory instruments exist that may be used as a basis for its construction.

Construction of a Social Licence Within the Financial System

The idea of building a social licence in the financial system leads us to integrate founding constitutional principles of any social structure – such as justice and equality – together with concepts associated with the function that financial services are called upon to fulfil. The generation of a positive social impact from the activities of the financial system is closely linked to the movement to strengthen ESG sustainability criteria.[9]

Such concepts as 'ESG', along with responsible investment and sustainable investment, refer to the incorporation of environmental, social, and governance considerations into investment decision-making, and their inclusion in investment portfolios.[10] As a point of reference, responsible investors[11] may take one of two positions: being inclined to (i) avoid or reduce the exposure of their investments that generate greater ESG risks, or to (ii) influence companies receiving investment so that they act to reduce ESG risks and generate a positive social impact. In this context, it is helpful to understand that the ESG movement has been motivated by social changes, regulatory changes after the global financial crisis, and for financial reasons.

Social transformations have arisen because small and large investors, due to generational changes, seek to make their investments more sustainable.[12] There is a great demand – from individual investors to institutional ones – that their money be used to create well-being, as well as positive and sustainable social and environmental impact in the long term.[13] Regulatory changes[14] have had effects on the performance of asset holders, the adoption of new codes of good governance or

9 Pedro Matos, *ESG and Responsible Institutional Investing Around the World: A Critical Review* (Kindle edn, CFA Institute Research Foundation, 2020) 83.

10 CFA Institute, 'Environmental, Social, and Governance Issues in Investing: A Guide for Investment Professionals', 2015. www.cfainstitute.org/-/media/documents/article/position-paper/esg-issues-in-investing-a-guide-for-investment-professionals.ashx accessed 11th November 2023.

11 See PRI, 'What are the Principles for Responsible Investment'. www.unpri.org/pri/what-are-the-principles-for-responsible-investment accessed 11th November 2023.

12 R. Aggarwal, I. Erel, M. Ferreira and P. Matos, 'Does Governance Travel around the World? Evidence from Institutional Investors', *Journal of Financial Economics* 100.1 (2011): 154–181.

13 R. Bénabou and J. Tirole, 'Individual and Corporate Social Responsibility', *Economica* 77.305 (2010): 1–19.

14 EU Sustainable Finance Taxonomy Regulation (EU) 2020/852.

stewardship[15] for institutional investors, and the implementation of rules for greater corporate transparency[16] established by governments and trading platforms such as stock exchanges. Financial motivations are associated with 'doing well by doing good',[17] and with the expectation of investors to maintain or improve their returns – the expectation that the factors included in the ESG and in its measurement will have an attractive performance, reflected in increased value of companies, and the reduction of other corporate risks.[18]

To the extent that most of the current regulatory efforts are focused on the development of environmental[19] risk identification and management instruments, our purpose is to contribute to the debate on the construction of social criteria, taking David Rouch's work[20] as a point of inspiration, and his formulation of a social licence for the financial system. In particular, we focus on his call that financial services must urgently regain the trust of consumers[21] and society in general, and that they must commit to creating social solidarity and avoid destroying it.[22]

We would assert that this is not a completely new phenomenon, since some historical facts have shown the level of influence the financial system has had in generating important social changes in the past. For example, although some participants in the system benefited from forced labour,[23] the financial sector was influential in the formal abolition of slavery in the 1830s. In fact, it was the largest syndicated loan in history underwriting manumission (the freeing of slaves) in the British Empire.[24] Today, we need the leadership and cooperation of the financial sector to help end various contemporary social problems, including modern slavery

15 Global Stewardship Codes Network. www.icgn.org/policy/global-stewardship-codes-network accessed 11th November 2023.

16 M. Becht, J. Franks, J. Grant and H. F. Wagner, 'Returns to Hedge Fund Activism: An International Study', *Review of Financial Studies* 30.9 (2017): 2933–2971.

17 M. A. Ferreira and P. Matos, 'The Colors of Investors' Money: The Role of Institutional Investors around the World', *Journal of Financial Economics* 88.3 (2008): 499–533.

18 ibid.

19 See Mark Carney, 'Breaking the Tragedy of the Horizon: Climate Change and Financial Stability', Speech given at Lloyd's of London, CFA Institute, 'Environmental, Social, and Governance Issues in Investing: A Guide for Investment Professionals', 29 September 2015. www.cfainstitute.org/-/media/documents/article/position-paper/esg-issues-in-investing-a-guide-for-investment-professionals.ashx accessed 10th November 2023.

20 David Rouch, *The Social Licence for Financial Markets: Reaching for the End and Why it Counts* (Palgrave Macmillan, 2020).

21 Mark Carney (Former Governor of the Bank of England), 'Foreword', in David Rouch (ed), *The Social Licence for Financial Markets: Reaching for the End and Why it Counts* (Palgrave Macmillan, 2020).

22 David Rouch, *The Social Licence for Financial Markets: Reaching for the End and Why it Counts* (n 20) 8.

23 Jasper Jolly, 'Bank of England Apologises for Role of Former Directors in Slave Trade', 18 June 2020. www.theguardian.com/business/2020/jun/18/bank-of-england-apologises-for-role-of-former-directors-in-slave-trade accessed 10th November 2023.

24 N. Draper, 'The City of London and Slavery: Evidence from the First Dock Companies, 1795–1800', *The Economic History Review: New Series* 61.2 (2008): 432–466. www.jstor.org/stable/40057514 accessed 10th November 2023.

and human trafficking, by 2030, in line with the commitments made under the UN SDGs.[25]

In this scenario, there are several criteria that go into configuring the notion of positive social impact from the financial sector. It would usually include the commitment of the industry and investors to the protection of human rights,[26] understanding that both the corporate sector and institutional investors must avoid causing, contributing to, or being directly or indirectly linked to any type of infringement or violation.[27] In this sense, the OECD (in the revision of the Guidelines for Multinational Companies) clarified that companies, including institutional investors,[28] may be subject to complaints cases through an OECD national contact point (NCP) if they do not comply with the standards. This is a formal grievance process, through which interested parties can file complaints in case of noncompliance. In response to the high volume of complaints against institutional investors, in 2017, the OECD issued new guidelines for multinational companies and investors to prevent or address adverse impacts related to human and labour rights, the environment, and corruption in their investment portfolios.[29] Additionally, there are initiatives led by investors, guided by the Principles of Responsible Investment, the UN Guidelines for Information Reporting, and joint initiatives with civil society such as the Corporate Human Rights Benchmark.[30] We observe that a regulatory framework has been created by various interest groups focused on the construction of standards of conduct required of financial institutions and investors, as fundamental actors in the context of protection of human rights.

Labour rights protection standards have also occupied investors in recent years – although to a lesser extent, if compared to the work carried out in human rights. Investors typically perceive that improving supply chain labour standards can help mitigate operational, legal, regulatory, and reputational risks. It also provides chances to capitalise on innovative suppliers, broaden market access and contractual opportunities, cultivate loyal customer relationships, engage committed and productive employees, and establish secure partnerships with suppliers.[31]

25 PRI, 'A Blueprint for Mobilizing Finance Against Slavery and Trafficking', Final Report of the Liechtenstein Initiative's Financial Sector Commission on Modern Slavery and Human Trafficking, September 2019, 2. www.unpri.org/download?ac=9773 accessed 10th November 2023.

26 UN Guiding Principles for Business and Human Rights UNGP.

27 See PRI, 'Why and How Investors Should Act on Human Rights', 22 October 2020. www.unpri.org/human-rights-and-labour-standards/why-and-how-investors-should-act-on-human-rights/6636.article accessed 10th November 2023.

28 Case Law of Violations of Human Rights Reported to the OCDE. https://mneguidelines.oecd.org/database/instances/kr0010.htm accessed 10th November 2023.

29 OCDE, 'Responsible Business Conduct for Institutional Investors: Key Considerations for Due Diligence Under the OECD Guidelines for Multinational Enterprises', 2017. https://mneguidelines.oecd.org/RBC-for-Institutional-Investors.pdf accessed 10th November 2023.

30 Corporate Human Rights Benchmark. www.worldbenchmarkingalliance.org/corporate-human-rights-benchmark/ accessed 10th November 2023.

31 PRI, 'From Poor Working Conditions to Forced Labour – What's Hidden in your Portfolio? A Guide for Investor Engagement on Labour Practices in Agricultural Supply Chains'. www.unpri.org/download?ac=1652 accessed 10th November 2023.

In this context, our argument seeks to formulate the concept of a social licence, urgently grounded in the delivery of financial services, and manifested through measurable actions. The discourse on the existence of a social licence has traditionally not held a prominent focus within the industry, nor has it been explicitly recognised by regulators – or at least, not under the designation of a 'social licence'. We acknowledge that certain market intervention mechanisms, whether stemming from participants through self-regulation tools, or resulting from regulatory authorities' initiatives, should be aligned with ensuring a positive social impact. It is important to note that the discourse on a social licence will evolve, recognising that sustainability extends beyond environmental aspects, (e.g., climate change control and the reduction of CO_2 emissions). Although these are the most urgent commitments, there are also other issues embedded in sustainability factors which, in turn, allow us to form a true notion of a social licence.

Features of a Social Licence

The recognition of influential regulators in the international arena explicitly mentioning the concept of a social licence[32] suggests that we are witnessing initial signs of a shift in perception from authorities. This shift reflects an acknowledgment of the challenges and adaptations required by the financial system to foster economic growth, navigate crises, and contribute to social development, while upholding and enhancing standards of dignity and justice. In this sense, in 2015, Mark Carney[33] anticipated that real markets must be resilient, fair, and efficient – that they are called upon to maintain their social licence, and they must build markets for the well-being of people and the community,[34] based on dynamism, the resilience, sustainability, justice, responsibility, solidarity, and humility.[35] We are drawing upon concepts that influence notions of justice, and are subject to change, based on the historical context, the economic system, and a language primarily shaped by regulation, but also by the alignment of private interests through financial contracts' negotiations.

While adhering to the imperatives of resilience, justice, and efficiency, the pursuit of a social licence becomes integral. This license must be concretely realised, through the establishment of markets that are well structured and function to the advantage of the community.[36] It is precisely the *idea* of society – and the need to protect its interests[37]– that leads us to spin the concept of social licence.

32 Mark Carney, 'Breaking the Tragedy of the Horizon: Climate Change and Financial Stability' (n 19).

33 Mark Carney, *Value(s): Building a Better World for All* (Signal McClelland & Stewart, Penguin Random House Canada, 2021).

34 Mark Carney, 'Breaking the Tragedy of the Horizon: Climate Change and Financial Stability' (n 19).

35 Mark Carney, *Value (s): Building a Better World for All* (n 33) 9.

36 J. C. de Swan, *Seeking Virtue in Finance: Contributing to Society in a Conflicted Industry* (n 3) 84.

37 Robert Schiller, *Finance and the Good Society* (Princeton University Press, 2012) 35.

Without intending to repeat the debates on capitalism[38] and a good society inspired by Marx,[39] Friedman,[40] and successor schools of thought, our purpose is to start by delimiting the notion of a licence, and then continue by setting the parameters that make up the social criteria.

The need to build the notion of a license for the financial system arises from the impossibility of assimilating this type of social permit with the licensing processes that exist, for example, in extractive activities.[41] We understand that the licence of the financial system cannot be limited to influential markets in the international context, or to certain domestic markets. Given the inherent nature of the financial system, the formulation of a licence must be comprehensive and international, ensuring its issuance is not fragmented nor exclusive to specific markets. This does not prevent local regulatory agencies from becoming protectors of the effectiveness of this social licence.

A first step towards building a social licence can focus on understanding the reasons behind the authorisation processes that all market institutions must comply with, in order to access the financial system.[42] While it is a widely recognised process, there are several reasons behind the decision to impose entry requirements into the system. Although it may not be precisely termed 'social licensing', it does encompass elements of selection, where those capable of providing services and products are chosen based on their ability to do so consistently, without compromising their stability. In addition to this first element, we must consider that the social licence of the financial system is inspired by its fundamental premise, centred on the fact that financing, as a social construction, is a socially contingent element.[43] It is called to be always present, not because it is constantly in use, but because it must be available to support any economic activity that requires it.[44] We place special emphasis on the notion of social construction,[45] because it deals with concepts and elements that a social group accepts as true. For example, the notion of what money and investment represent[46] arises from a common social consensus;

38 George Edwards, *The Evolution of Finance Capitalism* (Martino Fine Books, 1938, Reprint 2014) 162.

39 Karl Marx, 'The Capital', in F. Engels (ed) *Capital* 1.13 and 26: 365, 785 (Regnery Publishing, 1996).

40 Milton Friedman, *Capitalism and Freedom: With a New Foreword by Binyamin Appelbaum* (University of Chicago Press, 1962/2020) 132.

41 Julián Tole Martínez, *Desafíos para la regulación de los derechos humanos y las empresas* (Universidad Externado de Colombia, 2019).

42 John Armour, Dan Awrey, Paul Davies, Luca Enriques, Jeffrey N. Gordon, Colin Mayer and Jennifer Payne, *Principles of Financial Regulation* (OUP, 2016) 75.

43 Thomas Lagoarde-Segot, 'Sustainable Finance: A Critical Realist Perspective', *Research in International Business and Finance* 47 (2019): 3.

44 Judith Rodin and Saadiea Madsbjerg, *Making Money Moral: How A New Wave of Visionaries is Linking Purpose and Profit* (Wharton School Press, 2021) 101.

45 Janet Wilde Astington, 'What's New About Social Construction? Distinct Roles Needed for Language and Communication', *Behavioral and Brain Sciences* 27.1 (2004): 96–97; Paul A. Boghossian, 'What is Social Construction?', *TLS*, 2001. https://philpapers.org/rec/BOGWIS.

46 C. Deutschmann, 'Money as a Social Construction: On the Actuality of Marx and Simmel', *Thesis Eleven* 47.1 (1996): 1–19.

its function exists thanks to what we have all agreed to,[47] as well as the meaning given by common language.

The development of a social licence for finance must gradually emerge as a universally accepted concept, embodying a manifestation of the principle of solidarity.[48] Such a licence stems from the need to strengthen the financial system as a forum for mobilising resources and creating value. Both activities are necessary to support the functioning of the economy. In the process of building a social licence, we start from other common notions, such as the notion of value,[49] a concept that has been discussed and re-evaluated, but which in any case is at the centre of the financial system.[50] The concept of 'value' helps illustrate the inseparable link between the financial system and the economy. It underscores the imperative to bridge social consensus and solidarity with the realisation of the fundamental objectives of financial services. The convergence of these elements necessitates the adoption of a shared language and a unified understanding of value and solidarity, establishing common concepts that fortify the financial system's purpose.

We define a *licence* as a permission or authorisation granted to an individual or group to freely engage in an activity, serving as custodians of the common trust.[51] In the context of the financial system, such an activity involves the management and administration of public resources. In this context, the first question would be what kind of societies would be called upon to grant such a licence. Initially, they would be those organised ones[52] which, regardless of the type of structure they follow, can create the law and regulation that are the basis for any financial activity. Under this understanding, *any social group that has a regulatory basis*[53] *that enables the exercise of financial activity* could be considered capable of granting that social licence. However, the existence of a regulatory body is only one of the multiple sources that feed the process of granting a social licence.

In addition to establishing entry, permanence, stability, and prudential requirements, the concept of regulation extends beyond instruments issued by state agencies. It encompasses industry-developed standards that can elevate the levels of compliance.[54] Additionally, the international and transnational nature of financial

47 D. Roberts, 'Georg Simmel's Philosophy of Money: Reflexions on the Relation Between Philosophy and History', *Thesis Eleven* 44.1 (1996): 12–27.

48 Sotiria Theodoropoulou, 'What Solidarity in the Eurozone After the Greek Crisis of 2015?', *Social Policy in the European Union: State of Play 2016* (ETUI, The European Trade Union Institute, 2017) 36.

49 Mariana Mazzucato, *The Value of Everything: Making & Taking in the Global Economy* (Hachette Book Group, 2020).

50 Oliver Horn, *A History of Savings Banks* (OUP, 1947) 118–167.

51 David Rouch, *The Social Licence for Financial Markets: Reaching for the End and Why it Counts* (n 20) 64.

52 ibid.

53 John Armour, Dan Awrey, Paul Davies, Luca Enriques, Jeffrey N. Gordon, Colin Mayer and Jennifer Payne, *Principles of Financial Regulation* (OUP, 2016) 57.

54 H.-K. Chey, 'Do Markets Enhance Convergence on International Standards? The Case of Financial Regulation', *Regulation & Governance* 1 (2007): 295–311.

institutions means that they are obliged to observe different regimes in different jurisdictions, as well as intersectoral relationships.[55] Thus, regulatory sources help us understand who is behind the creation of this social licence, a phenomenon that goes beyond the issuance of regulatory standards by state agencies.[56]

The next question is aimed at resolving who would be the recipients of the social licence. The determination of who is granted the license considers the diversity and heterogeneity of the institutions, intermediaries, agents, and other participants in the financial system. In this sense, both financial institutions and the individuals who work within them are included. We emphasise *institutions and individuals* because of the way in which behaviour in the market is observed and controlled. Although, for the most part, conduct risk is usually linked to the behaviour of regulated and supervised institutions; the rise and strengthening of individual-responsibility schemes have promoted the debate on the need to establish individual conduct criteria, e.g., a 'Fit and Proper Standard'.[57] The objective is for the construction of a social licence for the financial system to be integrated with conduct-risk-management mechanisms for institutions and individuals.

Upon obtaining a social licence, mechanisms should be implemented to verify its efficacy. These are tools that make it possible to identify the degree of trust[58] that the public has in a system and its institutions. Normally, verification becomes possible in moments after a crisis, in which it is possible to know more clearly the perceptions of a social group regarding the functioning, failures, and virtues of the financial system.[59] Similarly, varying levels of trust in the system can be discerned when new players, services, and products prompt consumers to explore alternative mechanisms beyond traditional banking. We argue that, in the context of rethinking the role of financial derivatives for sustainability purposes, building trust is essential. Therefore, it is key to understand how enhancing transparency, improving transaction standardisation, and setting clear parameters for the drafting and measuring of ESG KPIs is pivotal to ensure that ESG derivatives contribute to achieving verifiable sustainability targets.

It is necessary to consider that changes in the behaviour of consumers and investors in the financial system may arise from consumer trends,[60] which is especially relevant in terms of sustainability tendencies, or due to new opportunities to

55 Satvros Gadinis, 'The Financial Stability Board: The New Politics of International Financial Regulation', *Texas International Law Journal* 48 (2012–2013): 157.

56 Robert Baldwin, Martin Cave and Martin Lodge, *Understanding Regulation: Theory, Strategy, and Practice* (2nd edn, OUP, 2012) 41.

57 See Danny Busch and Annick Teubner, 'Fit and Proper Assessments Within the Single Supervisory Mechanism', EBI Working Paper Series 2019 – No. 34. https://ssrn.com/abstract=3346976 accessed 11th November 2023.

58 Curtis C. Verschoor, 'Measuring Trust in Business', *Strategic Finance* 92.11 (2011): 14. Gale Academic OneFile.

59 Stijn Claessens, 'Access to Financial Services: A Review of the Issues and Public Policy Objectives', *The World Bank Research Observer* 21.2 (Fall 2006): 207–240.

60 Ver Robert Lempka and Paul D. Stallard, *Next Generation Finance: Adapting the Financial Services Industry to Changes in Technology, Regulation and Consumer Behaviour* (Harriman House Limited, 2 December 2013).

maximise profits. In both cases, the notion of trust and credibility depends both on the conception of justice[61] held by the groups of consumers and investors, as well as on the efficiency of the sector in satisfying the needs and interests of those social groups. Despite being social constructs, a widespread failure of trust has the potential to become a threat to the stability[62] and functioning of financial services. In this sense, the task of monitoring and controlling the behaviour of those who participate in the market arises for the regulator, to maintain trust levels.

In the process of building a social licence for the financial system, we now consider the terms in which such a license may be granted. As explained before, law and regulation emerge as primary sources which are not exclusive. The first is understood as any regulatory instrument issued by state agencies, and the second is comprehensive of various instruments, strategies, and principles that may arise from unions, industry regulation, and disposition of interests. In the context of sustainability, we understand that there are expectations that go beyond the regulatory debate, and that encourage its evolution. Self-regulation mechanisms[63] play a fundamental role in this construction, e.g., principles created by industry bodies, codes of conduct, corporate governance, voluntary reporting practices, and so on.

The dynamics of change and balance of the interests involved in the regulatory environment make behaviour change a continuous challenge. The setting of the 'rules of the game' is not exclusively in the hands of the regulatory authority. In the case of fixing the concept of interest and positive social impact as a central element of a social licence for the financial system, it is nourished by some commonly accepted elements – for example, the relationship of the financial institution to its employees, which involves conditions such as favourable remuneration, security, stability, and clear promotion mechanisms. All these aspects are considered not only as factors that concern the workforce, but also as criteria by which we will evaluate the institutions participating in the market, and the companies they finance.[64] In this scenario, when those who can grant the social licence identify behaviours contrary to the rights and welfare of workers, they will progressively choose to withdraw their resources from certain financial institutions.[65] In this way, the social licence can create an inherent incentive[66] for market institutions to commit to safeguarding and ensuring the exercise of workers' rights as the initial expression of positive social impact. We anticipate that this would sustain and potentially enhance their

61 Andrea Fejős, 'Social Justice in EU Financial Consumer Law', *Tilburg Law Review* 24 (18 December 2018/2019).

62 Garry J. Schinasi, 'Defining Financial Stability', IMF Working Paper No. 04/187, October 2004.

63 Saule Omarova, 'Rethinking the Future of Self-Regulation in the Financial Industry', *Brooklyn Journal of International Law* 35 (2010): 665.

64 Timothy M. Devinney, Pat Auger, Giana Eckhardt and Thomas Birtchnell, 'The Other CSR: Consumer Social Responsibility', Stanford Social Innovation Review, Leeds University Business School Working Paper No. 15-04, Fall/1 May 2006.

65 ibid.

66 T. Berglund, 'Incentives for Complexity in Financial Regulation', *Journal of Risk Finance* 15.2 (2014): 102–109.

consumer and investor base; realising such impact is contingent on the genuine interest of consumers and investors in scrutinising and evaluating the conduct of the institution handling their capital.[67] This expands the scope of interests for these groups, transcending purely economic considerations.

Thus, the change in behaviour generated as a result of the granting of the social licence is not directed exclusively at market participants and their workers, but would be reflected in the generation of greater awareness regarding the content of this expected positive social impact of the financial system.

In the dialogue for the construction of a social licence, attention must be paid to the role of some social groups that have constantly monitored[68] the conduct of market actors. We refer to initiatives promoted by think tanks that seek to investigate and disclose the greater or lesser degree of commitment that financial institutions have with the achievement of a positive social and environmental impact – for example, Bank Track,[69] whose mission is to prevent banks from financing harmful commercial activities. They promote a banking sector that respects human rights, and contributes to just societies and a healthy planet, as well as supporting other civil society organisations in their commitment to banks.[70]

Moreover, when discerning positive social impact, we draw upon certain traditional concepts of market operation. One such concept is the conviction that, while pursuing an economic objective, we aim to foster overall well-being,[71] interpreted in diverse ways contingent upon the social, political, and economic framework of the locale. Nonetheless, we may acknowledge, respecting differing viewpoints, that general welfare encompasses an effective allocation of resources, enabling all stakeholders to equitably partake in their benefits. Therefore, the efficiency in distribution of sources should not be measured exclusively in traditional economic terms.[72] It is not only a question of seeking the best distribution of available resources, but of guaranteeing that the distribution (which we qualify as efficient) considers the interests of different social groups,[73] thus observing the *Gapponshugi* principle mentioned at the beginning of this chapter.[74] In this scenario, the financial

67 M. A. Ferreira and P. Matos, 'The Colors of Investors' Money: The Role of Institutional Investors around the World', *Journal of Financial Economics* 88.3 (2008): 499–533.

68 Vicente Lazen and Cristian Eguiluz, 'Conflictos de Interés en Servicios Financieros: Taxonomía y Mecanismos de Control Regulatorio [Conflicts of Interest in Financial Services: Taxonomy and Mechanisms for Regulatory Control]', MPRA Paper 3891, University Library of Munich, 2006. https://ideas.repec.org/p/pra/mprapa/3891.html accessed 11th November 2023.

69 Bank Track. www.banktrack.org accessed 11th November 2023.

70 ibid.

71 L. Boone, N. Girouard and I. Wanner, 'Financial Market Liberalisation, Wealth and Consumption', in *OECD Economics Department Working Papers, No. 308* (OECD Publishing, 2001).

72 Keith A. Allman and Ximena Escobar de Nogales, *Impact Investment: A Practical Guide to Investment Process and Social Impact Analysis* (Wiley, 2015) 4.

73 Benjamin Lee and Randy Martin (eds), *Derivatives and the Wealth of Societies* (The University of Chicago Press, 2016) 175.

74 Patrick Fridenson and Kikkawa Takeo (eds), *Ethical Capitalism: Shibusawa and Business Leadership in Global Perspective* (University of Toronto Press, 2017) 35.

regulator not only intervenes to prevent or control market failures,[75] but also seeks to balance the economic and social benefit that financial services are called to generate.[76]

The parameters of a social licence presuppose that delineating regulation with a focus on safeguarding the public interest is one of the most intricate responsibilities for regulators. This complexity arises from the dynamic nature of the concept of public interest, which is directly influenced by the temporal, geographical, and culturally specific values of the social group in question.

Distributive Justice and Dignity

The reference to distributive justice addresses the need to find a protection mechanism for the most vulnerable within the financial system, and others affected by its operation. Rawls provides us with the foundational principles from which a social licence for the financial system is expected to materialise.[77] The notion of distributive justice entails the requirement that well-being be distributed among all the members of a social group, thus excluding the possibility that some are bound to benefit more than others.[78] Finding the equilibrium point in the distribution of well-being and the sources that generate it is not necessarily an easy task.[79] For example, as observed in the corporate context, conflicts of interest and the greater influence of a few versus the fate of the majority,[80] or in the regulatory dialogue, the capture of the regulator by power groups,[81] have led to the relegation of the weakest in the market, both in terms of recognition and the guarantee of rights. Recognising the evident inadequacy of the sector's regulation in the current context is evidence that the ideology of distributive justice in the financial system has yet to be successfully realised.[82] This calls us to explore complementary sources for inducing positive changes in the behaviour of market participants.

75 David Llewellyn, 'The Economic Rationale for Financial Regulation', FSA Occasional Papers in Financial Regulation, April 1999. www.researchgate.net/profile/David-Llewellyn-4/publication/247849804_The_Economic_Rationale_for_Financial_Regulation/links/53e3573d0cf23a7ff7493f9e/The-Economic-Rationale-for-Financial-Regulation.pdf accessed 11th November 2023.

76 S. Morris and H. S. Shin, 'Financial Regulation in a System Context', *Brookings Papers on Economic Activity* 2008.2 (2008): 229–274.

77 J. Rawls, *A Theory of Justice* (Clarendon Press/Oxford University Press, 1972).

78 ibid.

79 Andrés Murcia Pabón, 'Determinantes del Acceso al Crédito de los Hogares Colombianos', Borradores de Economía, Banco de la República, N 449 de 2007, 2. www.banrep.gov.co/sites/default/files/publicaciones/pdfs/borra449.pdf accessed 11th November 2023.

80 C. B. Ingley and N. T. Van Der Walt, 'Corporate Governance, Institutional Investors and Conflicts of Interest', *Corporate Governance: An International Review* 12 (2004): 534–551.

81 IMF, 'Regulatory Capture in Banking', vol. 2006, issue 34. www.elibrary.imf.org/view/journals/001/2006/034/article-A001-en.xml?ArticleTabs=fulltext accessed 11th November 2023.

82 David T. Llewellyn, 'Institutional Structure of Financial Regulation and Supervision: The Basic Issues', Paper presented at a World Bank Seminar Aligning Supervisory Structures with Country Needs Washington DC, 6 and 7 June 2006. http://citeseerx.ist.psu.edu/viewdoc/download?doi=10.1.1.503.2388&rep=rep1&type=pdf accessed 11th November 2023.

It is at this point that our argument focuses on defending the idea that the financial system's social licence is built from existing regulatory mechanisms, and complemented by the reconfiguration of financial contracting, in favour of value creation in the market.

The distribution of capital is called upon to focus on activities, products, and services that generate the greatest possible positive impact. Hence, the construction of a social licence for the financial system is presented as a mechanism aimed at achieving the general adoption of criteria such as distributive justice throughout financial services. The objective is that not only few,[83] but *all* market participants incorporate value-generation criteria in the execution of their activities, and a correlative decrease in value-extraction activities. In this scenario, both existing products and services, as well as those that will be created in the future, must comply with – in addition to technical market regulations and compliance standards – a verifiable positive social impact, e.g., efficient distribution of resources, generating greatest possible profit, financing of sustainable projects.[84] Thus, sustainability would no longer be reduced exclusively to a line of business tending towards partially promoting responsible practices,[85] but would become a transversal factor in all the activities of financial institutions.

The regulator would be called upon to lead a standardisation process to promote and facilitate the adoption of positive social impact criteria. This in turn would require the acceptance of social constructions, such as justice, equitable distribution of resources, and how these two elements generate well-being. Once these criteria have been established, they must be incorporated into the regulation of the sector, and internalised in the mechanisms for the mobilisation of capital – that is, financial contracts, in particular, financial derivatives. To the extent that the adoption of voluntary standards lacks strength to the degree of enforceability and compliance expected,[86] the call is directed towards the regulator taking advantage of the notion of social construction to accept a social licence.

In the context of the social licence for the financial system, just as we recognise and accept social constructions facilitated by the law in other scenarios, the regulator can employ a social construction to encourage its adoption. The regulator would utilise an instrument aimed at behavioural change, advocating for an expanded relationship between regulators and regulated entities in the financial sector. This transition aims to incorporate more comprehensive criteria, ensuring

83 Lv Jinfang and Qin Shusheng, 'Policy Support for Developing Green Economy and Promoting the Construction of Ecological Civilization', *Philosophy Study* 6.5 (May 2016): 282–288. www.davidpublisher.com/Public/uploads/Contribute/579b0cc340ca6.pdf accessed 11th November 2023.

84 S. Barua, 'Financing Sustainable Development Goals: A Review of Challenges and Mitigation Strategies', *Business Strategy and the Development* 3 (2020): 277–293.

85 Institut Rousseau, 'Fossil Assets: The New Subprimes?', June 2021. https://reclaimfinance.org/site/wp-content/uploads/2021/06/Report-Fossil-Assets-the-new-subprimes.pdf accessed 11th November 2023.

86 A. Nurse, 'Creative Compliance, Constructive Compliance: Corporate Environmental Crime and the Criminal Entrepreneur', *Contemporary Issues in Entrepreneurship Research* 5 (2015): 97.

that the design of regulatory tools embedding the social licence adequately considers all aspects related to social impact made by financial activities.

This standardisation process may draw from sectoral initiatives aimed at intertwining the criteria for measuring positive social impact. However, as the regulator is just one of the involved actors, its role involves constructing a framework that guides the formation and evolution of a social licence. The regulator's responsibility is to establish explicit expectations regarding the substance of positive social impact.

Along with distributive justice, parallel considerations arise regarding how the functioning of the financial system is expected to contribute, without compromising other constitutional principles, such as human dignity.[87] This includes directing capital through financial products and contracts towards activities that respect the dignity of members of social groups.[88] Entities in the sector are also expected to commit to preventing their channels from being used to legitimise money obtained through activities that violate human rights, or that (either directly or indirectly) contribute to perpetuating sources of social conflict.[89] Regulations against money laundering and terrorism financing[90] have been widely developed from a technical perspective. Nevertheless, the objective is for its implementation to proactively prevent the entry of capital associated with any form of human rights violation into the financial system.[91]

Achieving this objective is intricately tied to the reciprocal relationship between society and the financial market. Trust and freedom are bestowed upon market participants, with the expectation that the outcome is oriented toward mutual benefit rather than a conflict of interest.[92] This underscores the purpose of the financial system as a conduit for the realisation of common goods, particularly the ideals of justice, equitable resource distribution, well-being generation, and human dignity. In this context, its function is not solely confined to the area of monetary transactions, but is also intertwined with the embodiment of intrinsic human value.

The development of a social licence grounded in the concepts of value generation and extraction provides us with more tangible criteria for assessing the conduct of financial institutions, and reimagining the role of financial derivatives. Consequently, in determining whether an institution merits a social licence, scrutiny of its products and services in terms of value creation becomes essential. If the

87 Miguel Ángel and Gómez Ortiz, 'Globalización, derecho y dignidad humana en América Latina', *Anuario de Derecho* 30 (2013): 13.

88 Robert Shiller, *Finance and the Good Society* (Princeton University Press, 2012) 149.

89 Tony Addison, Abdur R. Chowdhury and Mansoob Murshed, 'By How Much Does Conflict Reduce Financial Development?', WIDER Discussion Paper No. 2002/48.

90 Richard Lowe, 'Anti-Money Laundering – The Need for Intelligence', *Journal of Financial Crime* 24.3 (2017): 472–479.

91 Z. Dobrowolski and Ł. Sułkowski, 'Implementing a Sustainable Model for Anti-Money Laundering in the United Nations Development Goals', *Sustainability* 12 (2020): 244.

92 Jed Emerson, *The Purpose of Capital: Elements of Impact, Financial Flows, and Natural Being* (Blended Value Group Press, 2018) Loc. 1515 Kindle Version.

institution's offerings are predominantly identified with value extraction, or lack identifiable value generation, such instances could raise alarm signals, prompting a reconsideration of the eligibility for a social licence. This assessment is pivotal in gauging the institution's commitment to the principles of social justice, equitable resource distribution, the promotion of general well-being, and the safeguarding of human dignity.

In the construction of a social licence from the promotion of regulatory standards, it is necessary to consider the costs associated with regulation. One of the most widespread misunderstandings is considering that regulation is a cost-free good and, to that extent, should and can be demanded without measure by consumers, and generously implemented by the state, limiting innovation and economic activity. The imposition of a regulation aimed at solving a problem can per se generate higher costs – both for those obligated to comply, and for the one who monitors compliance. Thus, in the construction of a social licence, the regulator is called upon to choose the regulatory instruments and strategies that contribute to the generation of greater value without this representing the assumption of excessive costs. Much of the success of these regulatory instruments is focused on putting into operation an incentive system that allows regulated entities to identify the benefits that arise for them from compliance with standards of conduct.

The Role of Conduct Regulation in the Construction of a Social Licence

The construction of a social licence is not simply a reformulation of the social contract of Hobbes and Locke.[93] While for the social contract, we start from a relationship of subordination and conflict,[94] for a social licence we want to avoid the unbalanced relationship that has existed between financial institutions and other market participants, such as consumers and investors. The license must be internalised by all those involved in the provision, use and monitoring of financial services. It should be reflected in each of the products offered and negotiated, not just in lines created exclusively to serve social objectives. Burdens are imposed upon institutions, the individuals who work in them, and users, consumers, and investors, all of whom are committed to ensuring that the financial system effectively contributes to the generation of well-being for all. The consumer and the investor will make the decision to use financial services only if they clearly involve value generation, not only for their individual interests, but also for the social group. Sector institutions will receive incentives to promote the adoption of transparent criteria for positive social impact.

The conduct regime[95] is a fundamental element in financial regulation and especially in risk-based regulation. However, there is no single definition of what

93 Christopher W. Morris, *The Social Contract Theorists: Critical Essays on Hobbes, Locke, and Rousseau* (Rowman & Littlefield Publishers, 1 January 2000) 23.

94 ibid.

95 A. F. Tuch, 'Conduct of Business Regulation', in *Oxford Handbook of Financial Regulation* (Oxford University Press, 2014) 537.

should be understood as a conduct regime.[96] In each country or jurisdiction, regulators design standards of conduct that usually include consumer protection, rules of conduct in the market, and some ethical standards that are included in codes of conduct. Some traditional elements included in the protection systems of those who are judged weak in market relations, i.e., consumers and investors, include: adequate levels of investor protection according to the different categories, promotion of high standards of integrity and probity, the duty imposed on authorised participants and intermediaries to act with diligence and care, contractual obligations with consumers, especially the delivery of information to make investment decisions, the duty to deposit and safeguard information.

The Reconfiguration of Financial Derivatives for the Construction of a Social Licence

In addition to the elements created by sectoral regulatory mechanisms, commercial and contract law also has a regulatory dimension, in terms of sanctions for noncompliance and in preventing abusive and harmful behaviour by market players. Our argument in this book focuses on understanding the reconfiguration of financial derivatives as a mechanism that promotes the strengthening of a social licence for the market – understanding that it rests on the generation of a positive social impact guaranteeing the ideas of justice, efficiency in the distribution of the resource, and generation of general well-being. To build this argument, we will refer to the need to redirect financial services and the purposes involved in entering ESG derivatives in the market *towards the generation of value and the progressive reduction of value-extraction activities*.[97]

According to Professor Mariana Mazzucato,[98] *value creation* involves ways in which different types of resources (human, physical, and intangible) are established and interact to produce new goods and services. *Value extraction* occurs through activities focused on moving around existing resources and their products, to gain disproportionately from their subsequent negotiation.[99]

Financial derivatives must focus on the clear identification of positive results for the economy.[100] This means understanding whether the conditions under which financial derivatives are entered into *generate profitability and well-being for the*

96 See Arias Barrera and Ligia Catherine, *Regulation and Supervision of the OTC Derivatives Market* (Routledge, 2018) ch. 3.

97 Jennifer A. Dlouhy, 'Federal Regulators Hear Call for Tighter Controls on Speculators', 29 July 2009. www.pressdemocrat.com/article/news/federal-regulators-hear-call-for-tighter-controls-on-speculators/ accessed 11th November 2023.

98 Mariana Mazzucato, *The Value of Everything: Making & Taking in the Global Economy* (n 49).

99 Lynn A. Stout, 'Why the Law Hates Speculators: Regulation and Private Ordering in the Market for OTC Derivatives', *Duke Law Journal* 48 (1999): 701–786.

100 Oliver Hart, 'Financial Contracting', *Journal of Economic Literature* 39.4 (December 2001): 1079.

economy, or if, on the contrary, they exclusively benefit some market participants. The foregoing implies judging derivatives contracts from the classification of productive activities and nonproductive activities, not to promote the former and outlaw the latter, but to understand how these activities can be shaped in response to the need to generate value. Naturally, the position adopted depends on the economic theory used as a point of reference. While a perspective close to Marx[101] would tend to criticise the existence of financial services to the extent that they do not create value, Lord Lauderdale and Nassaw Senior's[102] approach would suggest profit-generating financial activity deserves to be preserved – it is a reward for saving and reducing consumption. For their part, the leaders of the theory of marginal utility – Walras, Jevons, and Menger[103] – would understand that all economic activity, including finance, generates income as a reward for productivity. In the last two of these theories, there seems to be a direct connection between the effort made in carrying out the activity, and being rewarded by profits. Thus, under the current market circumstances, it would be difficult for us to judge financial activities as nonproductive and seek to proscribe them for not generating value, to the extent that in all of them, the allocation of resources to obtain a result is verifiable.

In this process of evolution of the notion of value, we owe a great deal to the work of Adam Smith[104] and Jeremy Bentham,[105] who began to disdain the concepts of *goodness* or *badness* in judging how productive an activity is; on the contrary, they directed their efforts to illustrating the common goods that may be achieved when pursuing individual interests. So, if we want to judge the financial activity instrumentalised in financial derivatives as productive and value-generating, we will have to look at the common goods to which it contributes, while, at the same time, serving the individual interests of the contracting parties.[106]

The advent of utility theory, initially proposed by Alfred Marshall,[107] brings with it the blurring of a sharp distinction between productive and nonproductive activities. Fundamentally, to the extent that each sector produces for the market and an exchange of products is generated, Marshall suggests there are no definitively unproductive sectors or activities. Thus, the success of economies depends on markets that guarantee competition between market participants, which is necessary for everyone to maximise their preferences and for companies to obtain profits. All of which, according to marginal utility theory, leads to the creation of general

101 Karl Marx, *Capital*, vol. 3 (Penguin Classics, 1992) chs. 38 and 39.

102 Mariana Mazzucato, *The Value of Everything: Making & Taking in the Global Economy* (n 49) 59.

103 ibid., 60.

104 See Adam Smith and A. Skinner (eds), *The Wealth of Nations* (Penguin, 1776/1999).

105 See Jeremy Bentham, *A Fragment on Government: Being an Examination of What Is Delivered, on the Subject of Government in General, in the Introduction to Sir William Blackstone's Commentaries: With a Preface, in Which Is Given a Critique on the Work at Large* (T. Payne, P. Elmsly, and E. Brooke, 1776).

106 Iren Levina, 'A Puzzling Rise in Financial Profits and the Role of Capital Gain-Like Revenues', Political Economy Research Institute Working Paper No. 347, April 2014, 24.

107 See Alfred Marshall, *Principles of Economics* (Macmillan, 1890/1920).

welfare. In this scenario, all financial contracts – whether they are used to provide access to credit, to obtain profitability, to speculate, to manage risks, or to promote savings – are legitimate sources of income. What really matters is that the market works in conditions of harmonious competition and thus, in principle, is creating a common good.

However, the reality of the development and dynamism of the market presents great difficulty, since there are several factors that prevent the normal functioning of the market in conditions of perfect competition. It should be noted that the pervasiveness of the problems associated with activity in financial markets is variable. For example, information asymmetry is greater in some markets than in others, due to the types of transactions and agreements, actors and intermediaries, and the level of experience and sophistication of each. Events of imperfect information and problems derived from contractual relations and the duties of banks with their clients (framed in well-known agency problems[108]) mean that consumers are not able to evaluate the financial situation of their bank, or to know the inherent value of the product they have purchased – for example, a bond or an insurance policy. Thus, in addition to the regulation of conduct explained before, to avoid the adverse consequences of the behaviour of financial institutions, individuals, consumers, and society in general, it is necessary to promote the notion of a social licence that requires contracting parties to recognise that the use they make of their derivatives contracts is called upon to contribute to the generation of general well-being and positive social impact.

In this discourse of economic theory around the notion of value, an additional concept is related to *income* as the main mechanism for extracting value.[109] Starting with neoclassical economists, profits and income are determined in a similar way, since the owners of capital lend it until the marginal utility is less than the utility of consuming or using that capital. Thus, the justification in the generation of profits derives from individual decisions. The concept of income holds significance, as it influences how economic growth is assessed, the evaluation of the role of financial activities, and the formulation of public policies aimed at promoting general well-being. In line with the theory of marginal utility, where value is derived from the given price, a high salary is indicative of an individual's high level of productivity and social value.[110] However, applying this notion to evaluate financial activities poses challenges. Without deeper analysis, traditional functions like attracting and deploying public resources may be deemed productive and value-generating, based solely on their remuneration.

However, the reality of financial activities instrumentalised in contracts is complex, and not all of them can clearly identify the generation of value. In the past,

108 See Michael Jensen and William Meckling, 'Theory of the Firm: Managerial Behavior, Agency Costs and Ownership Structure', *Journal of Financial Economics* 3.4 (1976): 305–360. Elsevier.

109 Mariana Mazzucato, *The Value of Everything: Making & Taking in the Global Economy* (n 50) 72.

110 Silvia Merler and Pia Hüttl, 'Welcome to the Dark Side: GDP Revision and the Non-Observed Economy', *Bruegel*, 2 March 2015. www.bruegel.org/blog-post/welcome-dark-side-gdp-revision-and-non-observed-economy accessed 11th November 2023.

financial institutions were divided between those that carried out banking activities and those that did not. With the evolution of modern financial institutions, a notable trend can be identified for these institutions to combine both types of services. The parameter that characterises banking activities is the acceptance of deposits and the role of intermediation between savers and lenders, including investment management. Similarly, the investment advisory function can be identified as a traditionally nonbanking activity. However, with the growth of internal offices dedicated to this activity, it has become an integral area of banking activities. Something similar happens with securities trading.

Before the Global Financial Crisis, there was a progressive growth of conglomerates in the financial sector executing banking and nonbanking activities. After the crisis, there was a movement towards specialisation in the provision of services, in addition to regulatory efforts tending to separate (using the figure of 'Ring-fencing'[111]) the typical banking activities of commercial banks, and those of private investment banks. We observe that more and more banks are dedicated to investing in the capital market, and obtaining profits derived from the movement or variation in the prices of the assets traded, or the underlying assets. To the extent that we are in a market whose operation implies price variations, there is always the positive or negative risk of obtaining profits or, conversely, suffering losses. In traditional banking activity, the risk derived from price fluctuations is minimal. However, as soon as banks begin to participate in the capital market, taking positions in their own name and not as agents of their clients, they are exposed to market risk.[112]

From our perspective, it is not feasible to rely on the theory of marginal utility[113] as a definitive reference point for distinguishing – within financial activities and contracts – which ones are designed to generate value and which are geared towards extracting value. Consequently, determining the type of activities that contribute to the generation of common well-being and positive social impact requires a more nuanced approach, beyond the simplistic framework of remuneration.

The scope of financial activities necessitates moving beyond general classifications of banking and nonbanking activities. This expansion is essential to discern whether the mobilisation of capital is directed toward safeguarding broader public interests (i.e., sustainability goals) or, as some scholars argue, if the goal is the prosperity of the financial institution executing such mobilisation. This critique leads us to consider the contradictory nature of the trend according to which economic progress requires the growth and expansion of the financial system as a sine qua non condition. Especially noteworthy is that even proponents of this notion,

111 Iain Hardie and Huw Macartney, 'EU Ring-Fencing and the Defence of Too-Big-To-Fail Banks', *West European Politics* 39.3 (2016): 503.

112 See Arias Barrera and Ligia Catherine, *Regulation and Supervision of the OTC Derivatives Market* (n 96) ch. 4.

113 George Stigler, 'The Adoption of the Marginal Utility Theory', *Nebraska Journal of Economics and Business (Lincoln, NE)* 11.4 (Fall 1972): 188.

such as Schumpeter[114] and Gerashchenko,[115] acknowledge that the contribution of financial institutions, particularly banks, to economic development is contingent upon the exercise of monopoly power, and the accrual of rents and profits for these institutions.

Thus, the intermediation activity between savers and lenders allows banks to capture value from others, rather than create it themselves. Traditionally, both commercial banks and investment banks obtain a large part of their income from the differences between the interest rates they charge their clients and those they must pay to the funds that provide them with financing. Usually, the charging of interest rates is explained by the need to remunerate the creditors, who, during the term of the credit relationship, lose the opportunity to use the capital, to the extent that they cede its use to the debtors. It is a remuneration for waiting. Furthermore, charging interest rates can be explained as a way of rewarding risk-taking.[116] Here, we are referring to the risk associated with not using the money at this time, which may lead to less satisfaction in using it in the future, or, eventually, the risk of default by the debtor and his inability to pay all or part of the capital loaned. Alternatively, the risk of not using the money in the present can materialise through the loss or decrease in its value. According to this approach, beyond being considered usurious, the interest charge can be interpreted as a remuneration to the creditor for assuming the risk of losing his money.

Although it is possible to understand the economic reasons behind charging interest rates, these constructs do not necessarily answer definitively the question of how financial institutions and financial contracts create value.[117] The generation of value must be determined from the content and function fulfilled by each activity and contract carried out in the sector. In this scenario, banking activities and contracts involve short-term deposit conversion services into long-term loans, such as mortgage loans and financing lines for productive activities. In addition, banking services are called upon to provide liquidity to companies and individuals. Likewise, banks oversee analysing the credit capacity of potential debtors and deciding if they meet the requirements to access credit. Also, they are sources of channelling resources between lenders and debtors. From these functions, typical of banking activities and contracts, we can easily identify risk management and administration, which defines financial intermediation. However, the difficulty arises when we try to distinguish between the justification for interest and other charges imposed on consumers of financial services, and the rationale behind obtaining rents as a form of value extraction.

Naturally, it is not possible to deny that the activities and contracts of the financial system facilitate the circulation of goods and services – a fundamental aspect

114 J. A. Schumpeter, *History of Economic Analysis* (OUP, 1954) 590.

115 Alexander Gerschenkron, *Atraso Económico e Industrialización* (Ariel, 2015) 86.

116 Andreas Christofi and A. M. Agapos, 'Interest Rate Deregulation: An Empirical Justification', *Review of Business and Economic Research (New Orleans, LA)* 20.1 (Fall 1984): 39.

117 Mariana Mazzucato, *The Value of Everything: Making & Taking in the Global Economy* (n 49) 110.

for the growth of the economy. However, there is a call for fundamental reform of the functioning of the financial system, and of the objectives that the contracts entered into the market are called upon to fulfil. This call is motivated by the practices associated with the excessive generation of profits that only benefit financial institutions, and that do not channel resources to alternative forms of investment, that in turn generate common well-being and positive social impact. William Baumol[118] defends the idea of reconfiguring financial services by virtue of which activities of strict value extraction must be progressively reduced, eliminated, and controlled. In a more restrained manner, and closer to the realities of the market, Mariana Mazzucato[119] argues that the real challenge is not exclusively the identification of financial services with the categories of value creation/extraction, but the fundamental transformation of the financial system as a genuine source of value creation.

Here, our argument focuses on promoting the construction of a social licence supported by financial derivatives. In our opinion, the fundamental transformation of financial derivatives for the generation of value[120] must be built based on collaboration between the actors involved. This implies the use and strengthening of the existing regulation regarding the management of conduct risk of market participants. As we anticipated in previous sections of this book, this category includes financial institutions, individuals, and financial products and services.

Additionally, in the process of building a social licence, we understand that the sources of regulation of the conduct of market participants are nourished by the instruments that individuals use to dispose of their interests – that is, *contracts*. In this regard, we understand that the contract is an instrument protected by the legal system, and in which power relations materialise, as explained by Professor Katharina Pistor.[121] Our argument is focused on understanding that a social licence for the financial system must be reflected in the objectives that inspire the execution of financial derivatives, which cannot exclusively attend to the individual interests of the contracting parties, but rather are called upon to contribute to the generation of positive social impact.

To shape the concept of a social licence concerning financial derivatives, we need to transcend certain social constructs that have been widely accepted as determining the functioning of financial services. One such construct posits that the industry will invariably strive to safeguard the unrestrained generation of profits – a notion integral to the economic literature's concept of the economically rational individual.[122] According to *homo economicus*, the market participant is motivated

118 W. J. Baumol, 'Entrepreneurship: Productive, Unproductive, and Destructive', *Journal of Political Economy* 98.5 (1990): 893.

119 Mariana Mazzucato, *The Value of Everything: Making & Taking in the Global Economy* (n 49).

120 M. E. Porter and M. R. Kramer, 'Creating Shared Value', *Harvard Business Review* 89 (2011): 62.

121 Katharina Pistor, *The Code of Capital: How the Law Creates Wealth and Inequality* (Princeton University Press, 2019) 206.

122 Malcolm Sparrow, *The Regulatory Craft: Controlling Risks, Solving Problems, and Managing Compliance* (Brooking Institution Press, 2000) 549.

solely and exclusively by obtaining profits and profits. Julia Black[123] suggests that it is necessary to separate from this notion, in order to understand that – even though obtaining profits is at the centre of any business – there are other aspects that must be considered and that can impose ethical and honest behaviour of market players, such as reputation, market pressure, and the culture of respecting the rules of the game. Thus, the criteria for judging the conduct of market participants cannot continue to attend exclusively to the generation of profits. It must include their interest in contributing to the generation of social welfare.[124] Naturally, the paramount incentive lies in the control and management of reputational risk.[125] As a financial derivatives market participant garners higher levels of recognition for dedication to generating a positive social impact, they secure a superior position in the market compared to other institutions.[126] This elevated standing resonates with consumers, investors, regulators, and society at large.

Given that one of the most relevant aspects in the construction of a social licence is *compliance with human rights protection standards*, our argument is focused on understanding that financial derivatives can become the instrument to ritualise the protection of human rights. From regulation theory, such ritualism is a way of adapting the normative order according to the five modes of adaptation of cultural values proposed by Robert Merton[127] (conformity, innovation, ritualism, withdrawal, and rebellion). In the context of human rights, ritualism implies the acceptance of institutional means to obtain regulatory objectives which, in our case, are focused on generating a positive social impact. The level of greater or lesser adherence to institutional mechanisms uses the motivational positions adopted by the recipients of human rights regulation. Charlesworth[128] affirms that ritualism seems to be more common in the face of the institutional discourse of protection of human rights than its open rejection. This is an apparent enforcement policy, aimed at avoiding scrutiny and accountability for ongoing abuses and violations. Of course, the main motivation is the reputational benefit associated with presenting oneself as a State or individual committed to the protection of human rights.

According to Charlesworth,[129] the implications of adapting aspects of the regulation theory to the human rights protection regime lie in the opportunity to create

123 Julia Black and Robert Baldwin, 'When Risk-Based Regulation Aims Low: A Strategic Framework', *Regulation and Governance* 6 (2012): 131.

124 Andrew MacInnes, *Sustainability and Capital Markets: Guide for US Companies* (A Brilluminant Publication, 2020) 124.

125 Dinah Heidinger and Nadine Gatzert, 'Awareness, Determinants, and Value of Reputation Risk Management: Empirical Evidence from the Banking and Insurance Industry', *Journal of Banking & Finance* 91 (2018): 108.

126 Christian Eckert, 'Corporate Reputation and Reputation Risk: Definition and Measurement from a (Risk) Management Perspective', *Journal of Risk Finance* 18.2 (2017): 145–158.

127 Robert Merton, *Social Theory and Social Structure* (Free Press, 1968).

128 Hilary Charlesworth, 'A Regulatory Perspective on the International Human Rights System', in Peter Drahos (ed), *Regulatory Theory: Foundations and Applications* (Australian National University, 2017) 359.

129 ibid.

response mechanisms and access to justice that respond to the circumstances of the protected subjects. In this context, existing rules and institutions are of great importance, but only as elements of a regulatory network that is incomplete, and must continue to adjust to the multiple sources and actors of human rights violations.[130] It is precisely in this aspect that the construction of a social licence for the financial system finds support. The objective of the internalisation of a social licence is that the development and offer of financial services instrumentalised through contracts responds to the general interest of creating well-being. The challenge is precisely to prevent this social construction of a license from becoming a purely ritualistic mechanism.

The success in the process of adoption of conduct regulation and the acceptance of the social licence in financial derivatives is verifiable, according to the way regulated institutions respond to the regulation.[131] If there is a culture of compliance,[132] there will consequently be a harmony and cordial relationship between the regulator and the regulated. The positive effects of cooperation mechanisms between the regulated and the regulator contribute to the proper functioning of the market,[133] and benefit corporates and investors. In those events where cooperation mechanisms and incentives-based regulation are not effective, the supervisor will be forced constantly to impose sanctions. In these cases, the regulatory environment is tense and usually inefficient. It is useful to note that excessively strict regimes[134] can be counterproductive, because profit margins can be considerably affected, so much so that financial derivatives participants may decide to calculate and include penalties for noncompliance.[135] Consequently, the construction of a social licence will only be successful if it results from a negotiation process led and monitored by regulatory agencies. It will need the support of derivatives market participants using contracts that are clearly directed towards the generation of value. This process necessitates dialogue and cooperation in defining the constitutive elements of such a license, and those criteria to be assessed as positive social impact. It also

130 See Laura Bernal Bermudez, 'Using Judicial Actions to Address Corporate Human Rights Abuses: Colombia, 2000–2014', in Pedro Fortes, Larissa Boratti, Andrés Palacios and Tom Daly (eds), *Law, and Policy in Latin America: Transforming Courts, Institutions, and Rights* (Palgrave Macmillan St. Antony's Series, 2017) 150.

131 A. Batory, 'Defying the Commission: Creative Compliance and Respect for the Rule of Law in the EU', *Public Admin* 94 (2016): 685.

132 M. Angelova, T. Dannwolf and T. König, 'How Robust Are Compliance Findings? A Research Synthesis', *Journal of European Public Policy* 19.8 (2012): 1269.

133 Jeffrey Checkel, 'Why Comply? Social Learning and European Identity Change', *International Organization* 55.3 (2001): 553.

134 Doreen McBarnet, 'When Compliance is not the Solution But the Problem: From Changes in Law to Changes in Attitude', Centre for Tax System Integrity (CTSI), Research School of Social Sciences, The Australian National University, Working Paper (Centre for Tax System Integrity) No. 18, August 2001, 8. https://openresearch-repository.anu.edu.au/bitstream/1885/154916/1/18.pdf accessed 11th November 2023.

135 See Doreen McBarnet, 'Questioning the Legitimacy of Compliance: A Case Study of the Banking Crisis', in Adam Crawford and Anthea Hucklesby (eds), *Legitimacy and Compliance in Criminal Justice* (Routledge, 2012) 103.

involves establishing mechanisms for measurement, enforcement, or verification of compliance.

Final Remarks

The construction of a social licence for the financial system relies on regulatory advancements that underscore the functions historically assigned to the sector's activities and contracts. We specifically allude to the efficient mobilisation of capital directed at safeguarding the general interest. The regulatory framework that has evolved around the concepts of justice, equality, and efficiency in resource distribution is undergoing a re-evaluation. In this context, regulatory instruments should strive to fortify the envisioned positive social impact of financial activities. Merely proclaiming that financial services must protect the public interest is no longer sufficient. *What is now imperative is the establishment of precise regulatory expectations that lend substance and a foundation to sustainability criteria.* All of this is aimed at elucidating the role that financial derivatives ought to play in discerning and mitigating ESG risks, encompassing both their inherent risks, and those of the entities and individuals they serve.

Our purpose is to contribute to the construction of the social criterion, making use of the idea coined by David Rouch around the need to build a social licence for the financial system. This involves actively engaging in the construction and definition of parameters that align the provision of financial services with positive social impact. It requires fostering a financial landscape that is not only economically sound, but also a creator of value for all stakeholders. In this context, ESG derivatives assume a pivotal role, by significantly bolstering the commitment to a distinct and positive social impact at the transactional level. The construction of the social licence relies on the interaction between *regulation* and *contract*, understanding that they are the two main sources of legitimacy that a social licence must possess, if its effectiveness is to be ensured.

Naturally, any social licence must build on existing regulatory advances. In this sense, we recognise that the role of conduct regulation as a bastion of market intervention is a good starting point. More precisely, the foundations of a social licence seek to strengthen the generation of common well-being as a regulatory objective. However, there is still another ingredient required for building a social licence: the role that financial contracts can play to complement and strengthen its construction and implementation.

Consequently, we defend the need to reconfigure ESG derivatives, based on the concepts of value generation and value extraction. Understanding that a social licence must focus on the generation of positive social impact (e.g., the protection of human rights, respect for labour rights, positive impact on communities, generation of common well-being, etc.) it is necessary to concentrate on the clear identification of the results that financial services deliver to the economy. In this sense, it is possible to establish whether the conditions under which ESG derivatives are negotiated generate profitability and well-being for all, or if, on the contrary, they benefit only a few market participants. Based on the foundations of economic theory and the redefinition of value proposed by Mariana Mazzucato, we affirm that the financial derivatives associated with the excessive generation of profits – that benefit financial institutions and do not channel public resources to serve investments that generate positive social impact – should be discouraged.

The success of the fundamental transformation of ESG derivatives must be built on the collaboration of all the actors involved. In this sense, it is not an exclusive movement of regulators and supervisors, but involves financial derivatives market participants. Achieving a transversal acceptance of a social licence – and its incorporation in each financial derivative in the market – helps us to avoid problems such as a ritualistic response to the protection of human rights.

In the quest for constructing a social licence, adherence to human rights protection standards emerges as a crucial factor. Our argument centres on the notion that financial derivatives can serve as instruments to formalise the safeguarding of human rights, adopting a ritualistic approach in the context of regulation theory. Ritualism, characterised by the acceptance of institutional means to achieve regulatory objectives, aligns with generating a positive social impact. Adapting aspects of regulation theory to the human rights protection regime provides an opportunity to create responsive mechanisms and access to justice for those protected. The construction of a social licence for the financial system finds support in this adaptation, aiming to ensure that financial services contribute to the general well-being. However, the challenge lies in preventing this social construction from becoming a mere ritualistic 'rubber-stamp' mechanism. The success of conduct regulation and the acceptance of the social license in financial derivatives are discernible through how regulated institutions respond to the regulation.

Bibliography

Books

Armour, J., Awrey, D., Davies, P., Enriques, L., Gordon, J., Mayer, C., and Payne, J., *Principles of Financial Regulation* (Oxford University Press 2016).
Carney, M., *Value (s): Building a Better World for All* (Signal McClelland & Stewart, Penguin Random House Canada 2021).
de Swaan, JC., *Seeking Virtue in Finance: Contributing to Society in a Conflicted Industry* (Cambridge University Press 2020).
Emerson, J., *The Purpose of Capital: Elements of Impact, Financial Flows, and Natural Being* (Blended Value Group Press 2018).
Lee, B., and Martin, R. (eds.), *Derivatives and the Wealth of Societies* (The University of Chicago Press 2016).
LiPuma, E., *The Social Life of Financial Derivatives: Markets, Risk, and Time* (Duke University Press 2017).
MacInnes, A., *Sustainability and Capital Markets: Guide for US Companies* (A Brilluminant Publication 2020).
Marx K, *Capital*, vol. 3 (Penguin Classics 1992)
Mazzucato, M., *The Value of Everything: Making & Taking in the Global Economy* (Hachette Book Group 2020).

Patrick, F., and Takeo, K. (eds.), *Ethical Capitalism: Shibusawa and Business Leadership in Global Perspective* (University of Toronto Press 2017).
Pistor, K., *The Code of Capital: How the Law Creates Wealth and Inequality* (Princeton University Press 2019).
Rawls, J, *A Theory of Justice* (Clarendon Press; Oxford University Press 1972).
Rouch, D., *The Social Licence for Financial Markets: Reaching for the End and Why It Counts* (Palgrave Macmillan 2020).
Shiller, R., *Finance and the Good Society* (Princeton University Press 2012).

Articles

Becht, M., Franks, J., Grant, J., and Wagner, H.F., 'Returns to Hedge Fund Activism: An International Study' 30(9) *Review of Financial Studies* (2017) 2933.
Claessens, S., 'Access to Financial Services: A Review of the Issues and Public Policy Objectives' 21(2) *The World Bank Research Observer* (Fall 2006) 207.
Eckert, C., 'Corporate Reputation and Reputation Risk: Definition and Measurement from A (Risk) Management Perspective' 18(2) *Journal of Risk Finance* (2017) 145.
Hart, O., 'Financial Contracting' 39(4) *Journal of Economic Literature* (2001) 1079.
Jinfang, L., and Shusheng, Q., 'Policy Support for Developing Green Economy and Promoting the Construction of Ecological Civilization' 6(5) *Philosophy Study* (2016) 282.
Morris, S., and Shin, H.S., 'Financial Regulation in a System Context' (2) *Brookings Papers on Economic Activity* (2008) 229.
Porter, M.E., and Kramer, M.R., 'Creating Shared Value' 89 *Harvard Business Review* (2011) 62.
Stigler, G., 'The Adoption of the Marginal Utility Theory' 11(4) *Nebraska Journal of Economics and Business* (1972) 188.
Stout, L.A., 'Why the Law Hates Speculators: Regulation and Private Ordering in the Market for OTC Derivatives' 48 *Duke Law Journal* (1999) 701.

Working Papers

Addison, T., Chowdhury, A., and Murshed, M., 'By How Much Does Conflict Reduce Financial Development?', WIDER Discussion Paper No. 2002/48.
Busch, D., and Teubner, A., 'Fit and Proper Assessments Within the Single Supervisory Mechanism', EBI Working Paper Series no. 34 (2019).
Levina, I., 'A Puzzling Rise in Financial Profits and the Role of Capital Gain-Like Revenues', Political Economy Research Institute Working Paper no. 347 (April 2014).

International Organizations Policy Documents and Reports

OECD, 'Responsible Business Conduct For Institutional Investors: Key Considerations for Due Diligence under the OECD Guidelines for Multinational Enterprises' (2017) <https://mneguidelines.oecd.org/RBC-for-Institutional-Investors.pdf> accessed 10th November 2023.
PRI, From Poor Working Conditions to Forced Labour – What's Hidden in Your Portfolio? A Guide for Investor Engagement on Labour Practices in Agricultural Supply Chains (2016). <www.unpri.org/download?ac=1652> accessed 10th November 2023.
World Bank, 'Institutional Structure of Financial Regulation and Supervision: The Basic Issues'. Paper presented by David T Llewellyn at a World Bank Seminar Aligning

Supervisory Structures with Country Needs Washington DC, 6th and 7th June 2006 <http://citeseerx.ist.psu.edu/viewdoc/download?doi=10.1.1.503.2388&rep=rep1&type=pdf> accessed 11th November 2023.

Conference Papers

Carney, M., ‘Breaking the Tragedy of the Horizon: Climate Change and Financial Stability’, Speech given at Lloyd’s of London (29 September 2015).

7 Beyond Traditional Governance Risks and Uncertainties in ESG Derivatives

In the context of globalisation, governance is perceived as a multi-actor process of building, coordinating, and establishing a common understanding in how a particular social group is expected to behave. In that sense, the regulatory space is fragmented. Usually, it includes regulatory agencies, market participants, investors, and consumers, among others. Cooperation involving all stakeholders is meant to ensure the protection of all interests and rights entangled in the regulatory process.

In the context of ESG criteria, financial institutions, intermediaries, and investors become surrogate regulators. They are called to create control and discipline in the process of allocating resources and providing risk-management tools to those that comply with certain standards. The difference with other instances of self-regulation is that the ESG appreciation of risk and uncertainties is more comprehensive and dynamic. Understanding that there is difference between governance as a *risk* and governance as an *uncertainty* requires stakeholders to apprehend new politics of accountability. We are not aiming for an impossible utopian scenario, where all governance drawbacks can be controlled and sanctioned. Instead, the focal point of the assessment of future events regarding governance is in the *distinction* between risk and uncertainty, and how to adopt both elements in structuring ESG derivatives.

We argue that the incorporation of ESG derivatives specifically for the *governance* factor is intricately tied to the ongoing discourse surrounding the correlation between the use of derivatives contracts and firm value. This interconnection is discerned by the extent to which derivatives play a role in mitigating market imperfections, which encompass challenges such as financial distress, funding constraints, and information misalignment. Consequently, derivatives can serve as a tool to strengthen governance within a firm when employed for hedging purposes. ESG derivatives should *not* be employed for speculative purposes – such use would not be conducive to investors' long-term interests. Indeed, in this context, any practices influenced by short-termism would contradict the fundamental aims of ESG goals.

Although the exclusion of speculative purposes in ESG derivatives is at the core of many industry and regulators' discussions, in short-selling (which might involve derivatives), some market actors see an opportunity to accomplish ESG

DOI: 10.4324/9781003365242-7

goals.[1] The notion is that short-selling as a trading strategy could potentially help to redirect capital away from high-emissions companies, while preserving and optimising investment performance.[2] In this way, investors seek to adopt a positive ESG engagement strategy. However – the inherently contradictory characteristics of short-selling impede its widespread acceptance as a robust and sustainability-aligned investment strategy. While regulators acknowledge its merits in terms of information processing within asset markets, the paradox emerges during periods of market turmoil.[3] While deemed beneficial for its role in efficiently incorporating information, short-selling may be prohibited during market distress, as it can amplify market volatility and contribute to destabilising the market overall.[4]

Against this background, this chapter explores the most salient features of the governance factor, from the perspective of risk and uncertainties. We then consider the interaction between financial derivatives and governance, and how it is adopted as a reference point for different sustainable investment strategies. Understanding the relevance of ESG reporting, we explore how some corporates and investors benefit from self-regulatory instruments drafted within capital markets. As the development of governance is closely related to investors' fiduciary duties, the final section considers whether such duties are called to be reconfigured, in line with broader ESG goals.

Introduction

The ESG movement transcends being merely a trend in which investors exert pressure on companies and financial institutions to address ESG risks.[5] Rather, it entails a *paradigm shift* whereby these entities proactively integrate alterations into the very fabric of their economic operations.[6] The movement signifies an acknowledgment of the growing significance of the interests and values of third parties (commonly referred to as stakeholders), in conjunction with safeguarding the interests of shareholders, encapsulated by the concept of shareholder value.[7]

To the extent that ESG criteria are dynamic, a singular definition is insufficient. However, in terms of governance, an initial formulation would include the following aspects:

1 Managed Funds Association, 'The Use of Short Selling to Achieve ESG Goals', 7 June 2022. www.managedfunds.org/industry-research/the-use-of-short-selling-to-achieve-esg-goals/#:~:text=Incorporating%20short%20selling%20as%20part,the%20most%20heavily%20polluting%20companies accessed 24th November 2023.

2 ibid.

3 Archana Jain, Pankaj K. Jain, Thomas H. McInish and Michael McKenzie, 'Worldwide Reach of Short Selling Regulations', *Journal of Financial Economics* 109.1 (2013): 177–197.

4 ibid.

5 Mozaffar Khan, 'Corporate Governance, ESG, and Stock Returns around the World', *Financial Analysts Journal* 75.4 (2019): 103–123.

6 World Economic Forum General Meeting 2019. www.weforum.org/events/annual-meeting-of-the-new-champions-2019/sessions/climate-change-the-next-financial-crisis accessed 11th November 2023.

7 R. Aggarwal, I. Erel, R. Stulz and R. Williamson, 'Differences in Governance Practices between US and Foreign Firms: Measurement, Causes, and Consequences', *Review of Financial Studies* 22.8 (2009): 3131–369.

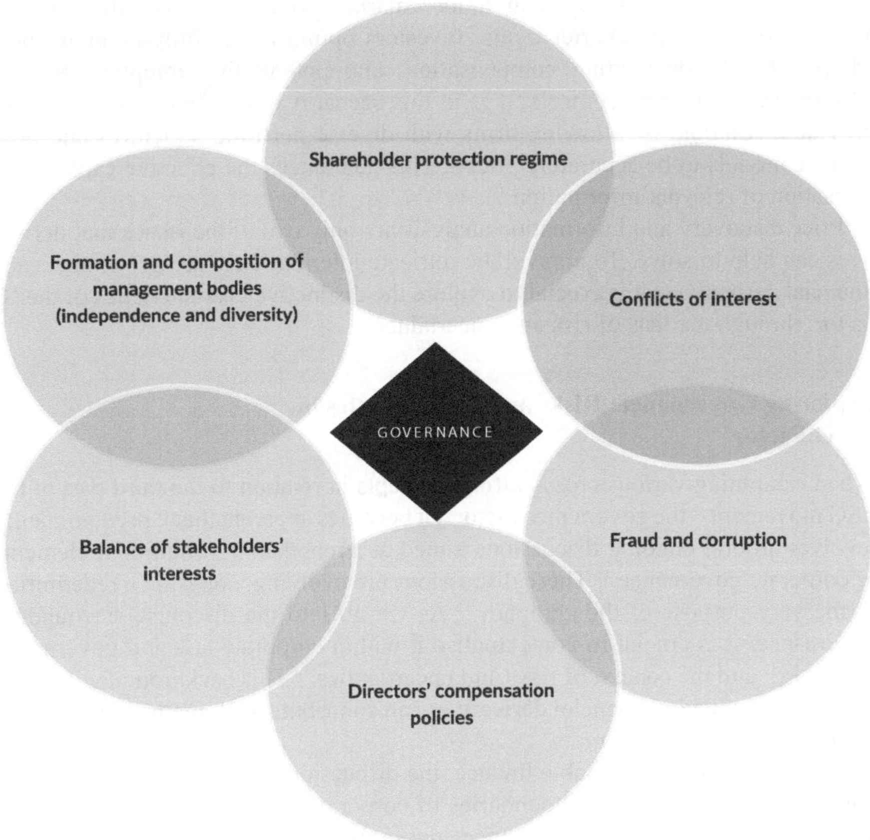

Figure 7.1 Elements of Governance
Source: Author

Corporates aiming to attract investment must establish governance structures perceived as valuable by investors, as poor governance impacts financing success and company performance.[8] The mechanism's effectiveness depends on accurately pricing securities from firms with diverse governance structures. Pricing inaccuracies may arise from limitations in securities-market price discovery, driven by factors like information constraints and the costly price-discovery process. Risk aversion can further contribute to pricing inaccuracies, if investors avoid adjusting portfolios to reflect all available information.[9] Excessive diversification, while

8 Rob Bauer, Jeroen Derwall and Colin Tissen, 'Private Shareholder Engagements on Material ESG Issues', *Financial Analysts Journal* 79.4 (2023): 64–95.
9 David Hirshleifer, 'Investor Psychology and Asset Pricing', *The Journal of Finance* 56.4 (2001): 1533–1597.

advised by portfolio theory, can hinder market price discovery, affecting the accuracy of corporate charter terms. Investors opting not to fully diversify bear additional risk, demanding compensation, and potentially prompting adverse adjustments to internal controls. It is in this scenario where financial derivatives provide a solution, by allowing firms with diverse portfolio structures and governance models to be accurately priced. This guarantees the effective capture and utilisation of relevant information.[10]

Price discovery and information analysis are only two of the issues that derivatives can help to solve. To unravel the intricate interplay between governance and financial derivatives, it is crucial to explore the distinctive characteristics of the 'G factor' through the lens of risk and uncertainty.

Exploring Governance: Risks and Uncertainties in the G Factor

When examining various cross-cutting concepts in relation to the third part of the ESG movement – the governance factor – it becomes apparent that it predominantly revolves around ongoing discussions aimed at strengthening traditional elements of corporate governance.[11] These discussions are evolving alongside a redefinition of the very purpose of the company.[12] As we go into the discourse surrounding governance, it is crucial to contextualise it within corporate law and governance practices,[13] and the context of risks and uncertainties.[14] This background will allow us to understand how financial derivatives can contribute to strengthen governance in line with broad ESG targets.

In the context of sustainable finance, the discussion surrounding the 'G factor' transcends the conventional boundaries of corporate law, going into the intricate dynamics that govern the interconnectedness of all external stakeholders linked to a company's business. This broadened perspective prompts an examination of how a company's internal structure and operations are called upon to play an active role in safeguarding the interests of not only the company and its shareholders, but also the myriad third parties associated with it (i.e., creditors, customers, suppliers, employees, and communities). This shift in focus underscores the expectation that

10 Frank Easterbrook, 'Derivative Securities and Corporate Governance', *The University of Chicago Law Review* 69.3 (2002): 733–747.

11 World Economic Forum, 'Defining the "G" in ESG Governance Factors at the Heart of Sustainable Business', June 2022. https://www3.weforum.org/docs/WEF_Defining_the_G_in_ESG_2022.pdf accessed 21st November 2023.

12 Lynn A. Stout, 'The Problem of Corporate Purpose', *Issues in Governance Studies* 48.1 (2012): 1–14.

13 See Michael C. Jensen and William H. Meckling, 'Theory of the Firm: Managerial Behavior, Agency Costs, and Ownership Structure', *Journal of Financial Economics* 3: 305.

14 Ian Brown, Adam Steen and Julie Foreman, 'Risk Management in Corporate Governance: A Review and Proposal', *Corporate Governance: An International Review* 17 (2009): 546–558.

companies actively contribute to the overarching goals of sustainable finance.[15] In turn, this entails an enhancement of both internal and external controls, to mitigate agency costs and elevate the transparency of financial and nonfinancial information, fostering a corporate environment where sustainability is not merely a buzzword, but a tangible commitment reflected in the company's actions and policies.[16]

Hence, pivotal issues – such as delineating the interests of shareholders, the company itself, and potential conflicts of interest – find a distinctive space in this context. Several of these concepts revolve around fundamental sustainability principles, notably the growing reliance on institutional investors – major stakeholders entering companies as shareholders. These institutional investors play a crucial role in spearheading the reinforcement of environmental and social criteria, thereby contributing to the ongoing redefinition of the governance criterion. However, adopting a 'stakeholderism' approach, in lieu of a shareholder governance model, carries significant drawbacks, imposing substantial costs on shareholders, stakeholders, and society.[17] This shift would amplify the detachment of corporate leaders from shareholders, diminish their accountability, and could adversely impact economic performance.[18]

An enduring question in economic studies is around the impact and significance of corporate social responsibility (CSR) and the emerging ESG trend on decision-making.[19] This inquiry extends to considering how investors engage with companies for funding, as well as the influence exerted by investors within companies, especially in steering impactful changes through active economic management.[20] Some economic studies[21] approach this question by juxtaposing theoretical concepts with empirical evidence, examining specific cases in particular markets. While these studies may not necessarily establish universal rules, they provide valuable insights into how we can effectively leverage the evolving phenomena of CSR, concepts related to corporate governance, and potentially strengthen the governance criterion.

15 See O. Weber, 'Finance and Sustainability', in H. Heinrichs, P. Martens, G. Michelsen and A. Wiek (eds), *Sustainability Science: An Introduction* (Springer, 2015) 119–129.

16 A. J. Hillman and T. Dalziel, 'Boards of Directors and Firm Performance: Integrating Agency and Resource Dependence Perspectives', *Academy of Management Review* 28.3 (2003): 383–396.

17 Hao Liang and Luc Renneboog, 'Corporate Social Responsibility and Sustainable Finance: A Review of the Literature', European Corporate Governance Institute, Working Paper No. 701/2020, September 2020.

18 Lucian Bebchuk and Roberto Tallarita, 'The Illusory Promise of Stakeholder Governance', *Cornell Law Review* 106 (26 February 2020): 91–178, Harvard Law School John M. Olin Center Discussion Paper No. 1052, Harvard Law School Program on Corporate Governance Working Paper 2020-1.

19 Roland Benabou and Jean Tirole, 'Individual and Corporate Social Responsibility', *Economica* 77 (2010): 1–19.

20 Harrison Hong, Jeffrey Kubik and Jose Scheinkman, 'Financial Constraints and Corporate Goodness', NBER Working Paper No. 18476, 2012.

21 See Rui Albuquerque, Yrjo Koskinen and Chendi Zhang, 'Corporate Social Responsibility and Firm Risk: Theory and Empirical Evidence', *Management Science*, 65.10 (2019): 4451–4949.

Certainly, to address the question of balance between shareholder value and stakeholder value, one could use a theoretical perspective, asserting that the traditional economic approach hinges on the concept of value generation.[22] This paradigm, encapsulated by the notion of 'shareholder value', has held sway in corporate law – particularly, though not exclusively, in the American context. The discourse surrounding shareholder value and its assessment has been pivotal in comprehending how it influences corporate practices.[23]

When examining the notion of value for shareholders, a critical consideration arises regarding whether the focus is exclusively on profit generation, or whether other interests of the shareholder should also be factored into the determination of greater value.[24] While the foundational principle often asserts that companies exist to generate profits, reflecting the notion of '*homo economicus*' – an entity driven by profit motives – it is imperative to acknowledge that shareholders are neither uniform in their responses nor their adherence to a single model.[25] We recognise that companies certainly aim to generate profits – and yet, a nuanced understanding emerges as we consider the evolving behaviour and interests of shareholders.

This dynamic has been acknowledged by domestic regulators, exemplified in legislative measures such as the UK Companies Act of 2006.[26] In this regulatory framework, the inclusion of the director's duty to act with due regard for stakeholders' interests signifies a recognition of the evolving landscape in corporate governance. This legal provision underscores the duty for directors to extend their fiduciary responsibilities *beyond* the exclusive pursuit of shareholder wealth. It emphasises a broader responsibility to consider the varied interests of stakeholders in the decision-making process. However, the level of uncertainty regarding the extent of the reconfiguration of directors' duties undermines the purpose of the provision.

Certain questions persist regarding the interplay between the obligation to consider stakeholders' interests, and the overarching requirement that directors promote the success of the company for the benefit of its shareholders. The nuanced challenge arises in situations where these two factors may be in conflict, prompting an exploration into how directors navigate and reconcile divergent interests. In such scenarios, the uncharted territory lies in understanding the practical and legal dimensions of directorial decision-making, especially when the pursuit of broader

22 Adam Edmans, 'The Link Between Job Satisfaction and Firm Value, with Implications for Corporate Social Responsibility', *Academy of Management Perspectives* 26.4 (2012): 1–19.

23 Ing-Haw Cheng, Harrison Hong and Kelly Shue, 'Do Managers Do Good with Other People's Money?', National Bureau of Economic Research, Working Paper 19432, September 2013. www.nber.org/system/files/working_papers/w19432/w19432.pdf accessed 21st November 2023.

24 William Lazonick and Mary O'Sullivan, 'Maximizing Shareholder Value: A New Ideology for Corporate Governance', *Economy and Society* 29.1 (2000): 13–35.

25 Linda Muswaka, 'Shareholder Value versus Stakeholders' Interests – A Critical Analysis of Corporate Governance from a South African Perspective', *Journal of Social Sciences* 43.3 (2015).

26 Section 172 Companies Act 2006.

stakeholder interests may appear at odds with the traditional emphasis of advancing the company's success for the exclusive benefit of its members.[27]

Despite slow regulatory response, litigation has been given form, to the extent of directors' liability regarding ESG factors. In a trend we might expect to continue for some years, there has been an increase in litigation involving boards.[28] Directors are facing legal actions amid allegations of negligence in addressing climate risks that pose a potential threat to the company's future prosperity. In the recent case, *Butler-Sloss v Charity Commission for England and Wales*,[29] the accusations against the Board include the failure to implement an energy transition strategy in alignment with the Paris Agreement, and the failure to progress toward achieving a 45% reduction in group-wide emissions by the end of the decade. These purported shortcomings are asserted to be violations of their duties as outlined in the Companies Act of 2006.

Acknowledging a complex landscape, we start to unravel the multifaceted nature of corporate governance, where profit generation aligns with the interests and preferences of consumers, employees, contractors, and the community, who ultimately constitute the beneficiaries of the company's economic activity.[30] This realisation prompts a more comprehensive approach, considering not only profit, but also the broader spectrum of stakeholders' interests, and the evolving dynamics shaping shareholder behaviour.

The pursuit and safeguarding of consumer interests, integral to the company's mission, are intertwined with the concept of economic efficiency. Economic efficiency transcends the mere pursuit of profits at any cost;[31] it goes beyond a mathematical exercise of projections and task execution, aimed solely at achieving anticipated financial gains.[32] In this context, the profit-generation process should consider not only shareholders' interests, but also those of fellow companies operating in the same sector and, crucially, the interests of consumers.[33] In our view, to clarify this trend would help to complete the concept of materiality, as explored in Chapter 5.

Well-crafted ESG regulations, efficient enforcement mechanisms, and a market commitment to voluntary compliance concur, to promote a desired generalised

27 Andrew Keay, 'Having Regard for Stakeholders in Practising Enlightened Shareholder Value', *Oxford University Commonwealth Law Journal* 19.1 (2019): 118–138.

28 WTW, 'Global Directors', Liability Survey Report 2022/2023, 30 March 2023. www.wtwco.com/en-in/insights/2023/03/directors-and-officers-liability-survey-2023 accessed 22nd November 2023.

29 *Butler-Sloss v Charity Commission for England and Wales* [2022] EWHC 974 (ch.).

30 David G. Yosifon, 'The Consumer Interest in Corporate Law', *UC Davis Law Review* 43 (2009): 253.

31 Richard C. Bishop, 'Economic Efficiency, Sustainability, and Biodiversity', *AMBIO* 22.2–3 (1993): 69.

32 Richard S. Markovits, *Truth or Economics: On the Definition, Prediction, and Relevance of Economic Efficiency* (Yale University Press, 2008) 19.

33 P. V. Balakrishnan, Rajan Nataraajan and Anand Desai, 'Consumer Rationality and Economic Efficiency: Is the Assumed Link Justified?', *Marketing Management Journal* 10 (2000): 1.

compromise towards the integration of ESG factors.[34] However, there remains the challenge that failures may not be promptly addressed or resolved at the required pace. Considering this, the concept of CSR has gained significant traction,[35] representing a self-initiated response within the market to the symptoms of several market imperfections, such as *the agency problem*.[36]

Rooted in corporate law and agency theory, the agency problem posits, among other cases, the inherent conflicts of interest in relationships between shareholders and company directors, and the various ways in which agency problems can manifest.[37] Tasked with managing a company, directors face constant temptations to prioritise their individual interests, potentially at the expense of shareholder interests.

In this context, seeking to solve market functioning problems (e.g., agency issues and information asymmetry), two approaches emerge: (i) state intervention through regulation and supervision; and (ii) initiatives within the corporate sector to develop tools that mitigate negative consequences arising from conflicts of interest.[38] CSR, initially conceived as a set of actions to harness a positive social impact, transcends traditional company interests and mandatory regulatory requirements. It aims to go beyond the baseline obligations imposed to companies by regulators.[39]

The Rise of CSR to Manage Risk in Corporate Behaviour

CSR emerges as a unique tool within the corporate landscape. It encompasses the adoption of self-regulatory instruments, aiming not just at rectifying market failures and elevating overall market participation, but also striving to provide customised solutions tailored to the distinctive characteristics of each company and sector.[40] These tools are intended to furnish resolutions and strategic navigational guidance, when conflicts of interest come to the forefront. We argue that the contextualisation of CSR serves as a vital complement to any comprehensive corporate sustainability strategy. In this regard, it plays a pivotal role in steering the assimilation of ESG financial instruments, thereby strengthening the realisation of specific ESG targets. Central to this paradigm is the pivotal function of *the G factor*, which stands as a cornerstone for reinforcing commitment towards both environmental and social objectives.

34 Michael J. Kelly, 'ESG: The 5th Element of Corporate Risk Assessment', *Michigan State Law Review* 2022 (2022): 811.

35 Hana Hlochova, 'The Origins of CSR in Theory and Practice: Chapter from CSR History in the CEE Region', *International Journal of Business Research and Management (IJBRM)* 84 (2019).

36 Walaa Wahid and El Kelish, 'Corporate Governance Risk and the Agency Problem', *Corporate Governance* 18.2 (2018): 254–269.

37 Clara Xiaoling Chen, Hai Lu and Theodore Sougiannis, 'The Agency Problem, Corporate Governance, and the Asymmetrical Behavior of Selling, General, and Administrative Costs', *Contemporary Accounting Research* 29.1 (Spring/March 2012): 252.

38 ibid.

39 ibid.

40 Nina Cankar, 'Transition Economies and Corporate Governance Codes: Can Self-Regulation of Corporate Governance Really Work?', *Journal of Corporate Law Studies* 5.2 (2005): 285–304.

The core impetus behind the CSR movement is to address what the state, through regulation and supervision, has been unable or unwilling to tackle comprehensively.[41] Whether due to limitations or strategic choices, existing regulatory frameworks are deemed insufficient. Consequently, the corporate sector endeavours to enhance the management of risks stemming from conflicts of interest. The challenge in the market lies in the diverse solutions pursued by different countries. This variability in problem-solving approaches results in the adoption of rules that can be hollow, inefficient, inconsistent, and burdensome in compliance.[42] Excessive costs incurred due to regulatory burdens create reluctance among regulated entities, contributing to the inefficiency of the rules.

Against this rationale, when confronted with inefficient governance structures, regulatory states, territorial challenges, or instances of regulatory capture by specific interest groups, CSR can take an alternative trajectory.[43] In such scenarios, where disagreement arises with the government's approach to a particular issue, businesses may perceive regulatory oversights or inadequacies. In response, the corporate sector leverages CSR initiatives to showcase more efficient and effective alternatives for addressing specific concerns,[44] serving as a demonstration of viable solutions to regulators.

Acknowledging the profound role of CSR in shaping the G factor, within the broader context of ESG considerations, it becomes imperative to recognise that ESG extends beyond a narrow focus on profit generation. Instead, it advocates for the integration of interests beyond the company itself, encompassing the environment, society, market, consumers, and the broader public interest – interests that may or may not align harmoniously. At this critical juncture, our inquiry shifts towards understanding the potential impact of adopting CSR regarding the company's purpose and the diverse nature of such impact.[45] The enduring concept of shareholder value, undergoing continual re-evaluation yet remaining central to a company's activities, assumes a pivotal importance in this discourse.[46]

A prevailing perspective suggests that 'doing well by doing good'[47] can yield positive ESG outcomes, while ensuring continued profitability in the market. Under

41 E. Wymeersch, 'The Enforcement of Corporate Governance Codes', *Journal of Corporate Law Studies* 6.1 (2006): 113–138.

42 Marc Goergen, 'What Do We Know About Different Systems of Corporate Governance?', *Journal of Corporate Law Studies* 7.1 (2007): 1–15.

43 Fang-Mei Tai and Shu-Hao Chuang, 'Corporate Social Responsibility', *iBussiness* 6 (2014): 117–130.

44 Lance Moir, 'What Do We Mean by Corporate Social Responsibility?', *Corporate Governance* 1.2 (2001): 16.

45 Phuong-Anh Nguyen, Ambrus Kecskés and Sattar Mansi, 'Does Corporate Social Responsibility Create Shareholder Value? The Importance of Long-Term Investors', *Journal of Banking & Finance* 112 (2020).

46 Paul Godfrey, Craig Merrill and Jared Hansen, 'The Relationship Between Corporate Social Responsibility and Shareholder Value: An Empirical Test of the Risk Management Hypothesis', *Strategic Management Journal* 30 (2009): 425–445.

47 Gaurav Talan and Gagan Sharma, 'Doing Well by Doing Good: A Systematic Review and Research Agenda for Sustainable Investment', *Sustainability* 11 (2019): 353.

this paradigm, a company has the capacity to expand its market share, strengthen its market position, and simultaneously serve broader societal interests. To ensure that shareholders can preserve sought-after benefits while concurrently fostering a positive impact through their investments in a company, influencing business activities, it is imperative to address the challenge of short-termism.[48] Characterised by a focus on immediate profits without due consideration for medium and long-term consequences, short-termism poses a significant obstacle to the realisation of positive environmental and social impacts.[49] It also undermines the purpose of the governance-related objectives.

Countering short-termism necessitates a shift in perspective, and sometimes a change in corporate governance,[50] urging shareholders and investors to reinvest not only their financial resources but also their commitment to long-term environmental and social projects. The transformational impact of strengthened governance, interlinked with positive environmental and social outcomes for third parties, requires the gift of time. For instance, effective legal philanthropy implies that companies demonstrating a dedicated commitment to specific social issues, especially those closely aligned with their consumers, should possess the capability to effectively measure the resulting changes in behaviour.[51] The increasing availability of such information to consumers not only empowers companies, but also offers them a concrete platform to demonstrate how their business activities prioritise criteria that have transformed into crucial considerations in their consumer relationships – criteria that may not have held the same level of importance before.[52] However, the fruits of this progress can only be realised after a sustained period of consistent corporate action.

Companies adopt varied approaches when addressing CSR and social impact issues. Some leverage CSR to position themselves as sustainable entities, aiming to generate a positive social impact in the market. For others, these efforts are considered worthwhile only if they also present viable business opportunities – a perspective not inherently negative.[53] In the pursuit of effecting change, particularly in rectifying negative impacts, it becomes imperative to align with the genuine interests of the intended audience.[54] If the primary motivation for behavioural

48 Philipp Haessler, 'Strategic Decisions between Short-Term Profit and Sustainability', *Administrative Sciences* 10 (2020): 63.

49 Ivar Kolstad, 'Why Firms Should Not Always Maximize Profits', *Journal Business Ethics* 76 (2007): 137.

50 Robert Anderson, 'The Long and Short of Corporate Governance', *The George Mason Law Review* 23 (2005–2016): 19.

51 Robert Grant, Rodney J. Clarke and Elias Kyriazis, 'Modelling Real-Time Online Information Needs: A New Research Approach for Complex Consumer Behaviour', *Journal of Marketing Management* 29.7–8 (2013): 950–972.

52 ibid.

53 Walentina A. Simkhovich, 'Motives Behind Corporate Social Responsibility Implementation by Belorussian Entrepreneurs', *European Management Studies* 8.2 (28) (2010): 93.

54 Peter Dahlin, Peter Ekman, Jimmie Röndell and Ossi Pesämaa, 'Exploring the Business Logic Behind CSR Certifications', *Journal of Business Research* 112 (2020): 523.

change lies in gaining a competitive advantage, it remains a valid incentive. The overarching objective is to bring about meaningful change, regardless of whether the incentive is singular or primary, if it contributes to the broader goal of creating a positive and sustainable impact.

Conversely, companies that neglect to genuinely prioritise CSR – engaging in superficial philanthropy[55] used solely for public relations, without substantively transforming their business practices – expose themselves to potential adverse consequences. As detailed in Chapter 2, the risk of 'ESG-washing' (encompassing a broader category akin to greenwashing) looms large when corporations fall short of committing to substantial behavioural change. Should these insincere practices come to light within the market, drawing attention from consumers, regulators, and supervisors, they can significantly impede the company's standing and participation in the market.[56] The repercussions of such disingenuous actions have the potential to cast a shadow on their overall reputation, and disrupt their market engagement.

This shift in perspectives has prompted a recent redefinition of a company's purpose,[57] extending beyond profit generation and financial value maximisation. Investors now seek companies that not only deliver financial results, but also contribute to achieving specific social objectives and upholding ethical standards.[58] Recognising this, companies and sectors are establishing self-regulation mechanisms, indicating their willingness to commit to social and ethical responsibility. Ideally, coherence should be sought between the minimum mandates set by state regulators which carry penalties for noncompliance, and mechanisms to reinforce self-regulation within the industry.

The Role of Reporting Nonfinancial Information

Within this framework, ESG emerges as a powerful tool, capable of shedding light on the authentic role a company is meant to fulfil. It operates as an informational resource, allowing us to decipher the behavioural trends of a company, and the preferences of potential investors engaging with it.[59]

55 Jedrzej George Frynas, 'The False Developmental Promise of Corporate Social Responsibility: Evidence from Multinational Oil Companies', *International Affairs* 81.3 (May 2005): 582.

56 Addisu Lashitew, 'Corporate Uptake of the Sustainable Development Goals: Mere Greenwashing or an Advent of Institutional Change?', *Journal of International Business Policy* 4 (2021): 184–200.

57 Hubert Joly, 'Creating a Meaningful Corporate Purpose', *Harvard Business Review*, 28 October 2021. https://hbr.org/2021/10/creating-a-meaningful-corporate-purpose accessed 24th November 2023.

58 Edward Rock, 'For Whom is the Corporation Managed in 2020? The Debate over Corporate Purpose', European Corporate Governance Institute – Law Working Paper No. 515/2020, NYU School of Law, Public Law Research Paper No. 20-16, NYU Law and Economics Research Paper, 1 May 2020.

59 Maria Aluchna, Maria Roszkowska-Menkes and Bogumil Kamiński, 'From Talk to Action: The Effects of the Non-Financial Reporting Directive on ESG Performance', *Meditari Accountancy Research* 31.7 (2023): 1–25.

This dynamic encapsulates two interrelated aspects. On one hand, there is the reporting of nonfinancial data, unveiling the extent of a company's commitment to each ESG criterion. However, the efficacy of this reporting obligation lies not just in compliance, but in how accurately the information reflects the company's actual operations.

On the other hand, ESG also delineates what the regulator deems essential for inclusion, and identifies market preferences among asset and capital owners, and managers who determine where to allocate their resources.[60] These actors gauge their commitment to ESG criteria based on societal and financial priorities,[61] arriving at a consensus on what should take precedence within each criterion. In essence, ESG serves as a dynamic and interconnected compass, guiding both transparency in reporting, and aligning market preferences with the broader goals of sustainability and responsible corporate behaviour.

Along with state regulation of nonfinancial data reporting, certain guiding principles have been embraced to steer the allocation of resources by investors – notably, the 'Principles for Responsible Investment' (PRI),[62] conceived in 2006 as a private sector initiative led by institutional investors, that have evolved into a significant force for responsible investment practices. The PRI were instituted with the explicit goal of injecting transparency and sustainability into the fabric of the capital market.[63] The period from their inception in 2006 to 2019 witnessed a transformative shift, elevating these principles from futuristic aspirations to indispensable benchmarks for any investor navigating the market. Throughout this evolution, more than 2,500 large institutional investors embraced the principles, committing to align their investment strategies increasingly with these foundational guidelines. The engagements they undertake with the companies they finance are intricately governed by these six core principles, solidifying the role of responsible investment as a cornerstone in contemporary financial practices.

Given the ample and comprehensive nature of these principles, each of the signatory investors may interpret and integrate them differently into their internal policies.[64] Such policies, adopted by diverse entities such as asset owners, investment managers, and service providers, reflect a broad spectrum of perspectives. Among asset owners, this encompasses pension funds, sovereign wealth funds, and entities managing sovereign debt portfolios – this range showcases the diverse landscape of responsible investment practices within the PRI framework.[65]

60 Virginia Harper, 'Comply or Explain and the Future of Nonfinancial Reporting', *Lewis & Clark Law Review* 21 (2017): 318.

61 ibid.

62 PRI, 'What are the Principles for Responsible Investment?'. www.unpri.org/about-us/what-are-the-principles-for-responsible-investment accessed 24th November 2023.

63 Jean-Pascal Gond and Valeria Piani, 'Enabling Institutional Investors' Collective Action: The Role of the Principles for Responsible Investment Initiative', *Business & Society* 52.1 (2013): 64–104.

64 A. Andrea Gasperini, 'Principles for Responsible Investment (PRI) and ESG Factors', in W. Leal Filho, A. M. Azul, L. Brandli, P. G. Özuyar and T. Wall (eds), *Climate Action. Encyclopedia of the UN Sustainable Development Goals* (Springer, 2020).

65 PRI, 'What are the Principles for Responsible Investment?' (n 62).

We anticipate that the PRI will steer the embracing of ESG investment strategies, allowing the integration of ESG considerations into investment decisions; as such, we note the importance of fostering transparent disclosure regarding ESG commitments. In this context, we argue that the traditional functions of financial derivatives, such as hedging and risk management, can be expanded to encompass broader areas, including corporate governance. This extension reflects a holistic approach, where financial tools not only mitigate risks, but also contribute to a more comprehensive and responsible corporate and societal landscape.[66]

Financial Derivatives and Governance

As explained in Chapter 4, the foundation of ESG derivatives lies in their purpose to actively contribute to the construction of sustainability-driven investment strategies, addressing market deficiencies in the process. Within this framework, derivatives play a vital role in enhancing risk-management effectiveness. They offer the means to align exposures more closely with both risk tolerance, and the requisites of comprehensive risk-management strategies.[67] Moreover, the derivatives market assumes a critical function in augmenting transparency, by furnishing forward information on underlying commodities, securities, or assets.[68] This transparency is not only instrumental in immediate risk management, but also significantly contributes to the realisation of overarching long-term sustainability objectives – among them the G factor. In essence, ESG derivatives not only serve as risk mitigation tools, but also act as catalysts in fostering a more transparent, responsible, and sustainable investment landscape.[69] Following this rationale, financial institutions and investors could employ ESG derivatives to wield influence over their counterparties, encouraging the adoption of high-quality corporate governance practices. The accessibility and cost-effectiveness of financial derivatives for corporates and investors create a dynamic landscape, in which markets present an extensive array of risk-return combinations. This, in turn, facilitates the seamless construction of tailored transactions to meet specific needs. The impact of this flexibility is particularly pronounced in OTC derivatives markets. Consequently, investors consistently prioritise the maximisation of expected value within each firm.

Moreover, the adoption of well-known derivatives can also enhance investment efficiency.[70] For instance, the effectiveness of commodities futures contracts in

66 Sumit Kumar, 'ESG Derivatives and Factoring Sustainability in Investment Management', *Academy of Marketing Studies Journal* 27.S4 (2023).

67 Karel Lannoo and Apostolos Thomadakis, 'Derivatives in Sustainable Finance', *CEPS-ECMI Study, Centre for European Policy Studies* 8 (2020).

68 ibid.

69 ibid.

70 Chee Kwong Lau, 'How Corporate Derivatives Use Impact Firm Performance?', *Pacific-Basin Finance Journal, Part A* 40 (2016): 109.

serving a robust price-discovery function is widely acknowledged.[71] Individuals with insights into the supply-and-demand dynamics of commodities can leverage this information more swiftly in futures markets, compared to spot markets for the physical commodity. As explained in Chapter 2, this underscores the significance of futures markets as the premier source for gauging asset value, emphasising their pivotal role in the broader financial landscape.

Investors involved in smaller projects can also enjoy the benefits of using derivatives.[72] This type of investor benefits from existing contractual protections, while larger firms with debt investors have more established safeguards. Governance is often seen as a secondary measure for those with residual claims in ongoing organisations. However, if uncertainty can be efficiently managed through derivatives markets, the production structure can be simplified.[73] This simplification facilitates the use of direct contracts – resembling many contemporary joint ventures – rather than relying on any form of overarching 'governance'. In essence, effective management of uncertainty through derivatives offers a pathway to more streamlined and direct contractual arrangements in project investments.

Likewise, those companies that are not publicly listed can benefit from derivatives trading. This falls under the umbrella of 'synthetic entities'[74] – business ventures designed for singular projects that do not conform to conventional governance structures. Here, the concept of 'governance' becomes pertinent primarily in the context of long-term, multiparty ventures. In this scenario, the principles of corporate governance function as guidelines for equity investors, compensating for the company's inability to make pay-out promises, due to inherent uncertainties.[75]

Derivatives play a role in evaluating the effectiveness of current governance systems.[76] By engaging in the trading of futures and options linked to yet-to-be-issued securities, investors can potentially fine-tune the pricing of securities associated with initial public offerings (IPOs).[77] This approach provides companies and investors with valuable insights into which governance mechanisms are particularly valued. Although markets for such purposes have not fully materialised, the conceptualisation and establishment of markets that assess the pricing of various governance terms are plausible endeavours.

71 Kenneth D. Garbade and William L. Silber, 'Price Movements and Price Discovery in Futures and Cash Markets', *The Review of Economics and Statistics* 65.2 (1983): 289–297.

72 René M. Stulz, 'Should We Fear Derivatives?', *The Journal of Economic Perspectives* 18.3 (2004): 175.

73 S. M. R. K. Samarakoon, P. Rudra, Rana P. Pradhan and Premjit Sahoo Maradana, 'What Determines the Success of Equity Derivatives Markets? A Global Perspective', *Borsa Istanbul Review* (2023): 56.

74 See Janet M. Tavakoli, *Credit Derivatives and Synthetic Structures: A Guide to Instruments and Applications* (John Wiley & Sons, 2001).

75 Katharine V. Jackson, 'Towards a Stakeholder-Shareholder Theory of Corporate Governance: A Comparative Analysis', *Hastings Business Law Journal* 7.2 (Summer 2011).

76 Karel Lannoo and Apostolos Thomadakis, 'Derivatives in Sustainable Finance' (n 67).

77 Oghenovo A. Obrimah, 'Innovation Futures, The Nature of Speculation, and Stock Valuations', SSRN, 19 January 2020. https://ssrn.com/abstract=3512441 accessed 17th December 2023.

Consider a scenario where a company contemplating an IPO communicates its intention to the market, allowing for a phase of trading in hypothetical securities.[78] Introducing futures contracts for shares, with and without features such as a staggered board[79] or poison pills,[80] enables entrepreneurs to extract valuable insights into investor preferences. This information equips investors and companies to make informed decisions about selecting governance devices that yield the best price, or to explicitly understand the trade-offs associated with different choices in relation to sustainability targets.[81]

Opting for a governance setup less favoured by investors carries an explicit cost, providing a transparent mechanism for companies. Importantly, if the pricing of a governance structure is accurate, investors are adequately safeguarded, even if the structure falls short of perfection.[82] This approach not only fosters transparency in decision-making, but also ensures a fair and protective environment for investors, enhancing the overall integrity of the financial system.[83] Moreover, it also contributes to align corporate finances with the idea of regenerative economy[84] – a concept that entails the creation of value for all within the financial activities.

Derivatives have the potential to directly impact managerial behaviour, potentially diminishing the significance of formal governance structures.[85] Managers – often risk-averse due to their lack of diversification in both financial and human capital – may select projects with lower variance.[86] This risk aversion contrasts with investors benefiting from broad diversification in financial markets, who therefore tend to prefer projects with the highest expected value, even if they come with higher risk.[87]

78 Merrit Fox, 'Regulating Public Offerings of Truly New Securities: First Principles', *Duke Law Journal* 66 (2016–2017): 673.

79 A staggered board has distinct classes of directors, with only one class open to elections in each term. See Yakov Amihud and Stoyan Stoyanov, 'Do Staggered Boards Harm Shareholders?', *Journal of Financial Economics* 123.2 (2017): 432.

80 A poison pill is a defensive strategy employed by a company to thwart potential hostile or unsolicited takeover attempts. See Aurelio Gurrea-Martínez, 'New Agency Problems, New Legal Rules: Rethinking Takeover Regulation in the US and Europe', Ibero-American Institute for Law and Finance, Working Paper Series No. 3/2016, 30 October 2019, 8.

81 Zhaohui Wu and Mark Pagell, 'Balancing Priorities: Decision-Making in Sustainable Supply Chain Management', *Journal of Operations Management* 29.6 (2011): 580.

82 Margaret M. Blair and Lynn A. Stout, 'A Team Production Theory of Corporate Law', *Virginia Law Review* 28.2 (March 1999): 247.

83 ibid.

84 Sandra Vilardy, 'Conference Launch of 2022 SDGs Index for Latin America and the Caribbean. Centro de los Objetivos de Desarrollo Sostenible para América Latina y el Caribe', Andes University, 27 November 2023.

85 George Allayannis, Ugur Lel and Darius P. Miller, 'The Use of Foreign Currency Derivatives, Corporate Governance, and Firm Value Around the World', *Journal of International Economics* 87.1 (2012): 70.

86 Mukesh Bajaj, Yuk-Shee Chan and Sudipto Dasgupta, 'The Relationship between Ownership, Financing Decisions and Firm Performance: A Signaling Model', *International Economic Review* 39.3 (1998): 723–744.

87 ibid.

In theory, derivatives offer a means for managers to hedge the risks they bear, making them more inclined to consider higher-variance projects with potentially greater returns.[88] However, firms might be cautious about managers hedging too effectively, as it could decouple their individual returns from that of the company. This could reduce their incentive to maximise firm value, particularly if they become risk neutral.[89]

Nevertheless, there is room to design compensation packages that strike an optimal balance between aligning interests and managing risk.[90] While some firms already utilise compensation packages involving derivatives (albeit often self-created),[91] the increasing prevalence of synthetic instruments in the market suggests the potential for more sophisticated approaches. For instance, certain firms might encourage their managers to use derivatives strategically to enhance the payoffs of their positions,[92] creating incentives for taking risks aligned with investor preferences. In the context of ESG targets, these preferences extend beyond purely financial returns, encompassing a comprehensive spectrum of sustainability objectives.

Derivatives offer firms a more cost-effective way to hedge their risks, particularly facilitating managers in addressing their risk aversion. It is worth noting that most derivatives are held by corporations, rather than individual investors.[93] The predominant custom-designed swaps market, constituting a substantial portion of total outstanding derivatives, is accessible primarily to banks, major corporations, and large institutional investors. In this scenario, there used to be questions around the reasons behind corporations and significant investment funds engaging in hedging activities.[94] The Modigliani-Miller theorem[95] has been challenged, as it entailed that investors, being diversified and essentially risk neutral (a condition upheld by the derivatives market), do not derive direct benefits from hedging at the firm level. The prevailing empirical evidence, however, generally aligns with the theory that

88 H. Kent Baker, J. Clay Singleton and E. Theodore Veit, 'Risk Management and Derivatives', in *Survey Research in Corporate Finance: Bridging the Gap between Theory and Practice, Financial Management Association Survey and Synthesis Series* (2010; online edn, Oxford Academic, 1 May 2011).

89 Mitchell A. Petersen and S. Ramu Thiagarajan, 'Risk Measurement and Hedging: With and Without Derivatives', *Financial Management* 29.4 (2000): 5–29.

90 Rangarajan K. Sundaram and David L. Yermack, 'Pay Me Later: Inside Debt and Its Role in Managerial Compensation', *The Journal of Finance* 62.4 (2007): 1557.

91 See Lim & Young Appraisal, 'Derivatives and Shared Based Compensation'. www.limandyoung.com/derivatives-share-based-compensatio accessed 24th November 2023.

92 Jie Chen, Woon Sau Leung, Wei Song and Davide Avino, 'Does CDS Trading Affect Risk-Taking Incentives in Managerial Compensation?', *Journal of Banking & Finance* 151 (2023).

93 ISDA, 'Policy Framework for Safe and Efficient Derivatives Activity in Emerging and Developing Markets', 22 May 2022. www.isda.org/a/YHVgE/Policy-Framework-for-Safe-and-Efficient-Derivatives-Activity-in-Emerging-and-Developing-Markets.pdf accessed 24th November 2023.

94 Kimberly D. Krawiec, 'Derivatives, Corporate Hedging, and Shareholder Wealth: Modigliani-Miller Forty Years Later', *University of Illinois Law Review* (1998): 1039.

95 See Neil Wallace, 'A Modigliani-Miller Theorem for Open-Market Operations', *The American Economic Review* 71.3 (1981): 267–274.

the hedging practices of most firms adhere to a rationale centred on maximising shareholder wealth.[96] In the context of ESG derivatives, such creation of value is expected to be augmented by sustainability factors that complement shareholders' interests.

As may be anticipated, derivatives play a pivotal role in shaping governance, by serving as instruments to either fortify existing structures, or incentivise companies to embrace transparent governance frameworks. The establishment of such structures, in turn, exerts a positive influence on a firm's overall value, and facilitates access to a myriad of investment strategies that now integrate a more expansive spectrum of sustainability objectives. Therefore, the aforementioned uses of derivatives for governance purposes will be engrained into large sustainable investment strategies.

Types of Sustainable Investment Strategies

Following a risk-based approach, it is pivotal to understand how a company delivers value to its clients or investors. This is the key feature for delineating diverse strategies in responsible investment.[97] The identification of risks and uncertainties starts with the screening process, where the initial set of strategies involves identifying companies deemed suitable for investment. Here, the spectrum ranges from a stringent approach – refraining from involvement with sectors carrying an unfavourable reputation due to their adverse environmental or social impact – to accepting certain levels of negative impact regarding environmental and social issues, with the expectation that such remaining effects could be solved within the life of the investment.[98] Therefore, there is a wide range of sustainable investment strategies that reflect diverse levels of commitment to ESG targets. Such strategies could be classified into two categories.[99] The first one considers the strategies adopted for the construction of the ESG portfolio (i.e., screening, integration, and thematic investing). The second category encompasses the techniques used to improve investees' ESG performance, known as active ownership or stewardship (i.e., engagement and proxy voting). In 2020, the prevailing sustainable investment strategy was ESG *integration*, followed by the strategies of *negative screening, corporate engagement, norms-based screening, and sustainability-themed investment*.[100]

96 Daniel J. H. Greenwood, 'Fictional Shareholders: For Whom Are Corporate Managers Trustees, Revisited', *Southern California Law Review* 69 (1996): 1021, 1074.

97 See Mirjam Staub-Bisang, *Sustainable Investing for Institutional Investors: Risks, Regulations and Strategies* (John Wiley & Sons, 2012).

98 Mauro Sciarelli, Silvia Cosimato, Giovanni Landi and Francesca Landolo, 'Socially Responsible Investment Strategies for the Transition Towards Sustainable Development: The Importance of Integrating and Communicating ESG', *The TQM Journal* 33.7 (2021): 39.

99 UNPRI, 'Screening'. www.unpri.org/download?ac=10608#:~:text=These%20criteria%20might%20be%20based,lowest%20emitters%20(positive%20screening) accessed 25th November 2023.

100 GSI Alliance, '2020 Global Sustainable Investment Review', 2020. www.gsi-alliance.org/wp-content/uploads/2021/08/GSIR-20201.pdf accessed 25th November 2023.

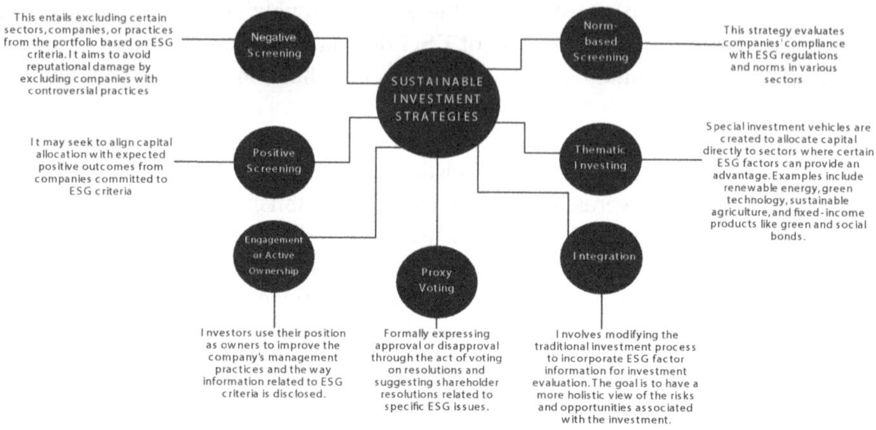

Figure 7.2 Sustainable Investment Strategies

Source: Author

Strategies for the Construction of ESG Portfolio

We will explore each strategy in turn, leaving integration for last. In the **negative screening** strategy, certain actors, companies, or practices are excluded from the investment portfolio, based on the information available regarding the adherence of the company to ESG criteria.[101] The overarching objective is to circumvent reputational harm, ensuring that financiers or investors remain untethered to actions that generate adverse effects on ESG issues. This strategic approach aims to uphold a commitment to responsible investment practices, and mitigate potential risks associated with reputational damage.

Conversely, in situations where outright dismissal of investment in a particular sector, company, or practice is not feasible, a more nuanced approach comes into play. In this **corporate agreement** scenario, the objective is to progressively align capital allocation with the positive outcomes generated by specific companies.[102] Here, the investor might be directly associated with an activity, sector, or company that currently yields negative impact without immediate objection. However, simultaneously, investors actively contribute to facilitate the gradual transformation of the company's operational practices. This involvement requires heightened investor engagement, where a deep understanding of the ESG risks and uncertainties

101 Magnus Jansson and Anders Biel, 'Motives to Engage in Sustainable Investment: A Comparison Between Institutional and Private Investors', *Sustainable Development* 19.2 (March–April 2011): 138.

102 Ming-Lang Tseng, Phan Anh Tan, Shiou-Yun Jeng, Chun-Wei Remen Lin, Yeneneh Tamirat Negash and Susilo Nur Aji Cokro Darsono, 'Sustainable Investment: Interrelated Among Corporate Governance, Economic Performance and Market Risks Using Investor Preference Approach', *Sustainability* 11.7 (2019): 2108.

inherent in each investee company serves as a guide.[103] Through this informed approach, the investor becomes a catalyst for incremental behavioural changes within the company, steering it towards a trajectory of positive impact over time.[104]

Investors might find it simpler to sidestep excessive value judgments, by grounding their financing decisions in something objective – measuring the degree of compliance a company or sector has with regulations pertaining to ESG.[105] However, we may question whether this **norm-based screening** constitutes a comprehensive investment strategy. The crux of the matter lies in the fact that not all countries adhere to identical standards for ESG protection. Comparing the behaviours of a company in one country with another becomes intricate, due to variations in regulatory frameworks. The absence of comparable benchmarks makes it challenging to gauge the extent of compliance between the two, rendering the norm-based screening less straightforward as a comprehensive metric.

Some investors embrace the **thematic-investing approach**, often facilitated using special purpose vehicles (SPVs) within the financial system.[106] These specialised investment entities are purposefully established to channel capital into specific sectors. The strategy aims at directing funds toward projects explicitly designed to generate a positive impact in alignment with certain criteria.[107] This entails investments in areas such as renewable energies, green initiatives, and sustainable agriculture. It signifies a commitment either to a transitional phase or the direct financing of projects, activities, or companies exclusively geared towards generating a positive impact. While this approach represents an ideal scenario, it is worth noting that not all sectors have reached this advanced stage, and the investment process targeting such activities remains specific and nuanced.[108]

Finally, **integration** involves adhering to traditional forms of investment decision-making in accordance with market standards.[109] However, in addition to traditional financial information, this approach includes the requisition of reporting, analysis, and other information pertaining to ESG criteria.[110] Acknowledging the

103 Nick Robins, 'The Emergence of Sustainable Investing', in *Sustainable Investing* (Routledge, 2012) 4.

104 ibid.

105 Felipe Arias Cunha, Fogliano de Souza, Erick Meira and Renato J. Orsato, 'Sustainable Finance and Investment: Review and Research Agenda', *Business Strategy and the Environment* 30.8 (2021): 3821.

106 Kara Nel, Nadia Mans-Kemp and Pierre D. Erasmus, 'Sustainable Thematic Investing: Identifying Opportunities Based on an Analysis of Stewardship Reports', *Sustainability* 15.10 (2023): 8411.

107 ibid.

108 Koye Somefun, Romain Perchet, Chenyang Yin and Raul Leote de Carvalho, 'Allocating to Thematic Investments', *Financial Analysts Journal* 79.1 (2023): 18–36.

109 Emiel Van Duuren, Auke Plantinga and Bert Scholtens, 'ESG Integration and the Investment Management Process: Fundamental Investing Reinvented', *Journal of Business Ethics* 138 (2016): 527.

110 Nicola Raimo, Alessandra Caragnano, Marianna Zito, Filippo Vitolla and Massimo Mariani, 'Extending the Benefits of ESG Disclosure: The Effect on the Cost of Debt Financing', *Corporate Social Responsibility and Environmental Management* 28.4 (2021): 1412.

equal importance of nonfinancial information in the decision-making process – alongside growth projections, profits, and other financial factors – the integration strategy underscores the significance of ESG considerations in shaping comprehensive investment decisions.[111]

Investors rely on pertinent information provided by the company in anticipation of their investment. However, they undertake a meticulous research phase to authenticate the veracity of the reported information.[112] This investigative process is pivotal, forming the foundation for constructing the portfolio and ensuring a nuanced understanding of how to prudently manage associated risks. It is imperative to acknowledge that, despite the initial commitment, there exists the possibility of nonfulfilment, introducing scenarios where investors' interests could potentially be adversely impacted. This underscores the necessity for ongoing diligence and risk management throughout the investment lifecycle.

According to the Global Sustainable Investment Review of 2018, screening used to be the most common strategy. As of 2018, negative screening accounted for assets under management totalling USD 19.8 trillion globally. Positive screening was applied to assets amounting to USD 1.8 trillion, while norms-based screening covered assets totalling USD 4.7 trillion.[113] However, between 2016–2020 there were considerable changes towards the adoption of integration and corporate engagement. The Global Sustainable Investment Review of 2020 (the latest available review at the time of writing) highlighted that sustainability-themed investing, ESG integration, and engagement had consistently seen growth. However, norms-based screening, positive screening, and negative screening have followed a more variable trajectory since 2016.[114]

Strategies for Improving Investees' ESG Performance

Engagement is another investment strategy that goes beyond mere reliance on regulatory compliance, granting investors the opportunity to engage directly with the company's management from the outset of the investment.[115] This direct engagement or active ownership empowers the investor to influence decisions and catalyse changes in how the business operates. In essence, the investor assumes the role of a guarantor, signifying that certain transformative changes within the company

111 ibid.

112 Li Yiwei, Mengfeng Gong, Xiu-Ye Zhang and Lenny Koh, 'The Impact of Environmental, Social, and Governance Disclosure on Firm Value: The Role of CEO Power', *The British Accounting Review* 50.1 (2018): 66.

113 GSI Alliance, '2018 Global Sustainable Investment Review', 2018. www.gsi-alliance.org/wp-content/uploads/2019/03/GSIR_Review2018.3.28.pdf accessed 25th November 2023.

114 GSI Alliance, 2020 Global Sustainable Investment Review (n 100) 11.

115 Elroy Dimson, Oğuzhan Karakaş and Xi Li, 'Active Ownership', *The Review of Financial Studies* 28.12 (2015): 3229.

would not be achievable without their active involvement.[116] The engagement strategy is one of the most common forms of investors' influence over the company's business. Indeed, as we explained in Chapter 3, the UK Stewardship Code considers it the most effective way for asset managers and asset owners to engage with investee companies.

The transition in institutional investor practices towards more 'active' forms of ownership signifies that institutional investors recognise that their fiduciary duty to clients and beneficiaries entails deliberate consideration, monitoring, and intervention, concerning ESG factors impacting investee companies.[117] Within this rationale, the PRI identifies three dynamics featuring corporate engagement: communicative, learning, and political.[118] We argue that the use of ESG-aligned financial products, particularly ESG derivatives, could be a manifestation of the political dynamics, as this enables the development of internal and external relationships for companies and investors to help advance the ESG agenda.

In this context, product creation (in the sense coined by George Serafeim)[119] entails investment instruments to intentionally allocate capital and influence investees with measurable financial and environmental, social – and, we would add, governance – outcomes. While Serafeim excludes governance, deeming it a process rather than an outcome,[120] we argue that governance *must* yield identifiable results throughout its transformative journey. Consequently, the challenge in designing a financial product aligned with the governance factor lies in determining how to adopt KPIs that facilitate the measurement of progress and periodic outcomes related to governance issues.

Despite the divergence in the treatment of governance results, we draw upon the essential features that ESG investment products should embody. As articulated by Serafeim,[121] these features include expressing intentionality, incorporating mechanisms to ensure accurate measurability, and adhering to the well-established principles of materiality and additionality. These attributes collectively contribute to enhancing the overall significance and effectiveness of ESG investment products. Consequently, they underscore the substantial impact expected from the political dynamics of corporate engagement. Engaging with companies not only helps foster relationships with investors, particularly long-term investors,[122] but also plays a pivotal role in achieving ESG targets. As part of an engagement strategy, the

116 Terry McNulty and Donald Nordberg, 'Ownership, Activism, and Engagement: Institutional Investors as Active Owners', *Corporate Governance: An International Review* 24.3 (2016): 348.

117 UNPRI, 'How ESG Engagement Creates Value for Investors and Companies', 2018. www.unpri.org/download?ac=4637 accessed 25th November 2023.

118 ibid.

119 George Serafeim, 'ESG: From Process to Product', Harvard Business School, Working Paper 23-069, 13 May 2023.

120 ibid.

121 ibid.

122 UNPRI, 'How ESG Engagement Creates Value for Investors and Companies' (n 117).

growing adoption of ESG-aligned financial transactions strengthens the foundation of trust, encouraging a trajectory toward the realisation of long-term ESG objectives.

The complex issue of active ownership is closely tied to the question of the proxy voting strategy. This entails navigating a landscape where a significant part of the market relies on trust in advisory and representation firms, known as *proxy advisory firms*. Catering to institutional investors, these entities specialise in research services, data collection, and recommendations related to representation proposals and governance bodies overseeing shareholder voting at corporate meetings. Essentially, they act as strategists for votes cast at general shareholders' meetings, on behalf of a group of enlisted shareholders.

Considering the type of ESG information analysed and managed by proxy advisory firms, it seems reasonable to argue in favour of consistent regulation of their activity – aiming to achieve a coherent oversight that has so far escaped the grasp of the SEC, in their most recently amended 2022 rules.[123] Proxy advisory firms have the potential to evolve into new market participants, directly influencing how shareholders and investors wield their voting rights concerning a company's commitment to ESG issues. Surely the minimum expectation would be the capacity to demand their genuine commitment, eventually enforced through regulation? The SEC developed rules and guidance regulating the provision of proxy voting services by such firms in 2020,[124] marking the most significant steps the Commission had taken to date in this area. The prevailing view was that the 2020 rule amendments made meaningful improvements to the proxy voting process, promoting accountability, and enhancing transparency regarding the advice of proxy advisory firms – however, these rules were never put into effect. In 2022, a new set of amendments was adopted;[125] the new rules were far from clear, and expert commentators agree that this latest version does not address the core issues debated in 2020.[126]

Beyond the US, the regulatory landscape for proxy voting firms is not markedly better.[127] Notably, the concept of voting as a fiduciary duty, well established in the US, only gained traction in the UK in the early 2000s, and is still absent in several international jurisdictions.[128] This deficiency in the proxy voting system

123 SEC, 'Proxy Voting Advice, Final Rule', 17 CFR Parts 240 and 276. www.sec.gov/files/rules/final/2022/34-95266.pdf accessed 7th December 2023.

124 See Exemptions from the Proxy Rules for Proxy Voting Advice, 85 Fed. Reg. 55,082 ('2020 Rule Amendments'), 3 September 2020.

125 SEC, 'Proxy Voting Advice, Final Rule' (n 123).

126 David A. Katz, Laura A. McIntosh and Lipton Wachtell, 'Regulatory Instability for Proxy Advisory Firms', Harvard Law School Forum on Corporate Governance, 29 July 2022. https://corpgov.law.harvard.edu/2022/07/29/regulatory-instability-for-proxy-advisory-firms/ accessed 25th November 2023.

127 Chris Mallin, 'Institutional Investors and Voting Practices: An International Comparison', *Corporate Governance* 9.2 (April 2001): 120.

128 ibid.

is exacerbated by outdated voting methods and a lack of transparency. Substantial reforms are imperative to ensure that proxy voting systems evolve into effective, efficient, and transparent mechanisms capable of enhancing corporate governance.[129]

Along with the uncertainty surrounding proxy voting regulation, there are also increasing queries around its real impact regarding ESG commitments. Proxy voting firms adopt guidelines that occasionally include sustainability provisions.[130] However, their implementation is considerably elastic and inconsistent. Proxy voting agents are tasked with adhering to these guidelines, yet some authors[131] have shown that instances of noncompliance are often rationalised by citing the vagueness of the guidelines, the opacity of existing proxy voting practices, and the divergence between portfolio managers' priorities and their clients' declared sustainability commitments.[132] Additionally, proxy voting agents may base their decisions on their perception of what best serves the interests of their clients.[133] Given the unresolved challenges in proxy voting, relying on this strategy may not be advisable for addressing the pressing needs related to ESG goals.

Finally, the most potent and resilient recourse available to investors in the context of investment strategies is the ability to undergo the process of divestment.[134] This is, in McKibben's terms,[135] a mainstay of transnational activism that surges in response to regulatory capture. In a moment where the market is collectively pivoting towards embracing ESG standards, investors find it imperative to disengage, withdrawing not only support from a specific company, but financial backing from a particular sector. While instances of such decisions have been observed with certain companies, it is crucial to note that very few possess the capacity to entirely sever ties with clients. This underscores the profound and impactful consequences of divestment processes, in signalling a commitment to aligning investments with evolving sustainable standards. Some empirical studies already evidence[136] that divestment serves not only as an ethical investment approach, but

129 ibid.

130 See ISS, 'Voting Policies', 2023. www.issgovernance.com/policy-gateway/voting-policies/ accessed 25th November 2023.

131 Julie Bernard, Olivier Boiral, Laurence Guillaumie and Marie-Christine Brotherton, 'Does Proxy Voting Really Promote Corporate Sustainability?', *Corporate Governance* 31 (2022): 445.

132 ibid.

133 Randall S. Thomas and Patrick C. Tricker, 'Shareholder Voting in Proxy Contests for Corporate Control, Uncontested Director Elections and Management Proposals: A Review of the Empirical Literature', *Oklahoma Law Review* 70 (2017): 9.

134 S. Pye and B. Gordon, 'Sustainable Investment Withdrawals', *Journal of Portfolio Management* 26.4 (Summer 2000): 77.

135 Gay W. Seidman, 'Divestment Dynamics: Mobilizing, Shaming, and Changing the Rules', *Social Research* 82.4 (2015): 1015.

136 Chelsie Hunt and Olaf Weber, 'Fossil Fuel Divestment Strategies: Financial and Carbon-Related Consequences', *Organization & Environment* 32.1 (2019): 41.

also as a strategy capable of mitigating financial risks[137] associated with climate change. Simultaneously, it offers the opportunity to reduce the carbon exposure of investment portfolios.

Despite the benefits tied to divestment, there are also shortcomings that reflect the level of risk and uncertainty entailed in this strategy. Recent studies in the fossil fuels sector reveal that the capacity of institutional investors to employ divestment as a strategy for shielding their holdings from GHG exposure is limited, and they face substantial financial risks associated with a low-carbon future across various sectors of the economy, extending beyond oil, gas, and coal producers.[138] Moreover, divesting from oil and gas producers to channel funds into renewable energy necessitates critical alterations to institutional investment policies and expectations. These limitations underscore the challenges associated with viewing divestment as a standalone approach for promoting corporate behavioural change.

Acknowledging the benefits and shortcoming of sustainable investment strategies leads us to consider the importance of the emerging developments aiming to strengthen both investment methodologies, and the overarching principle of responsible investment as a tool for improving corporate governance. The introduction of ESG reporting obligations, although controversial and in evolution, should be considered as a necessary tool for accessing and analysing material ESG data. Such data is central to further developing ESG-aligned financial products that are designed to deliver sustainable finance outcomes (e.g., valorisation of natural resources).[139]

The Importance of ESG Data for Decision-making

Navigating the complexities of ESG reporting poses a formidable challenge, primarily due to the inherent intricacies of the standardisation process. The attempt to apply a one-size-fits-all criterion across diverse sectors within the real economy proves unfeasible and overly ambitious. The key challenge lies in the daunting task of comparing the varied information disseminated by market players using distinct reporting standards. This diversity in standards not only complicates matters, but also subjects investors to excessive scrutiny. Faced with a plethora of seemingly accurate information, investors encounter the challenge of discerning differences among market players, making it difficult to arrive at well-informed investment decisions.

137 Jeff Rubin, 'The Case for Divesting from Fossil Fuels in Canada', (CIGI Papers No. 112). CIGI. 42, 2016.

138 Justin Ritchie and Hadi Dowlatabadi, 'Divest from the Carbon Bubble? Reviewing the Implications and Limitations of Fossil Fuel Divestment for Institutional Investors', *Review of Economics & Finance* 5.2 (2015): 61.

139 Sandra Vilardy, 'Conference Launch of 2022 SDGs Index' (n 84).

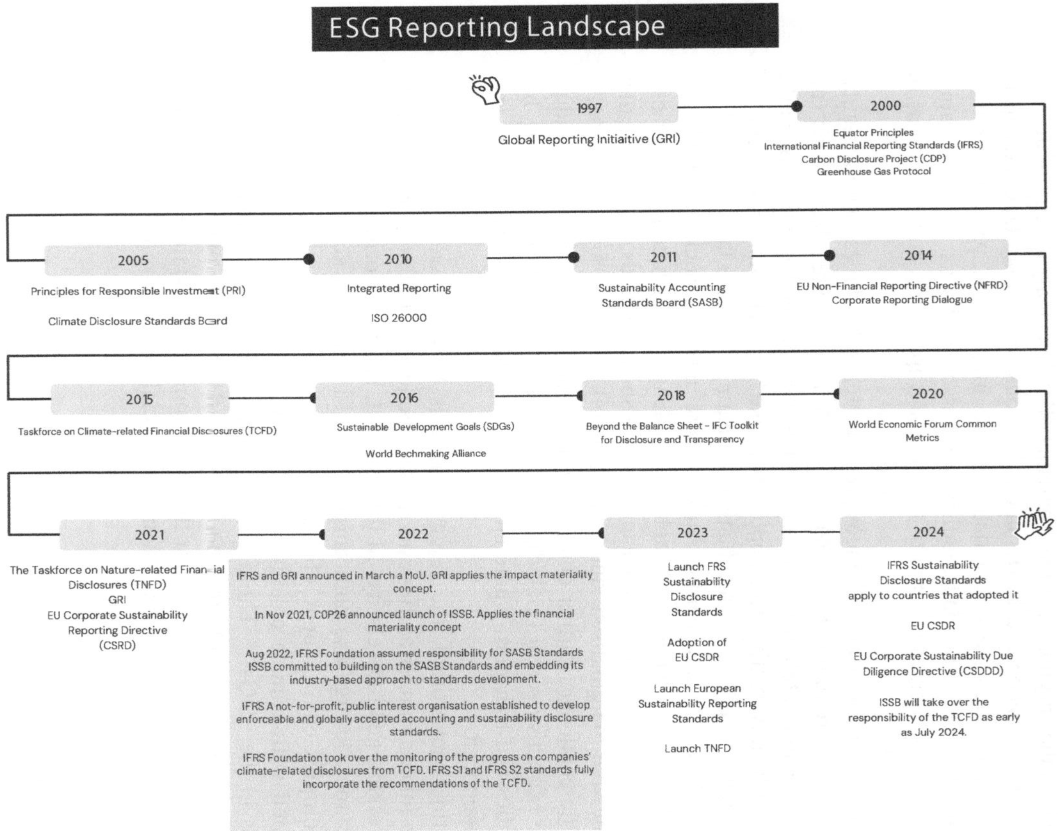

Figure 7.3 ESG Reporting Landscape

Source: Author, based on the diagram of the IFC, 2023.[140]

140 IFC, 'Understanding the Global Reporting Frameworks', 2023. www.ifcbeyondthebalancesheet.org/understanding-global-reporting-frameworks accessed 25th November 2023.

The current ESG reporting landscape is characterised by a multitude of regulatory instruments, intended to address the complexities of ESG factors. However, the diversity in these regulations poses a risk of undermining their intended purpose. Recognising this challenge involves considering factors such as company size, economic activity, geographical location, data availability, and conflicting standards. Imposing identical standards on large corporations and SMEs may be unrealistic, given the varying resources for data collection, analysis, corporate governance, and risk management. SMEs and micro-businesses may lack the capacity for dedicated teams to prepare meticulous ESG information, presenting a dual challenge: understanding ESG data requisites and associated risks, and formulating effective reporting strategies tailored to the diverse capabilities and limitations of different businesses.

Additionally, geographical challenges are heightened by the escalating regulatory complexities surrounding ESG issues.[141] While increased regulation adds valuable information as a reference point, a persistent lack of standardisation prevails, even in ostensibly universally agreed upon areas like human rights. This absence of uniformity extends to protective mechanisms, creating a diverse landscape in how companies are linked to safeguarding stakeholders' interests, such as compliance with human rights laws. These geographical challenges contribute to market discrepancies, as larger entities find it easier to adopt such standards, leaving smaller markets somewhat marginalised, due to their inability to meet similar criteria.[142] Sector-specific challenges further compound the issue, not only in certain industries like the extractive sector (including mining, oil, and energy production), but also in logistics and transport, where environmental and social concerns are particularly pronounced.

Against this background, the central query is how can we truly measure impact? The inherent uncertainties and risks embedded in ESG reporting underscore the pressing need for clarity. In this context, setting priorities emerges as a paramount tool, to organise both corporate and investment actions within an otherwise complex environment. However, transcending the immediate urgencies associated with climate change, the benchmark for assessing progress or setbacks lies in the SDGs.[143] These goals provide a continuous framework for evaluation and adaptation, offering the necessary flexibility to maintain compliance, and allowing additional time for the development of sustainable solutions. Encompassing 17 SDGs, spanning economic, social, and environmental targets,

141 Rumi Mahmood, 'How Do Different Regions Score on ESG Attributes?', ESG Clarity, 30 October 2020. https://esgclarity.com/how-do-different-regions-score-on-esg-attributes/ accessed 25th November 2023.

142 About the disparities of information in Latin America and the Caribbean: see CODS, 'Índice ODS 2022 para América Latina y el Caribe. Centro de los Objetivos de Desarrollo Sostenible para América Latina y el Caribe', 2023. https://cods.uniandes.edu.co/wp-content/uploads/2023/11/Indice-ODS-2022-para-America-Latina-y-el-Caribe-3.pdf accessed 27th November 2023.

143 UN, 'The Sustainable Development Goals Report 2023', 10 July 2023. https://unstats.un.org/sdgs/report/2023/ accessed 27th November 2023.

the framework aspires not only to control existing negative impacts but, more significantly, to prevent the emergence of new sources that could jeopardise the facets encapsulated within the SDGs.

The main argument in this context is that the financial system – especially the capital mobilisation sector – plays a crucial role in addressing challenges related to the SDGs. The focus shifts to investment managers who, beyond adhering to conventional risk profiles, are tasked with aligning their efforts with the SDGs.[144] This involves influencing the governance of investee companies. Investors aim to critically assess company initiatives and quantify their level of compliance with the SDGs. This has led to the introduction and discourse around KPIs as specific metrics within the industry and financial contracts, illustrating counterparties' commitment to one or more SDGs.

In the intricate exploration of SDGs, various tools play a crucial role in understanding their implementation across diverse markets. The commitment fostered through enhanced corporate governance aims at serving environmental and social objectives. Measurements such as governance and integration are anticipated to align with the goal of elevating the roles of investors, asset managers, and asset owners, to effectively contribute to achieving the SDGs.[145]

In this context, the Global Reporting Initiative (GRI) plays a pivotal role.[146] This instrument's scope extends beyond mere corporate information reporting, related to environmental and social issues. It encompasses the utilisation of performance indicators as a mechanism for companies, not only to present information, but also to facilitate an evaluation of their progress over time. This approach transcends a mere checklist,[147] delving into a deeper verification of whether companies are genuinely committed to instigating changes and adjustments in response to ESG risks.

Initially perceived as a tool for companies to be answerable to civil society, the GRI underwent a perceptible evolution.[148] With a reduction in civil society's participation, and a notable surge in institutional involvement, the dynamics guiding the formulation of reporting guidelines underwent a transformative shift: transitioning gradually from an accentuation on accountability, to a stance that was more accommodating and favourable toward companies.

144 PRI, 'Investment Mandates: Embedding ESG Factors, Improving Sustainability Outcomes', 14 October 2021. www.unpri.org/mandate-requirements-and-rfps/embedding-esg-factors-in-investment-mandates/8563.article accessed 27th November 2023.

145 UNEPFI, 'The Net-Zero Asset Owner Alliance Releases a Foundational Paper for Asset Owner Expectations of Asset Managers' Climate Engagement', 16 November 2023. www.unepfi.org/industries/the-net-zero-asset-owner-alliance-releases-a-foundational-paper-for-asset-owner-expectations-of-asset-managers-climate-engagement/ accessed 25th November 2023.

146 John Dumay, James Guthrie and Federica Farneti, 'GRI Sustainability Reporting Guidelines for Public and Third Sector Organizations', *Public Management Review* 12.4 (2010): 531–548.

147 ibid.

148 Denise English and Diane K. Schooley, 'The Evolution of Sustainability Reporting', *The CPA Journal* 84.3 (March 2014): 26.

Notwithstanding any critiques that may emerge from this evolutionary process,[149] the GRI retains its status as the most widely acknowledged reference framework. While extensively employed in the market, its ubiquity does not necessarily imply that it is the most exhaustive or efficient across all dimensions.[150] Recent market analyses (particularly focusing on companies listed on the S&P 500 in the US market) reveal that the GRI is just one among several guides consulted to determine the additional information that necessitates disclosure. Companies frequently integrate the GRI with other reporting guides,[151] highlighting that it is only one avenue, and not necessarily the most comprehensive, for conveying information to the market regarding their engagements with ESG issues.

Along with the GRI, capital markets participants have further guidelines issued by the International Organization of Securities Commissions (IOSCO).[152] Responding to criticisms, IOSCO established a starting point by considering anything within the ESG factors as constituting sustainability. Their adopted definition encapsulates the idea that ESG factors encompass considerations that can impact a company's ability to execute its business strategy, foster growth, create value, and enhance relationships with investors.

Embedded within this initiative are significant objectives aligned with compliance levels necessary for capital access, the measurement and sustenance of profitability and growth, profitability and investment considerations, company growth, regulatory compliance, risk management, reputation, or, more precisely, reputational, and corporate brand risk, information flow, and the enhancement of relationships with investors.[153] Consequently, a broad concept emerges, positing that a commitment to ESG factors not only generates value for businesses, but is integral to the broader notion of business value. We consider that the IOSCO approach contributes to set how capital markets instruments should be considered, in the design of corporate sustainability strategies. This initiative requires companies to integrate the well-being of various stakeholder groups into their operations, emphasising innovation, compatibility, and corporate reputation.[154] It aligns with guidance from stock exchanges, focusing on material aspects for investors and value creation for the company and stakeholders.

149 José M. Moneva, Pablo Archel and Carmen Correa, 'GRI and the Camouflaging of Corporate Unsustainability', *Accounting Forum* 30.2 (2006): 123.

150 Markc Mcelroy, 'Is It Possible That GRI Has Never Really Been About Sustainability Reporting at All?', Sustainable Brands, 2017. https://sustainablebrands.com/read/new-metrics/is-it-possible-that-gri-has-never-really-been-about-sustainability-reporting-at-all accessed 25th November 2023.

151 Oliver Boiral, 'Sustainability Reports as Simulacra? A Counter-Account of A and A+ GRI Reports', *Accounting, Auditing & Accountability Journal* 26.7 (2013): 1038.

152 IOSCO, 'Recommendations on Sustainability-Related Practices, Policies, Procedures and Disclosure in Asset Management', Final Report, November 2021. www.iosco.org/library/pubdocs/pdf/IOSCOPD688.pdf accessed 27th November 2023.

153 ibid.

154 ibid.

Key players in ESG derivatives markets, *exchanges* are part of another notable sustainability initiative led by sustainable stock exchanges.[155] Originating from a guide on ESG reporting criteria, this initiative involves global stock exchanges to recognise their role beyond trading facilitation. Collaborating with organisations like the UN Global Compact and UNPFI, the initiative offers practical insights aligned with the operational realities of stock exchanges. Strengthened by alignment with the World Federation of Exchanges,[156] the initiative highlights the growing importance of ESG factors in both company operations and investment decision-making. This reflects a significant catalyst in the broader framework of corporate sectors, CSR, and responsible investment.

In this context, there is the emergence of socially responsible investing (SRI) as the counterpart to the discourse, the inverse of the coin of CSR. Here, companies and investors engage in a reciprocal commitment to social impact. Unlike traditional investment models, SRI aims to influence corporate behaviour, emphasising investors' role in generating positive effects beyond mere profitability. The distinguishing feature lies in considerations beyond financial gains, incorporating moral foundations that vary, based on the specific market segment in focus. This aligns with the broader theme of investors driving positive change in corporate behaviour.

In the interaction of CSR, SRI, and ESG reporting, regulatory and self-regulatory mechanisms play a dual role. They not only facilitate the measurement process, but also influence the impact of these measurements. This transformative shift broadens the adoption of ESG standards, involving all market participants. A notable trend is the reconfiguration of fiduciary duties to encompass environmental and social interests, reflecting the evolving intersection and potential conflicts between shareholder interests, company goals, and broader societal concerns in the current ESG landscape.

Reconfiguration of Fiduciary Duties?

The examination of fiduciary duties within the ESG framework challenges the traditional notion that environmental and social interests are inherently at odds with the stringent responsibilities of directors and boards.[157] Two prevailing perceptions must be transcended: the idea that fiduciary duties hinder asset managers from considering these factors in decision-making, and the belief that the entire investment portfolio remains unaffected when pursuing a sustainable strategy.[158] Advocates for a paradigm shift recognise the flaws in these perceptions and call for a directional change in approach.

155 See Sustainable Stock Exchanges Initiative. https://sseinitiative.org accessed 27th November 2023.

156 WFE, 'WFE Sustainability Principles', 4 October 2018. www.world-exchanges.org/our-work/articles/wfe-sustainability-principles accessed 27th November 2023.

157 William Martin, 'Socially Responsible Investing: Is Your Fiduciary Duty at Risk?', *Journal of Business Ethics* 90 (2009): 549–560.

158 William Sanders, 'Resolving the Conflict between Fiduciary Duties and Socially Responsible Investing', *Pace Law Review* 35 (2014–2015): 535.

There is the need to consider these complexities to truly understand the intricacies directors face each time they fulfil their duties. The challenge lies in prioritising and effectively addressing ESG interests, while balancing the imperative to generate profits and enhance shareholder value.[159] The persistent question revolves around aligning with shareholders' interests or the company's interests, acknowledging that inherent conflict is present in any corporate setting. This factor can surface in decision-making processes and tasks undertaken by corporate directors. The reinforcement of corporate governance rules – the very structure and implementation mechanisms intended to strengthen corporate governance – should empower both the company and the investor with the tools to navigate conflicts of interest. A clear procedure is essential for managing these conflicts in the most effective way possible.

Moving into examining the portfolio,[160] we are considering an investment strategy that spans diverse sectors. If a portion of a portfolio is exclusively dedicated to projects, activities, or sectors that singularly generate a positive impact on social and environmental issues, then investors' long-term engagement, considering sustainability factors, can be equally profitable as traditional investment strategies.

In the context of reconfigured fiduciary duties, a crucial challenge arises: how to apply financial science concepts to ensure a comprehensive understanding, beyond subjective opinions or fleeting trends? The key focus is on clarifying the expansion of fiduciary duties to encompass a prudent investor.[161] This involves delving into investment theories and market dynamics. Despite their financial science origins, legal experts guiding these processes must acknowledge their evolving nature. The *Modern Portfolio Theory* serves as a pathway within finance, shedding light on risk scrutiny, management efforts, and the control of adverse effects, ultimately guiding the prudent investor.

The foundations of Modern Portfolio Theory were laid by Harry Markowitz,[162] a Nobel Laureate in Economics in the 1990s. Markowitz articulated that investment strategies undergo variations depending on, or in alignment with, the Efficient Market Theory.[163] These concepts, deeply rooted in economic theory, are intricate, and warrant a level of expertise and time that we may not delve into here. Nevertheless, at its core, Modern Portfolio Theory posits that, in accordance with Efficient Market Theory, and as we progressively seek heightened levels of market efficiency – whether through the pricing system or by considering the efforts and

159 Joakim Sandberg, 'Socially Responsible Investment and Fiduciary Duty: Putting the Freshfields Report into Perspective', *Journal of Business Ethics* 101 (2011): 143–162.

160 K. Johnson, 'Introduction to Institutional Investor Fiduciary Duties', *International Institute for Sustainable Development Report* 44 (2014).

161 Folarin Akinbami, 'The Fiduciary Duties of Institutional Investors', in *Routledge Handbook of Corporate Law* (Routledge, 2016) 108–123.

162 Harry M. Markowitz, 'Foundations of Portfolio Theory', *The Journal of Finance* 46.2 (1991): 469–477.

163 Amy Buttell, 'Harry M. Markowitz on Modern Portfolio Theory, the Efficient Frontier, and His Life's Work', *Journal of Financial Planning* 23.5 (2010): 18.

costs each link in the investment chain contributes to achieve optimal results – the yardstick for measuring efficiency lies within the functions performed within the financial system.

Within the context of Efficient Market Theory,[164] the overarching goal is to facilitate risk dispersion across the portfolio, rather than undertaking a specific analysis of the risk associated with each individual asset. Consequently, as we commit to making a positive impact on environmental and social issues, there will be instances where nonparticipation becomes inevitable. This nonparticipation, often termed negative screening, implies withholding the allocation of resources, and entails certain costs. To counterbalance this anticipated risk, a crucial emphasis is placed on diversification.

This strategic emphasis on diversification empowers investors to project returns and profitability levels that remain sufficiently attractive. Essentially, concepts of risk and risk management (exemplified by diversification) contribute to an exceedingly efficient risk-management approach. This considers not only the investor's profile, but also the unique characteristics of the markets in which they participate,[165] hence our reference to Efficient Market Theory and the criteria employed to assess efficiency. These criteria form the foundation for constructing an optimal strategy, aiming to generate environmental and social impact, without compromising economic interests. The 'prudent investor' perspective necessitates the inclusion of ESG factors, extending beyond a narrow focus on profits within specific time frames.

In this evolving landscape, disciplines from corporate and investor domains converge, to develop criteria integrating ESG considerations and associated risks into operational frameworks. Diverse risk assessment models are deployed, with financial institutions finding integration more straightforward. However, the challenge lies in identifying potential situations serving as indicators of environmental risks, and proactively navigating the adverse effects of transition risks. It is crucial to note that identified risks may not unfold as anticipated, and uncertainties persist in measuring their impact and understanding subsequent material effects. To address this, specialised risk assessment models have been created by sectors and associations.

The argument revolves around the notion that the features of Modern Portfolio Theory can aid in the reconfiguration of fiduciary duties.[166] The theory provides objective benchmarks to assess how directors' decisions can align not only with shareholders' interests, but also consider stakeholders' issues. It also serves as a crucial tool for evaluating the potential impact of adopting ESG factors on the distribution of dividends, fulfilment of financial obligations, cash flow generation, and

164 ibid.

165 William Menges, William Suley and Kevin Getii Moranga, 'Indirect Investment and Financial Performance of the Real Estate Sector in Nairobi County Kenya', *International Journal of Business Ecosystem & Strategy (2687–2293)* 1.4 (2019): 9–18.

166 Amy Buttell, 'Harry M. Markowitz on Modern Portfolio Theory, the Efficient Frontier, and His Life's Work' (n 163) 25.

the scope of implementation of the business judgement rule[167] within the operations of the recipient of the investment. Additionally, asset managers focus a significant portion of their efforts on comprehending the transition policies adopted by companies within their respective sectors. The adoption of such transition policies raises questions about potential reductions in profits, and increases in costs, particularly in sectors that draw heightened attention to environmental and social concerns.

Remarks

The integration of ESG derivatives, particularly in addressing governance risks and uncertainties, is intricately connected to the ongoing discourse surrounding the correlation between the use of derivatives contracts and firm value. This relationship hinges on the contribution of derivatives in rectifying market imperfections, such as information misalignment, and their role in resolving corporate governance issues – the 'G factor'. The discourse of corporate governance relies heavily on the lessons learned from CSR, and integration with SRI principles.

In the broader landscape of sustainable finance, a profound understanding of optimal strategies for capital mobilisation emerges as a crucial tool for achieving ESG targets. Such comprehension has the potential to expedite the transition process and elevate overall efficiency. The nuances embedded in the G factor serve as the foundation for fostering the success of the entire corporate sustainability strategy, subsequently influencing the selection of the most suitable sustainable finance approach.

The formation of sustainable investment strategies relies on the ESG data available in the market and analysed by investors. In this scenario, it is worth noting that considerations regarding company size, economic activity, geographical location, data availability, the sometimes conflicting nature of standards, are all areas that have an impact on how capital is allocated in the context of sustainability.

The corporate sector and investment community navigate a complex regulatory terrain. Compliance has undergone a transformation, moving away from a voluntary approach, and embracing a mandatory trend, particularly in ESG reporting. Nevertheless, the responsibility for shaping the trajectory, charting the course, and deciding on additional actions rests squarely with the company and the investor, adhering to existing regulatory expectations. In this dynamic context, the discussion extends beyond mere corporate or investor responsibility, with an emerging imperative to elucidate and redefine the fiduciary duties of company directors and investors.

We argue that the principles of Modern Portfolio Theory can assist the process of reshaping fiduciary duties. This theory offers objective benchmarks for evaluating directors' decisions, aligning them with both shareholder and stakeholder

167 Thilo Kuntz, 'ESG and the Weakening Business Judgment Rule', in Thilo Kuntz (ed), *Research Handbook on Environmental, Social, and Corporate Governance* (Edward Elgar, Forthcoming/21 October 2023).

interests. Additionally, the theory proves instrumental in assessing the potential effects of integrating ESG factors on dividend distribution, meeting financial obligations, and generating cash flow in the recipient's operations.

Bibliography

Books

Gasperini, A., 'Principles for Responsible Investment (PRI) and ESG Factors' in Leal Filho, W., Azul, A.M., Brandli, L., Özuyar, P.G., and Wall, T. (eds.), *Climate Action. Encyclopaedia of the UN Sustainable Development Goals* (Springer 2020).

Tavakoli, J., *Credit Derivatives and Synthetic Structures: A Guide to Instruments and Applications* (John Wiley & Sons 2001).

Articles

Albuquerque, R., Koskinen, Y., and Zhang, C., 'Corporate Social Responsibility and Firm Risk: Theory and Empirical Evidence' 65(10) *Management Science* (2019) 4451.

Allayannis, G., Lel, U., and Miller, D.P., 'The Use of Foreign Currency Derivatives, Corporate Governance, and Firm Value Around the World' 87(1) *Journal of International Economics* (2012) 70.

Bebchuk, L., and Tallarita, R., 'The Illusory Promise of Stakeholder Governance' 106 *Cornell Law Review* (2020) 91.

Buttell, A., 'Harry M. Markowitz on Modern Portfolio Theory, the Efficient Frontier, and His Life's Work' 23(5) *Journal of Financial Planning* (2010) 18.

Chen, J., Leung, W., Song, W., and Avino, D., 'Does CDS Trading Affect Risk-Taking Incentives in Managerial Compensation?' 151 *Journal of Banking & Finance* (2023) 10.

Easterbrook, F., 'Derivative Securities and Corporate Governance' 69(3) *The University of Chicago Law Review* (2002) 733.

Edmans, A., 'The Link Between Job Satisfaction and Firm Value, With Implications For Corporate Social Responsibility' 26(4) *Academy of Management Perspectives* (2012) 4.

Jain, A., Jain, P., McInish, T., and McKenzie, M., 'Worldwide Reach of Short Selling Regulations' 109(1) *Journal of Financial Economics* (2013) 177.

Jensen, M., and Meckling, W., 'Theory of the Firm: Managerial Behavior, Agency Costs, and Ownership Structure' 3 *Journal of Financial Economics* (1976) 305.

Kelly, M., 'ESG: The 5th Element of Corporate Risk Assessment' *Michigan State Law Review* (2022) 811.

Khan, M., 'Corporate Governance, ESG, and Stock Returns Around the World' 75(4) *Financial Analysts Journal* (2019) 103.

Krawiec, K.D., 'Derivatives, Corporate Hedging, and Shareholder Wealth: Modigliani-Miller Forty Years Later' *University of Illinois Law Review* (1998) 1039.

Lashitew, A., 'Corporate Uptake of the Sustainable Development Goals: Mere Greenwashing or an Advent of Institutional Change?' 4 *Journal of International Business Policy* (2021) 184.

Nel, K., Mans-Kemp, N., and Erasmus, P., 'Sustainable Thematic Investing: Identifying Opportunities Based on an Analysis of Stewardship Reports' 15(10) *Sustainability* (2023) 8411.

Sanders, W., 'Resolving the Conflict between Fiduciary Duties and Socially Responsible Investing' 35 *Pace Law Review* (2015) 535.

Stout, L.A., 'The Problem of Corporate Purpose' 48(1) *Issues in Governance Studies* (2012) 14.

Working Papers

Gurrea-Martínez, A., 'New Agency Problems, New Legal Rules: Rethinking Takeover Regulation in the US and Europe' Ibero-American Institute for Law and Finance, Working Paper Series 3/2016 (30 October 2019).

ISDA, 'Policy Framework for Safe and Efficient Derivatives Activity in Emerging and Developing Markets' (22 May 2022) <www.isda.org/a/YHVgE/Policy-Framework-for-Safe-and-Efficient-Derivatives-Activity-in-Emerging-and-Developing-Markets.pdf> accessed 24th November 2023.

Liang, H., and Renneboog, L., 'Corporate Social Responsibility and Sustainable Finance: A Review of the Literature', European Corporate Governance Institute, Working Paper No. 701/2020 (September 2020).

Rock, E., 'For Whom Is the Corporation Managed in 2020? The Debate over Corporate Purpose' (1 May 2020). European Corporate Governance Institute – Law Working Paper No. 515/2020, NYU School of Law, Public Law Research Paper No. 20–16, NYU Law and Economics Research Paper.

Serafeim, G., 'ESG: From Process to Product', Harvard Business School, Working Paper 23–069 (13 May 2023).

International Organizations Policy Documents and Reports

IOSCO, 'Recommendations on Sustainability-Related Practices, Policies, Procedures and Disclosure in Asset Management', Final Report, FR08/21 (November 2021) <www.iosco.org/library/pubdocs/pdf/IOSCOPD688.pdf> accessed 27th November 2023.

UN PRI Initiative, 'Blueprint for Responsible Investment' <www.unpri.org/about-us/a-blueprint-for-responsible-investment> accessed 13th June 2023.

UNEPFI, 'The Net-Zero Asset Owner Alliance Releases a Foundational Paper for Asset Owner Expectations of Asset Managers' Climate Engagement' (16 November 2023) <www.unepfi.org/industries/the-net-zero-asset-owner-alliance-releases-a-foundational-paper-for-asset-owner-expectations-of-asset-managers-climate-engagement/> accessed 25th November 2023.

WFE, 'WFE Sustainability Principles' (4 October 2018) <www.world-exchanges.org/our-work/articles/wfe-sustainability-principles> accessed 27 November 2023.

US Legislation and Policy Documents

SEC, Exemptions from the Proxy Rules for Proxy Voting Advice, 85 Fed. Reg. 55,082 (3 September 2020) ('2020 Rule Amendments').

SEC, Proxy Voting Advice, Final Rule, 17 CFR Parts 240 and 276 <www.sec.gov/files/rules/final/2022/34-95266.pdf> accessed 7th December 2023.

EU Legislation

European Commission, 'Guidelines on Non-financial Reporting (methodology for reporting non-financial information)' 26 June 2017. C (2017) 4234 final.

European Commission, 'Proposal for a Directive on Corporate Sustainability Due Diligence and Annex' 23 February 2022 <https://commission.europa.eu/publications/proposal-directive-corporate-sustainability-due-diligence-and-annex_en> accessed 17th October 2023.

European Commission, 'SME Relief Package' (12 September 2023) <https://single-market-economy.ec.europa.eu/system/files/2023-09/COM_2023_535_1_EN_ACT_part1_v12.pdf> accessed 17th October 2023.

European Commission, *Sustainable Finance: Investing in a Sustainable Future* (June 2023).

8 Final Remarks

This book, for the first time, uncovers the strategic role of ESG derivatives in sustainable investment strategies, providing valuable insights into the effective management of intricate ESG risks and uncertainties. This innovative study embraces a risk-based approach as the guiding methodology – to identify not only the challenges, but also the potential solutions that ESG derivatives bring to the inefficiencies of sustainable finance. Through a groundbreaking and comprehensive exploration of the fundamental risks and uncertainties associated with each ESG factor, this book presents the first legal analysis of the EU, UK, and US regimes for ESG derivatives, emphasising the imperative to enhance legal certainty regarding the characterisation of these transactions as sustainable financial instruments if aligned with the recommendations provided in the study.

Sustainable finance reflects a dedicated commitment to well-defined sustainability goals, with green finance prioritising environmentally positive investments, notably in nature-based finance and biodiversity finance. Blended finance, integrating public and private investments, becomes crucial for overcoming challenges and advancing transformative changes.

Companies are adapting economic practices, emphasising sustainability reports, stakeholder concerns, and shareholder interests. Robust reporting standards for comprehensive, transparent, and comparable data are still under development, and the uncertainty about materiality assessments must be further discussed. In this scenario, ESG derivatives play a significant role in addressing climate-related risks in sustainable finance, considering physical, transition, and liability risks, as well as in the actions needed to achieve the net-zero target, using carbon credit derivatives. In this context, given that greenwashing stands out as a pivotal risk in sustainable finance, delving into the various manifestations of this practice not only elucidates its nuances, but also underscores how ESG derivatives can serve as catalysts for encouraging positive corporate behaviour, aligned with explicit, substantive, and quantifiable sustainability objectives.

Acknowledging regulatory limitations and challenges in promoting behaviour change is crucial. Sustainable development requires the involvement of diverse stakeholders and legal institutions, with contracts serving as pivotal governance mechanisms. The focus should be on aligning contract objectives with specific and quantifiable sustainability metrics (KPIs) – rather than merely including

DOI: 10.4324/9781003365242-8

sustainability clauses. Financial derivatives, known for adaptability, present a significant opportunity for sustainable finance. Their flexibility aligns well with sustainability goals, addressing issues like price discovery, data collection, and transparency.

The sustainable finance regulatory landscape, particularly in the EU, involves instruments like the EU Taxonomy, SFDR, CSRD, ESRS, and the proposed CSDDD, providing clarity on disclosure and classification mechanisms. Various regimes oversee the prudential framework for green assets, with considerations for differentiating traditional derivatives from ESG-focused transactions. The UK framework covers a broad range of laws and regulations, including corporate governance, stewardship practices, and company law. The US approach relies on voluntary initiatives, with recent SEC regulations focusing on disclosing climate-related risks. The CFTC's Climate Risk Unit promotes new financial instruments for climate-related risks, giving the US market an advantage over the EU and UK. While these regulatory instruments lay the groundwork for the trading of ESG derivatives, a lingering sense of uncertainty persists, due to regulators' reluctance to explicitly acknowledge these transactions as financial instruments aligned with sustainability objectives.

The study of ESG derivatives considers traditional derivatives with specific ESG KPIs. This category highlights the general role of derivatives in sustainability, primarily focusing on risk management. This includes CDS, futures, options, and catastrophe weather derivatives, serving their core function of facilitating effective risk-management practices. However, challenges related to poor ESG data quality and endogeneity should be considered, especially in the case of CDS, where the strong connection between corporate sustainability and CDS spreads relies on improved ESG reporting transparency. Negotiating options and futures linked to an underlying ESG target raises concerns about potential home bias, as ESG data availability is not globally uniform. Developed economies have an advantage, exacerbating the home bias issue, and excluding developing markets from derivative transactions.

SLDs emerge as powerful tools for advancing sustainability and ESG objectives. With specific KPIs, SLDs offer adaptability, enabling the customisation of contracts to various ESG-related goals. The ISDA recommendations on drafting KPIs provide a solid foundation, ensuring that SLDs align with intended outcomes.

While carbon markets have experienced growth, their full potential remains untapped. Unlocking this potential necessitates increased demand, improved transparency, and streamlined certification processes. VCMs, emphasising co-benefits such as poverty alleviation and biodiversity conservation, provide a mechanism for addressing climate change and contributing to sustainable development. Collaborative efforts are needed to address challenges related to additionality, standardisation, and double counting. Derivatives in VCMs, with their enhanced transparency and standards, can play a transformative role in transitioning to a low-carbon economy.

The features of ESG derivatives must consider the particularities of each of the ESG factors. Adopting a risk-based approach in the examination of environmental risks presents a versatile and adaptable strategy that responds to the dynamic nature of regulatory requirements. This methodology, characterised by the categorisation of risks and uncertainties, offers regulatory authorities a clear and comprehensive framework for designing and implementing effective regulatory structures. The integration of risk and uncertainty perceptions not only promotes voluntary compliance, but also facilitates the identification of specific areas that demand regulatory attention. Within the scenario of environmental risks, the precision afforded by this approach in identifying and categorising risks becomes a crucial decision-making tool, particularly in situations characterised by knowledge gaps. The complexity introduced by regulatory frameworks such as the CSRD, with its double materiality concepts, further emphasises the importance of setting clear reporting expectations and risk identification tools for environmental impacts.

The risk-based approach, through its systematic identification of environmental risks, significantly influences the design of effective, sustainable investing methods. Moreover, it actively contributes to the evolution of ESG derivatives as potent instruments for effectively managing risks within the realm of environmental considerations. This comprehensive approach not only ensures a nuanced understanding of environmental risks, but also facilitates the creation of strategies aligned with sustainable investing practices, fostering the development of innovative financial instruments (e.g., ESG derivatives).

Positioned as solutions for addressing information and data deficiencies related to environmental issues, ESG derivatives play a crucial role in enhancing transparency and streamlining the price discovery process. Despite the risk-based foundation, the identification of material environmental risks may be influenced by specific market interests. A comprehensive risk-based approach, encompassing risk tolerance, identification, and assessment, aligns ESG derivatives with the SDGs, thus overcoming challenges hindering the growth of sustainable finance.

Viewed as a subset of regulatory risk, greenwashing can be effectively managed using ESG derivatives, contributing to environmental risk-management and regulatory objectives. Recognising the inherent limitations and ongoing evaluation post-implementation is crucial. This involves a focused examination of the direct correlation between regulatory objectives and risks emanating from regulated entities, as well as an assessment of how the risk-based approach influences their behaviour regarding environmental issues. Complementing the risk-based strategy with methodologies like regulatory-impact analysis ensures the establishment of a comprehensive and effective regulatory framework that addresses both risks and the behavioural dynamics of regulated entities.

The construction of the social factor in the context of sustainable finance is still a pending task. To contribute to the development of more specific features of the social impact, we adopt the concept of building a social licence for the financial system. Recognising the interaction between regulation and contract as the primary sources of legitimacy for such a licence, our goal is to ensure its effectiveness. While conduct regulation serves as a commendable starting point within a social licence framework, strengthening the generation of common well-being as a regulatory objective, the role of financial contracts should be added to complement and strengthen such a tool.

Here, we call for the imperative to reconfigure ESG derivatives based on the concepts of value generation and extraction. A social licence, with its focus on positive social impact, necessitates a clear identification of the outcomes that financial services deliver to the economy. The negotiation conditions of ESG derivatives must result in profitability and well-being for all, discouraging those associated with excessive profits benefiting only a select few market participants. Collaboration among *all* stakeholders, including regulators, supervisors, and market participants, is pivotal for the success of the fundamental transformation of ESG derivatives, mitigating issues such as ritualism in the protection of human rights.

Establishing a social licence for the financial system is contingent on regulatory advancements that underscore its historical functions, notably the effective mobilisation of capital for collective welfare. The ongoing reassessment of the regulatory framework, centred on principles of justice, equality, and efficient resource distribution, aims to reinforce a positive social impact from financial activities. Mere proclamations of protecting the public interest are no longer deemed adequate; precise regulatory expectations are deemed indispensable to imbue sustainability criteria with substance. Our paramount focus lies in elucidating the pivotal role of financial derivatives in discerning and mitigating ESG risks, encompassing both inherent risks, and those that impact the entities and individuals they serve.

Moreover, such regulatory evolution reflects a deepened understanding of the intricate interplay between financial transactions and broader social, economic, and environmental dynamics. It underscores the imperative to move beyond a narrow focus on profit generation, and consider the broader implications of financial activities on society. The goal is to ensure that the financial system actively contributes to social welfare, promoting fairness, and equality.

In this context, financial derivatives play a pivotal role – as instruments that can be harnessed not only for financial gain, but also for achieving broader societal objectives. Their strategic utilisation in managing ESG risks demonstrates a proactive approach to aligning financial operations with sustainability goals. Ongoing regulatory efforts are a recognition of the financial sector's transformative potential in shaping a more sustainable and equitable future. They signify a departure from conventional paradigms that narrowly focus on profit maximisation, and highlight a paradigm shift towards a financial system that actively contributes to societal well-being. In essence, the establishment of a social licence for the financial system is an evolution towards a more conscientious, responsible, and sustainable financial landscape.

In exploring the governance factor, this book underscores the critical significance of conceiving governance not merely as a facilitator of financial interests, but as a conduit to broaden the purpose of any economic activity. The incorporation of ESG derivatives – specifically in navigating governance risks and uncertainties – is intricately intertwined with the ongoing dialogue on the correlation between derivatives contracts and firm value. This correlation is rooted in the role played by derivatives in ameliorating market imperfections, particularly addressing information misalignment, and their pivotal function in resolving issues related to corporate governance. The discourse on corporate governance extrapolates insights from CSR and converges with the principles of SRI.

In the expansive area of sustainable finance, a profound grasp of optimal strategies for capital mobilisation becomes imperative for achieving ESG targets. This understanding not only expedites the transition process, but also elevates overall efficiency. The intricacies embedded in governance serve as bedrock for the success of the entire corporate sustainability strategy, shaping the selection of the most fitting sustainable finance approach. Sustainable investment strategies hinge on ESG data available in the market, subject to analysis by investors. Considerations encompassing company size, economic activity, geographical location, data availability, and occasionally conflicting standards intricately influence how capital is allocated within the sustainability context.

Within this intricate landscape, the corporate sector and investment community navigate a complex regulatory framework, witnessing a shift from voluntary to mandatory compliance, particularly in the context of ESG reporting. Nevertheless, the onus of shaping the trajectory, mapping the course, and deciding on additional actions rests squarely on the shoulders of both companies and investors, aligning with regulatory expectations. In this dynamic scenario, the discourse transcends mere corporate or investor responsibility, extending to the elucidation and redefinition of the fiduciary duties held by company directors and investors.

We recommend the adoption of the principles of Modern Portfolio Theory, as they can play an essential role in reshaping fiduciary duties. This theory furnishes objective benchmarks for evaluating director-level decisions, aligning them with the interests of both shareholders and stakeholders. Moreover, it is instrumental for assessing the potential impacts of integrating ESG factors on various facets such as dividend distribution, meeting financial obligations, and generating cash flow within recipient operations.

As the regulatory frameworks for ESG derivatives in the EU, UK, and US evolve, several areas emerge as potential subjects for future policy debate. Firstly, there is a need for clear definitions encompassing the diverse array of derivatives that play a substantial role in advancing sustainable objectives. This includes determining whether ESG derivatives should be exclusively aligned with hedging purposes, and not harbour speculative motives.

Additionally, there is a call for the enhancement of standards and transparency within the carbon market, aimed at fostering increased liquidity for carbon credit derivatives. The recently announced CFTC's guidance for the listing of Voluntary Carbon Credit Derivatives appears to be a measure aimed at minimising the vulnerability of these contracts to manipulation, thereby instilling confidence in their liquidity. Strengthening these aspects could contribute significantly to the effectiveness and efficiency of carbon credit derivatives.

Maintaining an ongoing dialogue with participants in the derivatives market is crucial. This dialogue will provide heightened certainty regarding the legal recognition of ESG derivatives as legitimate instruments within the area of sustainable finance. Clear communication and collaboration with market participants are integral to establishing a robust and well-understood framework to recognise and utilise ESG derivatives for sustainable finance initiatives. Finally, within the domain of ESG derivatives and, more broadly, sustainable finance, there is a pressing need for the continued exploration and development of the interconnections between derivatives, and social and governance risks and uncertainties.

Index

For Product Safety Concerns and Information please contact our EU representative GPSR@taylorandfrancis.com Taylor & Francis Verlag GmbH, Kaufingerstraße 24, 80331 München, Germany